THE ARDEN SHAKESPEARE

THIRD SERIES

General Editors: Richard Proudfoot, Ann Thompson,
David Scott Kastan and H. R. Woudhuysen

THE TEMPEST

REVISED EDITION

THE ARDEN SHAKESPEARE

ALL'S WELL THAT ENDS WELL	edited by Suzanne Gossett and Helen Wilcox
ANTONY AND CLEOPATRA	edited by John Wilders
AS YOU LIKE IT	edited by Juliet Dusinberre
THE COMEDY OF ERRORS	edited by Kent Cartwright
CORIOLANUS	edited by Peter Holland
CYMBELINE	edited by Valerie Wayne
DOUBLE FALSEHOOD	edited by Brean Hammond
HAMLET, Revised	edited by Ann Thompson and Neil Taylor
HAMLET, The Texts of 1603 and 1623	edited by Ann Thompson and Neil Taylor
JULIUS CAESAR	edited by David Daniell
KING EDWARD III	edited by Richard Proudfoot and Nicola Bennett
KING HENRY IV PART 1	edited by David Scott Kastan
KING HENRY IV PART 2	edited by James C. Bulman
KING HENRY V	edited by T.W. Craik
KING HENRY VI PART 1	edited by Edward Burns
KING HENRY VI PART 2	edited by Ronald Knowles
KING HENRY VI PART 3	edited by John D. Cox and Eric Rasmussen
KING HENRY VIII	edited by Gordon McMullan
KING JOHN	edited by Jesse M. Lander and J.J.M. Tobin
KING LEAR	edited by R.A. Foakes
KING RICHARD II	edited by Charles Forker
KING RICHARD III	edited by James R. Siemon
LOVE'S LABOUR'S LOST	edited by H.R. Woudhuysen
MACBETH	edited by Sandra Clark and Pamela Mason
MEASURE FOR MEASURE	edited by A.R. Braunmuller and Robert N. Watson
THE MERCHANT OF VENICE	edited by John Drakakis
THE MERRY WIVES OF WINDSOR	edited by Giorgio Melchiori
A MIDSUMMER NIGHT'S DREAM	edited by Sukanta Chaudhuri
MUCH ADO ABOUT NOTHING, Revised	edited by Claire McEachern
OTHELLO, Revised	edited by E.A.J. Honigmann, with an Introduction by Ayanna Thompson
PERICLES	edited by Suzanne Gossett
ROMEO AND JULIET	edited by René Weis
SHAKESPEARE'S POEMS	edited by Katherine Duncan-Jones and H.R. Woudhuysen
SHAKESPEARE'S SONNETS, Revised	edited by Katherine Duncan-Jones
SIR THOMAS MORE	edited by John Jowett
THE TAMING OF THE SHREW	edited by Barbara Hodgdon
THE TEMPEST, Revised	edited by Virginia Mason Vaughan and Alden T. Vaughan
TIMON OF ATHENS	edited by Anthony B. Dawson and Gretchen E. Minton
TITUS ANDRONICUS, Revised	edited by Jonathan Bate
TROILUS AND CRESSIDA, Revised	edited by David Bevington
TWELFTH NIGHT	edited by Keir Elam
THE TWO GENTLEMEN OF VERONA	edited by William C. Carroll
THE TWO NOBLE KINSMEN, Revised	edited by Lois Potter
THE WINTER'S TALE	edited by John Pitcher

THE ARDEN SHAKESPEARE

THE
TEMPEST

Edited by
VIRGINIA MASON VAUGHAN
and ALDEN T. VAUGHAN

THE ARDEN SHAKESPEARE
LONDON • NEW YORK • OXFORD • NEW DELHI • SYDNEY

THE ARDEN SHAKESPEARE
Bloomsbury Publishing Plc
50 Bedford Square, London, WC1B 3DP, UK
1385 Broadway, New York, NY 10018, USA
29 Earlsfort Terrace, Dublin 2, Ireland

BLOOMSBURY, THE ARDEN SHAKESPEARE and the Arden Shakespeare logo are
trademarks of Bloomsbury Publishing Plc

This edition of *The Tempest* by Virginia Mason Vaughan and
Alden T. Vaughan, first published by Thomas Nelson and Sons Ltd 1999
Reissued with additional material and a new cover
by Bloomsbury Publishing Plc 2011
Reprinted by Bloomsbury Arden Shakespeare 2011, 2012 (twice),
2013 (twice), 2014 (three times), 2015 (three times), 2016 (twice),
2017 (twice), 2018 (twice), 2019, 2020, 2021 (twice)

The general editors of the Arden Shakespeare have been
W. J. Craig and R. H. Case (first series 1899–1944)
Una Ellis-Fermor, Harold F. Brooks, Harold Jenkins and
Brian Morris (second series 1946–82)
Present general editors (third series)
Richard Proudfoot, Ann Thompson, David Scott Kastan
and H. R. Woudhuysen

A catalogue record for this book is available from the British Library.

A catalog record for this book is available from the Library of Congress.

ISBN: HB: 978-1-4081-3348-4
PB: 978-1-4081-3347-7
ePDF: 978-1-4081-3930-1
ePUB: 978-1-4081-3931-8

Series: The Arden Shakespeare Third Series

Additional material typeset by Country Setting, Kingsdown, Kent
Printed and bound in India

To find out more about our authors and books visit
www.bloomsbury.com and sign up for our newsletters.

The Editors

Virginia Mason Vaughan, Professor of English and former Chair of the English Department at Clark University in Worcester, Massachusetts, has published essays on Shakespeare's history plays and three books on Shakespeare's *Othello*: the annotated bibliography in the Garland Shakespeare series, compiled with Margaret Lael Mikesell (1990); an anthology, *'Othello': New Perspectives*, coedited with Kent Cartwright (1991); and *'Othello': A Contextual History* (1994). Among her more recent works are *Performing Blackness on English Stages, 1500–1800* (2005), and *'The Tempest'* in Manchester University Press's 'Shakespeare in Performance' series (2011).

Alden T. Vaughan, Professor Emeritus of History at Columbia University, has published widely on England's American colonies in the seventeenth and eighteenth centuries, especially on their racial perceptions and policies. His most recent historical book is *Transatlantic Encounters: American Indians in Britain, 1500–1776* (2006). Earlier titles include *New England Frontier: Puritans and Indians, 1620–1675* (1965, 3rd edn 1995); *American Genesis: Captain John Smith and the Founding of Virginia* (1975); *Puritans Among the Indians: Accounts of Captivity and Redemption, 1676–1724* (1981), co-edited with Edward W. Clark; and a collection of his essays, *Roots of American Racism* (1995).

The Vaughans are the coauthors of *Shakespeare's Caliban: A Cultural History* (1991) and the coeditors of *Critical Essays on Shakespeare's 'The Tempest'* (1998).

To the staff of the
Folger Shakespeare Library

'Thou hast done well'
(*The Tempest*, 1.2.495)

CONTENTS

ILLUSTRATIONS

GENERAL EDITORS' PREFACE

The Arden Shakespeare is now one hundred years old. The earliest volume in the series, Edward Dowden's *Hamlet*, was published in 1899. Since then the Arden Shakespeare has become internationally recognized and respected. It is now widely acknowledged as the pre-eminent Shakespeare series, valued by scholars, students, actors and 'the great variety of readers' alike for its readable and reliable texts, its full annotations and its richly informative introductions.

We have aimed in the third Arden edition to maintain the quality and general character of its predecessors, preserving the commitment to presenting the play as it has been shaped in history. While each individual volume will necessarily have its own emphasis in the light of the unique possibilities and problems posed by the play, the series as a whole, like the earlier Ardens, insists upon the highest standards of scholarship and upon attractive and accessible presentation.

Newly edited from the original quarto and folio editions, the texts are presented in fully modernized form, with a textual apparatus that records all substantial divergences from those early printings. The notes and introductions focus on the conditions and possibilities of meaning that editors, critics and performers (on stage and screen) have discovered in the play. While building upon the rich history of scholarly and theatrical activity that has long shaped our understanding of the texts of Shakespeare's plays, this third series of the Arden Shakespeare is made necessary and possible by a new generation's encounter with Shakespeare, engaging with the plays and their complex relation to the culture in which they were – and continue to be – produced.

THE TEXT

On each page of the work itself, readers will find a passage of text followed by commentary and, finally, textual notes. Act and scene divisions (seldom present in the early editions and often the product of eighteenth-century or later scholarship) have been retained for ease of reference, but have been given less prominence than in the previous series. Editorial indications of location of the action have been removed to the textual notes or commentary.

In the text itself, unfamiliar typographic conventions have been avoided in order to minimize obstacles to the reader. Elided forms in the early texts are spelt out in full in verse lines wherever they indicate a usual late twentieth-century pronunciation that requires no special indication and wherever they occur in prose (except when they indicate non-standard pronunciation). In verse speeches, marks of elision are retained where they are necessary guides to the scansion and pronunciation of the line. Final -ed in past tense and participial forms of verbs is always printed as -ed without accent, never as -'d, but wherever the required pronunciation diverges from modern usage a note in the commentary draws attention to the fact. Where the final -ed should be given syllabic value contrary to modern usage, e.g.

> Doth Silvia know that I am banished?
> *(TGV* 3.1.214)

the note will take the form

 214 **banished** banishèd

Conventional lineation of divided verse lines shared by two or more speakers has been reconsidered and sometimes rearranged. Except for the familiar *Exit* and *Exeunt*, Latin forms in stage directions and speech prefixes have been translated into English and the original Latin forms recorded in the textual notes.

COMMENTARY AND TEXTUAL NOTES

Notes in the commentary, for which a major source will be the *Oxford English Dictionary*, offer glossarial and other explication of verbal difficulties; they may also include discussion of points of theatrical interpretation and, in relevant cases, substantial extracts from Shakespeare's source material. Editors will not usually offer glossarial notes for words adequately defined in the latest edition of *The Concise Oxford Dictionary* or *Merriam-Webster's Collegiate Dictionary*, but in cases of doubt they will include notes. Attention, however, will be drawn to places where more than one likely interpretation can be proposed and to significant verbal and syntactic complexity. Notes preceded by * involve editorial emendations or readings in which the rival textual claims of competing early editions (Quarto and Folio) are in dispute.

Headnotes to acts or scenes discuss, where appropriate, questions of scene location, Shakespeare's handling of his source materials, and major difficulties of staging. The list of roles (so headed to emphasize the play's status for performance) is also considered in commentary notes. These may include comment on plausible patterns of casting with the resources of an Elizabethan or Jacobean acting company, and also on any variation in the description of roles in their speech prefixes in the early editions.

The textual notes are designed to let readers know when the edited text diverges from the early edition(s) on which it is based. Wherever this happens the note will record the rejected reading of the early edition(s), in original spelling, and the source of the reading adopted in this edition. Other forms from the early edition(s) recorded in these notes will include some spellings of particular interest or significance and original forms of translated stage directions. Where two early editions are involved, for instance with *Othello*, the notes will also record all important differences between them. The textual notes take a form that has been in use since the nineteenth century. This comprises, first: line reference, reading adopted in the text and closing square bracket; then: abbreviated reference, in italic, to the earliest edition to adopt the accepted reading, italic semicolon and noteworthy alternate reading(s), beginning with the rejected original reading, each with abbreviated italic reference to its source.

Conventions used in these textual notes include the following. The solidus / is used, in notes quoting verse or discussing verse lining, to indicate line endings. Distinctive spellings of the basic text (Q or F) follow the square bracket without indication of source and are enclosed in italic brackets. Names enclosed in italic brackets indicate originators of conjectural emendations when these did not originate in an edition of the text. Stage directions (SDs) are referred to by the number of the line within or immediately after which they are placed. Line numbers with a decimal point relate to entry SDs and to SDs more than one line long, with the number after the point indicating the line within the SD: e.g. 78.4 refers to the fourth line of the SD following line 78. Lines of SDs at the start of a scene are numbered 0.1, 0.2, etc. Where only a line number and SD precede the square bracket, e.g. 128 SD], the note relates to the whole of a SD within or immediately following the line. Speech prefixes (SPs) follow similar conventions, 203 SP] referring to the speaker's name for line 203. Where a SP reference takes the form e.g. 38 + SP, it relates to all subsequent speeches assigned to that speaker in the scene in question.

Where, as with *King Henry V*, one of the early editions is a so-called 'bad quarto' (that is, a text either heavily adapted, or reconstructed from memory, or both), the divergences from the present edition are too great to be recorded in full in the notes. In these cases the editions will include a reduced photographic facsimile of the 'bad quarto' in an appendix.

INTRODUCTION

Both the introduction and the commentary are designed to present the plays as texts for performance, and make appropriate reference to stage, film and television versions, as well as introducing the reader to the range of critical approaches to the plays. They discuss the history of the reception of the texts within the theatre and scholarship and beyond, investigating the interdependency of the literary text and the surrounding 'cultural text' both at the time of the original reproduction of Shakespeare's works and during their long and rich afterlife.

PREFACE

This edition of *The Tempest* is based on the play's first known printing, the Folio of 1623. We have modernized the spelling and punctuation according to the ground rules laid out in the General Editors' Preface and in the Text section of our Introduction. Because the precise orthography of the Folio is sometimes crucial to the points we make in our Introduction and commentary notes, we have reproduced all quotations from the Folio as closely as possible to the original; in quotations from other early modern texts we have, for the reader's convenience, adhered to present-day usage of 'i', 'j', 'u' and 'v', reduced the long 's' and substituted 'th' for the thorn. Quotations and citations of other Shakespeare dramas are from *The Riverside Shakespeare*, 2nd edn (Boston, 1997), ed. G. Blakemore Evans and John J.M. Tobin.

Editing a Shakespearean play is in many ways a cumulative process, begun in the author's own day and layered by generation after generation of editors from whom the next generation learns. Sometimes the lessons are unintentionally negative: not every edition improves unfailingly on its predecessors. Most editions nonetheless make a few contributions, and some make a great many, to the better understanding of a document written nearly four hundred years ago in a context that can only partly be reconstructed and in a language that has changed immeasurably. Today's editors accordingly owe a lasting debt to all previous editors for suggesting ways to (or not to) modernize, to gloss, to interpret and to introduce the text at hand.

In the preparation of this edition of *The Tempest*, we have perused dozens of editions and read very carefully the major scholarly versions. We are especially appreciative of Morton Luce's path-breaking first Arden edition (1901) and appreciate even more Frank Kermode's second Arden edition (1954). We gladly acknowledge also our indebtedness to the perceptive recent editions by Anne Barton (1968), Stephen Orgel (1987), David Bevington (1988) and Barbara Mowat (1994); readers will find frequent references to their contributions throughout this edition. And, reaching back more than a century, we are thankful for the indefatigable H.H. Furness's variorum edition of 1892, which is still useful and edifying on many specific points. Of course the Arden 3 edition of *The Tempest* reflects our own preferences – with essential help from the many scholars cited below – on all the editorial matters, large and small, that collectively distinguish an edition from a reprint.

The dedication of this volume to the staff of the Folger Shakespeare Library in Washington, D.C., underscores our profound indebtedness to the institution in which we conducted most of the research for this edition of *The Tempest*. Especially during the academic year 1996–7, when a sabbatical leave from Clark University enabled Virginia Vaughan to be released from teaching duties, but also on frequent visits over a six-year span, the Reading Room staff, ably headed by Elizabeth Walsh, assisted us with unfailing expertise, efficiency, patience and courtesy. Georgianna Ziegler, Reference Librarian, tracked down the arcane information editors need, while Julie Ainsworth, head of Photographic Services, and Theresa Helein assisted with illustrations. Librarian Richard Kuhta always took a friendly interest in our progress, and daily conversations with fellow readers spurred us on. For us, as for countless other scholars, the Folger Library provides a wealth of information about Shakespeare and early modern Europe in a supportive, attractive environment.

We are also grateful to other libraries and librarians. At our home base, the Reference staff of the Robert Hutchings Goddard Library of Clark University (Mary Hartman and Irene Walch, in particular) provided vital assistance. On less frequent forays to the Library of Congress, the Harvard Theatre

Collection and the British Library, we also encountered efficient and helpful staff. Our thanks to all.

Just as we could not have conducted our research without access to libraries, we could not have modernized the play's text and written our Introduction and commentary without the friends and colleagues who critiqued our work. The greatest debt is to our general editors, Richard Proudfoot, Ann Thompson and David Kastan, who read repeated drafts of the edition. Any mistakes that escaped their eagle eyes are, of course, our responsibility. James Bulman and R.A. Foakes, fellow Arden editors, each read a draft of our introduction with friendly but forthright candour; the final version is not quite what either of them would wish for, perhaps, but it is substantially improved by their comments.

We are also grateful to Shakespeareans who contributed their particular expertise: Peter Blayney on printing, Leslie Thomson on stage directions, Susan Snyder on genre, Barbara Mowat on magic and on editing in general, Peggy Simonds on alchemy, Dympna Callaghan on Ireland, Naomi Liebler on Richard Johnson's *The Most Famous History of the Seven Champions of Christendom*, Jonathan Bate on 'water with berries', Richard Levin on Stephano's 'bald jerkin', T.W. Craik on 'telling the clock', Reginald Rampone on Derek Jarman, A.R. Braunmuller on early Shakespeare editions, George Wright on metre and Katherine Duncan-Jones and Valerie Wayne on the 'wise'/ 'wife' crux. Ann and John Thompson alerted us to the bas-relief at Burford Church.

During six years of intensive work on *The Tempest*, we were privileged to talk about our evolving edition with a variety of audiences whose questions and comments stimulated our thinking. We are especially grateful to the colleagues who organized our presentations: Lois Potter at the University of Delaware, James Bulman at Allegheny College, William Sherman and Peter Hulme at the University of Maryland, and Robert Madison at the U.S. Naval Academy.

Essential to any scholarly endeavour is the tedious business of production and publication. We owe a special thanks to the 'Ariel' of this edition, the stage manager who co-ordinated all the actors and timed the production: Jessica Hodge of Thomas Nelson and Sons Ltd. Our copy-editor, Judith Ravenscroft, paid meticulous attention to detail, saving us many embarrassments. We are also grateful to the policy-makers at Thomas Nelson and Sons Ltd for maintaining the high standards that have been associated with the Arden Shakespeare for the past one hundred years; we feel privileged to be part of such a professional enterprise.

On the home front in Worcester, Massachusetts, we owe thanks to Felice Bochman for a transcription of F1, our basic text, and to Jacquelyn Bessell for valuable assistance and good cheer. Discussions with Virginia Vaughan's students and colleagues at Clark University frequently stimulated fresh insights. We also thank our own canine 'Ariel' (better known as Becca) and her playmate Caliban for love and support through the entire project. Though their wistful eyes often wondered 'Is there more toil?' – especially on fine days we spent at the library instead of walking in the countryside – they always greeted us joyfully when we returned. And last, but not least, we thank each other, for patience, good humour and love that 'frees all faults'. In that spirit, we remind our readers of Prospero's final request: although we accept responsibility for any shortcomings they find in this edition, 'As you from crimes would pardoned be, / Let your indulgence set [us] free'.

Virginia Mason Vaughan
and Alden T. Vaughan
Worcester, Massachusetts

INTRODUCTION

First performed in 1611 and first printed as the opening play in
Shakespeare's collected works of 1623, *The Tempest* has long
dazzled readers and audiences with its intricate blend of magic,
music, humour, intrigue and tenderness. It charmed Jacobean
audiences, played (in substantially altered form) to packed
houses from the Restoration through the eighteenth century,
emerged (in its original form) as a focal point in nineteenth-
century European debates about the nature of humanity, and
served disparate symbolic roles in twentieth-century writings on
western imperialism and its demise. *The Tempest* has been a play
for all eras, all continents and many ideologies.

What several centuries of readers, watchers and critics have
found so fascinating in Shakespeare's last solo play is perhaps
less the story of the shipwreck, island refuge, murderous cabals
and happy ending than it is *The Tempest*'s vibrant but ambiguous
central characters: the admirable or detestable Prospero (who,
some critics contend, reflects the author himself), the bestial or
noble Caliban, the loyal or resentful Ariel, the demure or
resilient Miranda. Such antithetical extremes and their many
intermediate positions exemplify *The Tempest*'s endlessly arguable nature. Even the play's narrative context is disputable.
Some critics, for example, champion *The Tempest*'s likely New
World sources, claim Bermuda or some other colonial setting as
its island and find in Caliban the personification of American
Indians. Other critics, with equal urgency, insist that the play's
most meaningful analogues, its geographical context and its
major characters are emphatically European.

Controversy has marked *The Tempest* almost from the outset.

Beginning with Ben Jonson's quip in 1614 about a '*Servant-monster*' (clearly Caliban), through centuries of changing interpretations by legions of scholars – whether from a Romantic, Christian, Darwinian, Freudian, allegorical, autobiographical, cultural materialist or post-colonial perspective – *The Tempest* has resonated with unusual power and variety. It has also appealed diversely to a wide range of visual artists, including William Hogarth, Henry Fuseli, Walter Crane and Arthur Rackham; to musicians Henry Purcell, Michael Tippett, and (too late in life) Verdi and Mozart; and to such disparate poets and novelists as Robert Browning, Herman Melville, T.S. Eliot, W.H. Auden, George Lamming and Edward Kamau Brathwaite. Sociopolitical writers like Ernest Renan, José Enrique Rodó, Octave Mannoni and Roberto Fernández Retamar have employed *The Tempest* metaphorically to epitomize their sometimes antithetical cultural perceptions. And although other Shakespearean plays enjoy worldwide recognition in the aftermath of the British Empire, *The Tempest* has been uniquely adopted by formerly colonized nations in refashioning their post-colonial identities.

This Introduction reviews the necessary backgrounds from which a reader or viewer of *The Tempest* may assess its multiplicity of interpretive perspectives and appreciate its appeal to diverse eras and cultures. The first section discusses the play itself, addressing formal elements such as structure, plot, language and characterization. The second section examines the various historical, literary and dramatic contexts that may have shaped the play's plot and characters. The third section surveys the play's afterlife – four centuries of critical interpretations, theatrical and literary adaptations, and metaphoric appropriations in Britain and North America especially, but also throughout the world in response to the rise and fall of colonialism. The Introduction's final section summarizes current knowledge about the printing of the Folio text, its typographical peculiarities and most problematic textual cruxes, and this edition's editorial practices.

THE PLAY

In Act 5 of the Folio *Tempest*, a stage direction instructs: '*Here Prospero discouers Ferdinand and Miranda playing at chess*' (5.1.171.1), whereupon the actor playing Prospero pulls aside the arras from the 'discovery space' – the alcove at the back of the stage – so that Ferdinand and Miranda can suddenly be seen. That action, *The Tempest*'s final spectacle of discovery, provokes open-mouthed wonder in the onstage spectators, most of whom thought Ferdinand had drowned. Gonzalo attributes this joyous discovery to deities who have 'chalked forth the way / Which brought us hither', and marvels that

> in one voyage
> Did Claribel her husband find at Tunis,
> And Ferdinand, her brother, found a wife
> Where he himself was lost; Prospero his dukedom
> In a poor isle; and all of us ourselves,
> When no man was his own.
>
> (5.1.203–4, 208–13)

Gonzalo's wonder at discovering what had been unknown or, if known, what was assumed to be irretrievably lost, epitomizes *The Tempest*'s enduring power, for to audiences and readers alike the play prompts us to 'rejoice / Beyond a common joy' (5.1.206–7) at unexpected discoveries of people, places and events. The play is a theatrical wonder cabinet, a collection of exotic sights and sounds that parallels in many respects the gatherings of natural and man-made rarities from around the world that fascinated Shakespeare's contemporaries.

Wonder and discovery are, of course, no strangers to Shakespeare's late plays. *Pericles* offers two scenes in which the hero first finds his long-lost daughter and then his wife; both reappear almost miraculously after being lost for about fifteen years. In *The Winter's Tale* Perdita's discovery evokes 'a notable passion of wonder' (5.2.15–16), and Hermione's sudden resurrection after sixteen years stupefies the audience as well as the onstage characters. But as wonderful as these moments are, they pale beside the manifold surprises of *The Tempest*, where shipwrecked Stephano and Trinculo encounter a monstrous islander, strange shapes produce a banquet and then make it disappear, a terrible figure of a harpy maddens the shipwrecked Neapolitans, and the beauteous masque of celestial deities performed for his betrothal amazes young Ferdinand.

Despite the play's unique panoply of visual wonders, very little happens on Prospero's enchanted island. *The Tempest*'s spectacular opening storm ostensibly splits a ship and all its passengers drown, but we soon learn that the storm was only an illusion crafted by Prospero and that the castaways are all safe. For the remainder of the play, the shipwrecked Europeans and the savage Caliban wander in clusters around the island, while Ariel flits from one group to another; Prospero and Miranda barely budge. The last scene brings everyone to Prospero's cell for a final revelation, but they were always nearby.

A sense of newness, of wonder, of exciting discovery nonetheless pervades the play, transcending its restricted geography and paucity of action. Those limitations notwithstanding, the island to some degree epitomizes Europe's age of discovery. Gonzalo's amazement at Ferdinand and Miranda's sudden appearance, as well as Miranda's joyous surprise at a 'brave new world' with 'such people in't' (5.1.183–4), echo the response of European explorers to exotic peoples, fauna and flora in a remote new world. While *The Tempest* is not primarily about America (despite many attempts to Americanize it reductively (see pp. 98–108)), the play's wondrous discoveries link the drama thematically to the travellers' tales that so delighted readers of Richard Hakluyt's *Principal Navigations* (1589, 1598–1600) and, a bit later, of Samuel Purchas's *Purchas his Pilgrimage* (1613) and, later still, *Purchas his Pilgrimes* (1625). Caliban's / Prospero's island lies literally in the Mediterranean between Tunis and Naples, but its geographical location is less important than the fact that it is nameless, uncharted and largely un-explored. This enchanted island harbours two Milanese cast-aways (Prospero and Miranda), two remarkable natives (Caliban and Ariel) and assorted spirits unlike anything the Europeans (and we, the audience) have ever seen. Our sojourn on this enchanted island is akin to a trip to a distant planet, where we find a world dramatically unlike our own.

Gonzalo's assertion that all the Neapolitans have 'found' themselves during their afternoon on this enchanted island is overly optimistic, but he correctly judges that most of them were radically changed by the experience. Ferdinand, heir to the throne of Naples, has undergone a sea-change by falling in love with Miranda and finding a father-in-law in Prospero, the deposed Duke of Milan. His father Alonso has also been trans-formed; shipwreck, despair at the presumed loss of his son and pangs of guilt have brought repentance for his part in the con-spiracy against Prospero twelve years earlier. Whether Alonso's brother Sebastian and Prospero's brother Antonio have also changed is uncertain, but at least their lust for kingly office has been contained by Prospero's surveillance. And the play's final scene previews further transformations. Ariel will be free as the wind; Caliban will be wise, seek for grace and (probably) reinherit the island; Miranda will become a wife and the mother of future kings; and Prospero will be restored to his dukedom in Milan.

Whether Prospero has indeed found himself during the play's course is a matter of intense critical debate. At the beginning of Act 5, Ariel instructs him to forgive his enemies, which he pro-fesses to do. His willingness to relinquish magical powers so great that he could raise the dead signals, perhaps, an acceptance of his limited humanity, but this determination might also stem from a recognition that magic distracts from the political power he must wield as Duke.

Despite *The Tempest*'s exploitation of the conventional comic ending in the betrothal of a young couple and the reconciliation of their fathers, its conclusion is remarkably open-ended. From the opening storm to the closing epilogue, the play challenges the boundaries between illusion and reality. Actors and audiences alike are 'such stuff / As dreams are made on' (4.1.156–7), their lives transient, their aspirations ephemeral. In his final words Prospero erases the distinction between actor and audience, island world and our world:

> As you from crimes would pardoned be,
> Let your indulgence set me free.
> (Epilogue, 19–20)

Prospero, the wronged Duke of Milan who forgives his enemies, however reluctantly, is now the one seeking forgiveness from the audience. And all of us, on the stage and off it, need the 'Mercy itself' that 'frees all faults' (Epilogue, 18).

Genesis and early performances

In the summer of 1609 an English ship was wrecked in the uninhabited Bermuda islands; several narratives of that accident and its fortunate aftermath reached London in the later months of 1610. Shakespeare probably wrote *The Tempest* between the arrival of those accounts and the play's first recorded performance about a year later. According to a rare surviving record of performances on 1 November 1611 ('Hallomas nyght'), Shakespeare's acting company 'presented att Whithall before the kinges Majestie a play Called the Tempest'.[1] During the winter of 1612–13, *The Tempest* had a second royal performance as part of the festivities celebrating Princess Elizabeth's betrothal to the Elector Palatine (Chambers, 1.490–4).

Like the other thirteen plays selected for the wedding ceremonies, including *Othello*, *The Winter's Tale* and *Much Ado About Nothing*, *The Tempest* was almost surely written originally for performance at one of the King's Company's

---

1 The sparse surviving evidence of early performances is reproduced in the appendices to E. K. Chambers's biography of Shakespeare. See especially Chambers, 2.342–3.

playhouses[1] – probably the indoor Blackfriars Theatre, though it could easily have been mounted at the open-air Globe (Sturgess).[2] And while there is no evidence of textual changes during its early years, *The Tempest* may, like other plays, have been modified by the author between its initial, probably pre-Whitehall, performance in 1611 and Shakespeare's death in 1616 or by other hands from then until the printing of the Folio in 1623.[3]

The Tempest appeared at an exciting and prosperous time for the King's Company. They played in the summer months at the Globe Theatre, a public playhouse that could accommodate up to 3,000 spectators and, from October to May, at the Blackfriars, an intimate indoor theatre for a smaller, more aristocratic and relatively homogeneous audience (Fig. 1). Among the King's Company's many productions in the years following 1610–11, *The Tempest* appears to have been popular. John Dryden claimed in the Preface to the fanciful adaptation that he and William Davenant produced in 1667 that its precurser '*had formerly been acted with success in the* Black-fryers' (Dryden & Davenant, sig. A2ᵛ). Ben Jonson, though no fan of the play, judging from his (perhaps tongue-in-cheek) Induction to *Bartholomew Fair* (1614), implied that Shakespeare's play was well known, bragging of his own play: 'If there bee never a *Servant-monster* i'the *Fayre*; who can helpe it? he sayes; nor a nest of *Antiques*? Hee is loth to make Nature afraid in his *Playes*, like those that beget

1 In 1603, Shakespeare's acting company came under the patronage of King James; thereafter it was known as the King's Company or the King's Men.

2 In an intriguing case against the accepted wisdom that *The Tempest* was intended for performance at the Blackfriars Theatre and was produced only incidentally at court, Demaray contends that Shakespeare had a court performance in mind while writing, responding 'to a fascination at court with staged spectacles that embraced all of the theatrical arts – song, speech, scenery, dance and costume iconography – and that featured strange or unusual character-types in exotic locales' (16). But *The Winter's Tale* was also performed at court on 5 November 1611; since Simon Forman recorded seeing this play at the Globe on 11 May of the same year, it seems more likely that the court performances at Whitehall were special productions of plays already in the public repertoire (Chambers, 1.489).

3 For a discussion of several arguments in favour of a much earlier date of composition that have been almost wholly rejected by modern scholarship, and for suggestions about possible early alterations to the play, see Ard², xv–xxiv.

7

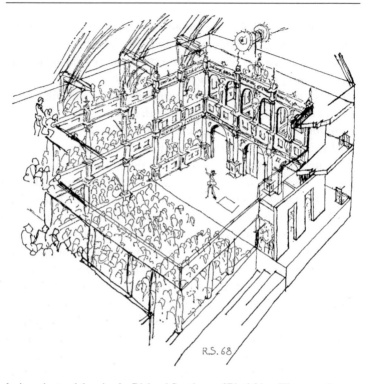

1 A conjectural drawing by Richard Southern of Blackfriars Theatre as it appeared after 1596

Tales, Tempests, and such like *Drolleries*' (Jonson, *Works,* 6.16). Unfortunately, Jonson's contemporaneous reference provides no information about *The Tempest*'s early staging.

If early performances of *The Tempest* conformed closely to the Folio text, they required thirteen men and four boys; because all the adult actors assemble at the finale, there is little opportunity for doubling. The stage directions also call for spirits, nymphs, reapers and hunting dogs, functions that could have been filled by extras, or perhaps by child singers attached to the royal household. The staging itself – most notably the tempest, the disappearing banquet and the masque – could easily have been created on the non-scenic, platform stage of the Blackfriars (Sturgess). Because Ariel obeys Prospero's direction to 'make thyself like a nymph o'th' sea' (1.2.302, 317.1), there is no need for the actor to fly, though in modern productions he[1] often appears to, either by the use of wires or, more often, by graceful movements aloft or up and down ladders.

The play also calls for an assortment of sound effects: thunder, confused noises, soft music, solemn music, a noise of hunters, dogs barking. Drums or rolling cannonballs probably evoked the thunder, squibs (an early variety of fireworks) may have created the effect of lightning, and a small orchestra most likely supplied the music. At the Blackfriars, an organ could have added the island's eerie music. Except for the opening storm scene, which could be recreated with appropriate sounds on a platform stage, Shakespeare limits the scene of his action to one fictional island, where characters can readily come and go without changes of scenery. The resulting simple staging could easily have been transferred to the Banqueting House at Whitehall for performances before King James.

Genre

The editors of the First Folio grouped *The Tempest*, along with *The Winter's Tale*, with Shakespeare's earlier comedies, which must have satisfied most seventeenth-century readers. Comedies typically traced the trials of young lovers at the hands of a blocking agent (usually her father) and ended with the celebration of their engagement and a parental blessing. The main plot was often paralleled in the comic subplot, for example the antics of Launce and Speed in *The Two Gentlemen of Verona*, Dogberry and Verges in *Much Ado About Nothing*, Sir Toby and Maria in *Twelfth Night*. *The Tempest* at first glance follows this pattern: Prospero pretends to block Ferdinand's courtship of Miranda

---

1 We employ male pronouns when referring to Ariel, although the character is essentially without sexual identity. The Folio's sole relevant pronoun is 'his' (1.2.193); and, of course, the role was originally played by a boy or young man.

but finally blesses their marriage; the lovers' wooing is juxtaposed with scenes of clowning by the drunken servants Stephano, Trinculo and Caliban. But in other respects, *The Tempest* is quite different from Shakespeare's earlier comedies. The audience's attention is consistently focused on the father, not the young lovers, and their betrothal is planned before they even meet. The comic clowning threatens the very life of the play's protagonist, and the peril of assassination permeates the plot. The darker themes of Shakespeare's tragedies - regicide, usurpation and vengeance – are always near this comedy's surface. To most twentieth-century critics, *The Tempest* (along with *Pericles*, *The Winter's Tale*, *Cymbeline* and *The Two Noble Kinsmen*) has seemed qualitatively different from Shakespeare's earlier comic works, and many have sought to explain the change.

The Winter's Tale, *Cymbeline*, *The Tempest* and the collaborative *Two Noble Kinsmen* were written in a changing theatrical climate; the more affluent audiences of the Blackfriars called for a different kind of drama than had long been customary at the Globe and other playhouses. By 1610–11, Francis Beaumont and John Fletcher had begun a productive literary collaboration, specializing in mixed-mode plays that were often labelled 'tragicomedies'. Fletcher, influenced by Giovanni Battista Guarini's defence of tragicomedy in *Il compendio della poesia tragicomica* (1601), adapted the Italian's experimental drama *Il Pastor Fido* to the English stage as *The Faithful Shepherdess* (1609–10). In a preface 'To the Reader', Fletcher defined the new genre:

> A tragie-comedie is not so called in respect of mirth and killing, but in respect it wants deaths, which is inough to make it no tragedie, yet brings some neere it, which is inough to make it no comedie.
>
> (Beaumont & Fletcher, 3.497)

Shakespeare's last plays generally adhere to this definition: several major characters suffer grievously yet eventually enjoy familial reunions and reconciliations. Still, the deaths of Cloten (*Cymbeline*), Mamillius and Antigonus (*The Winter's Tale*) contradict the Guarini / Fletcher notion that such a play 'wants deaths'; and, as a recent critic contends, *ex post facto* readings of Fletcher's preface (in a play that attracted meagre audiences) can distort our understanding of a popular dramatic form which appeared in many variations (McMullan & Hope, 4).

That Shakespeare was experimenting with a mixed mode of drama before Fletcher came on the scene seems apparent from *Pericles* (1608), which includes all the plot elements Shakespeare exploited later:

> a royal child is lost and rediscovered; sea journeys change men's lives; scenes occur in different countries, most of them remote; the main characters struggle against adversity and are rewarded in the end; characters thought dead are miraculously resurrected; and the final reconciliation is achieved through the agency of young people.
>
> (Hartwig, 4)

These narrative components are the stuff of romance, so it is unsurprising that although the dramatic category was unknown in Shakespeare's era, for most of the twentieth century *Pericles*, *Cymbeline*, *The Winter's Tale* and *The Tempest* have been regrouped as 'Shakespeare's romances'.

A standard definition of 'romance' is 'a fictitious narrative in prose of which the scene and incidents are very remote from those of ordinary life, *esp.* one of the class prevalent in the 16th and 17th centuries, in which the story is often overlaid with long disquisitions and digressions' (*OED* 3). Drawing on third-century AD Greek narratives about the extraordinary adventures of lost and wandering lovers, interlaced with strange monsters, savage beasts and supernatural apparitions, Elizabethan writers – John Lyly, Thomas Lodge, Robert Greene and, in the posthumously published *Arcadia*, Philip Sidney – brought such stories to the reading public. Dramatists combed the narratives for new plots. Shakespeare, for one, used Sidney's story of the Paphlagonian king for the Gloucester subplot in *King Lear* and in the process, according to Hallett Smith, began a period of experimentation with dramatizations of romances that culminated in *The Tempest* (H. Smith, 55).

The *commedia dell'arte* of continental Europe was well known in England and may also have influenced Shakespeare's plot and characters. In 1934 Kathleen M. Lea made a case for his use of a scenario from the *commedia dell'arte*, arguing that

> the favourite setting is either the coast of Arcadia or a lost island; the dramatis personae consists of a magician who has a somewhat malicious interest in the love-affairs of a group of nymphs and shepherds among whom one may be his daughter and another the lost son of the Magnifico or the Doctor who are shipwrecked onto the coast with the Zanni. The magician's attendants are satyrs, demons, or rustics of the cruder sort . . . At the denouement the magician discovers the relationship between himself, the lovers, and the strangers, ends the play by renouncing his magic and sometimes agrees to leave the island and return to civic life.
>
> (Lea, 2.444–5)

The similarity to Prospero (the magician), Miranda (his daughter), Ferdinand (the son of a duke instead of a magnifico), Ariel (a benign satyr) and Caliban (a demonic and rustic attendant) is clear. Though Stephano and Trinculo obviously share the comic qualities of the *zanni* – Trinculo is a court jester, Stephano a comic drunk – the extent of Shakespeare's indebtedness to this continental scenario is necessarily hypothetical (see Fig. 2).

Categories of dramatic works are useful but not essential. Whether *The Tempest* is labelled a tragicomedy (Hartwig) or a romance (Edwards, H. Smith, Felperin), neither typology tells us whether Shakespeare initiated a change in theatrical offer-

2 A. Younge as Stephano and H. Nye as Trinculo, with the latter wearing the customary jester's costume, uniform of the *zanni*

ings or seized upon contemporary fashions, or effectively did both. In any case, the play's content and structure are characteristic of the last years of the dramatist's career and of a highly popular Jacobean dramatic form.

Structure

Except for *The Comedy of Errors*, *The Tempest* is Shakespeare's shortest play; and like *The Comedy of Errors*, it roughly conforms to the unities of time, place and action. As Prospero's instructions to Ariel make clear (1.2.240–1; 5.1.4–5), the plot consumes the hours between 2 p.m. and 6 p.m.[1] (the events of twelve years ago and earlier are recounted rather than enacted in 1.2), and, aside from the initial storm scene, the events occur on one mysterious island. The plot's various strands are Prospero's interventions in the other characters' lives and psyches.

The Tempest may indeed be Shakespeare's most tightly structured play, an appropriate characteristic for a story in which the central character is so concerned with disciplining his minions. Composed of nine separate scenes, the play begins with a shipwreck and ends with the restoration of the ship that had seemed earlier to split. The rest of the play is comparably symmetrical. Scenes 2 (1.2) and 8 (4.1) involve Prospero, Miranda and Ferdinand; in scene 2 Ferdinand thinks he has lost his father forever; in scene 8 he assumes a new father in Prospero through marriage to Miranda. Scenes 3 (2.1) and 7 (3.3) develop Antonio and Sebastian's plan to kill Alonso and usurp his throne; in both scenes their conspiracy is postponed, in scene 3 by Ariel's intervention and in scene 7 by the mysterious arrival of a banquet. Scenes 4 (2.2) and 6 (3.2) display the drunken antics of Caliban, Stephano and Trinculo, and their plot to kill Prospero and take

---

1 With musical interludes between the acts (see Taylor, 30), *The Tempest* would have lasted approximately four hours – the same amount of time that Prospero suggests the action takes. But cf. Alonso's 'three hours since / Were wrecked upon this shore' (5.1.136–7), and the Boatswain's 'but three glasses since we gave out split' (5.1.223); perhaps Prospero allows an hour for the storm.

over the island (foiled in the last lines of 4.1). The central scene 5 (3.1) showcases Ferdinand and Miranda's betrothal.[1]

Within this tight pattern, several roles and events are parallel; *The Tempest*'s 'symmetric structure of correspondences gives it the multiplicity of a hall of mirrors, in which everything reflects and re-reflects everything else' (Brooks, 37). Prospero's overthrow in Milan twelve years earlier is nearly repeated, first in Antonio and Sebastian's plot to murder Alonso, and second in Caliban, Stephano and Trinculo's plan to assassinate Prospero. Each of these plot strands leads to a seemingly miraculous spectacle. Prospero's ultimate goals, the restoration of his rightful place and a proper marriage for his daughter, are celebrated in the masque he stages for Ferdinand and Miranda in 4.1. Alonso, Sebastian and Antonio are stunned by a disappearing banquet and Ariel's sudden appearance as a harpy in 3.3. Trinculo and Stephano are diverted from their murderous intent at the sight of Prospero's 'trumpery' hanging on a line; their appearance near the end of the play in stolen finery provides an antimasque which parodies Ceres and Juno's formal personations in 4.1. And, as the Epilogue reminds us, the play is itself a spectacle that will soon disappear.

Shakespeare's adherence to the unity of time is particularly problematic. Instead of evolving his plot across the vasts of time and space so common in Greek romance, the dramatist insists that his characters merely *remember* the events of the twelve years preceding. Although Miranda cannot recall enough to challenge Prospero's account, Caliban and Ariel do remember early events on the island; Caliban's recollections, in some particulars, challenge his master's, leaving the audience to speculate as to what really happened.[2]

---

1 See Mark Rose, *Shakespearean Design* (Cambridge, Mass., 1972), p. 173, for a scenic diagram that demonstrates the play's symmetry.
2 For further discussion of memory in *The Tempest*, see especially Günter Walch, 'Metatheatrical memory and transculturation in *The Tempest*', in Maquerlot & Willems, 223–38.

The compression of events to one afternoon also leaves many loose ends. Anne Barton observes that 'a surprising amount of *The Tempest* depends upon the suppressed and the unspoken' (Penguin, 16). The introduction of Antonio's son in 1.2.439, a figure who is not mentioned elsewhere in the play, is a case in point. Audiences may also wonder about the absence of Prospero's wife, the fate of Claribel in Tunis, Sycorax's life before she was banished to the island, Antonio's silence in the final scene and other gaps in the narrative. Antonio's son may be a loose end, an omission in the heat of composition; but these other conundrums appear to be deliberate silences on Shakespeare's part. *The Tempest* provokes dozens of questions for which the text provides no certain answers.

It also provokes questions about place. *The Tempest*, like *The Winter's Tale*, is a pastoral romance, but its opposition of court and country is affected by Shakespeare's adherence to the unity of place. We never see the courts of Milan and Naples (as we do Leontes' Sicily); rather they come to the island in the persons of Alonso, Antonio, Sebastian and others. These courtiers do not find themselves in a stylized world of sonnet-citing shepherds and shepherdesses, but discover instead an island replete with brine pits, hissing adders and stinging urchins. Alonso is mortified by his encounter with Ariel the harpy, but Antonio, and perhaps Sebastian, seem psychologically unchanged by their sojourn in the natural world. Shakespeare uses the pattern of pastoral, but as with other patterns in the play, unanticipated events disrupt expectations.

More than a simple setting, the island takes on a life of its own. Caliban creates its mythic resonances with his evocations of exotic flora and fauna: 'berries', 'clustr'ing filberts', 'pignuts', 'the nimble marmoset' and the ambiguous 'scamels' (2.2.157–69). His perspective is shaped by physical responses to night and day, moon and stars, emptiness and fullness, silence and music. The Neapolitans see the island differently. To Gonzalo it has possibilities as a golden-age plantation. To Sebastian and Antonio it evokes travellers' tales of unicorns and the phoenix. To Prospero it is a temporary if unwanted haven from the cares of office. To the audience it is the stuff that dreams are made on, an imaginative world of words and music.

The action on this island, as we suggested earlier, is mainly geographic movement writ small. The first four acts conclude with an invitation to move on: 'Come, follow' (1.2.502); 'lead the way' (2.2.183); 'Follow, I pray you' (3.3.110); 'Follow and do me service' (4.1.266) (see Aercke, 148). The characters perambulate in small groups from one part of the island to another; only at Prospero's final invitation, 'Please you, draw near' (5.1.319), do they join in one place. Although their physical and psychological journeys through the island's maze have ended, the play concludes with plans for a sea journey back to Milan that roughly parallels the journeys that brought all the Europeans to the island.

This sense of continual movement contributes to *The Tempest*'s elusiveness. Within its tightly organized scenes it switches from one view of human nature to another; each can be said to be 'true'. Stanley Wells observes that '*The Tempest* is a romance containing built-in criticism of romance; not a rejection of it, but an appreciation of both its glories and its limitations' (Wells[1], 76). This tension is most apparent in the counterpoint among Gonzalo, Antonio and Sebastian in 2.1.52–106. Gonzalo sees grass that is green and lusty; the cynical courtiers find only docks and nettles. Prospero's wry response to Miranda's discovery of a 'brave new world' – ''Tis new to thee' (5.1.183–4) – frames a similar opposition. Such contradictory visions are characteristic of Shakespeare's late plays. By yoking tragic themes and comic resolutions, realistic characterizations and exotic tales, the romances highlight the paradoxes of human experience.

Music

The atmosphere of *The Tempest*'s enchanted island is created largely through sound. The stage directions call for a variety of auditory effects, including Ariel playing on a tabor and pipe

(3.2.124SD), '*Solemn and strange music*' (3.3.17.1), '*soft music*' (3.3.82.1 and 4.1.58SD), '*a strange hollow and confused noise*' (4.1.138.3–4) and '*Solemn music*' (5.1.57SD). Moreover, Prospero manifests his power in music throughout *The Tempest*; akin in many ways to Orpheus, Prospero employs music to civilize his island's discordant elements (Simonds, 'Music').

Ariel must have originally been performed by an adept musician, for in addition to playing on his tabor and pipe, he sings four songs. Throughout the play, his songs are a vehicle for Prospero's magic: they guide Ferdinand to his meeting with Miranda in 1.2, waken Gonzalo in time to prevent regicide in 2.1 and lead the drunken conspirators into the horse pond in 4.1. Ariel's final tune, 'Where the bee sucks', accompanies Prospero's donning of ducal robes while the airy spirit exults in the merry life he will lead in liberty.

The two settings of Ariel's songs that survive, 'Full fathom five' and 'Where the Bee sucks' (reproduced in Figs 3 and 4), were composed by Robert Johnson, a lutenist attached to James I's court and in the service of Prince Henry.[1] Compared to Ariel's songs, the rest of the music in *The Tempest* is entertaining but of scant importance to the plot. Stephano enters singing a scurvy tune, Caliban chants a freedom catch, and the three drunks join in a round, 'Flout 'em and scout 'em'. In a more sober vein, music accompanies the masque, parts of it are sung, and it is followed by a dance of Reapers and Nymphs.

Of greater import than the individual songs announced by the stage directions is the pervasiveness of music conveyed in the text. Caliban assures his companions that the island is full of 'Sounds and sweet airs' (3.2.136). When he hears Ariel's song, Ferdinand wonders, 'Where should this music be? I'th' air, or th'earth?' (1.2.388). Few of Shakespeare's plays require so much music, 'and none of them puts so much emphasis on "dis-

---

1 For a musicological analysis of Johnson's songs, see Howell Chickering, 'Hearing Ariel's songs', *Journal of Medieval and Renaissance Studies*, 24 (1994), 131–72.

Cantus Primus.   R. Johnson.

Full fathome five thy Father lyes, of his bones are Corrall made

those are pearles that were his eyes, nothing of him that doth fade but doth

suffer a Sea change into something rich and strange.

Sea Nymphs hourly ring his knell, Hark now I heare them

Ding Dong Bell Ding Dong Ding Dong Bell

3 Robert Johnson's musical setting for 'Full fathom five', from *Cheerfull Ayres or Ballads*, 1660

persed" music, performed as if it came from all over the stage'
(Seng, 252). At the Blackfriars, Shakespeare had access to
instrumentalists and boy singers who could create a magical
island out of sheer sound.

4 Robert Johnson's musical setting for 'Where the Bee sucks', from *Cheerfull Ayres or Ballads*, 1660

Language

The Tempest's language is no less elusive than the island and its music. Its poetry 'seduces the audience into a state of stylistic suspension, an intuitive zone between sleep and wake, . . . a marginal condition between expectation and understanding,

20

affirmation and skepticism, comedy and tragedy' (McDonald, 27). The language itself creates the island's dreamlike effect, contributing to the audience's sense of suspension from time and space.

Like the play's action, the verse is often elliptical.[1] Apostrophes are used to omit syllables from words, not simply to suit the iambic pentameter line but in all likelihood to compress the language and reveal the emotions boiling beneath. Prospero's speeches to Miranda in 1.2, as he recounts his past, repeatedly use elisions, such as 'hearts i'th' state' (84), 'out o'th' substitution' (103) and 'in lieu o'th' premises' (123). Words are also conspicuously omitted, leaving the observer to make the line coherent by supplying an all-important noun, pronoun, verb or adverb. Consider, for example, 'there is no soul –' (1.2.29), short for 'there is no soul *perished*'; 'and his only heir' (1.2.58), short for 'and *you* his only heir'; 'urchins / Shall forth' (1.2.327–8), short for 'urchins shall *go* forth'. Sometimes key words are delayed, the flow of thought interrupted by a complex dependent clause, as in Prospero's description of Sycorax:

> This damned witch Sycorax,
> For mischiefs manifold and sorceries terrible
> To enter human hearing, from Algiers,
> Thou knowst, was banished.
>
> (1.2.263–6)

Audiences and readers automatically supply 'sorceries *too* terrible' and then wait for the final verb. This compression gives the poetry a 'stripped-down quality, more extreme than anything in Shakespeare's previous work. . . . [T]he verse achieves an uncanny eloquence by way of what it omits or pares away' (Penguin, 13).

---

1 The following analysis of Shakespeare's verse draws heavily on an unpublished paper by Russ McDonald, 'Shakespeare's late line', which was delivered at the March 1997 meeting of the Shakespeare Association of America, and on Anne Barton's introduction to The New Penguin *Tempest*.

Editors of *The Tempest* frequently note its unusual reliance on compound words such as 'sight-outrunning', 'sea-change', 'bemocked-at stabs', 'sea-marge', 'pole-clipped', 'cloud-capped', 'weather-fends', 'spell-stopped', to name just several. The words are joined without syntactical relationships, as if they have been 'left to work out their complex and unstable union within the reader's mind' (Penguin, 14). They add to our sense of the play's compression, collapsing several sentences of meaning into two or three words.

Other passages rely on repetition for effect. Miranda's 'I have suffered / With those that I saw suffer' (1.2.5–6) underscores her compassion, much as Prospero's 'Twelve year since, Miranda, twelve year since' (1.2.53) bespeaks his growing agitation. Like a musical theme with variations, the verse replicates the play's structural repetitions and variations – usurpation, killing the king, spectacle.

Despite the text's suggestions of movement, most of *The Tempest*'s scenes are static expositions of the past or plans for the future, a quality that makes Shakespeare's use of shared and run-on lines all the more important. The play's longest scene (1.2), consisting almost entirely of recollections, would be tedious indeed were it not for the frequent give and take between the central narrator, Prospero, and his listeners. One-fifth of *The Tempest*'s verse lines are short or shared, an effect that promotes tension and highlights interpersonal conflicts (G. Wright, 119, Appendix C).

The Tempest's high proportion of irregular lines and the frequent use of an extra unaccented syllable at the end of lines repeat at the linguistic level the plot's underlying tension between harmony and disruption, between utopian longings and the chaos caused by human nature. That chaos is perhaps best typified by Caliban, and discussions of the play's language often focus on his speeches. Miranda (with Prospero's assistance, surely) taught him their language, so it is not surprising that his major speeches – even in scenes with Trinculo and Stephano, who use the characteristic prose of clowns and jesters – are in blank verse. Caliban's diction differs, however, from Miranda's and Prospero's; his words express unique apprehension of the natural world, gleaned from his physical experience of island life in the sound of storms, the sting of porcupines, the hiss of adders and the music of the wind. The other characters have little, if anything, to say about Caliban's world; the function of much of their 'civilization' (clothing, utensils, cells) is to protect them from its rigours. Caliban's rhetoric invests the island with reality.

Characters

Like the location of the enchanted island, the origins of the play's characters are elusive. There are, to be sure, links to Shakespeare's earlier endeavours: Prospero has often been compared to *Measure for Measure*'s Vincentio, Miranda to the late romances' Marina, Imogen and Perdita. Despite the echoes of past creations, the characters in *The Tempest* are as much *sui generis* as the play's structure and language.

Ben Jonson included a Prospero and a Stephano in the first version of *Every Man in his Humour* (1598), which makes it tempting to imagine that Shakespeare, who appears in *Every Man*'s cast list, once performed Jonson's Prospero. But the resemblance between the two characters is in name only. Prospero, ironically enough, means 'fortunate' or 'prosperous' but, like Shakespeare's magician, the name has often belied reality. For example, William Thomas's *Historie of Italie* (1549), sometimes suggested as a direct source for *The Tempest* (Bullough, 8.249–50), describes the fate of Prospero Adorno, who was established by Ferdinando, Duke of Milan, as the Governor of Genoa. According to Thomas, Prospero was deposed; the citizens '(remembryng how thei were best in quiet, whan they were subjectes to the Duke of Millaine) returned of newe to be under the Milanese dominion: and than was Antony Adorno made governour of the citee for the Duke' (Thomas,

182). Whether or not Shakespeare took the names of Ferdinand and the brothers Prospero and Antonio from Thomas, the latter's account of a brother's treachery provides an intriguing analogue.

Prospero is 'fortunate' in that after twelve years of suffering on a lonely island he sees his daughter happily betrothed and is at long last restored to his dukedom. He is clearly the play's central character; he has far more lines than anyone else[1] and manipulates the other characters throughout. One's reaction to Prospero almost inevitably determines one's response to the entire play. In the eighteenth century, when the magus was perceived as an enlightened and benign *philosophe*, the play seemed a magical comedy; by the late twentieth century, when Prospero had come to be viewed as a tetchy, if not tyrannical, imperialist, the play itself seemed more problematic (see pp. 103–8).

Congruent with these changing interpretations were different physical images of the magus. From the eighteenth century into the twentieth, he was customarily depicted on stage and in visual representations as an old, grey-bearded sage; in many late twentieth-century commentaries, he is presented as middle-aged, which reflects partly a better knowledge of Renaissance royal culture and partly the influence of Freudian theories. Renaissance princes usually married early. Since Miranda is apparently his only offspring (whose mother presumably died giving birth) and is now approximately 15, Prospero could be as young as 35. The range of his emotions attests to a nature still in development, and his comment at the play's finale that 'Every third thought shall be my grave' is most likely the mature reflection of middle age that time is not limitless. When Richard Burbage (1567–1619) performed Prospero's role in 1611, he was 44 (Shakespeare was 47), which reinforces our impression of Prospero as between 40 and 45, but no older. If this is indeed the

---

1 Prospero has nearly 30 per cent of the lines; the next highest figure is Caliban's at less than 9 per cent. See Marvin Spevack, *A Complete and Systematic Concordance to the Works of Shakespeare*, 9 vols (Hildesheim, Germany, 1968–80), 1.36–62.

case, an underlying motive for his urgency for the match with Ferdinand may be incestuous feelings for his own daughter. As some recent critics and performances have emphasized, he needs to get her off the island and married, for his own sake as well as hers (see pp. 118, 123).

Throughout the play Prospero displays 'a superb combination of power and control' in his relations to others (Kahn, 239). His stance throughout is authoritarian, which may explain the changing reaction to his role over the centuries. As Duke, he was reponsible for the health of his duchy; his inattention to politics invited Antonio's *coup d'état* twelve years before the play begins; when Prospero resumes his ducal robes at the play's conclusion, there is some question as to what kind of ruler he will be now. His willingness to relinquish his books, the source of his earlier distraction, suggests that he will take a more 'hands-on' approach, perhaps replacing the information gathered by Ariel by using his own surveillance techniques to monitor Antonio and Sebastian.

Prospero is also, as briefly discussed above, a magician. He wears magic robes, uses a magic staff and refers to his books on magic. Magic is his technology, a means to the end of getting what he wants. But a central ambiguity in the play is *what* he wants. Does he plan a spectacular revenge against his enemies? His disjointed language and palpable anguish in 1.2.66–132 suggest the rage that has festered for twelve years, but his plan for Miranda's marriage to Ferdinand makes it less likely that he intends real harm to her future father-in-law. Prospero's angry outburst in the midst of the masquers' festive dance in 4.1 reveals a mind distempered by crimes he cannot forgive, yet he claims to have forgiven the courtiers at the play's conclusion, partly in response to Ariel's remonstrance and partly because he must if Miranda's union with Ferdinand is to succeed. Prospero's darker side, moreover, is emphasized by his being the mirror image to Sycorax. Like Prospero, she arrived with a child, though hers (Caliban) was still in the womb; like him, she used her magic (witchcraft) to control the elements. But Sycorax's powers are presented as demonic, and until he echoes the sorceress Medea's invocation in 5.1.33–50, Prospero construes his own magic as benign: 'There's no harm done' (1.2.15). Still, the parallel underlies the play and casts an ambiguous shadow on the magician.

Perhaps Prospero's most controversial role is that of master. In his service are Ariel, who serves under oral contract for an unstated period (1.2.245–50), and Caliban, enslaved by Prospero a year or two earlier, the text implies, for his sexual assault on a recently pubescent Miranda. Although Prospero handles both subordinates with threats of confinement and bodily pain, and although he is, in many modern interpretations, unduly strict and often petulant towards them, at the end he sets Ariel free ahead of schedule and, perhaps, leaves Caliban to fend for himself when the Europeans return to Italy. Prospero is equally impatient with Ferdinand, whom he temporarily forces to do manual labour. Ferdinand's service is short-lived, however, and he is rewarded with Miranda as a bride.[1]

In the effort to control his fellows, Prospero also seeks to monopolize the narrative. He burdens Miranda in 1.2 with one of the lengthiest expositions in all Shakespearean drama, and at his concluding invitation to the courtiers to pass the night in his cave, he promises to recount the events of his twelve-year exile. His anger at the plot devised by Caliban, Stephano and Trinculo may result in part from their threat to set up a competing narrative; Caliban wants to get his island back (even if Stephano is king), just as Prospero wants to get his dukedom back, and Caliban's plot to kill Prospero would, if successful, destroy the magus's plans. Caliban's and Prospero's conflicting perspectives produce contrary accounts of key events.

If Prospero can be said to 'prosper', Miranda is also aptly named with the feminine form of the gerundive of the Latin verb

---

1 *The Tempest*'s master–servant relations are explored in Andrew Gurr, 'Industrious Ariel and idle Caliban', in Maquerlot & Willems, 193–208.

miror, 'wonder'. Ferdinand exclaims, 'O, you wonder!' when he first meets her, and her response to her newly discovered relatives in the famous line, 'O wonder! . . . O brave new world!' (5.1.181–3), bespeaks her own amazement at a world now opening before her.

Miranda's role within *The Tempest*'s authoritarian framework is first as a daughter and then as a future wife. But even though she conveniently (or magically) falls in love with the man of her father's choice, Miranda is not as meek and submissive as she is often portrayed. She clandestinely (she thinks) meets Ferdinand without permission and then disobeys her father's command not to reveal her name. Earlier, her stinging rebuke of Caliban (1.2.352–63) reveals an assertive young woman.[1] Still, despite occasional disobedience and outspokenness, Miranda remains the chaste ideal of early modern womanhood. Central to Prospero's 'obsession with themes of chastity and fertility' (Thompson, 47), Miranda is his *raison d'être*, her marriage and future children his promise of immortality.

Although Miranda is central to *The Tempest*'s story line, Prospero's two servants play more vocal and dynamic roles; both have problematic names. 'Ariel' must have had rich resonances for a Jacobean audience: 'Uriel', the name of an angel in the Jewish cabala, was John Dee's spirit-communicant during his ill-fated experiments with magic (French, 111–17). Even richer are the biblical nuances. Although the Bishops' Bible equates Ariel with the city of Jerusalem, marginalia to Isaiah, 29, of the Geneva Bible observe that 'The Ebrewe worde Ariel signifieth the lyon of God, & signifieth the altar, because the altar semed to devoure the sacrifice that was offred to God'. Ariel is thus an appropriate appellation for the powerful magus's agent who contrives a storm and a disappearing banquet. In the Bishops' Bible, the prophet declares that the altar of Jerusalem 'shall be visited of the Lord of hostes with thundre, and shaking, and a great

---

1 For the debate over the assignment of this speech, see pp. 135–6.

noyse, a whirlwinde, and a tempest, and a flame of devouring fyre'. Ariel describes his activity in the storm:

> Now in the waist, the deck, in every cabin
> I flamed amazement. Sometime I'd divide
> And burn in many places – on the topmast,
> The yards and bowsprit would I flame distinctly,
> Then meet and join.

> (1.2.197–201)

The prophet Isaiah continues, 'And it shalbe like as an hungrie man dreameth, and beholde, he eateth: and when he awaketh, his soule is emptie . . . For the Lord hath covered you with a spirit of slomber and hath shut up your eyes' – metaphors that are reified in 2.1 when a 'strange drowsiness' possesses the Neapolitans and in 3.3 when '*the banquet vanishes*'. By 1610 Shakespeare probably had heard Isaiah, 29, expounded in church and perhaps had read it at home; whether he turned directly to the Bible or drew on subconscious recollections while he wrote, the image of Ariel as the 'lyon of God' speaking through flood and fire reverberates in *The Tempest*.

Prospero describes Ariel as 'quaint', 'delicate', 'dainty', and 'tricksy' (1.2.318; 4.1.49; 5.1.95, 226). Although Prospero is angered by the sprite's momentary rebellion in 1.2, usually master and servant seem fond of each other, and for most of the play Ariel gladly and expeditiously complies with his master's requests. (In some recent performances, however, such as Simon Russell Beale's in the 1993–4 production by the Royal Shakespeare Company, Ariel is palpably resentful of Prospero (see Fig. 5).) As an airy spirit, Ariel can be seen as one pole in a neo-Platonic dualism: Air as opposed to Caliban's Earth. Thus Ariel is usually portrayed in illustrations as airborne, sometimes with wings (see Fig. 6), and is often attached to ropes or wires in stage performances. Caliban, in stark contrast, is usually hunched and close to the earth, often, in illustrations and stage productions, emerging from a rocky or subterranean cave. Ariel

5 Simon Russell Beale as Ariel confronts Alec McCowen as Prospero in the
1993 Royal Shakespeare Company production of *The Tempest*

is also associated with water: the spirit implements the tempest
and is disguised as a 'nymph o'th' sea' (1.2.302). Air and water
connote lightness, fluidity and grace of movement. Accordingly,
Ariel is often enacted by performers trained to be dancers;
Caliban is contrastingly awkward, often impeded by fins, or a
hunched back, or even, as in the Trinity Repertory production
of 1982, in Providence, Rhode Island, with his feet strapped to
the tops of stools three feet high.

Although *The Tempest*'s cast of characters and the text itself
identify Ariel as a non-human, though rational, spirit, he has
independent thoughts and feelings. He refused, says Prospero,
to enact Sycorax's 'earthy and abhorred commands' (1.2.272–4),
and he urges Prospero to choose forgiveness over vengeance
(5.1.16–19). Still, Ariel once served the sorceress and is the main

29

6 Priscilla Reed Horton, a popular nineteenth-century Ariel, sporting wings
for the role

instrument of Prospero's illusionistic power. The magician even
calls Ariel a 'malignant thing' (1.2.257), though admittedly in a
moment of pique. In sum, he should not be seen simply as the
'Virtue' to Caliban's 'Vice', but as a complex character who asks
for Prospero's affection: 'Do you love me, master? No?' (4.1.48)

Caliban's nature and history are more controversial than his fellow servant's, as is the source of his name. A rough consensus has long prevailed that because Caliban is an anagram for 'cannibal', Shakespeare thereby identified the 'savage' in some way with anthropophagism. Cannibals were topical in Shakespeare's day (though probably less than in the previous century), partly because reports from the New World insisted that some natives consumed human flesh and partly because simultaneous reports from sub-Saharan Africa, often drawing on ancient myths, made similar claims. In America, the association of anthropophagism with the Carib Indians provided the etymological source for 'cannibal', a term that in the sixteenth century gradually replaced the classical 'anthropophagi'. Simultaneously, 'Caribana' soon became a common geographical label, widely used by cartographers for the northern region of South America, while other forms of 'Carib' were associated with various New World peoples and locations.[1] Shakespeare might have borrowed 'cannibal' or one of its many variants from narratives of New World travel, or from contemporary maps, or, as has often been proposed, from the title and text of Montaigne's 'Of the Caniballes', to fashion an imprecise but readily recognizable anagram. The necessity of dropping a superfluous 'n' or 'e' and of substituting 'l' for 'r' – the latter was frequent in transliterations of native languages – would not, perhaps, have interfered with an audience's awareness of the anagram.

If Shakespeare intended an anagrammatic name for his deformed savage, it was too obvious or too cryptic for printed comment until 1778, when the second edition of Samuel Johnson and George Steeven's *Tempest* attributed to Richard Farmer, a prominent Cambridge University scholar, the notion that Caliban was 'cannibal' in verbal disguise. Although adherents to Farmer's exegesis have increased markedly in the succeeding two centuries, sceptics continue to challenge the anagram's theatrical feasibility. As Horace Howard Furness asked in the 1892 Variorum edition:

1 The best discussion of cannibalism and *The Tempest* is in the first two chapters of P. Hulme.

> [W]hen *The Tempest* was acted before the motley audi-
> ence of the Globe Theatre, [was] there a single auditor
> who, on hearing Prospero speak of Caliban, bethought
> him of the Caribbean Sea, and instantly surmised that the
> name was a metathesis of Cannibal? Under this impres-
> sion, the appearance of the monster without a trace of his
> bloodthirsty characteristic must have been disappointing.
>
> (Var, 5)

The usual retort is that Shakespeare meant not a literal cannibal
but a morally and socially deficient savage. Nonetheless, the evidence of authorial intentionality is at best inferential.

Several alternative etymologies have been offered. Among
them is the African placename 'Calibia', which appeared near
the Mediterranean coast on some sixteenth-century maps and is
mentioned in Richard Knolles's *Generall Historie of the Turks*
(1603), a book that Shakespeare unquestionably plumbed for
Othello only a few years before he wrote *The Tempest*. A classical
possibility is the 'Chalybes', a people mentioned by Virgil
(*Aeneid*, Bk 10, 174). Still other proposed sources for Caliban's
name are an Arabic word for 'vile dog', *Kalebon*; the Hindi word
for a satyr of Kalee, *Kalee-ban*; and, more plausibly, the Romany
(Gypsy) word for black or dark things, *caulibon*. Gypsies were a
major social concern throughout sixteenth- and seventeenth-
century England, as numerous laws, plays, tracts and sermons
attest; '*caulibon*' may have been an effective theatrical signifier
of unruliness, darkness and licentiousness (Vaughan, *Caliban*,
33–6). But the Gypsy word, like the other proposed etymologies
– including cannibal, Carib and Caribana – has no contemporary
corroboration.[1]

The Folio's '*Names of the Actors*' describes Caliban as a
'*saluage and deformed slaue*', words that may not be Shakespeare's but which do set rough parameters for his characteriza-

---

1 Another etymological possibility is *Kalyb*, a female character in Richard Johnson's
Most Famous History of the Seven Champions of Christendom (1596–7), a widely disseminated book and a likely influence on *Coriolanus*.

tion though not for his poetic language. Surely in Prospero's and Miranda's eyes, Caliban is a savage, as she specifically calls him (1.2.356); to Prospero he is a creature 'Whom stripes may move, not kindness' (1.2.346). Prospero accuses Caliban of being the son of a witch (Sycorax)[1] and 'the devil' (1.2.263, 320–1; 5.1.269), but the magus's angry words, especially about Caliban's paternity, are not necessarily true; Caliban was conceived before Sycorax's exile from Algiers. Her 'freckled whelp' (1.2.283), an islander by birth, grew for his first twelve or so years without the benefits of European culture, religion and language; to Prospero he resembles the bestial wild man of medieval lore – unkempt, uneducated and thoroughly uncivilized. His 'savagery' is thus opposed to the 'civility' brought to the island by Europeans (see Vaughan, *Caliban*, 7–8).

The extent of Caliban's 'deformity' is woefully imprecise. Prospero describes him as 'Filth', 'Hag-seed', 'beast' and 'misshapen knave' (1.2.347, 366; 4.1.140; 5.1.268) and claims that 'with age his body uglier grows' (4.1.191), but these vituperative terms are doubtless coloured by the magician's anger at Caliban's attempted rape of Miranda and his subsequent rebelliousness. Trinculo initially mistakes Caliban for a fish and later labels him a 'deboshed fish' and 'half a fish and half a monster' (3.2.25, 28), epithets that may reflect Caliban's smell instead of his shape, which may also be the case when Antonio calls him a 'plain fish' (5.1.266). Stephano and Trinculo persistently demean Caliban as 'monster', combining the term with various qualifiers: 'shallow', 'weak', 'scurvy', 'most perfidious and drunken', 'howling', 'puppy-headed', 'abominable', 'ridiculous' and, in a more positive (but surely sarcastic) vein, 'brave'. More suggestive of grotesqueness is Alonso's quip that Caliban is 'a strange thing as e'er I looked on' (5.1.290). But Caliban is nonetheless of human form and, in most respects, of human qualities. Prospero reports that *except for* Caliban, the island was 'not honoured with / A

---

1 Prospero's insistence that Sycorax is a witch (1.2.258, 263, 275–9, 289–91) is confirmed by Caliban (1.2.322–4, 340–1).

human shape' (1.2.283–4) when he and Miranda arrived; and she includes Caliban in her list of three human males when she calls Ferdinand 'the third man that e'er I saw' (1.2.446), although she implicitly modifies that comparison when she later attests that she 'may call men' only Ferdinand and her father (3.1.50–2). Once again *The Tempest* is indeterminate, yet the bulk of the evidence points to a Caliban who is, despite his possibly demonic parentage and unspecified deformity, essentially human.

Throughout *The Tempest*'s long history, Caliban has nonetheless been burdened with a wide variety of physical aberrations, sometimes in eclectic combination, including fins, fish scales, tortoise shells, fur, skin diseases, floppy puppy ears and apelike brows, to name just a few. The common thread here is, of course, difference. The simple fact of aboriginal nakedness in Africa and America, and to some extent in Ireland, contrasted with early modern Europe's obsession with ornate clothing and reinforced English notions of the natives' inherent otherness. In Prospero's and Miranda's eyes, Caliban was unalterably 'other', probably from the beginning but surely after the attempted rape, and the numerous pejorative epithets hurled at him by all the Europeans throughout the play reflect their assessment of his form and character as fundamentally opposite to their own.[1]

That Caliban is a slave for the play's duration is indisputable, by Caliban's testimony as well as Prospero's. The slave's resentment of his master is also indisputable, as evidenced by Caliban's curses, by his reluctant service (according to Prospero and Miranda), and by his plot with Stephano and Trinculo to kill Prospero and take over the island. Yet this slave seems more determined to gain liberation from his current master than from

---

1 We calculate Caliban's age to have been 24 at the time of the play's action, based on the following clues: Sycorax was pregnant with Caliban when she arrived at the island; sometime after, she pinioned Ariel in a tree, where he was confined for twelve years before Prospero arrived and set him free, which in turn was twelve years before the play's action begins (1.2.263–93). Only if there was a lengthy gap, not implied in the text, between Caliban's birth and his mother's imprisonment of Ariel can he be appreciably older than 24.

servitude in general. He shows no reluctance until the denoue-
ment in 5.1 to serve 'King' Stephano, and even Caliban's
'Freedom high-day' song is deeply ambivalent:

> Ban' ban' Ca-caliban,
> Has a new master, get a new man.
>
> (2.2.179–80)

Such clues to Caliban's ingrained dependency have encouraged
some actors and artists to portray him as a wistful re-inheritor of
the island[1] and have reinforced theories of a native dependency
syndrome, most notably in Octave Mannoni's emblematic
Caliban (see pp.103–5, and Appendix 2.3).

The Tempest offers only shorthand sketches of the remaining
dramatis personae. Ferdinand, the handsome prince who deserves
the heroine not just by birth but by merit, is descended from a
long line of heroes from Orlando through to Florizel. The court
party comprises similarly recognizable types, representative of
early modern political discourse. Gonzalo, like Polonius, is a garrulous counsellor whose moral platitudes are often ignored, but
there the similarity ends. Gonzalo never resorts to Polonius's
Machiavellian intrigues but speaks his mind openly and honestly
to whoever will listen. Antonio,[2] the ambitious Machiavel, tries
to corrupt Sebastian into murder in a scene remarkably akin to
Lady Macbeth's temptation of her husband; Sebastian is
Antonio's less imaginative partner in crime. Both are reminiscent
of Cleon and Dionyza in *Pericles*. Alonso, like Leontes, is a ruler
of mixed qualities – guilty of conspiracy against Prospero but
capable of repenting and wishing he had acted differently.

The court party is parodied by its servants: Stephano, the
drunken butler, and Trinculo, the court jester. Trinculo's name

---

1 The text is silent about Caliban's fate, suggesting neither that he is left behind nor that
he accompanies Prospero to Milan. Both scenarios have figured prominently in imaginative extensions of *The Tempest*.

2 *The Tempest*'s Antonio was Shakespeare's fourth. They are fully discussed in Cynthia
Lewis, *Particular Saints: Shakespeare's Four Antonios, Their Contexts, and Their Plays*
(Newark, Del., 1997).

aptly comes from the Italian verb, *trincare*, to drink greedily, while Stephano is a more generic Italian name that may, in this instance, derive from a slang word (*stefano*) for stomach or belly. His 'celestial liquor' roughly parallels Prospero's magic – it mysteriously transforms people and provides visions of delight. When the two clowns join Caliban in a conspiracy to kill Prospero and take over the island, they parody Antonio's actions of twelve years earlier, not to mention his current plot to kill Alonso. More important, their stupidity in dawdling over Prospero's fancy robes instead of murdering him contrasts with Caliban's superior knowledge that the clothes are 'but trash'.

The two pairs of disreputable Europeans – Antonio and Sebastian, Stephano and Trinculo – differ in many respects from Caliban to illustrate the issues Montaigne contemplated in his famous essay on Brazilian Indians (see Appendix 1.2): which is more barbarous, the educated European who makes a sham of his Christian upbringing, or the 'savage' who responds honestly to his natural instincts? Does civilization uplift or corrupt? In contrast to Antonio, Caliban finally learns from his experience to 'seek for grace'; in contrast to Stephano and Trinculo, he seems to have an innate understanding of nature, of music and of how to achieve his goals.

THE CONTEXT

The Tempest's historical debut (1610–23) – the time of its composition, initial performances and first publication – is, like most aspects of the play, open to conflicting assessments, especially as scholarly understanding of the period expands. In this section we place *The Tempest* within its historical context, as best we can reconstruct it – a reconstruction that must include more than the obvious imperial and political discourses. Aesthetic, scientific, social and philosophical texts (to the extent that such documents can be meaningfully categorized) formed essential parts of Shakespeare's world and often resonate in the play.

While issues of state surely influenced those other concerns, they are not one and the same; *The Tempest* 'is structured around . . . oppositions between courtly discourse and wider linguistic contexts' (Norbrook, 21). To set *The Tempest* in its comprehensive context is to work spatially from Shakespeare's personal milieu (the King's Company at the Globe and Blackfriars theatres) outward to Jacobean London, to the rest of the British islands, to continental Europe and on to the outer perimeter – the global framework of North Africa, Bermuda, Jamestown and the Virginia Company's explorations. The Jacobean milieu of *The Tempest* also includes literary influences far removed in time from Shakespeare's immediate era: a vast intellectual tradition – classical and medieval, and more often of continental than English origin – that shaped the work of playwrights and poets, as did past and present scientific and philosophical treatises, iconographic traditions and religious controversies.

No one knows why and how the dramatist drew, consciously or unconsciously, from such rich resources. Scholars can, however, indicate likely connections between *The Tempest*'s language and characters and the political, social and intellectual climates in which Shakespeare lived and worked. Such connections mitigate our human tendency to see only the present era's concerns mirrored in Shakespeare's text. When *The Tempest* is situated within its early seventeenth-century historical framework, cultural and literary resonances that were transparent to Shakespeare's original audiences but opaque to subsequent generations are often clarified.

Domestic politics

Court performances were routine. As we mentioned earlier, *The Tempest*'s inclusion in the celebration of Princess Elizabeth's wedding did not necessarily carry any political significance, but there are nevertheless suggestive parallels between the play and events at court. While Shakespeare was crafting *The Tempest*, negotiations were under way for the marriages of both Prince

Henry and Princess Elizabeth; the political problems of royal marriages and dynastic arrangements were on the public's mind. James hoped to establish his reputation as a peacekeeper by balancing a Catholic marriage for Henry with a Protestant alliance for Elizabeth. Negotiations for the Princess's marriage were well along by the autumn of 1611 and reached their final stage the following summer. In late October 1612, Prince Henry suddenly took ill; his death on 6 November sent England into profound mourning for the popular royal heir. In the wake of Henry's funeral, Elizabeth's wedding to the Elector Palatine was postponed until Valentine's Day (14 February) the following year. As David Scott Kastan observes, 'Alonso's sadness at having apparently lost his son and married his daughter to a foreign prince might well have seemed a virtual mirror of the [royal] situation' (Kastan, 96–7).

The poignant history of Elizabeth, 'the winter Queen', could not have been foreseen by Shakespeare or his audience, but it has affected responses from later critics (New Cambridge Shakespeare, xlvi–xlvii). Instead of flourishing and building a new dynasty – as Miranda promises at *The Tempest*'s conclusion – Elizabeth's fate was to be like Claribel's, far from her father's protection and lost to England. As she prepared to leave for Bohemia, Elizabeth lamented: 'I shall perhaps never see again the flower of princes, the king of fathers, the best and most amicable father, that the sun will ever see' (quoted in Bergeron, 117). Events proved her right. Elizabeth spent the rest of her life embroiled in the politics of the Habsburg empire. But other aspects of Bohemian history may have influenced Shakespeare. The plight of Rudolph II, Holy Roman Emperor and King of Bohemia, parallels Prospero's story. In 1608 Rudolph's brother usurped from him the crowns of Austria, Hungary and Moravia; and in April 1611 Rudolph also lost the throne of Bohemia. His interest in the occult was widely known; in the 1580s the English magus John Dee had briefly enlisted his support in a quest for the philosopher's stone. Beset by political troubles, Rudolph, much like Prospero, retreated to his palace library and consoled himself with books (Kastan, 98).

In addition to these contemporary European analogues, *The Tempest* has often been viewed as a mirror image of the Jacobean court, with Prospero partly reflecting James. In the *Basilikon Doron* (published in Latin in 1599, in English in 1603), James had warned his son:

> it is necessarie yee delight in reading, and seeking the knowledge of all lawfull things; but with these two restrictions: first, that ye choose idle houres for it, not interrupting therewith the discharge of your office: and next, that yee studie not for knowledge nakedly, but that your principall ende be, to make you able thereby to use your office.
>
> (James I, *Political*, 38)

Yet James seems not to have practised much of what he preached, often neglecting his kingly duties for hunting. Like Prospero, he was concerned with the marriage of his children, the future of his dynasty and the management of his people.[1]

Brave new world

Although continental and domestic politics provide important historical contexts for *The Tempest*, there may be more relevance in Tudor and Stuart England's incipient empire. The extensive and varied discourses of colonialism, many critics argue, are deeply embedded in the drama's language and events. Prospero commandeers a distant island and imposes his superior technology (books, magic) and his language as tools of conquest and domination. Ariel wants his 'liberty' from the servitude Prospero imposes as his price for liberating the sprite from an earlier thraldom, but the best Ariel can expect is that his master

---

1 An alternative model for Prospero is Sir Robert Dudley, whose case is vigorously argued in Richard Wilson, 'Voyages to Tunis: new history and the Old World of *The Tempest*', *English Literary History*, 64 (1997), 333–57.

will 'bate [him] a full year' (1.2.249–50). Caliban, 'Which first was mine own king' (1.2.343), is initially well treated by the newcomers but is later enslaved and his island appropriated for his attempted rape of Miranda (1.2.332–63). Thereafter, Europeans control the land, its resources, its inhabitants: a theatrical microcosm of the imperial paradigm.[1]

Shakespeare's and his audiences' familiarity with American colonization was not restricted to England's toeholds on the North American coast. For more than a century, reports of discoveries and settlements to the west by Spanish, Portuguese, French, Dutch and eventually English chroniclers produced a growing flood of fact and myth – some of it in print, much of it oral – that formed a huge 'linguistic and narrative force-field', to borrow Charles Frey's apt expression (Frey, 'New World', 33). One early account on which Shakespeare perhaps drew for incidental items in *The Tempest* was Antonio Pigafetta's short account of the Magellan expedition's circumnavigation in 1519–22, originally published on the Continent but subsequently translated into English in Richard Eden's travel anthologies of 1555 and 1577.[2] The Patagonians of lower South America, Pigafetta reported, worshipped a 'greate devyll *Setebos*' (mentioned several times) – the first known precursor of Sycorax's deity. Pigafetta also described St Elmo's fire, great tempests and (perhaps partial prototypes of Caliban and his name) assorted giants and 'Canibales' (Eden, 216^v–21^r). Commentators since the late eighteenth century have generally agreed that *The Tempest* reveals Shakespeare's incidental indebtedness to this highly accessible source. But as Walter Alexander Raleigh observed in 1904, and Frey argued more recently and extensively, much of that detail could have

1 For disparately focused interpretations of *The Tempest*'s colonial themes, see especially Greenblatt; P. Hulme; Gillies; Halpern; Cheyfitz; Brown; Knapp; and Leo Salingar, 'The New World in "The Tempest"', in Maquerlot & Willems, 209–22. Several of these works are critically analysed in Skura's essay.

2 A few English narratives appear in Eden's first anthology (1555) and far more in his second (1577). Similarly, but on a far grander scale, Hakluyt's collection of 1589 is greatly expanded in his three-volume edition of 1598–1600, although the latter omits a few important documents that appeared in its predecessor.

come instead from a later English source: Francis Fletcher's journal of Sir Francis Drake's circumnavigation of 1577–80. In a manuscript that must have circulated widely, Fletcher described (perhaps derivatively from Eden), 'a most deadly tempest', a deity called 'Settaboth' or 'Settaboh', a native suddenly addicted to European wine, and other events and phrases that may be reflected in *The Tempest*.[1] In any case, the voluminous literature of European exploration was rife with tempests, wrecks, miracles, monsters, devils and wondrous natives. Although many of Shakespeare's contemporary playwrights drew on that literature more overtly than he did, *The Tempest* may nonetheless be his oblique dramatization of Europe's age of discovery.

Shakespeare's borrowings from several sixteenth-century travel narratives are overshadowed by his almost certain familiarity with William Strachey's 'True Reportory of the Wracke, and Redemption of Sir Thomas Gates' on Bermuda in July 1609. Strachey had been aboard Admiral George Somers's *Sea Venture*, flagship of a relief expedition en route to the English outpost in Virginia, when a hurricane scattered the fleet, sank one ship and drove *Sea Venture* on to Bermuda's rocky coast. All passengers and crew reached shore safely. Despite a disgruntled faction's abortive revolt, the survivors flourished for nine months in Bermuda's salubrious climate and on its abundant provisions before sailing to Virginia in two newly constructed vessels. In early September 1610, Sir Thomas Gates arrived back in England with Strachey's epistolary 'True Reportory', written during and immediately after the events. Although it was not published until 1625 in Samuel Purchas's *Hakluytus Posthumus, or, Purchas his Pilgrimes*, the manuscript was probably read by many of London's cultural and political leaders.[2] If, as

---

1 For the texts and their contexts, see Raleigh, 112; Frey, 'New World', 35–7; and Fletcher, 41, 48–9.

2 S.G. Culliford, *William Strachey, 1572–1621* (Charlottesville, Va., 1965), 151–4. For doubts about the influence of Strachey's letter, and support for James Rosier's *True Relation* (1605), see Arthur F. Kinney, 'Revisiting *The Tempest*', *Modern Philology* 93 (1995), 161–77.

modern scholars generally believe, Shakespeare was acquainted with several prominent members of the Virginia Company of London (most notably the Earl of Southampton) and other dignitaries, perhaps with Strachey as well, the 'True Reportory' very likely came to the playwright's hands in the autumn of 1610 or soon thereafter.[1]

Among the Strachey letter's linguistic echoes are '*A most dreadfull Tempest*' ('tempest', of course, was a common term in the sixteenth and seventeenth centuries for a violent storm, and Shakespeare had used it in several earlier plays), a long and vivid description of St Elmo's fire, names that suggest Gonzalo and Ferdinand, and some specific words or phrases evocative of *The Tempest*. More thematically significant are the seemingly miraculous survival of the mariners and passengers, their almost magical rejuvenation on the enchanted island's bounteous flora and fauna, and their governance by a dominant and resourceful leader who overcame 'divers mutinies' (see Appendix 1.1).

About the time Shakespeare was probably reading Strachey's 'True Reportory', Sylvester Jourdain's *A Discovery of the Barmudas, otherwise Called the Ile of Divels* and Richard Rich's *Newes from Virginia: The Lost Flock Triumphant* were published in London. The former, a thin narrative, adds a few details to Strachey's account – most relevant perhaps, its report that some on board sought solace in alcohol during the storm (cf. 1.1.55–6: 'We are merely cheated of our lives by drunkards', and, of course, Stephano's 'celestial liquor' in 2.2 and elsewhere) – but is otherwise undistinguished, although Malone gave it a privileged position among the Virginia tracts. Rich's text, a brief

---

1 The late publication date of Strachey's manuscript misled scholars before the twentieth century into overlooking its probable influence on *The Tempest*. Early in the nineteenth century, Edmond Malone recognized the contextual affinity between the play and several pamphlets on the English settlement in Virginia and the shipwreck on Bermuda, but even he missed 'True Reportory's' probable importance. Twentieth-century editors and critics beginning with Ard[1] are almost unanimous in assigning Strachey's letter a major role in inspiring *The Tempest*.

tetrameter poem about the shipwreck, spells the island 'Bermoothawes', which approximates the Folio spelling, but has few other affinities with *The Tempest*. Both texts, however, reinforce the timeliness of a dramatic performance in 1611 that included shipwreck, miraculous survival and an enchanted island refuge.

Still other London publications of 1608–10 heightened *The Tempest*'s topicality and could have provided additional dramatic details. *A True Relation of Such Occurrences and Accidents of Noate as Hath Hapned in Virginia* (1608), an eyewitness account by Captain John Smith, describes the struggling Jamestown settlement's first year, emphasizing disruptive colonists, inept aristocratic leaders and resentful natives. The next year (1609), a Virginia Company of London pamphlet lamented *Sea Venture*'s loss in 'The Tempest' (the survival of its passengers and crew was not yet known) and gave further particulars of the Jamestown colony's troubles. In late 1610 another Company pamphlet hailed the remarkable deliverance of Admiral Somers's party and, attempting to put a happy face on Jamestown's continuing misfortunes, called the episode 'this tragicall Comaedie' – a phrase that might have jogged the dramatist's imagination (*True Declaration*, 11).

From these assorted New World texts may have come the play's title, its storm scene, its exotic island setting, its unruly factions, its beleaguered natives, and a multitude of details of plot, character and dialogue. Yet the bulk of information in the Bermuda and early Virginia tracts is not directly relevant to *The Tempest*, and there is little scholarly consensus on Shakespeare's indebtedness to any specific text or passage. Nor is there agreement about Caliban's affinity to portrayals of American natives in the extensive writings about the New World. Indians abound in English and continental publications, and Shakespeare, like any literate Londoner of his day, must have been familiar with many of those texts and, very likely, had seen – perhaps even conversed with – one or more of the approximately 25 American natives who lived for a time in early seventeenth-century England.[1]

The temptation to see Caliban as an American Indian stems partly from *The Tempest*'s ambiguous geography: if the play is set in America or is metaphorically about New World colonization, Caliban must be to some degree an American native. Separate from this assumption, but sometimes offered to reinforce it, is a reading of 2.2 in which Trinculo (often) and Stephano (occasionally) are said initially to have identified Caliban as an Indian. But in fact, Trinculo guesses first that the creature under the gaberdine is 'A strange fish!' – either a true fish of the monstrous kind or, figuratively, an odd, odoriferous creature. 'Were I in England . . . and had but this fish painted', Trinculo surmises, he could earn a small fortune, for while its people 'will not give a doit to relieve a lame beggar, they will lay out ten to see a dead Indian' (2.2.24–33) – a comment on tightfisted English folk and their attraction to exotic exhibits rather than a description of the gaberdine-covered creature. Two lines later, after inspecting the creature's limbs and touching its skin, Trinculo concludes that 'this is no fish, but an islander that hath lately suffered by a thunderbolt'. When Stephano stumbles upon the gaberdine a moment later, Trinculo is under it too. The drunken butler wonders if the creature is a devil or perhaps a trick put on by 'savages and men of Ind'; but that too is more a speculation about Trinculo (probably on top) than about Caliban, and is primarily about a hazily perceived 'monster of the isle, with four legs' (2.2.56–65).

If Shakespeare nonetheless had American Indians in mind when he fashioned Caliban, the range of contemporaneous verbal and visual representations was immense, from near-beasts, ugly and immoral, at one extreme, to golden-age innocents, handsome and virtuous, at the other. To the extent that Caliban is barbarous, lustful and prone to intoxication, Shakespeare may

1 Lee, 'Indian'; Alden T. Vaughan, 'Trinculo's Indian: American natives in Shakespeare's England', in Peter Hulme and William Sherman, eds, *The Tempest and Its Travels* (London, 2000).

44

have mined sixteenth-century images, both continental and English, such as André Thevet's description of American natives of the far north as 'wild and brutish people, without Fayth, without Lawe, without Religion, and without any civilitie: but living like brute beasts' (Thevet, 43) (see Fig. 7). To the extent that Caliban is in tune with nature and lord of the island until overthrown by Prospero and later corrupted by Stephano and Trinculo, Shakespeare may have borrowed from Montaigne's description of Brazilians, in John Florio's translation of 1603, who 'are yet neere their originall naturalitie. The lawes of nature do yet commaund them, which are but little bastardized by ours' (Montaigne, 102) (see Fig. 8). Several English reports preceded and reinforced Montaigne's relatively benign assessment of New World natives. Captain Arthur

7 A bearded European (upper right) watches American cannibals carve and cook their victims; engraving from Theodor de Bry's *America*, Volume I, 1590

8 The tomb (1569) in Burford, Oxfordshire (25 miles from Stratford) of
Edward Harman, a former barber to Henry VIII and local official, featuring
four Brazilian Indians. Harman's connection to the New World is unclear,
but the Indians may suggest his participation in overseas mercantile
adventures

Barlow's narrative of 1584, for example, describes the natives of
Roanoke Island and vicinity as 'most gentle, loving, and faithful,
voide of all guile and treason, and such as live after the manner
of the Golden age' (Hakluyt, 1598–1600, 8.305); a few years
later, Thomas Hariot's account of Roanoke Island and its

46

accompanying vivid illustrations by John White conveyed a similar message.[1]

Neither the deeply pejorative nor the completely laudable descriptions of American natives could have been the sole model for Caliban's complex form and character. More likely – if Shakespeare indeed had American 'savages' in mind – was what Sidney Lee, the prolific English biographer and ambivalent admirer of American Indians, would describe three centuries later as an imaginative composite of various geographical and cultural types that formed 'a full length portrait of the aboriginal inhabitant of the New World' (Lee, 'Caliban', 341). But like Caliban's name, his physical and social prototype remains unproven and endlessly arguable. And Caliban aside, *The Tempest* unquestionably has American overtones. It may not be Shakespeare's American play, as some have proposed, but it nevertheless reflects to an indefinable extent the issues and events that had captured European imaginations since the late fifteenth century and had recently acquired new significance for England.

Africa and Ireland

Two other geopolitical contexts and their abundant literary reflections may also have influenced Shakespeare's writing of *The Tempest*. Encroachments in Africa by various European nations, including England, in the second half of the sixteenth century and the early years of the seventeenth, and, simultaneously, a resurgence of English efforts to subdue and govern Ireland, made the history of both places highly topical and wholly compatible with themes of colonization, appropriation and resistance. Africa appears explicitly several times in the play; Ireland is never mentioned but may have been implied in

---

1 White's paintings, now in the British Museum, may have circulated as early as the late 1580s; engraved versions by Theodor de Bry appeared in the second edition of Hariot's book *A Briefe and True Report of the New Found Land of Virginia* (Frankfurt, 1590), which was Part 1 of de Bry's *America*, published that year in English, French, German and Latin editions.

some of *The Tempest*'s themes and perhaps in one or more of its characters and specific references.

The play's most obvious African connection is the island's location: if plotted literally, it must have been within a hundred or so miles from a line between Naples and Tunis. Although its precise location is unspecified – 'an vn-inhabited Island' says the Folio – several nineteenth-century literary critics debated the most likely Mediterranean isle, based on the imaginary intersection point of a drifting 'rotten carcass of a butt' (1.2.146) from the coast near Milan and, twelve years later, of a tempest-tossed ship en route from Tunis to Naples.[1] To further identify the location, critics culled *The Tempest* for topographical clues: 'fresh springs, brine pits, barren place and fertile' (1.2.339), 'clust'ring filberts' (2.2.168) and the like (see Elze; Hunter; Var, 1–4). Whatever such sleuthing uncovers – Corfu, perhaps, or Pantalaria, or Lampedusa – it is (if one reads the play literally) not very far from the African coast. Helping to underscore the notion of Africa's proximity are the courtiers' banter in 2.1 about the recent marriage of Alonso's daughter Claribel to an African king, and their extended repartee about widow Dido, all prompted by the court party's recent departure from Tunis.

More significant is Caliban's African genesis. Sycorax, Prospero reports, was an Algerian witch, who conceived the 'freckled whelp' before her banishment to the island. (Her voyage from Algiers to the island is, of course, another suggestion of proximity to the African continent.) The play never describes Caliban's complexion, but 'this thing of darkness' (5.1.275) may refer to a dusky skin; his enslavement by the European intruder reinforces Caliban's thematic tie to Africa; his name, if derived from the town of Calibia, is emphatically African, and if 'Caliban' is instead a purposeful anagram of cannibal, it is as symptomatic of English perceptions of Africans as of Native

1 Jerry Brotton contends that colonialist readings of *The Tempest* have under-emphasized the text's Mediterranean setting.

Americans. Some critics have accordingly seen Caliban as wholly or partly African. Morton Luce, for example, in the first Arden edition of *The Tempest* (1901) saw him as, among other things, 'an African of some kind', probably 'a (negro) slave' (Ard[1], xxxv).

The topicality of a south Mediterranean setting and characters of African origin would not have been lost on *The Tempest*'s early audiences. Information was abundant about western Europe's ongoing exploration of Africa and its brazen enslavement of African people, some to labour in European nations, most in overseas colonies. And for more than half a century before 1611, Englishmen had travelled intermittently to the Barbary coast and increasingly to sub-Saharan regions, where they seized and carried to England small numbers of natives as early as 1555 and where they joined in the transatlantic slave trade as early as 1562.

English commentators in Shakespeare's day were almost wholly indifferent to the plight of captured Africans but not to the fate of captured English sailors. In the late sixteenth and early seventeenth centuries, several North African nations became notorious for their enslavement of Europeans, including hundreds, perhaps thousands, of Englishmen; viewers of a play that was ostensibly set near the African coast would have recognized some topicality in an exiled Sycorax and an embryonic Caliban from Algiers, as well as a widow Dido (anciently) and a Claribel (recently) from Tunis. Some in the audience – perhaps the author himself – might have read John Evesham's brief account of a voyage to North Africa in 1586, published in Hakluyt's *Principal Navigations* twelve years before *The Tempest*, which mentioned within a few lines 'the great Citie of Carthage where Hannibal and Queen Dido dwelt', and the 'Towne of Argier . . . inhabited with Turkes, Moores, and Jewes' and 'a great number of Christian captives, wherof there are of Englishmen [now] onely fifteene' (Hakluyt, 1598–1600, 6.38). In order to have ignited a spark of interest in an English audience, the association of *The Tempest* need not, in sum, have been with Africa's sub-Saharan regions nor with dark-hued natives.

Yet many of the travel narratives available to English readers as individual tracts, or in the compendia by Richard Eden and later by Hakluyt, did describe sub-Saharan areas such as Guinea, Nubia and the Congo. (Perhaps the best-known text, Leo Africanus' *Geographical Historie of Africa*, translated into English in 1600 and culled by Shakespeare for *Othello*, addressed nearly the whole continent.) Some of the literature was indifferent towards sub-Saharan Africans and some of it was ambivalent, but many English assessments, especially of Africans with dark skin, were decidedly pejorative and some were vituperative – 'fiends more fierce then those in hell', one Englishman insisted after a voyage to Guinea (Hakluyt, 1589, 134). More ambiguous but largely derogatory representations of Africans appeared on the Elizabethan stage in George Peele's *Battle of Alcazar*, the anonymous *Lust's Dominion* and Shakespeare's *Titus Andronicus*. Nor was the evidence of England's widespread contempt for Africans confined to books and the stage. Britain harboured only a small fraction of the black Africans who were enslaved elsewhere in Europe, on the islands to the west of Africa, and in the Iberian nations' American colonies; nevertheless, the presence in England, especially in London, of scores, perhaps hundreds, of sub-Saharan Africans was well known and sometimes deplored. By the end of the sixteenth century, an economic slump spurred complaints about the 'great number of negars and Blackamoores'; they had become a 'great annoyance', said the Privy Council, to the English people. Royal proclamations at the turn of the century called for the Africans' owners to relinquish them to a crown-appointed agent for expulsion from the realm.[1] Most owners apparently evaded the decree.

---

1 See *Tudor Royal Proclamations*, ed. Paul L. Hughes and James F. Larkin, 3 vols (New Haven, 1964–9), 3.221–2; and Vaughan, 'Africans', 42.

In light of government policy and the portrayal of Africa and its people in many literary and dramatic works, an English audience would have understood Sebastian's disapproval of Claribel's marriage to an African and Prospero's contempt for 'The foul witch Sycorax' from Algiers (1.2.258), and would have readily seen in Caliban's ethnic origin, his physical and social monstrosity, and possibly in his name, the source of his moral shortcomings. Africans, an English author had sneered during Elizabeth's reign, were 'blacke, Savage, Monstrous, & rude' (Cuningham, fol. 185).

But one need not leave the British isles to find pejorative prototypes for Caliban, or an example of English imperialism, or an array of *Tempest* themes and tropes. In the same year that Shakespeare's play opened, the historian–cartographer John Speed's comprehensive study of the 'British Empire' described profusely the regions 'now in actuall possession', including England, Scotland, Wales, Ireland and even the Isle of Man, but barely mentioned the fledgling colony in Virginia.[1] For it was in Ireland, of course, not Virginia, that England's major efforts at 'plantation' had long been invested. Not for several decades would England's New World outposts command the financial and literary attention that by 1611 had been lavished on the island across the Irish Sea.

English descriptions of the Irish were almost always defamatory. In the absence of any clear-cut prototypes for Sycorax and especially for Caliban, those characters may partly reflect the invective that Edmund Spenser, Barnabe Rich and many of their literary contemporaries heaped on the inhabitants of the island that England sought vigorously but unsuccessfully to subdue, culturally as well as militarily. English writers in the late six-

---

1 Speed, 1.1; 2.157. On the emerging concept of the British Empire, see David Armitage, 'Literature and Empire', in Canny, 99–123. Speed seems to foreshadow a later usage of 'empire' by including the American colonies, however briefly, in his editions of 1611 and 1627.

teenth and early seventeenth centuries castigated 'the wilde Irish' as thoroughly as they did the Africans and (less consistently) the American natives. *A New Description of Ireland* by Barnabe Rich (who earlier had influenced *Twelfth Night*), published the same year that Shakespeare probably concluded *The Tempest*, is symptomatic. Rich complained that the Irish were 'rude, uncleanlie, and uncivill, . . . cruell, bloudie minded, apt and ready to commit any kind of mischiefe', even 'to rebel against their [English] princes; . . . [N]either may age nor honour so protect any [person], that Rape be not mingled with murder, nor murder with Rape' (B. Rich, 15–16, 19). And while the Irish people epitomized English notions of incivility, unruliness and political disorder, the Irish island provided a real-life stage for Elizabethans and Jacobeans of various social strata to vent their imperial ambitions and to suppress indigenous plots and rebellions. Ireland may well have served Shakespeare as a topical example of the complex issues of overseas settlement, political legitimacy, revenge and repentance. Caliban's suitability for English perceptions of Irish men as uncouth, unlettered, rebellious and intoxicated is readily apparent (see Fig. 9).

Although Ireland as an analogue for Caliban's / Prospero's island may have been readily apparent in 1611, the case was not articulated until the late twentieth century. The most comprehensive account is offered by Dympna Callaghan, who posits several specific and significant affinities between the play and English accounts of Ireland, besides the general circumstances – an overseas island, dispossession, exploitation of the natives, and their profound resentment and resistance. Some specifics, according to Callaghan, reflect the imperialists' vision of Caliban: their fear of his attempted miscegenation; their contempt for his language ('gabble', a word of Irish provenance, first appears in a sixteenth-century Anglo-Irish description of Irish speech); their efforts to displace his culture; their curtailments of his freedom and territory. Some English descriptive literature even accused the Irish of cannibalism. More significant are sev-

The Wilde Irish man

9 A 'wilde Irish man' as depicted in a border illustration to the map of Ireland in John Speed, *The Theatre of the Empire of Great Britaine*, 1611

eral persistent parallels between Ireland and *The Tempest*: the importance of music in Irish folk life and in Shakespeare's most musical play; the English imperialists' efforts to control memory and to reshape the narrative to reflect their (in *The Tempest*, Prospero's) perceptions; and the patriarchal quality of the imposed colonial rule on Ireland and on Shakespeare's imaginary island.[1] Ireland, in sum, 'might be understood as the

---

1 On an even more specific level, a possible source for the elusive 'Young scamels' (2.2.169) may be the Irish *scallachan* ('an unfledged bird'), and a possible analogue for Sycorax may be County Mayo's Granuaile (Grace O'Malley) – a notorious troubler of English colonial authorities encountered by Sir Henry Sidney and Sir Philip Sidney (Callaghan).

sublimated context for colonial relations in *The Tempest*' (Callaghan).[1] More likely, we believe, Ireland meshed eclectically in the playwright's mind with colonial and other contextual concerns about Africa, America and Europe.

Literary forerunners

While the Virginia pamphlets, Montaigne's essays and travel narratives by Pigafetta or Fletcher are probable if not certain New World sources for *The Tempest* (Bullough, 8.275–99), Shakespeare's indebtedness to sixteenth- and early seventeenth-century Old World sources is less clear. Here again, what may have been obvious to Shakespeare's contemporaries is generally obscure to later eras. Accordingly, when source-hunting was fashionable, especially during the late nineteenth and early twentieth centuries, frustrated scholars scoured English and continental literature for the play's prototype or, at the very least, for a text that might have inspired its basic structure. Two of their findings display sufficient resemblances to *The Tempest* to merit contemporary attention, but neither has been classified by twentieth-century editors as a direct source.

Shakespeare almost certainly knew the popular *Mirror of Knighthood*, an English translation of the lengthy Spanish romance *El espejo de principes y caballeros* (Bullough, 8.247). The first part, translated by Margaret Tyler in 1580, was soon followed by seven more parts, some translated by Robert Parry and some by Thomas Purfoot. Part I's interwoven narrative includes the story of Palisteo, second son to the King of Phrygia. Because he was not born to inherit, Palisteo decides not 'to trouble himselfe with the care of governing' but to study the 'Arte Magicke' (*Mirror*[1], 148[r]). After his wife dies, Palisteo escapes with his infant son and daughter (Lindaraza) to a magic island. When Lindaraza falls in love with the picture of the

---

1 In addition to Callaghan's recent study, see the slightly older essays by Baker; Brown; and Andrew Hadfield, ' "The Naked and the Dead"; Elizabethan perceptions of Ireland', in Maquerlot & Willems, 32–54.

Emperor Trebacio, her father's magic brings him to her. For a time Lindaraza and Trebacio live blissfully on an enchanted island, a 'paradise' populated with deer, rabbits, squirrels, birds 'and the faire Unicorne' (*Mirror*[1], 137[v]), but after twenty years the Knight of the Sun arrives to rescue Trebacio and restore him to his lawful wife, Princess Briana. The third part of Book I, published in 1586, continues the Knight of the Sun's adventures. After a storm so terrible 'that the cunning of the marriners did not serve for the government of the ship' (*Mirror*[2], 58[v]), he lands on the Island of the Devil, inhabited by the witch Artimaga and Fauno, a monster 'that the divell was within', and their offspring, 'the divellish or possessed Fauno'. But the second-generation devilish monster is no Caliban. Without any semblance of human form, he is as big as an elephant and (like his father, but 'much more horrible') has the shape of a lion, the face of a man but with a huge horn in his forehead, and carries 'a whole legion of divels within his bodie' (*Mirror*[2], 60[v]–61[v]).

The Mirror of Knighthood is characteristic of the prose romances that circulated in early modern Europe; its heroes are precursors of Sidney's Arcadian knights and Spenser's allegorical champions. It provides an intriguing intertextual framework for Shakespeare's *Tempest*, but the resemblances are too fleeting for it to be considered more than a tangential source.

Similar problems burden the case for Jacob Ayrer's *Die Schöne Sidea*, published in Nuremburg in 1618, which may be an adaptation of an English play performed in Germany by English actors (Bullough, 8.248). Ayrer died in 1605, so the text of *Die Schöne Sidea* was unquestionably extant before Shakespeare composed *The Tempest*, although it is highly unlikely that Shakespeare used it. When H.H. Furness translated the entire play, he found nothing but chance resemblances (Var, 324–43). *Die Schöne Sidea* begins with a pitched battle between two German princes, Leudegast and Ludolff; Ludolff is defeated and escapes with his daughter Sidea to a distant island, where he dabbles in magic and conjures the devil to do his bidding. When

Leudegast's son Engelbrecht goes hunting, the vengeful Ludolff captures him, immobilizes his sword by means of a magic staff and sentences him to carry logs. Unlike Miranda, Sidea initially scorns the young man, but his pitiful plight eventually softens her heart and she agrees to marry him. The couple become separated in episodes that have no counterpart in *The Tempest*, but eventually they reunite and their love inspires a reconciliation between their feuding fathers. We concur with Bullough that '*Die Schöne Sidea* throws little light upon Shakespeare's play', despite its intriguing parallels, and more generally with Frank Kermode's conclusion that 'Ultimately the source of *The Tempest* is an ancient *motif*, of almost universal occurrence, in saga, ballad, fairy tale and folk tale' (Bullough, 8.249; Ard², lxiii). *The Mirror of Knighthood* and *Die Schöne Sidea* do demonstrate, however, Renaissance Europe's fascination with exotic tales of magicians, wizards, strange beasts, enchanted islands and romantic love – a broad intertextual framework that underlies Shakespeare's play.[1]

Classical models

English Renaissance humanism was founded in the early sixteenth century on the principle of teaching great classical authors to every schoolboy; the educated Blackfriars audience and many in the Globe audience would have recognized allusions to the prominent Latin texts of the sixteenth century, especially Virgil's *Aeneid* and Ovid's *Metamorphoses*. Both Roman poets are plausibly identified as sources for *The Tempest* because echoes of their major works are easily detected in the play's themes and patterns as well as in some specific words and phrases.

Like many other elements of *The Tempest*'s context, recognition of its classical sources that may have been obvious to early readers and audiences did not receive extensive critical attention

---

1 See Chambers, 1.493–4, and Ard², lxiv–ix, for other analogous texts that, in those authorities' opinions and ours, had slight influence, if any, on *The Tempest*.

until the twentieth century. Only in 1948 did J.M. Nosworthy identify the *Aeneid* as an unquestionable narrative source and 'pervasive influence' on *The Tempest* (Nosworthy, 288–93). The most direct allusion is, of course, Gonzalo's reference to 'widow Dido'; *Aeneid*, 1.343–52, describes Dido's marriage to Sychaeus, his murder by her brother Pygmalion, and Dido's escape to northern Africa, where she supervised the founding of Carthage. Despite Antonio's scepticism ('Widow? A pox o'that' (2.1.78)), she was indeed a widow, and in accounts other than Virgil's she lived in devotion to her dead husband and committed suicide lest a second marriage be forced upon her.

While many specific passages from the *Aeneid* have clear parallels in Shakespeare's language, several thematic similarities are more important (Nosworthy, 288–93). One critic terms the Virgilian presence ' "spectral" – a half-seen image of death, or damnation, or despair at the back of an episode, a line, or even a single word' (Pitcher, 197). The Dido passage evokes the tragic story of lovers ruined by passion; Ferdinand and Miranda are imaginative reworkings of the ancient lovers, but their destiny is not tragic because their love is chaste and sanctioned by marriage. Another scholar deepens the case for Virgil's influence, arguing that Shakespeare's play is an imitation of the main patterns of Virgil's epic in its beginning, middle and end. Both stories commence with a tempest in which ships are lost and heroes wrecked, yet the narratives later reveal supernatural agency at work – Venus in the *Aeneid*, Prospero's magic in *The Tempest*. In the storm's aftermath the heroes are hopelessly lost, confused and subject to strange visions. Aeneas suffers the pain of the underworld; Ferdinand is initially lost and until the end of the play is tormented by his father's presumed death, though Ferdinand has the joy of finding and wooing Miranda. In the final section of each text a new society is founded, new bonds are established. Presiding over both works is the idea of a metaphorical tempest – humanity buffeted by forces it does not understand and cannot control (Wiltenburg).

Shakespeare's imitation of Virgil may be reflected in the issues of power and colonial domination highlighted in the historical contexts outlined above. Donna B. Hamilton describes *The Tempest* as a 'formal and rigorous rhetorical imitation of the major narrative kernels of *Aeneid*, 1–6' (Hamilton, x). In addition to the analogy between Aeneas the private man and Ferdinand the lover, Hamilton finds a parallel between Aeneas the nation-builder and Prospero, Duke of Milan (though Prospero's nation-building consists merely of finding the right husband – the future King of Naples – for his daughter). Both protagonists are analogous to James I, whose struggles to manage Parliament were as difficult as Prospero's efforts to dominate Caliban and reform Antonio. That there are Virgilian resonances in *The Tempest* should come as no surprise, nor should such echoes be over-schematized.

Shakespeare and a large portion of his audience also knew Ovid's *Metamorphoses*, many in the original Latin, still more in Arthur Golding's English translation. Shakespeare drew frequently on Ovid throughout his career, and *The Tempest* is no exception. Prospero's farewell to his magic (5.1.33–57) is a fairly direct translation of Medea's invocation to Hecate in Ovid, through Golding's mediation:

Ye airs and winds; ye elves of hills, of brooks, of woods alone,
Of standing lakes, and of the night, approach ye every one,
Through help of whom (the crooked banks much wondr'ing at
    the thing)
I have compelled streams to run clean backward in their spring.
(Ovid, 7.265–8)

Shakespeare repeats the 'elves of hills' and 'standing lakes' from Golding but, as Jonathan Bate notes, his 'rifted Jove's stout oak' comes directly from Ovid's 'convulsaque robora' (Bate, *Ovid*, 8). This familiar Ovidian passage recurs in Thomas Heywood's reworking of Roman myth in *The Brazen Age*, a play performed by Queen Anne's Company in the same period as *The Tempest* was first performed. Heywood's Medea exclaims:

> The night growes on, and now to my black Arts,
> Goddess of witchcraft and darke ceremony
> To whom the elves of Hils, of Brookes, of Groves,
> Of standing lakes, and cavernes vaulted deepe
> Are ministers.

(Heywood, sig. G1ᵛ)

Medea's invocation to Hecate was associated with witchcraft in the popular imagination. In the scene described by Ovid (and Heywood), the sorceress uses her magic to invert the forces of nature and destroy her enemies. Prospero appropriates her language but ultimately renounces magic altogether, choosing virtue over vengeance.

Aside from these famous lines, *The Tempest* has no direct borrowings from Ovid, yet Bate's contention that metamorphosis is a recurring theme in the drama is surely correct. During their stay on the island, nearly all of the characters undergo some sort of 'sea-change'. The play's episodic construction, focusing first on one set of characters, then another, is akin to Ovid's storytelling technique. Depictions of the penalties for greed and passion are Ovidian indeed.

The 'salvage man'

The Tempest's exploration of what makes us civilized and free is characteristic not only of the greatest texts of the ancient world but also of medieval folklore and legend.

The contrast between 'civility' and 'barbarism' had been reified in tapestry, wood-carvings, paintings, poetry and pageants from the middle ages into the Renaissance, throughout Europe, in the (usually) ominous figure of the wild man. In Germany he was the *Wildeman*, in France *l'homme sauvage*, in Italy *huomo selveggio* and in England the wodewose or green man, but wherever he appeared this man–beast, clad in animal skins or vines and bearing a huge club, represented forces of raw nature that threatened civilized society. The wild man lived in the borderlands – the forests or mountains; his brutish behaviour contrasted sharply with prescribed standards of human morality and decorum. As Hayden White observes, 'in whatever way he is envisaged, the Wild Man almost always represents the image of the man released from social control, the man in whom the libidinal impulses have gained full ascendancy' (White, 21). He could, however, be tamed by a beautiful maiden or taught 'civilized' language.

The wild man (Spenser's 'Salvage Man') appeared frequently in English Renaissance pageantry and drama. As late as 1610 he was staged as Bremo in *Mucedorus*, an anonymous play printed many times, beginning in 1598, and revived at court by the King's Company (Vaughan, *Caliban*, 69). Bremo carries a club, lives in the forest and savagely attacks all who come within his reach. He is a cannibal, but when smitten by the fair Amadine he refuses to devour her. Eventually the forces of civility reassert themselves; a valiant knight, Mucedorus, slays Bremo and rescues the maiden.

Although Caliban differs in many ways from this figure, they share some qualities. On the admirable side, Caliban knows the 'qualities of the isle' and is attuned to its music; he has also learned from Prospero and Miranda a European language and some rudimentary science. But he cannot subdue his ferocity, for he is (according to Prospero's hostile account) the son of a witch and a devil 'on whose nature / Nurture can never stick' (4.1.188–9). The lustful savage tries to ravish Miranda and regrets only the failure. After Prospero enslaves him, Caliban lives in a cave, isolated from Prospero's and Miranda's domesticated space. Yet, like the wild man, he is essentially human, even while representing humankind's most bestial qualities.

Caliban's complex role was likely influenced by Montaigne's 'Of the Caniballes', which challenges the prevailing binary opposition between 'savages' of the New World and 'civilized' peoples of Europe: 'I thinke there is more barbarisme in [figuratively] eating men alive', he muses, 'than to feede upon them being dead' (Montaigne, 104), and regrets that Europeans see the mote in the eye of Indian culture, ignoring the beam of greed and corruption in their own. In words that Shakespeare borrows almost verbatim for Gonzalo's explanation of how he would organize a colony on Prospero's island (2.1.148–65), Montaigne idealizes the indigenous culture of Brazil:

> It is a nation . . . that hath no kinde of traffike, no knowledge of Letters, no intelligence of numbers, no name of magistrate, nor of politike superioritie; no use of service, of riches, or of poverty; no contracts, no successions, no dividences, no occupation but idle; no respect of kinred, but common, no apparrell but naturall, no manuring of lands, no use of wine, corne, or mettle. The very words that import lying, falshood, treason, dissimulation, covetousnes, envie, detraction, and pardon, were never heard of amongst them.
>
> (Montaigne, 102)

Later in the essay, Montaigne contends that the Indians never fight to gain more lands because they have no need for extra territory; nature has supplied all their needs (see Appendix 1.2).

Shakespeare may have been influenced by more than the phrasing of a few passages; his rhetorical strategy of exploring different, often opposite, perspectives, never settling on a definitive view, also echoes Montaigne's. In 2.1 Gonzalo's idealism is a counterpoint to Antonio and Sebastian's cynicism, yet neither attitude seems completely appropriate to the situation. Moreover, the principal thrust of Montaigne's essay – that barbarousness is determined by behaviour, not ethnicity – is crucial to Shakespeare's portrayal of the shipwrecked courtiers. Antonio and Sebastian's cynical interruptions of Gonzalo's reverie remind the audience of the European corruption Montaigne exposed. Antonio and Sebastian 'eat men alive' through usurpation and murder. Caliban may be a 'salvage man', but as *The Tempest* unfolds, he proves to be more rational and sympathetic than the two Neapolitan conspirators or the two drunken servants who represent European culture's corrupt underside.[1]

Magic

The Folio capitalizes 'Art' when it denotes Prospero's magic. Although some scholars argue that the upper case A was a deliberate signal that the word was used in a technical sense to denote Prospero's magic (e.g. Berger), similar capitalizations were characteristic of manuscripts prepared for publication by scrivener Ralph Crane and therefore not necessarily significant (Howard-Hill, *Crane*, 109–10). Even without the capital A, Prospero's strange powers have provoked emphatic critical opinions about their nature – benign, or evil, or a precarious balance of both.[2]

The roots of Prospero's magic art may lie in the neo-Platonic authors translated by Marsilio Ficino: Plotinus, Porphyry and Iamblichus. Prospero is often described as a theurgist, a practiser of 'white magic', a rigorous system of philosophy that allows the magician 'to energize in the gods or to control other beneficent spiritual intelligences in the working of miraculous effects'. The antithesis of theurgy is 'goety' or 'black magic': 'its evil practitioner produces magic results by disordering the sympathetic relationships of nature or by employing to wicked ends the powers of irrational spirits' (Curry, 167). While practitioners such as Dr John Dee may have viewed themselves as theurgists, the Anglican Church and King James condemned magical studies as damnable (Pearson, 255). To James, witches and magicians

---

1 Evidence of Shakespeare's indebtedness to Montaigne has grown in recent years, and not only for 'Of the Caniballes' as an influence on *The Tempest*; several other essays also influenced it, and other plays too owe a great deal to Montaigne. See especially Arthur Kirsch, 'Virtue, vice, and compassion in Montaigne and *The Tempest*', *Studies in English Literature*, 37 (1997), 337–52.

2 There is an abundant literature on Prospero's magic. Curry, Traister and Mebane see the magician's role as essentially benign, while Pearson argues emphatically that Shakespeare's audience would have condemned it. Mowat, 'Hocus', relates Prospero to the street magicians who frequented marketplaces and fairs.

served 'both one Master, although in diverse fashions' and both should be punished by death (James I, *Daemonologie*, 32).

Ben Jonson's *The Alchemist*, performed by Shakespeare's company a year before *The Tempest*, dramatizes the negative view of magic expressed by James I. This satiric comedy depicts the predatory shenanigans of Subtle, a con man, and his familiar, Face, the trusty servant who manipulates the gulls. Subtle was probably performed by the King's Company's leading actor, Richard Burbage, who most likely appeared as Prospero in *The Tempest*. Both plays tap the popular interest in alchemy and magic but, while Jonson ruthlessly exposes their practice as flim-flam, Shakespeare allows his magician abundant success before he renounces his art (see H. Levin). But *The Alchemist* was not just a biting satire on alchemy; it was also an attack on any form of occult learning (Yates, 119). Although Jonson's protagonist is a charlatan rather than a consorter with diabolic spirits, the play strongly reveals the dramatist's contempt for the occult. But even if Jonson's view of magic was entirely negative, his fellow dramatist might have taken a different tack.

In creating *The Tempest*'s magical elements, Shakespeare might also have been influenced by the street wizard, a figure from legend and contemporary society. Street magicians, jugglers and conjurers were a frequent feature of Jacobean urban life and were often depicted on London stages. Shakespeare's audience would have recognized the ubiquitous type in Prospero and would have expected him to renounce his magic eventually. As a combination of serious magician and carnival illusionist, Prospero manipulates with characteristic legerdemain what the audiences – and the characters on the island – observe (Mowat, 'Hocus'). In that, of course, he is akin to the playwright.

The Tempest itself can be compared to one form of magic, the alchemical process. The title is the alchemical term for the boiling of the alembic to remove impurities and transform the base metal into purest gold (Mebane, 181); if we see Prospero's goal as the transformation of fallen human nature – Caliban,

Antonio, Sebastian and Alonso – from a condition of sinfulness to a higher level of morality, the play's episodes mirror the alchemical process. Note particularly Prospero's alchemical language at the beginning of Act 5 ('My charms crack not') to describe his project; by 'boiling' his enemies' brains (5.1.60), he attempts to transform their characters (Simonds, 'Charms').

Prospero bears the physical signifiers a Jacobean audience would have associated with power: books, staff and robe (see Fig. 10). In his first appearance he plucks off his magic garment and assures Miranda that the tempest she has just witnessed is really an illusion. He then explains how he lost the duchy of Milan. Reputed for his knowledge of the liberal arts, and

> those being all my study,
> The government I cast upon my brother
> And to my state grew stranger, being transported
> And rapt in secret studies.
>
> (1.2.74–7)

The final line evokes Faustus's exclamation: ''Tis magic, magic that hath ravished me' (Marlowe, 110); more than simply being 'deeply engaged or buried in', 'rapt' also connoted rapture or ravishment, a state of being transported or carried away in spirit (*OED ppl.* 3, 4). In his treatise on demonology, James had warned how the love of 'secret studies' could lead to the diabolic:

> For divers men having attained to a great perfection in learning, & yet remaining overbare (alas) of the spirit of regeneration and frutes thereof: finding all naturall thinges common, aswell to the stupide pedants as unto them, they assaie to vendicate unto them a greater name, by not onlie knowing the course of things heavenlie, but likewise to clim to the knowledge of things to come thereby. Which, at the first face appearing lawfull unto them, in respect the ground thereof seemeth to proceed of naturall causes onelie; they are so allured

The Tragicall Hiſtorie of the Life and Death of Doctor Fauſtus.

With new Additions.

Written by C H. M A R.

Printed at London for *Iohn Wright*, and are to be ſold at his ſhop without Newgate. 1631.

10   The title page to Christopher Marlowe's *Dr Faustus* (1631; reprinted from 1619) showing the magician in his customary robes, holding a book and using his staff to mark a circle, with a devilish figure as his familiar

thereby, that finding their practize to proove true in sundry things, they studie to know the cause thereof: and so mounting from degree to degree, upon the slipperie and uncertaine scale of curiositie; they are at last entised, that where lawfull artes or sciences failes, to satisfie their restles mindes, even to seeke to that black and unlawfull science of *Magic*.

(James I, *Daemonologie*, 10)

Here there is no distinction between theurgy and goety: from this point of view, Prospero's 'secret studies', like Adam's forbidden fruit, would eventually damn him.

Prospero nonetheless tries to make such a distinction by attributing the demonic power of magic to his enemy and alter ego, the witch Sycorax. Although she died before he arrived at the island, Prospero learned of Sycorax's powers through Ariel, left behind in a cloven pine. Sycorax's charms – 'wicked dew', 'toads, beetles, bats' (1.2.322, 341), according to Caliban – represent a more rudimentary form of magic than Prospero's art. Though she was sufficiently powerful to trap Ariel in the tree where he languished for twelve years, she 'Could not again undo' the spell. Prospero arrogantly asserts that 'It was mine art, / When I arrived and heard thee, that made gape / The pine and let thee out' (1.2.291–3). Prospero believes that just as his art is more potent than Sycorax's witchcraft, it is also morally superior.

The distinction between the two types of magic is erased, however, in Prospero's speech of renunciation. As Jonathan Bate has argued, having his protagonist openly speak words that some in his audience would recognize from Medea's speech in Ovid's *Metamorphoses* was Shakespeare's signal that the magician's power is not really benign and must be rejected (Bate, *Ovid*, 254). Aside from the temptation to use his magic for vengeance, study of the occult had distracted Prospero from his princely duties twelve years earlier; if he is to return to Milan and resume his ducal powers, he must abandon it.

Masque

Prospero's magical art creates illusions (usually with Ariel as actor and producer) that repeatedly evoke awe and wonder. The magician's art, like the dramatist's, lies in the creation of illusions, particularly the audience's belief that they have seen something that was apart from everyday life. John Dee, astrologer to Queen Elizabeth and believed by some critics to be Shakespeare's model for Prospero, learned this analogy early in his career. When he produced Aristophanes' *Pax* at Trinity College, Cambridge, the stage effect of '*Scarabaeus* his flying up to Jupiter's pallace, with a man and his basket of victualls on his back' caused 'great wondring, and many vaine reportes spread abroad of the meanes how that was effected'.[1] For the rest of his life Dee attributed the reports that he was a conjurer and magician to his early career as a producer of stage spectacles.

Stage spectacle was the essence of the Jacobean court masque, a form embedded in *The Tempest* not just in the musical interlude of Iris, Ceres and Juno but in other scenes as well. Masques were the original multimedia event, requiring 'painting, architecture, design, mechanics, lighting, music of both composer and performer, acting, choreography, and dancing both acrobatic and formal' (Orgel, 'Poetics', 368). Staged at great expense for special court occasions – weddings, birthdays, investitures – masques treated the audience to a vision of court ladies and gentlemen dressed in lavish costumes within spectacular moving sets.

Because Ben Jonson, the leading librettist for court masques, was also writing for the King's Company in 1611, Shakespeare must have been familiar with the form and its cultural impact. And, as Andrew Gurr contends, masques within plays 'became a conspicuous feature of King's Men's plays after 1610' (*Philaster*, xxxix–xl). Plays from that period frequently include elaborate choreography, such as the 'dance of twelve satyrs' in the sheepshearing scene of *The Winter's Tale*. Jonson listed the

---

1 Quoted in French, 24, from Dee's *Compendious Rehearsal*.

King's Company as performers in the 1612 masque *Love Restored*, and actors from Shakespeare's company were probably also involved in Jonson's earlier efforts.

As the masque form developed, the idealized figures of the court were grotesquely mirrored in 'antimasques' performed by professional actors. *The Masque of Queens* (1609), for example, began with 'twelve women in the habit of hags or witches, sustaining the persons of Ignorance, Suspicion, Credulity, etc., the opposites to good Fame'; Queen Anne, portraying Lady Fame, then drove out the hags and witches, restoring good fame to the court. In *Oberon* (1611) satyrs played the opposing role, ending their dialogue with 'an antic dance full of gesture and swift motion'; these antimasque figures dispersed with the entry of the court ladies and gentlemen, whose allegorical roles signalled the triumph of virtue, reason and grace over the forces of disorder (Jonson, *Masques*, 81, 109).

Jonson's *Hymenaei*, performed at court in 1606 for the wedding of the Earl of Essex and Lady Frances Howard, contains many of the elements Shakespeare used later in *The Tempest*. Jonson's stage directions describe the appearance of Juno:

> sitting in a throne supported by two beautiful peacocks; her attire rich and like a queen, a white diadem on her head from whence descended a veil, and that bound with a fascia of several-colored silks, set with all sorts of jewels and raised in the top with lilies and roses; in her right hand she held a scepter, in the other a timbrel; at her golden feet the hide of a lion was placed; round about her sat the spirits of the air, in several colors, making music . . . [B]eneath her [was] the rainbow, Iris, and on the two sides, eight ladies, attired richly and alike in the most celestial colors, who represented her powers (as she is the governess of marriage).
>
> (Jonson, *Masques*, 54–5, italics removed)

11   Masque scene from the 1951 production of *The Tempest* at the Shakespeare
Memorial Theatre in Stratford-upon-Avon.

Prospero's masque, performed in celebration of Ferdinand
and Miranda's betrothal, continues Jonson's hymeneal theme
but with several important differences. Instead of Jonson's
lengthy epithalamium exalting the joys of the marriage bed,

Shakespeare's masque is shaped by Prospero's insistence on continence: 'Do not give dalliance / Too much the rein . . . Be more abstemious' (4.1.51–3). His concern for his daughter's chastity is linked to his hopes for her fruitful marriage and the legitimacy of his dynasty. Ceres, in her insistence on the orderly processes of nature, echoes this theme.

Critics have sometimes dispraised the verse Shakespeare created for his masque, or even derided the entire episode as an interpolation by someone else (see Ard[1], xxii–iv; Oxf[1], 61–2). But the language of the court masque was highly stylized and artificial. Gods and goddesses, princes and queens, do not speak conversational blank verse; they are elevated high above the audience and speak an elite language (see Fig. 11). Prospero's masque serves *The Tempest* in the way that various cantos serve Spenser's books of *The Faerie Queene*, as an allegorical core that symbolizes ideas which pervade the play (see Lewis, 335). Ceres, Iris and Juno present a double image of the cosmic union of earth and air, fire and water, with a vision of the union of Ferdinand and Miranda as the return of universal harmony (Peyre, 54–5).

The threat to this harmony – lack of chastity or self-control – is represented mythologically by Ceres' inquiry about the whereabouts of Venus, goddess of sensual love, and her son Cupid, purveyor of passion:

> Since they did plot
> The means that dusky Dis[1] my daughter got,
> Her and her blind boy's scandaled company
> I have forsworn.
>
> (4.1.88–91)

---

1 Dis's rape of Proserpina mirrors the theme of miscegenation that runs through the play: Claribel had been 'loose[d] . . . to an African' (2.1.126) and, had Caliban's assault on Miranda not been thwarted, he'd have 'peopled else / This isle with Calibans' (1.2.351–2). Stephano's desire to bed Miranda transgresses class lines as well. Miscegenation was thus a threat to Prospero's dynastic project.

Venus and Cupid are banished from the world of Prospero's masque. Instead, the songs of Ceres and Juno celebrate chaste love, a temperate union that eschews extremes of passion (see Peyre, 57). If the earth is to bring forth 'foison plenty', it must be through cultivation and avoidance of extreme heat and cold. Ceres' wish for the lovers is an eternal spring that arrives just as harvest ends. As in Spenser's mythological Garden of Adonis, fertility flourishes without the killing blast of winter; the seasons of planting and reaping miraculously fuse. The dance of temperate nymphs and reapers signals this conflation, their graceful movement epitomizing concord and heavenly harmony. Through the union of Ferdinand and Miranda, Prospero hopes to see his dynasty continue in peace and prosperity, with his grandchildren as heirs to both Milan and Naples.

The mythological figures chosen for Prospero's masque resonated richly for an audience steeped in classical lore. Iris, signified by the rainbow, was messenger to the gods (particularly Juno) and sister to the harpies. Vincenzo Cartari, an Italian commentator on the ancient myths, whose work was translated into English in 1599 as *The Fountain of Ancient Fiction*, described Iris as 'the daughter of Thaumante, which signifieth admiration'. She is also responsible for 'the changes and alterations of the aire, making it sometimes faire, sometimes tempestuous, rainie, and cloudie, and some other times sending down haile, snow, thunder, and lightening' (Cartari, sigs Lii^v–Liii^r). Iris's airy qualities and relation to the harpies associate her with Ariel, while the wonder evoked by her rainbow colours is reminiscent of Miranda.

The Roman goddess Ceres represented the fecundity of the cultivated earth. Wheat and barley were sacred to her. She presided over the labours of ploughing, tilling, planting and harvesting, and was known as a maternal fertility goddess. Her daughter, Proserpina, had been abducted by Pluto (Dis) and taken to the underworld. As a result – in the words of Golding's translation of the *Metamorphoses* – 'The worlde did want . . . She marrde the seede, and eke forbade, the fieldes to yeelde their frute' (Ovid, 5.578–97). The rest of the story was well known to the well-educated in Shakespeare's audience: Juno allowed Ceres to rescue her daughter on the condition that Proserpina had not eaten anything during her sojourn in the underworld; but alas, she had consumed seven pomegranate seeds. Juno negotiated Pluto's desire to keep his bride and Ceres' wish to have her returned:

God *Jove* . . . parteth equally the yeare betweene them both;
And now the Goddesse *Proserpine* indifferently doth reigne
Above and underneath the Earth: and so doth she remaine
One halfe yeare with hir mother and the resdue with hir Feere.
(Ovid, 5.700–3)

Thus is the year divided between seasons of barrenness and fruitfulness.

Juno, Jove's sister and wife, was the goddess of light and childbirth. Cartari reports that 'shee is also oftentimes pictured with a scepter in her hand, to shew that shee hath the bestowing of governements, authorities, & kingdomes'; the peacock is sacred to her 'as the diverse-coloured fethers of this bird, enticeth the beholders eyes more and more to view & to gase upon them' (Cartari, sig. Lii^v). Most importantly, she represented the maternal side of marriage:

Some have depictured the Statue of Juno in Matrones habite, holding in one hand the head of the flower Poppie, and at her feet lying a yoke as it were, or a paire of fetters: by these was meant the marriage knot and linke which coupleth the man and wife together; and by the Poppie the innumerable issue of children, which in the world are conceaved & brought forth, alluded to in the numberlesse plentie of seed contained in the head of that flower.

(Cartari, sig. Mii^r)

Juno represents fecundity, the iconographic theme of the magician's masque.

While the traditional court masque began with grotesque antimasque figures and ended with their dispersal by idealized images of virtue, Prospero's masque inverts this order, ending abruptly with his recollection of Caliban's conspiracy. In a parody of the formal masque in which actors assume the roles of goddesses, Stephano and Trinculo in Act 4 seize the magus's clothing, prance about in borrowed robes and adopt an identity not their own. This parodic vision instantly disappears when spirits in the guise of dogs chase the conspirators from the stage.

In the absence of any clear-cut source for *The Tempest* as a whole, the precise literary and experiential influences on the play's plot and characters must remain conjectural. That the dramatist studied Virgil's *Aeneid* and Ovid's *Metamorphoses* at school; that he heard the Bible in church; that he read other texts – Montaigne, Strachey, Pigafetta – seems virtually certain. Echoes within *The Tempest* of classical texts, contemporary concerns, as well as dramas and court masques (some performed by his own acting company) may be the result of deliberate borrowing or subconscious reference. The discourses that inform Shakespeare's play remain part of a complex cultural milieu that we can probe, in part, but never wholly recuperate.

THE AFTERLIFE

The Tempest's extensive afterlife across the centuries, around the globe, and in a wide variety of genres and media suggests that the play is uniquely adaptable. We have already touched on some of the reasons for its continuing vitality; here we expand that discussion before tracing the play's multifaceted interpretive and adaptive post-history.

The Tempest's indefinite setting in time and place lends it uncommon transportability. Although Milan and Naples are constructed as autocracies within the play, Shakespeare provides no specifics that tie the reigns of Prospero and Alonso to a particular era or location. The usurpation of Prospero's throne – unlike that of Richard II, for example – could occur in any culture that has a hereditary ruler. Prospero's enchanted island could be almost anywhere – and, indeed, in modern productions and appropriations has been set in several continents and even in outer space.

The play's imprecise location attracts writers and artists to *The Tempest* for what science-fiction writers call a 'second world' structure, in which faraway islands, imaginary and often 'enchanted', are ideal. Isolated geographically or psychologically from the first world, and usually distanced as well by climate (tropical breezes, lush foliage) and way of life (holiday ease rather than daily toil), the island setting provides artists and writers with an opportunity to comment on human relations without reality's constraints. Prospero's island is already such an outpost, which Shakespeare used to full advantage; it also implicitly invites future utopian or dystopian reimaginings and reimagings of the same or other islands.

The Tempest's characters, moreover, embody the most basic human relationships: father and daughter, king and subject, master and servant. In all three interactions, the play emphasizes the dynamics of freedom and restraint, obedience and rebellion, authority and tyranny. These fundamental relationships and interactions, like the play's imprecise location, encourage almost limitless artistic adaptation.

This is especially true of Ariel and Caliban. Although in most appropriations Prospero and the court party remain European white males whose roles resist broad reinscription, *The Tempest*'s two most original characters are endlessly malleable because Shakespeare described them so sparsely and ambiguously. Ariel is by definition a spirit but, unlike Puck, he is not tied to the woods or any specific mythological framework. Androgynous by nature, he (or she, or it) can fly from the Mediterranean to the Bermudas and back in a blink. When invisible, he appears as a nymph of the sea – whatever that looks like. At other times, he might resemble anything or nothing at all. Earth-bound Caliban is almost as flexible. He can be portrayed as a reptile, an ape, an Indian (East or West), a black African, a European wild man or an eclectic combination. And both Ariel and Caliban have flexible histories, including their priority of occupancy of the island, their affinity for its environment and their resistance to Prospero's control, qualities that invite a wide range of symbolic identifications. In sum, *The Tempest*'s central characters and their relationships to each other are simultaneously specific enough to form an effective story and vague enough to allow new formulations that are at once drastic deviations from Shakespeare's play yet recognizably derivative.

And as we noted earlier, *The Tempest*'s action is elliptical, leaving readers and audiences to speculate about events that happened before the play begins and to wonder about what will happen after it ends. In implicit disagreement with the observation that Shakespeare begins *The Tempest* at nearly its end, in many adaptations the play is merely an interlude between the events of the previous twelve years and the time since Prospero sailed home. 'What's past is prologue' (2.1.253).

The text's loose ends also invite speculation. Antonio's lack of response in the play's final moments, for example, leaves the question of change – to his character at least – up in the air. And while all the Europeans will presumably leave the enchanted island and return to Italy after the play's conclusion, Prospero's epilogue asks the audience to use its imagination and applause to waft the Europeans homeward – almost an invitation to complete a story that seems naggingly unfinished. No wonder so many *Tempest* appropriations attempt to fill the narrative gaps by providing new information about Claribel or Sycorax, new adventures for the Europeans after their return to Italy, or future destinies for Ariel and Caliban, either on the island or as newcomers to Milan or elsewhere.

Finally, Shakespeare's emphasis on art, spectacle, magic and poetic language in *The Tempest* encourages artists to recreate the drama in their own terms through non-dramatic media. Many other Shakespearean plays have stimulated verbal and visual imitations, of course, but rarely, if ever, has a single play inspired so many painters and poets, musicians and film makers, novelists and political writers, to produce such a variety of representations. The following pages sample *The Tempest*'s rich and continuing afterlife.

Restoration rewritings

Davenant and Dryden's radical revamping of *The Tempest* in 1667 (published in 1670) retained the play's title but added *or, The Enchanted Island*. Seven years later, Thomas Shadwell created an operatic version of the Dryden–Davenant text with the same title. For the next century and a half, these rewritings of Shakespeare's play were performed frequently and dominated stagings and popular conceptions. Although textual editors like Nicholas Rowe early in the eighteenth century and Samuel Johnson later in the century reprinted the Folio text with minor editorial embellishments for the literary elite's enjoyment and edification, most English readers and audiences apparently assumed that the Dryden–Davenant–Shadwell versions were identical to Shakespeare's drama. Samuel Pepys, who attended numerous performances in the late 1660s, knew it as '*The Tempest*, an old play of Shakespeares'.[1]

Dryden and Davenant courted upper-class Restoration audiences by rewriting *The Tempest* to emphasize the royalist political and social ideals underlying Shakespeare's original: monarchy was presented as the natural form of government, patriarchal authority prevailed in matters of education and marriage, and patrilineality ruled the ownership and inheritance of property. But in addition to its ideological reflections, the Dryden–Davenant–Shadwell *Enchanted Island* tells much about

1 For Pepys's usually enthusiastic response to the play, see Pepys, 8.521–2 (quotation), 527, 576; 9.12, 48, 133, 179, 195, 422.

the acting traditions that, once established, affected its later stage history as well as popular perceptions of Shakespeare's characters. Besides, audiences liked it. Pepys considered it 'full of so good variety, that I cannot be more pleased almost in a comedy', and several visits later, it 'still pleases me mightily'. He memorized the words to 'the Seamens dance'.[1]

In his Preface to the first printed version of *The Enchanted Island*, Dryden claimed that Davenant 'design'd the Counterpart to Shakespear's Plot, namely that of a Man who had never seen a Woman; that by this means those two Characters of Innocence and Love might the more illustrate and commend each other' (Dryden & Davenant, A2^v, italics removed). Miranda now has a sister, Dorinda, and Prospero a foster son, Hippolito, the rightful Duke of Mantua. Because of a prophetic vision that a woman would cause Hippolito's downfall, Prospero has hidden him on the island, away from Miranda and Dorinda. Hippolito is naive both sexually and culturally.

Dryden and Davenant's comic subplot satirizes Restoration concerns. In a parody of the sexual intrigue of the main plot, Trincalo (Shakespeare's Trinculo, but here the boatswain instead of the jester) and Stephano (the ship's master) seek to possess Sycorax (Caliban's twin sister) and argue about who shall be duke on the island and who the viceroy. Their aspersions on the Commonwealth are palpable. Stephano proclaims, for example, 'we will have no Civil war during our Reign; I do hereby appoint you both to be my Vice-Roys over the whole Island' (Dryden & Davenant 20). The sailors' plot 'becomes chief instrument of the revisers to prove that all republican experiments are inevitably bound to fail' (Auberlen, 77).[2] The mariners cannot govern because they were not born to it, and their drunken discourse exposes the futility of democratic impulses.

1 Pepys, 8.527; 9.48, 179.
2 Insightful discussions of *The Enchanted Island*, in addition to Auberlen, include Maus and Wikander.

Although the Restoration Ariel was generally true to Shakespeare's original, the operatic version more obviously needed an actor, usually female, who could capably sing and dance. Contrary to the modern custom of casting male actors in the role,[1] Ariel seems to have been performed often in the Restoration by Mary (Moll) Davis, who later became a mistress of King Charles II. Richard Flecknoe described her in 1669:

> Who wou'd not think to see thee dance so light,
> Thou wer't all air? or else all soul and spirit . . . all men
>   must admire
> To see thee move like air, and mount like fire.
>   (Highfill, 4.224, italics removed)[2]

The operatic version of *The Tempest* concluded with a singing Ariel suspended over the stage.

While Dryden and Davenant's Ariel is more important than the Folio's, Caliban's role is drastically reduced. Mainly because the issues surrounding the 'salvage' or natural man in Shakespeare's original are displaced on to Hippolito, Caliban is merely a buffoonish monster. Coupled with his sluttish sister, he is humanity's bestial side (see Vaughan, *Caliban*, 91–5).

Dryden and Davenant's Prospero is also a different character from Shakespeare's original. Eckhard Auberlen summarizes the changes:

> In Shakespeare, Prospero firmly controls the outer events, but has to see the limits of his power in bringing about a moral regeneration on others and himself; in the adaptation, Prospero loses control over the outer events and is reduced to the status of a Polonius-like overbusy

---

1 The appearance of Aunjanue Ellis in the New York Shakespeare Festival's 1995 production of *The Tempest* surprised many who were used to male Ariels. Ellis's overt female sexuality added an extra dimension to her relationship with Patrick Stewart's Prospero.

2 Orgel argues that Dryden and Davenant's Ariel must have been enacted by a male since at the finale Ariel is accompanied by Milcha, a female spirit (Oxf[1], 70). But given the entries in Pepys's *Diary* praising Moll Davis's dancing, many theatre historians believe she performed either a *travesti* Hippolyto or the fairy spirit's role.

father, intent on protecting the chastity of his two sexually naive daughters while planning advantageous
dynastic marriages for them.

(Auberlen, 74)

The Restoration Prospero is a moralist, bent on controlling
events and people. He undergoes no change of heart. As the
play's final scenes make clear, if Ariel's salves had been ineffective and Hippolito had died from the wounds inflicted by
Ferdinand, Prospero would have executed Miranda's fiancé.
Only the fairy's intervention ensures a happy ending.

Thomas Shadwell's operatic version of the Dryden–
Davenant adaptation of *The Tempest* added more songs and
spectacular scenery and became an extremely popular entertainment (see Van Lennep; Guffey, ix). According to John Downes
in 1708, the opera provided tremendous variety, including:

Scenes, Machines; particularly, one Scene Painted with
Myriads of *Ariel* Spirits; and another flying away, with a
Table Furnisht out with Fruits, Sweetmeats, and all
sorts of Viands; just when Duke *Trinculo* and his
Companions were going to dinner; all was things per-
form'd in it so Admirably well, that not any succeeding
Opera got more Money.

(Downes, 34–5)

Downes uses 'Opera' in the late seventeenth-century sense of a
dramatic extravaganza rather like a modern musical comedy,
with dialogue interrupted by carefully choreographed songs
and dances. The published version of the operatic text offers
descriptive stage directions that reveal the Restoration *Tempest*'s
un-Shakespearean quality. The opening storm, for example, was
accompanied by music:

The Front of the Stage is open'd, and the Band of 24
Violins, with the Harpsicals and Theorbo's which
accompany the Voices, are plac'd between the Pit and

the Stage . . . [T]he Scene . . . represents a thick Cloudy
Sky, a very Rocky Coast, and a Tempestuous Sea in
perpetual Agitation. This Tempest (suppos'd to be
rais'd by Magick) has many dreadful Objects in it, as
several Spirits in horrid shapes flying down amongst the
Sailers, then rising and crossing in the Air. And when
the Ship is sinking, the whole House is darken'd, and a
shower of Fire falls upon 'em. This is accompanied with
Lightning, and several Claps of Thunder, to the end of
the Storm.

> (Shadwell, *Enchanted Island*, 1,
> in Guffey; italics removed) (see Fig. 12)

When the storm subsides and everyone is stranded on the island,
the locale divides in two. The 'Beautiful part of the Island'
where Prospero lives is 'compos'd of three Walks of Cypress-
trees, each Side-walk leads to a Cave, in one of which Prospero
keeps his Daughters, in the other Hippolito: the Middle-Walk is
of great depth, and leads to an open part of the Island'. In contrast to this cultivated space, Caliban and his maritime visitors
appear in a 'wilder part of the Island', which is 'compos'd of
divers sorts of Trees, and barren places, with a prospect of the
Sea at a great distance' (Shadwell, *Enchanted Island*, 5, 14, in
Guffey; italics removed). This visual opposition emphasizes the
play's careful distinctions between courtly and lower class, civilized and uncivil.

The Dryden–Davenant–Shadwell adaptation of *The Tempest*
was so successful at the Duke's Theatre that the rival King's
Company soon countered with a burlesque by Thomas Duffett.
The Mock Tempest (1675) begins with what seems to be a storm
but is actually a riot in a brothel. Prospero and Miranda appear
at Bridewell, where he informs her that fifty years ago he was
'Duke of my Lord Majors Dogg-kenne'. Alonso and Gonzalo
are frightened by a pageant of devils who sing a parody of the
opera's 'Arise, ye Subterranean winds' – 'Arise, ye Subterranean

12 The frontispiece to Nicholas Rowe's 1709 edition of *The Tempest*, the first known illustration of the play, may suggest the visual impact of the Dryden and Davenant storm scene

fiends!' Prospero successfully pairs Dorinda with Hypolito and Miranda with Quakero (Ferdinand), and the play concludes with a Chorus of pimps and bawds. Interlaced with Shakespearean allusions, this scabrous satire did nothing to deter the popularity of the Dryden–Davenant–Shadwell operatic version of *The Tempest*; rather, it added another pseudo-Shakespearean version that further deflected attention from the Folio text.

Eighteenth-century ambivalence

Eighteenth-century adaptations of *The Tempest* continued the Restoration's spectacular tradition. On 6 January 1716, for example, the Drury Lane Theatre paid three shillings for 'The Shower of Fire', six pence for Lightning and three pence for 'white wands'. Stephano and Trincalo also required bottles of white wine and a pint of sack (Van Lennep, 2: Pt 1, cvi). Eighteenth-century playbills advertised a *Tempest* with songs and dances, 'Scenes, Machines, Habits, Flyings, Sinkings, and other Decorations proper to the play' (24 January 1733, Drury Lane).

The London Stage consistently lists young actresses in the role of Ariel, except for two instances when a young male dancer or singer played the part.[1] Like Miss Lindar, who moved over to Dorinda in 1723, the actresses sometimes outgrew it. Ariel needed to have a superb voice and light and graceful movements. Caliban, by contrast, was usually a comedian's part. Ben Johnson took the role in the early part of the century and was succeeded by Charles Macklin and Edward Berry, actors known for their awkward figures. The century ended with Charles Bannister, another huge man skilled at dramatic singing, as the savage monster. Prospero was performed by the lead actor of the moment; though his role was the most prominent, his lines were usually contracted to allow more music and spectacle.

---

1 Master Woodward played Ariel on 2 June 1731, and Master Arne, presumably a son of the composer, took the role on 22 October 1734.

During the first half of the century, playgoers usually saw the Dryden–Davenant–Shadwell version of *The Tempest*. In 1756 actor–manager David Garrick countered with his own operatic *Tempest* at the Drury Lane Theatre. This three-act extravaganza with music by John Christopher Smith included the drunken seamen Mustacho and Ventoso but omitted the other Dryden–Davenant characters – Hippolito, Dorinda, Sycorax and Milcha. The text was cut to make room for thirty-two songs. When the early performances were not successful, Garrick dropped his adaptation from the repertory (see Stone).

The next year (1757) Garrick presented a restored (though heavily cut) Shakespearean *Tempest*, a revival that was profitably performed from time to time for the rest of the century. In 1789, John Philip Kemble reintroduced Dorinda and Hippolito to his acting version of *The Tempest,* but this was to be their last gasp on the English stage.

The eighteenth-century *Tempest* on stage and in artists' renderings underlined a neoclassical emphasis on human rationality and morality in Shakespeare's work. William Hogarth's painting of a composite scene dating from the mid-1730s (see Fig. 13) demonstrates these themes at work: posed like Joseph behind the Virgin Mary, Prospero protectively shelters Miranda from the bestial Caliban to her left, while a cherubic Ariel hovers overhead. Hogarth's Prospero is typical of eighteenth-century representations. Portrayed most commonly as a grey-bearded magus, Prospero controls the disorderly political forces in Antonio and Sebastian and the corrupt moral forces embodied in Caliban. Henry Fuseli's 1789 painting, commissioned for the Boydell Shakespeare Gallery in London (see Fig. 14), depicts similar relationships. Prospero, his extended hand pointing to the devilish figure of Caliban, signifies patriarchal protection of his innocent daughter from the threats of a born devil. A spectator gazing at this picture, or attending a production at Drury Lane, would presumably have accepted Prospero's wisdom and authority and interpreted the play

13 William Hogarth's composite scene from *The Tempest* (*c.* 1736), the first
    major artistic rendition of the play

through his eyes. Throughout the eighteenth century, amidst
operatic spectacles and comic distractions, *The Tempest*
remained Prospero's play.

Romanticism

The Tempest's perceived focus changed significantly with the
dawn of the nineteenth century. Partly under the impetus of
lectures, letters and essays by Romantic poets such as Samuel
Taylor Coleridge, William Wordsworth and John Keats, and
partly from the French Revolution's restructuring of social
values, a new generation of writers rejected neoclassical rules
and decorum. Wordsworth's 'Preface to the Lyrical Ballads'
(1800) called instead for poems about everyday life coloured by
the poetic imagination. Poetry, declared Wordsworth, is the
'spontaneous overflow of powerful feelings', and the poet, by

14 An engraving of Henry Fuseli's painting of *The Tempest*, commissioned for the Boydell Shakespeare Gallery (1789), featuring a magisterial Prospero, innocent Miranda and devilish Caliban

definition, 'has a greater knowledge of human nature, and a more comprehensive soul, than are supposed to be common among mankind' (Wordsworth, 448, 453). To Wordsworth and the Romantics who followed him, creative imagination, genius and poetry were intimately associated.[1] Shakespeare had by the late eighteenth century been apotheosized as England's greatest writer; the Romantics hailed his work as the ultimate example of creative imagination and the dramatist himself as the untutored genius who followed nature rather than the ancients' rules.

Poetry thus changed from Samuel Johnson's 'just representations of general nature' (S. Johnson, 491) to the individualized expression of the author's soul. Shakespeare's plays were no

1 For a full discussion of the influence of Shakespeare on the Romantic poets, see Jonathan Bate, *Shakespeare and the English Romantic Imagination* (Oxford, 1989).

longer considered as acting scripts for a public theatre but as expressions of his personal feelings. Accompanying this emphasis on the texts as poetry rather than drama was the assumption that Shakespeare's genius could only be realized in the reader's imagination. Charles Lamb contended that *The Tempest*, in particular, could not be embodied on stage:

> It is one thing to read of an enchanter, and to believe the wondrous tale while we are reading it; but to have a conjuror brought before us in his conjuring-gown, with his spirits about him, which none but himself and some hundred of favoured spectators before the curtain are supposed to see, involves such a quantity of the *hateful incredible* that all our reverence for the author cannot hinder us from perceiving such gross attempts upon the senses to be in the highest degree childish and inefficient. Spirits and fairies cannot be represented, they cannot even be painted.
>
> (Lamb, 191)

Thus began a split between the literary analysis of Shakespeare's text and assessments of Shakespeare in performance, two distinct threads that, even at present, are usually separate in academic discourse and institutional structure. With some notable exceptions (William Hazlitt, for example, frequently attended the theatre and occasionally referred to performances he had seen), nineteenth-century writers who discussed *The Tempest* relied on their private readings, not on public performance.

Coleridge, for example, found *The Tempest* to be a 'purely romantic drama' that 'addresses itself entirely to the imaginative faculty' (Coleridge, 1.118). Hazlitt concurred: 'the preternatural part has the air of reality, and almost haunts the imagination with the sense of truth', while the 'real characters and events partake of the wildness of a dream'. The enchanted island with its exotic furze, marmosets and water with berries appealed to the Romantic affinity for stark yet beautiful natural landscapes. The characters of Ariel and Caliban seemed spun from imagination alone. To Hazlitt, Ariel was 'imaginary power, the swiftness of thought personified'. Caliban, too, displayed the power and truth of the poet's imagination; his character grows 'out of the soil where it is rooted, uncontrolled, uncouth, and wild, uncramped by any of the meanness of custom' (Hazlitt, 82, 86, 84).

Ariel's songs, which Samuel Johnson had criticized for expressing 'nothing great, nor reveal[ing] any thing above mortal discovery' (S. Johnson, 531), conveyed to Hazlitt a 'peculiar charm'; they seemed 'to sound in the air, and as if the person playing them were invisible', sometimes resembling 'snatches of half-forgotten music' (Hazlitt, 86). Coleridge described Ariel in his ninth lecture: 'in air he acts; and all his colours and properties seem to have been obtained from the rainbow and the skies . . . He is neither born of heaven, nor of earth; but, as it were, between both' (Coleridge, 2.136–7). And in one of the earliest poems based on *The Tempest*, Percy Bysshe Shelley identified Ariel with the poet, the sprite's songs with poetry. 'With a Guitar, To Jane' begins with Ariel speaking:

> Ariel to Miranda: – Take
> This slave of Music, for the sake
> Of him who is the slave of thee,
> And teach it all the harmony,
> In which thou canst, and only thou,
> Make the delighted spirit glow[.]

Instead of being imprisoned in Sycorax's mighty oak, Shelley's Ariel is caught inside the guitar he presents to Jane, where he sings the harmonies:

> Of the plains and of the skies,
> Of the forests and the mountains,
> And the many-voicèd fountains;
> The clearest echoes of the hills,

> The softest notes of falling rills,
> The melodies of birds and bees,
> The murmuring of summer seas.
> (Shelley, 428–30)

Shelley's simple diction – the language of the common man that Wordsworth valued – here conveys Ariel's oneness with nature and imitates the straightforward beauty of Shakespeare's original songs.

Partly because the magus created Ariel's music, the Romantics identified him with Shakespeare. Coleridge called Prospero a 'mighty wizard, whose potent art could not only call up spirits of the deep, but the characters as they were and are and will be, [he] seems a portrait of the bard himself' (Coleridge, 2.253). If Prospero speaks for Shakespeare, and if, as the Romantics believed, poetry is personal expression, it followed that Prospero's feelings were Shakespeare's. This identification between the magus and the dramatist persisted, culminating in the notorious claims of Edward Dowden in 1875 that the romances reveal biographical information about Shakespeare's later life. '[T]he temper of Prosper', Dowden declared, 'the grave harmony of his character, his self-mastery, his calm validity of will, his sensitiveness to wrong, his unfaltering justice, and, with these, a certain abandonment, a remoteness from the common joys and sorrows of the world, are characteristic of Shakspere as discovered to us in all his latest plays'. By the end of *The Tempest*, Prospero / Shakespeare 'has also reached an altitude of thought from which he can survey the whole of human life, and see how small and yet how great it is' (Dowden, 371–2). Prospero, like Shakespeare, was a genius, an artist who understood the truths of human nature and whose words could arbitrate morality and wisdom.

Dowden's biographical approach to *The Tempest* led many – not only in the late nineteenth century but throughout the twentieth – to interpret Prospero's famous lines, 'Our revels now are ended . . .' (4.1.148–63), as Shakespeare's retirement speech and his 'Ye elves' passage (5.1.33–57) as his assessment of illusion's power and danger. *The Tempest*, in sum, was often perceived as Shakespeare's last and best expression of human reality.

But not everyone adopted Prospero's viewpoint. Several early nineteenth-century writers re-examined Caliban and found some merit in his rebellious claims to ownership of the enchanted isle. In his ninth lecture, Coleridge had argued that 'Caliban is in some respects a noble being: . . . a man in the sense of the imagination: all the images he uses are drawn from nature, and are highly poetical' (Coleridge, 2.138). To Hazlitt, Caliban's 'deformity whether of body or mind is redeemed by the power and truth of the imagination displayed in it' (Hazlitt, 83). Sympathy for Caliban became still more palpable after William Charles Macready produced *The Tempest* in Shakespeare's original text at Drury Lane in 1838. George Bennett's representation of the savage slave seems to have aroused his audience's feelings, including those of Patrick MacDonnell, who saw Caliban as 'maintaining in his mind, a strong resistance to that tyranny, which held him in the thraldom of slavery'. MacDonnell even defended Caliban's morals, suggesting that he tried to rape Miranda only after Prospero imprudently lodged the two together. The 'noble and generous character of Prospero, therefore, suffers, by this severe conduct to Caliban, and I confess, I have never read, or witnessed this scene, without experiencing a degree of pity for the poor, abject, and degraded slave' (MacDonnell, 16–19) (see Fig. 15).

It was perhaps predictable that after Dryden and Davenant cut Caliban's role so drastically, he should be revitalized in Macready's uncut version. Although the abolition of slavery in England coincided with the year of Macready's production, human bondage was still a sensitive topic in England and was, of course, legal through much of the world, including many of the United States. As a 'salvage and deformed slave', Caliban could

15 An 1820 engraving of John Mortimer's 1775 painting of a soulful, puppy-headed Caliban

be cast as 'hereditary bondsman' in Robert and William Brough's burlesque, *The Enchanted Isle* (1848), or as an aggrieved slave in political cartoons and broadsides (see Vaughan, *Caliban*, 105–9).

Enter Darwin

Caliban's deformity and incivility made him a useful symbol for mid-nineteenth-century challengers of traditional theology. Under the impact of Charles Darwin's evolutionary theories, humankind's place within the natural world and its relationship to God were newly debatable. Robert Browning's poem 'Caliban upon Setebos' (1864) explored such issues.[1] In a long monologue based on the principle of analogy (as I do, so does Setebos), Caliban speculates on Setebos's nature and motives. This god, according to Caliban,

> doth His worst in this our life,
> Giving just respite lest we die through pain,
> Saving last pain for worst, – with which, an end.
> Meanwhile, the best way to escape His ire
> Is, not to seem too happy.
>
> (Browning, 159; see Appendix 2.1)

Note that Caliban, not Prospero, is the speaker who ponders theological and philosophical questions. For the Victorian age, the slave was often more important than the master.

Caliban's importance expanded further in Daniel Wilson's *Caliban: The Missing Link* (1873), which identified him as Darwin's 'missing link' and tied his (presumed) amphibious nature to the increasingly accepted view that human life had evolved from some sort of aquatic animal. Caliban's form, however, remained essentially human, akin to early modern explorers' accounts of New World inhabitants. At the same time, Wilson sympathized with Caliban: 'We feel for the poor monster, so helplessly in the power of the stern Prospero, as for some caged wild beast pining in cruel captivity, and rejoice to think of him at last free to range in harmless mastery over his island solitude' (D. Wilson, 91). Caliban's struggle for knowledge and independence mirrors Victorian notions of progress, in

---

1 See especially Ortwin de Graef's essay in *Constellation*, 113–34.

which humankind inched towards nineteenth-century European civilization's full flowering. Artistic representations of Caliban in this period assigned him aquatic or apelike features (see Vaughan, *Caliban*, 238–43).

Unlike English writers who focused almost exclusively on Caliban, the French philosopher Ernest Renan gave equal weight to Prospero and Ariel in his closet drama *Caliban: Suite de La Tempête* (1878). In this sequel to Shakespeare's play, Ariel ('role for a woman') has followed Prospero to Milan and remains steadfastly loyal. When Caliban, who spends his time drinking in the palace wine cellar, rebels, Ariel protests that her master Prospero 'believes that God is reason, and that one should work towards the means by which God . . . governs the world more and more'. When Caliban spearheads a palace coup and becomes the new ruler of Milan, Prospero ruefully declares, 'Enlightened, little by little, through living in my house, he at last came to the power of thought and reflection, but all his thought was employed to plan my ruin . . . Oh! what a mistake it was to educate a brute who would turn my very instruction into a weapon against me' (Renan, 14, 20, 57).[1] Mistake or not, when Caliban becomes duke he actively imitates his former master's virtues and even tries to save him from the Inquisition.

Lost in the era's philosophical speculation is Miranda. Browning has her sleep through Caliban's monologue and Renan drops her altogether. Mary Cowden Clarke also omitted Miranda from her description of *The Girlhood of Shakespeare's Heroines* (1852). And although the nineteenth century had largely restored Shakespeare's original text, Miranda's most outspoken lines (1.2.352–63) continued to be assigned to Prospero on the grounds of decorum, and her remaining words and actions perhaps struck Victorian audiences as appropriately demure but uninteresting. John Forster praised Helen Faucit's Miranda in the 1838 Macready production for her modest

---

1 See also Koenraad Geldof's essay in *Constellation*, 85–94.

expression of love to Ferdinand: 'She seemed to us to second the gentlemanly love of Mr. Anderson with just such tones of trusting impulse as peculiarly fitted her for Miranda' (Forster, 71). Ariel, played by Priscilla Horton, was the wilful, interesting female. Miranda's diminished roles on stage and her omission from the most prominent philosophical appropriations of *The Tempest* reflect the nineteenth century's patriarchal perspective.

There were exceptions. Miranda appeared prominently in Anna Jameson's compendium of *Shakespeare's Heroines: Characteristics of Women Moral, Poetical, and Historical*, first published in 1832 under the title, *Characteristics of Women*. Classified along with Juliet, Helena, Perdita, Viola and Ophelia as a 'Character of Passion and Imagination' (in contrast to Portia's intellect and Desdemona's affection), Miranda was to Jameson a picture of 'feminine beauty', not only beautiful but 'so perfectly unsophisticated, so delicately refined, that she is all but ethereal' (see Fig. 16). In contrast to Ariel, she is a true human being with a woman's heart yet distinguished by her upbringing without the trappings of civilization. All who behold her, Jameson proposed, are struck with wonder at her 'soft simplicity, her virgin innocence, her total ignorance of the conventional forms and language of society' (Jameson, 147–55). But even to so enthusiastic an admirer as Jameson, Miranda's most salient feature is a void – a lack of experience, knowledge and sophistication.

With Miranda and Prospero in critical eclipse, Caliban dominated late nineteenth- and early twentieth-century stage productions. Leading actors selected the role for themselves and employed antic stage business to attract audiences to the deformed slave. The athletic Frank Benson played Caliban as an apish missing link by imitating monkeys and baboons he had observed at the zoo. On stage he climbed a tree, hung upside down and gibbered. Beerbohm Tree donned fur and seaweed and sported waist-length hair and an unkempt beard. In the play's final tableau, he stood alone, watching Prospero's ship

16 Miranda, as engraved by W.H. Mote from John Hayter's painting, in *The Heroines of Shakespeare . . . engraved under the direction of Mr. Charles Heath*, London, 1848

depart. Tree described the scene: as he stretches out his arms towards the empty horizon, 'we feel that from the conception of sorrow in solitude may spring the birth of a higher civilization' (Tree, xi). Tree's apelike Caliban, part-animal, part-human,

17 Herbert Beerbohm Tree as a hirsute, apprehensive Caliban in Tree's
    production of 1904, painted by Charles A. Buchel

symbolized primitive man before his evolution to a more
civilized stage (see Fig. 17).

In the last major Darwinian appropriation of *The Tempest*,
Caliban journeyed towards self-discovery in Percy MacKaye's

community masque, *Caliban by the Yellow Sands*, at Lewisohn Stadium in New York City in 1916 and later at the Harvard University stadium in Massachusetts. MacKaye proclaimed that his goal was 'to present Prospero's art as the art of the theater culminating in Shakespeare and to lead Caliban step by step from his aboriginal path of brute force and ignorance to the realm of love, reason and self-discipline' (Franck, 159). The theme, claimed MacKaye, was 'Caliban seeking to learn the art of Prospero – . . . the slow education of mankind through the influences of cooperative art' (MacKaye, xvii).

In addition to its huge cast of dancers and masquers, *Caliban by the Yellow Sands* foregrounded Ariel, Prospero and Miranda as the forces of civilization against Caliban, Lust, Death and War – the representations of evil (see Fig. 18). The pageant begins with Ariel and Caliban caught under Sycorax's evil spell; Miranda discovers Ariel imprisoned by darkness. Prospero releases Ariel and his spirits, who help the magician to display a 'pageant of his art' – a sampling of Shakespearean drama, from the Roman plays' portrayals of ancient Greece and Rome to the history plays' depictions of early modern England. As Caliban watches the unfolding pageantry, he and Prospero discuss the action; but despite the magus's educational efforts, Caliban's rebellious spirit, inspired by a recitation of *Henry V*'s militaristic rhetoric, refuses to die. Shakespeare, looking much like Prospero, appears in a final procession of the world's greatest dramatists and takes the magus's cloak. As the pageant concludes, a repentant Caliban cries for more knowledge:

> A little have I crawled, a little only
> Out of mine ancient cave. All that I build
> I botch; all that I do destroyeth my dream.
> Yet – yet I yearn to build, to be thine Artist
> And stablish this thine Earth among the stars –
> Beautiful!
>
> (MacKaye, 145)

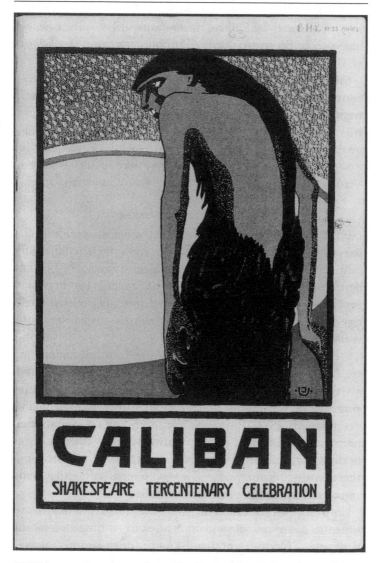

18 The programme cover to Percy MacKaye's *Caliban by the Yellow Sands*,
1916

Looking tenderly at Caliban, Shakespeare delivers the masque's final speech, Prospero's farewell to the stage from *The Tempest* (4.1.148–63).

MacKaye's identification of Prospero with Shakespeare as a figure of omniscient wisdom epitomizes the nineteenth and early twentieth century's romanticization of Shakespeare's last play. In 1916 Caliban's aspirations to build a new world of truth and beauty still seemed plausible to New York audiences, but like Prospero's insubstantial pageant, they were a final vestige of Victorian belief in the inexorable progress of humankind.

Perspectives on imperialism

Caliban was often the key player in two other major interpretations of *The Tempest* which first appeared in the late nineteenth century and flourished in the twentieth: an insistence (1) that the play is essentially about the New World, and (2) that it symbolizes European or United States imperialism, or a related ideology – materialism, for example, or racism – wherever in the world it appears.

During the long span from 1611 to 1898, critical commentary on *The Tempest* rarely emphasized its possible American sources or resonances. Edmond Malone's early nineteenth-century emphasis on the Virginia and Bermuda pamphlets is a notable exception. In 1892, Furness's Variorum edition summarized more than a century of random musings about American connections but did not favour their importance. Until the eve of the twentieth century, *The Tempest* seemed only tangentially connected to Europe's American ventures.

Emphatic identifications of *The Tempest* with the New World began suddenly and almost simultaneously in England and the Americas – North, Central and South. In the former Spanish colonies, the focus was almost entirely on Caliban, beginning with a Nicaraguan journalist, Rubén Darío, who in 1893 likened New York City's crudity and materialism to Caliban's. Five years later, Darío's short essay on 'The Triumph of Caliban' berated what many Latin Americans considered the United States' blatant aggression in the Spanish-American War of 1898; that same year an Argentine writer dubbed Anglo-Americans 'Calibanesque'. Such metaphorical borrowing from *The Tempest* expanded appreciably in 1900, when the Uruguayan philosopher–statesman José Enrique Rodó's short book, entitled simply *Ariel*, contrasted – cautiously but unmistakably – the noblest traits of Latin American civilization, symbolized by Shakespeare's gentle sprite, with the most regrettable characteristics of Anglo-American civilization, epitomized in Caliban's 'brutal sensuality' (see Appendix 2.2). *Ariel* quickly became a major socio-intellectual statement, hailed throughout Spanish-speaking America and attracting numerous disciples, many of whom exaggerated Rodó's application of metaphors from *The Tempest*. In 1918, for example, the Venezuelan writer Jesús Semprúm encapsulated the Hispanic nations' view of their northern neighbours as 'rough and obtuse Calibans, swollen by brutal appetites, the enemies of all idealisms, furiously enamoured of the dollar, insatiable gulpers of whiskey and sausages – swift, overwhelming, fierce, clownish' (Semprúm, 132).

While Latin American writers loosely applied symbols from *The Tempest* to the western hemisphere's history and culture, Sidney Lee and a growing number of English and American scholars insisted, from a very different perspective, that the play was 'a veritable document of early Anglo-American history'. Shakespeare, Lee argued in 1898 and for three decades thereafter in numerous editions of his *Life of William Shakespeare* and in several essays on American Indians, had intended *The Tempest* to reflect England's early colonial experience and the play's characters to epitomize colonization's representative participants.[1] The play, he contended, took place on an island along

---

1 More than a dozen editions of Lee's biography of Shakespeare appeared between 1898 and the author's death in 1926, and it remained a standard 'life' for many more years. Lee's most relevant work on Indians appeared first in 1907 in *Scribner's Magazine*, was largely incorporated in 1913 into an article in *Cornhill Magazine* and was reprinted in 1929 in a collection of his essays.

the North American coast or in a conflated English America, and Prospero, though probably modelled initially on one or more characters in European dramas, had unmistakable colonial elements. 'Every explorer', Lee assumed with undisguised Victorian pride, 'shared Prospero's pity for the aborigines' inability to make themselves intelligible in their crabbed agglutinative dialects, and offered them instruction in civilised speech'. Caliban, Lee concluded, was 'a creature stumbling over the first stepping-stones which lead from savagery to civilization' (Lee, 'Indian', 326–8).

Although Lee spearheaded the Americanization of *The Tempest* and was its most articulate and productive proponent, his numerous allies on both sides of the Atlantic reinforced and expanded the play's American connections. In the same year (1898) that Lee in England first linked characters from the play with early seventeenth-century ethnohistorical events, and Darío in Nicaragua proclaimed that Caliban personified the United States, an American cleric-scholar declared that *The Tempest* 'has an entirely American basis and character', and that Caliban 'is an American'. Also that year, Rudyard Kipling inaugurated a popular trend by insisting that Bermuda was, in fact, the play's location (Bristol, 51, 82; Kipling, 25–32).

The Americanization of *The Tempest* gained momentum in the early twentieth century. Morton Luce's Arden edition (1901) estimated that 'nine-tenths of the subjects touched upon by Shakespeare in *The Tempest* are suggested by the new enterprise of colonisation', and Caliban is to a considerable extent 'a dispossessed Indian' (Ard[1], xlii, xxxvi). A few years later, the British scholar Walter Alexander Raleigh declared in his introduction to a major reissue of Hakluyt's *Principal Navigations* that '*The Tempest* is a fantasy of the New World', in which:

> Shakespeare, almost alone, saw the problem of American settlement in a detached light ... The drunken butler, accepting the worship and allegiance of

Caliban, and swearing him in by making him kiss the
bottle, is a fair representative of the idle and dissolute
men who were shipped to the Virginian colony. The situation of Miranda was perhaps suggested by the story of
Virginia Dare, . . . the first child born in America of
English parents . . . And the portrait of Caliban, with
his affectionate loyalty to the drunkard, his adoration of
valour, his love of natural beauty and feeling for music
and poetry, his hatred and superstitious fear of his task-
master, and the simple cunning and savagery of his
attempts at revenge and escape – all this is a composition wrought from fragments of travellers' tales, and
shows a wonderfully accurate and sympathetic understanding of uncivilised man.

(Raleigh, 112–13)

In 1926 an American scholar, Robert Ralston Cawley, summarized the case for *The Tempest*'s essential Americanness by printing in sequential passages from the major travel accounts and
Shakespeare's play every plausible similarity of word, phrase or
speech.

A few sceptics found the evidence fragmentary and incon-
sequential. The most outspoken was the American scholar Elmer
Edgar Stoll, who complained to the annual meeting of the Modern
Language Association in 1926 that 'Spenser, Daniel, Drayton, and
the rest [of Shakespeare's contemporary writers] sing of the New
World and Virginia, but not Shakespeare . . . There is not a word
in *The Tempest* about America or Virginia, colonies or colonizing,
Indians or tomahawks, maize, mocking-birds, or tobacco. Nothing
but the Bermudas, once barely mentioned as a faraway place, like
Tokio or Mandalay' (Stoll, 212–13). Stoll notwithstanding, *The
Tempest* seemed by overwhelming consensus to be Shakespeare's
American play. The occasional doubters during the first half of the
twentieth century usually ignored the Americanist proponents
rather than refuted them.

Until the middle of the twentieth century the Americanization of *The Tempest* remained bifurcated. The critical interpretations promulgated principally by Lee, Raleigh and Cawley held sway in Britain and the United States; the emblematic appropriations popularized by Darío, Rodó, and Semprúm had little opposition in Latin America. In the latter region, versions of noble Ariel in conflict with ignoble Caliban appeared in social, political and cultural statements but seldom in dramatic or literary interpretations of Shakespeare's whole play; *The Tempest*'s usefulness was pragmatic and symbolic rather than aesthetic. Shakespeare specialists in Great Britain and the United States meanwhile worked from different assumptions. Ostensibly concerned with authorial intentions and the 'true' meaning of Shakespeare's text, yet heavily influenced by the political and cultural climates that were creating, at long last, a rapprochement between the two most populous Anglophone democracies, British and North American scholars persuaded themselves and most (apparently) of their generation that *The Tempest* had an essentially American setting, predominantly American themes and, at least in Caliban, a truly American character. Yet, like their Latin American counterparts, English-language commentators usually stressed Caliban's basest qualities: he was more savage than noble, more an aggressor than a victim.[1] Although Prospero was virtually absent from Latin American symbolic appropriations, Anglo-American literary critics kept him near centre stage and implicitly praised his introduction of English culture to the western hemisphere. He was the benign imperialist, the conduit of language, learning, refinement and religion – the uplifter of 'uncivilized man'.

Half a century after the emergence of separate Latin American and Anglo-American versions of *The Tempest*'s relevance to the

---

1 Two further examples of Caliban as an emphatically pejorative symbol in the first half of the twentieth century are Arnold Zweig, *Caliban, or Politics and Passions* (Potsdam, 1927), in which he personifies German antisemitism, and Leonard Barnes, *Caliban in Africa: An Impression of Colour-Madness* (London, 1930), in which Dutch South Africans are dubbed 'Calibanesque' for their racially exploitive 'apartheid'.

western hemisphere, new critical perspectives reversed the symbolism of the first paradigm, sharply modified the second paradigm and brought them closer to a consensus. Beginning in the 1950s and 1960s, Latin American appropriators of *The Tempest* recast Caliban as the emblem of South and Central American peoples and substituted Prospero as the imperialist, arrogant United States. Anglo-American critics and appropriators soon adopted a similar strategy. It differed from the earlier interpretation of Sidney Lee and his followers less in its realignment of the play's location or themes than in its recognition of new qualities in the central characters. Prospero was still a colonist; Caliban remained an American Indian or perhaps, now, an African–American slave; Trinculo and Stephano continued to be (occasionally) unruly settlers. But English and North American critics and performers now chastised Prospero for seizing the natives' land, enslaving their bodies and imposing an alien, unwanted culture. Caliban, by contrast, was ennobled and to some extent empowered. The victim had emerged victorious.

The radical shift in Latin American and Anglo-American readings of *The Tempest* emerged from different circumstances. The former reflected to a considerable extent the rise in South and Central America, and especially on the Caribbean islands, of an intellectual class whose ethnic and cultural ties were less to Spain or another continental nation than to a Native American or African (or both) heritage. In England and the United States, the new paradigm echoed an emerging scepticism about European imperialism and its impact on colonized people (dispossession and often death) and on the colonizers (insensitivity and often brutality). A major impetus towards paradigmatic reassessment in both hemispheres also came from a French social scientist's analysis of his own nation's administration of the African island of Madagascar: Octave Mannoni's *Psychologie de la colonisation*, first published in 1950 and six years later translated into English, with a provocative new title – *Prospero and Caliban*.

Seldom has a work about non-literary matters so profoundly influenced actors, directors, critics and teachers. (For their impact on readings, stagings and artistic reflections of *The Tempest*, the only comparable texts are Darwin's and Freud's.) Mannoni examined the basic patterns of temperament and behaviour of Madagascar's French colonizers and its indigenous population (Malagasies), which, as a trained psychoanalyst and experienced civil administrator on the island, he seemed uniquely qualified to render. Mannoni also had a keen eye for English literary symbols. In a brief but suggestive chapter on 'Crusoe and Prospero' he employed those fictional islanders to illustrate some of his major findings (see Appendix 2.3).[1]

Although Mannoni's book was a complex analysis of colonial interaction in Madagascar alone, its ultimate concern was with the personality types he believed to be generated by colonial contexts: on the one hand were domineering, callous, neurotic colonizers; on the other were submissive natives, racked by ambivalence over their acceptance of western values and their rejection of indigenous culture, and subconsciously resentful of their conquerors and even of themselves. Despite some heated criticism, especially of its portrayal of the Malagasies, social and political commentators eagerly applied *Prospero and Caliban* to modern colonial contexts in Africa, Asia and Latin America. Literary critics simultaneously applied Mannoni's models to seventeenth-century Anglo-America. Prospero's 'inferiority complex', a common phenomenon (according to Mannoni) among French colonists, explained his irritability, authoritarianism and manipulation; Caliban's 'dependency complex', like that of the Malagasies, shaped his early devotion to Prospero and Miranda, his pandering to Stephano and Trinculo, and his eventual rebellion. Soon after 1950, post-colonial interpretations of *The Tempest*, often with acknowledgement of Mannoni's influence, dominated stages and studies around the world.

1 Mannoni had been writing for several years before 1950 about the personality types he believed to be connected with colonialism, but he did not apply *The Tempest* metaphor until his book of that year.

Invigorated partly by *Prospero and Caliban* and partly by the social turbulence of the 1960s and 1970s, American scholars took renewed interest in *The Tempest*'s sociohistorical implications. Leslie Fiedler's 'prophetic' interpretation reflects one type of response. Fiedler saw in Prospero's rout of the Caliban–Trinculo–Stephano cabal 'the whole history of imperialist America', and in Caliban 'a kind of subhuman freak imagined in Europe even before the discovery of red men in America: the *homme sauvage* or "savage man", who in the nightmares of Mediterranean humanists, had been endowed with sexual powers vastly in excess of their own. Such monstrous virility Shakespeare attributes to Caliban, associating him not with cannibalism, after all, but with unbridled lust' (Fiedler, 238, 234; see also Marx).

American and English scholars continue to incorporate the colonial paradigm, though seldom with Fiedler's expansiveness and sometimes with as much indebtedness to Lee as to Mannoni. A few examples will illustrate the point. *The Tempest* is 'about colonisation', Philip Brockbank wrote in 1966, and Caliban is partly a personification of the anarchic colonists but partly too 'the epitome of the primitive and uncivilised condition of the native American' (Brockbank, 184, 192). Nearly a decade later, Gordon Zeeveld adjudged Caliban to be 'Shakespeare's sole representation of the human population of the New World' (Zeeveld, 250). The influence of Mannoni and of prophetic readings are more palpably expressed by an American historian who suggested that '[i]n an uncanny way, America became a larger theater for *The Tempest* . . . As Englishmen made their "errand into the wilderness" of America, they took lands from red Calibans and made black Calibans work for them'. Caliban, however, need not be limited in time, place, or ethnicity; as a representative figure of America's exploited peoples, he 'could be African, Indian, or even Asian' (Takaki, 12, 11).

The metaphoric appropriations of *The Tempest* in Latin

America after 1950 acknowledged Ariel's and Caliban's roles but emphatically altered them. The most prolific and influential advocate of the new model is a Cuban, Roberto Fernández Retamar, whose essay 'Caliban' initially appeared in Spanish and subsequently in several English editions. Speaking for Latin Americans generally but for Caribbean peoples especially, Fernández Retamar proposed in 1969 that:

> Our symbol ... is not Ariel, as Rodó thought, but Caliban. This is something that we, the *mestizo* inhabitants of these same isles where Caliban lived, see with particular clarity: Prospero invaded the islands, killed our ancestors, enslaved Caliban, and taught him his language to make himself understood. What else can Caliban do but use that same language – today he has no other – to curse him, to wish that the 'red plague' would fall on him? I know no other metaphor more expressive of our cultural situation, of our reality ... [W]hat is our history, what is our culture, if not the history and culture of Caliban?
>
> (Fernández Retamar, 24)

Elsewhere in the Caribbean, George Lamming of Barbados had already published a quasi-autobiographical novel, *The Pleasures of Exile* (1960), that drew abundantly on *The Tempest*'s plot and characters. Edward Kamau Brathwaite, also of Barbados, titled one poem 'Caliban', another 'Letter Sycorax' (an epistle to his own mother, thereby identifying himself with Caliban); in an essay on the Jamaican slave revolt of the 1830s, he expanded the customary colonialist metaphors to include Alonso as representative of the British parliament and Gonzalo of the well-meaning but misguided Christian missionaries (see Brathwaite, 'Caliban', *Islands*).[1] Aimé Césaire of Martinique recast Shakespeare's play

---

1 Brathwaite's poems have many *Tempest* allusions, not only in his early works but also in his later publications, especially *Middle Passages* (Newcastle-upon-Tyne, 1992), which includes 'Letter Sycorax'.

into his own *Une Tempête*, with Caliban an African field hand and Ariel a mulatto house servant (Césaire; Vaughan, *Caliban*, 156).

In 1971 the *Massachusetts Review* celebrated the new Latin American appropriation of *The Tempest* in a special issue, subtitled 'Caliban'. The journal contains a score of articles (including a reprint of Fernández Retamar's essay), poems, short stories and reproductions of original art; all contributions, the editor proclaims, are 'a contemporary echo of the rebellious Antillean slave in Shakespeare's final play', in which Caliban symbolizes 'a struggle for liberation and cultural authenticity . . . [a]gainst the hegemonic, europocentric, vision of the universe' (see Márquez).

Tempest metaphors, especially of Caliban and Prospero, also emerged in the 1970s in Africa. Taban lo Liyong of Uganda observed ironically that:

> Bill Shakespeare
> Did create a character called Caliban,
> The unwilling servant of Prospero,
> And this Caliban would have had Miranda
> – She who is a marvel to behold – a girl
> So much in need of love and for whom
> Ferdinand was a wonder from a brave new world,
> And who would have helped Caliban populate the island
> With little Calibans smelling like fish
> Had Prospero not fouled their plan.

The poet then identified his own writing with Caliban cursing in another culture's language (Liyong, 41). Also within the decade, Lemuel Johnson of Sierra Leone titled a collection of his poems *Highlife for Caliban*; Ngugi Wa Thiong'o (James Ngugi) of Kenya invoked *Tempest* themes in his *Homecoming*; and a play by David Wallace of Zambia, *Do You Love Me, Master?*, incorporated *Tempest* characters and borrowed its title from Ariel's query to Prospero in 4.1.48. The almost universal identification of Caliban with dispossessed Native Americans or Africans has meant that he is often portrayed on stage by a black actor, that productions emphasize his anger and victimization, and that he often, by himself or in juxtaposition to Prospero, is *The Tempest*'s central symbol.[1]

Only in Anglophone Canada and occasionally in Australia and New Zealand did Caliban fail to dominate late twentieth-century symbolic borrowings from *The Tempest* or to share the spotlight with Prospero. Although some Canadian scholars, especially those of African, Caribbean or French ancestry, adopted Caliban as their emblem of colonial victimization, his role in late twentieth-century literary symbolism was often subordinated to Miranda's.

Re-enter Miranda

In the conclusion to his 1987 analysis of post-colonial appropriations of *The Tempest*, Rob Nixon speculated that 'the play's declining pertinence to contemporary Africa and the Caribbean has been exacerbated by the difficulty of wresting from it any role for female defiance or leadership' (Nixon, 577). Miranda, after all, is the only female figure who actually appears in the text: Claribel and Sycorax are referred to but never materialize, while Ariel's sex – if spirits have sexual identity – is ambiguous. Miranda is the dutiful daughter of the white colonizer; she eagerly agrees to marry the man he has selected for her and relishes her role as the foundress of Prospero's future dynasty.

Yet for feminist writers, as for post-colonial adapters, *The Tempest* proved a rich resource for appropriations that revise, reshape and refocus. As early as 1949, the imagist poet H.D. (Hilda Doolittle) adopted Claribel as her spokeswoman in a two-part poem, *By Avon River*. Because Claribel's marriage to the African King of Tunis precipitates the Neapolitans' sea voyage

---

1 The literature from Latin America and Africa that borrows from *The Tempest* is far more abundant than the sample given here. Insightful discussions include Nixon; Cartelli; Saldívar; and L. Johnson, *Africa*.

and subsequent adventures, she is, for H.D., 'the figure of the exiled, alienated woman'; abandoned in an alien world, Claribel represented the plight of the twentieth-century female artist (Chedgzoy, 109).

Several late twentieth-century Canadian novelists found in Miranda a model for their experience as Anglophone women. To Diana Brydon, Miranda's situation is Canadian; she is 'attempting to create a neo-Europe in an invaded land, torn between Old World fathers and suitors while unable to ignore the just grievances of those her culture is displacing' (Brydon, 'Sister', 166). Morag, the Miranda-like heroine of Margaret Laurence's *The Diviners*, never openly rebels, but bides her time instead. This temporizing, Brydon suggests, is how the Empire worked itself out in Anglophone Canada and New Zealand. In Constance Beresford-Howe's *Prospero's Daughter*, the Canadian-born Prospero figure has two daughters: Paulina (named perhaps for her outspoken counterpart in *The Winter's Tale*) is the outgoing, wayward sibling, an actor with a botched personal life; her shy sister Nan acts as a servant, cooking meals and cleaning for her father. Prospero's self-obsession is wrong-headed, arrogant and ultimately destructive. The figure of a resistant Miranda is also central to Sarah Murphy's *The Measure of Miranda*, which describes the young Canadian Miranda's sacrifice of her own life to blow up a Central American dictator after she discovers photographs of the tortures he has committed. In Brydon's words, for 'Murphy's Miranda violent rebellion must entail self-destruction, because she is part of the system she rejects' (Brydon, 'Sister', 176). All three Canadian Miranda figures remain trapped by the patriarchal structure.

Another way to make *The Tempest*'s narrative reflect the feminine voice is to create a human, female Ariel. In *Indigo*, by the British writer Marina Warner, Shakespeare's sprite is an Arawak Indian who sleeps with the invading white enemy, Sir Christopher Everard (Warner's Prospero figure), and bears his child. Ariel becomes complicit with the colonizer when she rescues Everard from the black slave Caliban's armed rebellion. The novel's conclusion shifts 350 years to the future; Ariel and Everard's descendant, a mulatto Miranda, successfully finds a multiracial identity despite colonialism's painful legacy.

Yet another tactic, adopted by the Indian-born poet Suniti Namjoshi, is to feminize Caliban. In her poetic sequence, 'Snapshots of Caliban', Namjoshi uses *The Tempest*'s characters to explore issues of gender identity. Namjoshi's Miranda and Caliban, a female childhood playmate, grow through immature misunderstandings into lesbian lovers whom Prospero can never understand or acknowledge as his own.

Post-colonial authors such as Laurence, Beresford-Howe, Murphy, Warner and Namjoshi reminded their readers that appropriations of *The Tempest* need not be male-centred. For women as well as men, Shakespeare's text can be a catalyst for imaginative reconsiderations of the role of formerly colonized peoples in a post-colonial world.[1]

Freudian influences

Adaptations and appropriations of *The Tempest* have not been limited to the sociopolitical realm; the play is equally susceptible to modern conceptions of human psychology. Not surprisingly, then, as Freud's theories about the subconscious mind seeped into twentieth-century culture, they were bound to reshape interpretations of Shakespeare's characters. Ariel and Caliban came to be seen as embodiments of Prospero's subconscious mind; in its most reductive form, Ariel is his superego, Caliban his libido.

W.H. Auden's poetic commentary on *The Tempest*, composed during the dark days of World War II, focuses on Prospero's relationship to the libidinous Caliban. He begins his poem with Prospero's words to Ariel after the play's finale; as he packs and

---

1 The emergence of a feminist perspective on appropriations of *The Tempest* in Latin America is suggested by *Daughters of Caliban: Caribbean Women in the Twentieth Century*, ed. Consuelo López Springfield (Bloomington, Ind., 1998).

prepares to leave for Milan, Prospero concludes that 'In all, things have turned out better / Than I once expected or ever deserved'. Now Prospero claims he knows what magic is: 'the power to enchant / That comes from disillusion'. His only disappointment with the way things have sorted themselves out is with Caliban, his 'impervious disgrace'. After Prospero says good-bye to Ariel, the poem shifts to the supporting actors who reflect *sotto voce* on their experiences. Antonio begins, resigned to his loss but determined never to yield, to remain '*By choice myself alone*' (Auden, 312–14, 318). Caught up in their individual worlds, the other characters echo this theme. These dramatic monologues depend, of course, on the reader's knowledge of Shakespeare's original: Alonso advises Ferdinand how to be a good king; Ferdinand and Miranda profess their mutual devotion; the Boatswain extols the sailor's life; Trinculo resolves to continue fooling; and so forth. Gone from Auden's poetic commentary is MacKaye's buoyant optimism; in its place are lowered expectations and the willingness to make do with the 'darkness that we acknowledge ours'.

Auden's representation of Caliban as Prospero's mirrored face – the magus's dark and secret self – embodies libidinous forces that are normally repressed behind veneers of civility.[1] Caliban as 'id' became a palpable thread in twentieth-century psychoanalytic interpretations of *The Tempest*, a notion more dramatically presented in the 1956 science-fiction film, *Forbidden Planet*. Now a cult classic, this postwar film transports its Prospero figure to Altair–IV, a distant planet, where Professor Morbius (Walter Pidgeon) continues his scientific investigations, builds robots (Robby, the film's Ariel) and raises his daughter Altaira (the Miranda figure played by Anne Francis). When a spaceship from Earth invades the planet, Altaira falls in love with its handsome captain (Leslie Nielson), but their romance is threatened by an invisible force that nearly

---

1 On Auden's poem, see Herman Servotte's essay in *Constellation*, 199–210.

destroys the spaceship and kills several of its crew. The dramatic finale reveals that the mayhem is caused by the Professor's own inner psyche, projected on to an electromagnetic force (Caliban), which implements Morbius's repressed anger at the man who would take his daughter and jealousy at her love for another man. Only with the destruction of Professor Morbius can the Calibanic force be quelled (see *Constellation*, 211–29).[1]

The most successful twentieth-century musical adaptation of *The Tempest* also adopted a Freudian theme. Mangus, the psychoanalyst in Michael Tippett's 1971 opera, *The Knot Garden*, uses situations from *The Tempest* in his therapy sessions and pretends to be Prospero. Mel, the Caliban figure, represents sexual desire, while Dov, the opera's Ariel, is a musician who is associated with imagination in the opera's libretto. In the finale, Mangus abandons his therapy and addresses the audience:

> Enough! Enough!
> We look in the abyss.
> Lust for Caliban will not save us.
> Prospero's a fake, we all know that.
> (Tippett, 14)

Despite this disillusionment, Mangus's therapeutic tempest succeeds, and the opera concludes with a harmonious scene between Faber and Thea, the patients he had been trying to help.

'The Tempest' on stage and film since 1900

The interpretive patterns outlined here were bound to affect stage interpretations if only by cultural osmosis. A brief survey of memorable performances of *The Tempest* in the twentieth century illustrates how directors and actors have been affected by the broad interpretive trends that shaped the era's adaptations.

---

1 In the mid-1980s, Bob Carlton's rock-and-roll musical, *Return to the Forbidden Planet*, capitalized on the film's popularity, but also incorporated lines from several other Shakespeare plays (see Carlton).

For the first third of the century, the Darwinian approach suggested by Tree and MacKaye remained dominant. Robert Atkins's Caliban at the Old Vic (1920-5) was praised for showing 'with superlative art the malevolent brute nature with the dim, half-formed, human intellect just breaking through' (Crosse, 58). As late as 1957, Alec Clunes's Caliban for Peter Brook's *The Tempest* at the Royal Shakespeare Theatre in Stratford and later at Drury Lane was described variously as a 'gorilla', 'apish', 'anthropoid' and a 'missing-link'. The reviewer for the *Barnet Press* (21 December 1957) wondered 'why, when every reference to Caliban (Alec Clunes) is "Fishy," should he be so ape-like?' Contrasting with missing-link Calibans was Prospero, the arch representative of European civilization. At the Old Vic in 1930, for instance, John Gielgud's costume for his first venture in the role included a turban; he later confessed that he tried to look like Dante (Hirst, 46).

As the Darwinian Caliban faded, the role opened to modern nuances. In 1934 Roger Livesey (opposite Charles Laughton's Prospero) was probably the first actor to use black makeup in the role, according to Trevor R. Griffiths, but 'this excited virtually no comment, except for complaints that the black came off on Trinculo and Stephano' (Griffiths, 175). In 1945 the African–American actor Canada Lee performed Caliban in Margaret Webster's *The Tempest* for the Theatre Guild, New York. Lee's wife described him: 'In a costume of fish scales and long fingernails, Lee first appeared onstage bent over in a hump back position akin to Richard III; the audience subsequently thought of him only in that curved position, even when he stood tall'.[1] In 1960 Earle Hyman took the role at the American Shakespeare Festival in Connecticut, dressed with padded legs and torso, and with a grotesque headdress; in 1962 James Earl Jones played the monster as a lizard with darting red tongue.

While the presence of black actors in Caliban's role, however

---

1 Glenda E. Gill, 'The mercurial Canada Lee', in *White Grease Paint on Black Performers* (New York, 1988), 41.

grotesque their costuming, subtly implied black–white power relations in the play, not until 1970 did *The Tempest*'s colonial themes fully emerge on stage. Director Jonathan Miller read Mannoni's *Prospero and Caliban* before preparing his production; Miller's goal, reported by David Hirst, was to represent 'the tragic and inevitable disintegration of a more primitive culture as the result of European invasion and colonisation' (Hirst, 50). Prospero was the colonial governor, Ariel his mulatto house servant and Caliban his darker field hand. Graham Crowden's Prospero showed the magus's dictatorial side. In a final scene reminiscent of Tree but laden with new meaning, Caliban shook his fist at the departing ship as Ariel lifted Prospero's bent staff and began to straighten it: one native rejected western technology, the other sought to appropriate it.

The RSC's 1978 *The Tempest*, directed by Clifford Williams, broadened the colonial concept by making David Suchet's Caliban into a generic third-world 'primitive', with characteristics of both West Indian and sub-Saharan Africans. *The Times* of London (3 May 1978) saw Caliban as 'a sympathetic emblem of imperialistic exploitation, . . . a noble black . . . speaking the language with the too-perfect precision of an alien'. Michael Hordern's Prospero wore an academic gown and exuded a 'schoolmasterly' manner but, in contrast to Prosperos of the previous century, his control of the island's inhabitants was tenuous.

As these productions demonstrate, modern directors have found *The Tempest*'s colonial overtones appealing, and they are still evident in some directors' political perspectives. More difficult to translate to the stage are twentieth-century psychoanalytic readings of the play influenced by Freud. Director Gerald Freedman attempted one in 1981 at the American Shakespeare Theatre. In the programme notes he professed to:

> see Caliban and Ariel . . . as aspects of Prospero's character. Some of the libidinal aspects of his feelings are

embodied in Caliban, and it breaks Prospero's heart that
he cannot control them. . . . Ariel represents the best
aspects of the artist – the creative muse – the part that
takes wing at thought.

(Review in *SQ*, 31 (1980), 190–1)

Freedman depicted this psychic opposition by having Ariel performed by a white actor in silver, Caliban by a black actor in
brown. But as the reviewer for *Shakespeare Quarterly* noted, the
allegorical meaning was not clear to an audience that had not
been alerted to it in advance.

The RSC's 1982 *The Tempest*, directed by Ron Daniels, suggested a similar psychological approach. Mark Rylance's Ariel –
punk-haired and clad in a rainbow-hued body suit – was accompanied by five doubles who served as the play's nymphs, dogs and
the like. Bob Peck's Caliban, naked except for a loin cloth, wore
Rastafarian dreadlocks. The *Oxford Mail*'s reviewer took
Rylance's quicksilver Ariel and Peck's earthy Caliban to be 'extensions of Prospero's own personality' (12 August 1982). The colour
coding of Ariel (white body-paint) and Caliban (charcoal body-
paint) in Adrian Noble's 1998 RSC production may also have
been an effort to show the characters as opposing aspects of
Prospero's psyche, but the resulting contrast remained superficial.

The most successful psychoanalytic performance of *The
Tempest* may have occurred when its text was almost wholly
abandoned. Peter Brook's 1968 experiment at the Round House
in London suggested the play's plot and themes through mime
and movement. Sycorax was 'portrayed by an enormous woman
able to expand her face and body to still larger proportions – a
fantastic emblem of the grotesque'; she '[s]uddenly . . . gives a
horrendous yell, and Caliban, with black sweater over his head,
emerges from between her legs: Evil is born' (Croyden, 127). As
the action progresses, Caliban takes over the island and leads his
followers in a wild orgy. They capture Prospero and attack him
in a scene suggestive of homosexual rape until Ariel diverts the

devils with ribbons, costumes and trinkets. After Ferdinand and Miranda are married, Prospero admits to forgetting the rest of the plot and the play ends with an epilogue recited by all the actors, who then depart, leaving an empty space with no dimmed lighting and no curtain. This experimental adaptation, like a nightmare come to life, suggested the violent impulses below the surface of Shakespeare's text.

Brook's abandonment of Shakespeare's words for miming actors in turtlenecks and kimonos took the play outside its text. Other directors have been more concerned to restore to the play some of its original impact. At particular issue is the masque, a form that was richly nuanced to a Jacobean audience but whose iconographic significance is often lost on modern viewers. Influenced by the recent publication of Stephen Orgel and Roy Strong's compendium of Inigo Jones's drawings, Peter Hall costumed his Prospero in the 1974 National Theatre production to resemble the Elizabethan astrologer John Dee and, in an elaborately staged masque, made Juno resemble the dead Queen Elizabeth. Hall tried to recreate the masque's exploitation of visual symbolism by directing Gielgud never to look at Ariel, who appeared suspended on a trapeze-like object, or behind the magician as part of Prospero's consciousness, and by having Caliban (Dennis Quilley) appear in bisected makeup; 'one half of his face presented the ugly deformed monster, the other an image of the noble savage' (Hirst, 48).

John Wood's Prospero at the RSC (1988), directed by Nicholas Hytner, emphasized the magician's human complexity. Described in the *Financial Times* (28 July 1988) as 'a demented stage manager on a theatrical island suspended between smouldering rage at his usurpation and unbridled glee at his alternative ethereal power', Wood's modern-dress magus was awkward and uneasy with people, plagued by internal conflicts that he could never wholly resolve.

Sam Mendes' 1993 RSC production also emphasized the play's fusion of magic and spectacle. Although the most controversial stage business – Ariel (Simon Russell Beale) spitting at Prospero (Alec McCowen) after he is granted freedom – was dropped early in the run, Ariel's resentment remained palpable (see Fig. 5); Caliban's (David Troughton's) fleshy malevolence could not compete. The production's self-reflexive use of theatrical magic was also notable. The play began with Ariel, clad in a blue Mao-style suit, rising like a jack-in-the-box from a theatrical trunk; the storm commenced when he gently pushed a lantern overhead, its sway suggesting the ship's movement. Trinculo was a Yorkshire ventriloquist, complete with talking dummy. *The Guardian* (13 August 1993) described Prospero as 'a Victorian dramatist–director writing his own script as he goes along' and the play as 'a series of shifting illusions'. The set was minimal: piles of books and a ladder represented Prospero's study, and most of the action took place on a bare stage. The masque, by contrast, was performed from an elaborately painted Victorian toy stage with twirling mechanical dolls.

Unlike theatrical productions which run for a short season to limited audiences, twentieth-century screen versions of *The Tempest* have been more widely disseminated. A 1905 film of the play's opening shipwreck may have been initially designed to be shown with Beerbohm Tree's touring productions of *The Tempest*, saving the cost of transporting heavy sets and equipment (see pp. 93–5), but under the sponsorship of film entrepreneur Charles Urban, the two-minute film was shown for 143 performances in London and taken to America for independent exhibition (Ball, 30–2).

Like many Shakespearean plays, *The Tempest* was a staple of early BBC productions for television, but those renditions were essentially filmed stagings. The last major effort in this vein was the BBC / Time-Life version of 1979, a straightforward and mundane performance featuring a befuddled Prospero (Michael Hordern), a hairy, apish Caliban (Warren Clarke) and an androgynous, disappearing gold-laméed Ariel (David Dixon). Despite the production's lack of imagination, it demonstrates

Prospero's recent unravelling. No longer all-wise and benevolent, the modern Prospero is troubled by anxiety and anger. He seeks revenge for past wrongs; self-centred, he shows little patience or sensitivity with Ariel, Miranda or Caliban. He often seems aloof at the play's happy conclusion.

More imaginative and 'contemporary', Paul Mazursky's 1982 film adaptation of *The Tempest* chronicles a late twentieth-century, conflicted, middle-aged Prospero; New York architect Phillip Dimitrious (John Cassavetes) is fed up with his job, his boss and his wife. With his teenage daughter Miranda (Molly Ringwald), Phillip flees to an abandoned Greek island where, through interactions with the island's only inhabitant, Kalibanos (Raul Julia), and with Aretha (Susan Sarandon), a newly acquired companion, he finds himself. This adaptation hints strongly at the dangerous possibility of incest on Phillip's secluded island. In a noisy confrontation Kalibanos asks Phillip which of them is going to have sex with Miranda. Ferdinand's timely arrival, by yacht, resolves the dilemma of Miranda's blooming sexuality and Phillip's incestuous temptation.

Derek Jarman's 1980 film of *The Tempest* keeps more of Shakespeare's language, but it, too, is more overt about the play's multiple sexualities than was the original text. Jarman's focus is unabashedly gay. In a mimed flashback he shows Caliban (Jack Birkett) practising obscene rites with his naked mother Sycorax, while a tied-up Ariel looks on. Karl Johnson's Ariel projects the image of a feminized gay male, while Caliban seems more like an aging 'queen'. Toyah Willcox's Miranda, unlike most stage versions, is too sophisticated to take Caliban seriously. Annoyed, not frightened, she throws a sponge at him when he sneaks up on her while she's bathing.

Tension between a tyrannical Prospero and an openly rebellious Ariel animates Jarman's film. Heathcote Williams was a dabbler in the occult himself, and his Prospero is a dark, brooding figure who takes pleasure in exploiting both his servants. Filmed in the Palladian Stoneleigh Manor, this *Tempest* exudes an atmosphere that reflects the magus's inner life – dark and shadowy. Only the vibrant masque scene is brilliantly lit for Elisabeth Welsh's stunning rendition of 'Stormy Weather'. As the film ends, Prospero falls asleep in his chair while Ariel sneaks away to freedom.[1]

The most flamboyant twentieth-century representation of Prospero was Peter Greenaway's 1991 film, *Prospero's Books*. To Greenaway, Prospero is not simply a 'master manipulator' but a 'prime originator' (Greenaway, 9). Greenaway presents the text of *The Tempest* as Prospero's vision and creation; through a changing panorama of mirror images, the magus creates the characters and the action, writing the play's text in calligraphy as he thinks it, voicing the lines of characters as he imagines them (see Fig. 19). John Gielgud, who had performed Prospero many times in Stratford and London, was assigned in Greenaway's film the ultimate acting opportunity: in a vehicle screened all over the world, he could, like Bottom, play all the parts.

The keys to Prospero's power in Greenaway's version are the books Gonzalo rescued from his library and shipped with Prospero and Miranda to the island. Twenty-four in all (plus the *Tempest* text Prospero is writing), they include books on water, mirrors, mythology, colour, geography, travel, architecture, languages, biology, botany, love, pornography – everything, in short, that a Renaissance intellectual was likely to find of interest. Images from these books form the connecting tissue of the film; as Prospero moves from memories of his past to plotting vengeance in the present and, finally, to forgiveness and reconciliation, his ideas emanate from the pages of his books.

1 For more information on Jarman's *The Tempest*, see his autobiography, *Dancing Ledge* (New York, 1994); Michael O'Pray, *Derek Jarman: Dreams of England* (London, 1996); Colin McCabe, 'A post-national European cinema: a consideration of Derek Jarman's *The Tempest* and *Edward II*', in *Screening Europe: Image and Identity in Contemporary European Cinema*, ed. Duncan Petrie (London, 1992), 9–18; and David Hawkes, '"The shadow of this time": the Renaissance cinema of Derek Jarman', in *By Angels Driven: The Films of Derek Jarman* (Westport, Conn., 1996), 103–16. Far less successful was a made-for-television adaptation of *The Tempest* aired in the United States on 13 December 1998, and set during the American Civil War. Prospero's (Peter Fonda's) magic was African voodoo, learned from Ariel's mother, a slave on his Louisiana Plantation; Caliban was white, swamp-bound 'gator man'.

19 A still from Peter Greenaway's film *Prospero's Books* showing Prospero (John Gielgud) contemplating his work in progress, the text of *The Tempest*

Greenaway explores visually the play's interrogation of 'civility'. His islanders are naked, partly to suggest the naked Indians of Roanoke painted by John White, partly to represent Renaissance conceptions of mythological figures. In contrast to the islanders' uninhibited nudity are the Europeans' extravagant costumes; their dark colours, huge ruffs and high hats suggest Rembrandt's heavily attired aristocrats.

Throughout the film, Gielgud's majestic voice delivers all the play's speeches. The dramatic climax comes in the final scenes, when the perspective shifts: Ariel usurps Prospero's writing tables, takes over the script and writes the lines from 5.1.17–20: 'Your charm so strongly works 'em. . .'. After quietly agreeing that his affections will also become tender – 'mine shall' – Prospero (Greenaway explains) 'closes all the books in his study . . . blows out the candles, picks up his staff/crozier . . . and leaves the study and closes its curtains' (151). In the shots that follow, he throws his books into the ocean; except for *Thirty-Six*

Plays by William Shakespeare and the script of *The Tempest*, which are grabbed by Caliban, all sink. The film closes as it began, with a single drop of water. To Greenaway, the island is an illusion as evanescent as that single drop:

> an island full of superimposed images, of shifting mirrors and mirror-images – true mirages – where pictures conjured by text can be as tantalisingly substantial as objects and facts and events, constantly framed and re-framed. This framing and re-framing becomes like the text itself – a motif – reminding the viewer that it is all an illusion constantly fitted into a rectangle . . . into a picture frame, a film frame.
>
> (Greenaway, 12)

The visual influence of Greenaway's conception seemed readily apparent in the American Repertory Theatre's (A.R.T.'s) 1995 stage production in Cambridge, Massachusetts, when the Neapolitans appeared in similar be-ruffed black costumes. The natives (Ariel, Caliban and Miranda) in contrast wore very little, though they did not resort to frontal nudity. This eclectic production, directed by Ron Daniels, combined Greenaway's visual imagery with a colonial theme in which the masque imitated a South American carnival dance and Ferdinand resembled a Spanish conquistador.

The A.R.T. production was also reminiscent of George C. Wolfe's production in Central Park for the New York Shakespeare Festival. That *Tempest* sported a Prospero as Robinson Crusoe in cut-offs, beads and an open shirt (see Fig. 20). Science-fiction fans flocked to see *Star Trek*'s Patrick Stewart as Prospero in this outdoor production and found a magus 'whose intellect and emotions were in conflict, still enraged and resentful after all these years, perpetually between simmering fury and boiling point' (Ranald, 10). The casting of the sensual African–American actress Aunjanue Ellis as Ariel charged the production with erotic tensions that made Prospero's release of his servant all the more

20 Patrick Stewart as a pensive Prospero in George C. Wolfe's 1995
production for the New York Shakespeare Festival

difficult. Prospero's masque was memorably rendered by three Brazilian stiltwalkers as the goddesses Iris, Ceres and Juno; they were accompanied by dancers with puppets that moved and chanted to calypso beat. After awkwardly joining the dancers, Prospero remembered Caliban's conspiracy; the figures vanished as quickly as they had appeared.

The Shakespeare Theatre's (Washington, D.C.) 1997 production, directed by Garland Wright, presented Prospero's cell as the library of an eighteenth-century *philosophe*. In addition to stacks of books, like a *Wunderkabinet* its glassed-in shelves stored bones, fossils and other natural curiosities. Ted van Griethuysen's Prospero took emotional charge of the play, exuding vengeful anger from his first appearance. Inspired by Wallace Acton's compassionate Ariel, this humanized Prospero anguished over the decision to forgive but found he had no choice. Despite casting an African–American actor as a dreadlocked Caliban, Wright's *Tempest* eschewed colonial resonances in favour of an exploration of Prospero's psychology.

Many late twentieth-century productions also highlighted *The Tempest*'s underlying sexual tensions, in various combinations: Prospero and Miranda, Prospero and Ariel, Miranda and Caliban, even Caliban and Trinculo, and, newly eroticized, Miranda and Ferdinand. This emphasis on the play's sexuality marks a striking change from eighteenth-century and Victorian *Tempest*s, which were almost perversely asexual. But in adaptations and appropriations of the 1970s and beyond, such as Jarman's homo-erotic Ariel and Caliban, Greenaway's close-up images of naked islanders and Namjoshi's feminized, lesbian Caliban, the erotic component is palpable. Even in late twentieth-century commentaries on the Folio version, *The Tempest*'s implicit sexual tensions often achieved a level of attention that sharply set them off from earlier analyses – the gay perspectives, for example, of Kate Chedgzoy's *Shakespeare's Queer Children* and Jonathan Goldberg's 'Under the covers with Caliban'.

Modern productions are equally candid about the painful legacy of Europe's colonial past. Though the colonial theme is far less prominent than it was during the 1980s, it nevertheless underlies most theatrical productions and appropriations. Critical commentary has not generally followed suit, with the New Historicist insistence on *The Tempest*'s colonialist inspiration and controlling energy coming increasingly under question for underestimating the play's classical roots and European contexts.[1]

The Tempest for the twenty-first century, in sum, may be more conflict-ridden than ever before. Recent productions have emphasized the visceral over the lyrical, the text's underlying violence rather than its reconciliations, and the modern prophetic political context more than the politics of Shakespeare's day. Whether it is set on a distant planet or a tropical island, the contemporary *Tempest* embodies the pertinent issues of our time: the brutal realities of individual and collective power, the bitter legacy of colonialism and slavery, the difficulty of releasing the female body from male inscription and control, and the misunderstandings and violence that often accompany cultural exchange. *The Tempest* has evolved in diverse and sometimes radical ways from the polite *double entendres* of Dryden and Davenant and, indeed, from the optimistic progressivism of Percy MacKaye.

THE TEXT

Why *The Tempest* was given pride of place in the Folio of 1623 is one of the book's minor mysteries. *The Tempest*'s relative brevity may have made it a fitting starter for the Folio's compositors or, perhaps, a late play that had not been printed previously appeared more likely to convert browsers into buyers than would an old standby. The Folio's preface reminded readers

1 See especially Skura; McDonald; and Kastan.

that 'the fate of all Bookes depends vpon your capacities: and not of your heads alone, but of your purses . . . [W]hat euer you do, Buy'. In any event, *The Tempest* was the first text that the blind printer, William Jaggard, assigned to his compositors in February 1622 when work began on John Heminge and Henry Condell's collection of thirty-six dramas by their late theatrical colleague. After nearly two years of labour, with William Jaggard's son Isaac by then in charge after his father's death, *Mr. William Shakespeares Comedies, Histories, & Tragedies. Published according to the True Originall Copies* was available to the public for approximately fifteen shillings unbound and perhaps a pound for a copy in calf binding (Blayney, *Folio*, 25–32).

More than three centuries later, Charlton Hinman, the foremost authority on the mechanics of printing the Folio, demonstrated persuasively that special care was given to *The Tempest* and particularly to its first page. In a deviation from the normal order of printing that worked from the inside of the first twelve-page gathering (of the nineteen pages used for *The Tempest*) to the outer pages, Jaggard's compositors set the opening page first and then corrected the proofs at least four times, as revealed by subsequent changes in the surviving copies. Such a sequence and such proofing were not characteristic of the volume as a whole; *The Tempest* is generally acknowledged to be the cleanest of Shakespeare's early printed texts.[1]

Three compositors worked on *The Tempest*. Hinman's 'Compositor B', an experienced but sometimes careless journeyman in Jaggard's shop, who may have been given special responsibility for the entire volume, set the opening page and six more (Blayney, *Folio*, 11). The play's other compositors, Hinman's C and F, were also full-time employees and experienced printers. Each worked from his own type case, and once the play's

---

1 The major modern works on the Folio are Charlton Hinman's exhaustive comparison of fifty-five of the Folger Shakespeare Library's copies; Peter W.M. Blayney's Catalogue to the Folger Library's exhibition on 'The First Folio of Shakespeare'; and Blayney's Introduction to the second edition of *The Norton Facsimile* of the Folio.

opening page was deemed acceptable, there seems to have been little difficulty in dividing up the text so that it came out fairly evenly and clearly. Only a few pages (Folio, 15, for example) show the crowding of text and stage directions that reflect a misjudgement of the required space.[1]

Ralph Crane's manuscript

The manuscript used by the compositors has been identified as one of six prepared in the early 1620s by the legal scrivener Ralph Crane specifically, it seems certain, for the Folio project. (The others are *The Two Gentlemen of Verona*, *The Winter's Tale*, *Merry Wives of Windsor*, *Measure for Measure* and, as E.A.J. Honigmann recently established, *Othello* (Honigmann, 59–76).) Crane probably copied from Shakespeare's own rough draft, or possibly a copy of it, rather than from prompt copy, which would have been more helpful to actors than to readers (Jowett, 109). Prompt copy, with its barely legible insertions, deletions and impromptu stage directions would have posed serious problems for the typesetters.

Thanks to important research on his extant manuscripts by Trevor Howard-Hill and Ernst Honigmann, Crane's habits are now fairly clear, and speculation about how they shaped Shakespeare's printed texts can be made with some confidence. Because Crane started his career as a lawyer's clerk and only turned late in life to dramatic copying (in his sixties when work began on the Folio), he was old enough to have his own opinions about dramatic format and may accordingly have served to some degree as an 'editor'. Influenced by Ben Jonson's classicism, Crane apparently sought to impose regularity upon the texts – Shakespeare's and others' – that he copied. Howard-Hill concludes that *The Tempest* was among Crane's 'first play[s] prepared for publication', that the transcripts were 'literary by design not accident' and were modelled on Jonson's Folio of 1616 (Howard-Hill,

---

1 Improperly casting off copy occasionally caused difficulties elsewhere in the Folio; the resulting pages are either jammed with crowded lines or padded with extra space.

'Editor', 128), which Jonson himself had supervised. Honig-mann observes that 'Crane was neither humble nor faithful; he "improved" his transcripts, as he would see it, a creative or destructive role, depending on one's point of view' (75).

Crane's tidying of (presumably) Shakespeare's rough manuscripts is perhaps reflected in the division of the texts into acts and scenes, often – though not in *The Tempest* – with massed entries at a scene's beginning which list all of the characters who will appear by its conclusion. Crane also habitually listed the play's *dramatis personae* at the end of the text. Like *The Two Gentlemen of Verona*, *Measure for Measure*, *Othello* and *The Winter's Tale*, the Folio's *The Tempest* concludes with a complete listing and brief description of each character or group of roles, sometimes with important information that appears to reflect his own judgement (see Fig. 21). The frequently quoted depictions of Caliban as *'a saluage and deformed slaue'* and Ariel as *'an ayrie spirit'*, for example, may be Crane's interpretations of what he saw in performance rather than Shakespeare's descriptions of what he envisioned, although they could be both.[1]

Another of Crane's telling traits is idiosyncratic punctuation. Most often noted are the frequent parentheses, especially for phrases of direct address; Crane seems to have reproduced the parentheses in the text he was copying and probably added to them.[2] He also employed numerous hyphenated forms, as in the Folio's 'wide-chopt-rascall', and made lavish use of apostrophes, often to indicate elision (e.g. 'do'st' for 'doest'). The scribe sometimes even 'used different forms of elision in transcripts of the same text' (Howard-Hill, *Crane*, 39–44, 106). The frequent compression of lines through elision sometimes poses difficulties for actors and editors, as in such tongue-twisting clusters as 'out

---

1   On these matters, see Howard-Hill, *Crane*; and Roberts, 'Crane'.

2   See Howard-Hill, 'Parentheses'. Persuasive evidence that the parentheses are Crane's rather than the compositors' is found in Kermode's tabulation of the distribution of the parentheses, which reveals no significant variation from one compositor to another; they were therefore probably present in the printer's clean copy (Ard[2], lxxxix); see also G. Wright.

The Tempeſt. 19

And ſeeke for grace: what a thrice double Aſſe
Was I to take this drunkard for a god?
And worſhip this dull foole?
   Pro. Goe to, away.   (ſound it.
   Alo. Hence, and beſtow your luggage where you
Seb. Or ſtole it rather.
   Pro. Sir, I inuite your Highneſſe, and your traine
To my poore Cell: where you ſhall take your reſt
For this one night, which part of it, Ile waſte
With ſuch diſcourſe, as I not doubt, ſhall make it
Goe quicke away: The ſtory of my life
And the particular accidents, gon by
Since I came to this Iſle: And in the morne
I'le bring you to your ſhip, and ſo to *Naples*,

Where I haue hope to ſee the nuptiall
Of theſe our deere-belou'd, ſolemnized,
And thence retire me to my *Millaine*, where
Euery third thought ſhall be my graue.
   Alo. I long
To heare the ſtory of your life; which muſt
Take the eare ſtrangely.
   Pro. I'le deliuer all,
And promiſe you calme Seas, auſpicious gales,
And ſaile, ſo expeditious, that ſhall catch
Your Royall fleete farre off: My *Ariel*; chicke
That is thy charge: Then to the Elements
Be free, and fare thou well: pleaſe you draw neere.
Exeunt omnes.

EPILOGVE,

ſpoken by *Proſpero.*

NOw my Charmes are all ore-throwne,
   And what ſtrength I haue's mine owne.
Which is moſt faint: now 'tis true
I muſt be heere confinde by you,
Or ſent to *Naples*, Let me not
Since I haue my Dukedome got,
And pardon'd the deceiuer, dwell
In this bare Iſland, by your Spell,
But releaſe me from my bands
With the helpe of your good hands:
Gentle breath of yours, my Sailes
Muſt fill, or elſe my proiect failes,
which was to pleaſe: Now I want
Spirits to enforce: Art to inchant,
And my ending is deſpaire,
Vnleſſe I be relieu'd by praier
Which pierces ſo, that it aſſaults
Mercy it ſelfe, and frees all faults.
   As you from crimes would pardon'd be,
Let your Indulgence ſet me free.   *Exit.*

The Scene, an vn-inhabited Iſland

Names of the Actors.

Alonſo, K. of Naples:
Sebaſtian his Brother.
Proſpero, the right Duke of Millaine.
Anthonio his brother, the vſurping Duke of Millaine.
Ferdinand, Son to the King of Naples.
Gonzalo, an honeſt old Counceller.
Adrian, & *Franciſco, Lords.*
Caliban, a ſaluage and deformed ſlaue.
Trinculo, a Ieſter.
Stephano, a drunken Butler.
Maſter of a Ship.
Boate-Swaine.
Marriners.
Miranda, daughter to Proſpero.
Ariell, an ayrie ſpirit.
Iris
Ceres
Iuno   Spirits.
Nymphes
Reapers

FINIS.

THE

---

21 The final page of *The Tempest* in Shakespeare's *Comedies, Histories, & Tragedies* (1623), with the 'EPILOGVE' and '*Names of the Actors*' and, bleeding through from the verso side of the sheet, part of the title and text of *The Two Gentlemen of Verona*

o'th' substitution' (1.2.103) and 'wi'th' King' (1.2.112).[1] As A.C. Partridge contends, some of the contractions may have resulted from Crane's efforts 'to make the freer accentual measures more respectable in the eyes of Renaissance syllabic prosody; and behind this seems to loom the authority of Ben Jonson' (A.C. Partridge, 85). Crane's efforts to tidy the text, in sum, may have extended to the metre as well as to act and scene divisions. Whether the elided forms resulted from Shakespeare's effort to compress language, Crane's attempt to regularize the metre, or a compositor's desire to save space can never be absolutely known. In any case, *The Tempest* includes a high proportion of irregular lines, a characteristic shared with Shakespeare's other late plays.[2]

In copying dramatic manuscripts, Crane often inserted information that would have been especially helpful to a reader rather than an actor. Such interventions are also apparent in *The Tempest*'s elaborate stage directions, which are 'qualitatively different from those of any other Shakespeare play' and would be 'peculiarly ineffective in instructing the players' (Jowett, 107). When, for example, the Folio calls for a banquet set before the Neapolitans to disappear suddenly, the stage direction describes what a reader might expect in a theatrical spectacle:

> *Thunder and Lightning. Enter Ariell (like a Harpey) claps his wings upon the Table, and with a quient deuice the Banquet vanishes.*

> (Folio, 13)

Instead of prescriptive stage directions such as one might find in a prompt book, here we have the suggestion of a 'quaint device' – a vague reference to stage machinery by someone who knows little about theatre mechanics. Such unfamiliarity with

---

1 Howard-Hill suggests that 'Crane is more likely than the author to have contributed the apostrophe' to 'wi'th' King' (*Crane*, 105).
2 G. Wright notes that 'the lines in Shakespeare's later plays diverge from what we think of as regular meter about twenty percent of the time' (105).

technicalities is not surprising in a literary scribe who sought to infuse the stage directions with a literary flavour (Howard-Hill, *Crane*, 24), but it is not what we expect of Shakespeare in 1611.

In rewriting the stage directions for the reader rather than the actor, Crane may have adopted the style developed for Ben Jonson's Folio of 1616. Jowett lists fifteen stage directions in *The Tempest* which seem more likely to have been Crane's than the dramatist's, but he cautions that the case for non-Shakespearean intervention remains unproven and thus recommends a conservative editorial strategy (Jowett, 111–14). Whether *The Tempest*'s stage directions were written by Shakespeare or a prompter, or were interpolated later by Crane, they represent the earliest evidence we have of how the play was staged by the King's Company.

Editorial practices

Because the Folio's *The Tempest* is necessarily the basic text for this edition, our editorial interventions are less numerous and problematic than they would be for plays with one or more quarto editions. Yet even the relatively well-printed and carefully proofread Folio version, like any early seventeenth-century text, presents innumerable peculiarities to the modern eye.

In Shakespeare's day, spelling had not yet been fully regularized. Many words, even names, are spelled two or more ways in the play (e.g. Prospero, Prosper; Ariel, Ariell); 'u' and 'v' were used interchangeably (as in 'braue Vtensils'); 'y' often served for the modern 'i' ('noyses', 'waytes') as did, occasionally, 'i' for 'j' (Iupiter); and the Old and Middle English thorn (represented in type by 'y') sometimes substituted for 'th' ('ye'), though only in *The Tempest* to save space in a tight line. Capital letters and italics were sometimes employed for emphasis but more often for no discernible reason.

Even more problematic was Renaissance punctuation. Commas are interspersed throughout the Folio *Tempest* with (again, to the modern eye) apparent indiscrimination. Dashes and colons, many of them probably added by Compositor B, frequently indicate pauses that are now more often signified by commas, or pauses of greater length that are now indicated by semicolons or periods. By modern standards, some passages have too much punctuation, others too little, for the meaning to be clear.

The frequency of elisions in the Folio's *The Tempest* creates another kind of editorial conundrum. Although Crane may have tidied some of Shakespeare's irregular lines to improve the metre, there is no way of verifying such interventions, however likely they are. We have accordingly taken a conservative approach to lineation, altering lines only where a compositor's error seems apparent (e.g. 1.2.305). Problematic cases are cited in the textual notes.

Our editorial decisions about the play-text inevitably pit the Folio's chronological authority against the readers' need for a grammatically and orthographically coherent text. Further complicating the issue is the Folio's questionable authority on specific matters; it was a highly mediated document. Honigmann demonstrates that Crane repunctuated the texts he transcribed, and 'the Folio compositors also changed the punctuation of their texts quite drastically' (Honigmann, 179, n.6). There is, in short, no unimpeachable authority, no truly reliable basic version of the play – no 'pure' Shakespeare. In the preparation of this edition of *The Tempest* we have therefore attempted to create the clearest and most readable version of the play that simultaneously expresses our sense of the author's intentions. Our editorial interventions are, as with any mediated text, open to differing interpretations by readers and actors.

The alterations we have made to the Folio text can be summarized as (1) the modernization of spelling and capitalization according to guidelines established by the general editors; (2) the introduction of modern rules of punctuation; (3) the removal of superfluous italics; and (4) the insertion, occasionally, of brief supplementary stage directions where the Folio seems ambiguous. A representative sample of the difference between the

Folio's text and ours is the final speech before the Epilogue, which in the Folio appears as:

> *Pro*. I'le deliuer all,
> And promise you calme Seas, auspicious gales,
> And saile, so expeditious, that shall catch
> Your Royall fleete farre off: My *Ariel*; chicke
> That is thy charge: Then to the Elements
> Be free, and fare thou well: please you draw neere.
>
> (Folio, 19; see Fig. 21)

This edition reads:

> PROSPERO   I'll deliver all,
> And promise you calm seas, auspicious gales
> And sail so expeditious that shall catch
> Your royal fleet far off. [*aside to Ariel*] My Ariel, chick,
> That is thy charge. Then to the elements
> Be free, and fare thou well!
> [*to the others*]   Please you, draw near.
>
> (5.1.314–19)

This brief passage illustrates the four categories of modernization listed above: spelling, which here most notably omits the Folio's superfluous letters (as in 'calme', 'saile', 'farre'); punctuation, which here substitutes periods and an exclamation mark for many of the original's commas and colons; the omission of extraneous italics ('*Ariel*'); and the addition of stage directions to indicate, in this instance, the alternating recipients of Prospero's instructions.

In the preparation of this edition of *The Tempest*, we followed the usual practice of consulting all earlier major versions and have summarized the differences in the textual notes on the bottom of each page of text. Our collation differs from previous editions of *The Tempest* by including Dryden and Davenant's adaptation of 1670. Although *The Enchanted Island* adds characters and action foreign to Shakespeare's text, when it does follow

F directly (as in the first half of 1.2) its spelling, punctuation and occasional emendations illuminate ways in which the generation after Shakespeare interpreted *The Tempest*. Collation with Dryden and Davenant can only be sporadic, of course, in scenes that were freely adapted, such as 1.1, but even there, Dryden and Davenant's decision to keep some words and phrases while deleting others is indicative of what those two Restoration playwrights thought was obscure or ineffective in the original text and what they believed was theatrically useful. It should be borne in mind that each of the other Folio editions of Shakespeare's dramas – the second (1632), the third (1663) and the fourth (1685) – relies on its predecessors but commits additional compositorial errors while occasionally, but inconsistently, correcting earlier errors. It is nonetheless instructive to know what changes were made before Nicholas Rowe began the editorial practices that have persisted, and evolved, since the early eighteenth century.

Our collation is also the first to include a proof-sheet, extant in the British Library, of the first eight pages (through 1.2.181) of *The Tempest: A Comedy*, 'Printed in the YEAR 1708'. This sheet was most likely a preliminary sample of the octavo format that publisher Jacob Tonson planned for Rowe's edition of Shakespeare and was probably intended to pique the interest of potential subscribers. Because several of its readings differ from those in both of Rowe's 1709 editions, it is here regarded as an independent, if fragmentary, edition (see Fig. 22).

Cruxes

Perhaps as a result of Crane's careful inscription, there are fewer textual cruxes in *The Tempest* than in most of Shakespeare's plays. We discuss them briefly in our commentary notes, but two bear further explanation here because they illustrate how the editorial process is often influenced by editors' cultural attitudes and, in particular, how changing gender roles can affect editorial decisions.

22 A proof-sheet of *The Tempest: A Comedy*, 1708

The earlier crux is the speech prefix for 1.2.352–63: Miranda's (according to the Folio) angry denunciation of the 'Abhorred slave' Caliban. Beginning with Dryden and Davenant and for the next two and a half centuries, editors reassigned this speech to Prospero, principally because it seemed to them indecorous for a young lady to speak so frankly. In the mid-eighteenth century, Lewis Theobald contended, for example, that it would be 'an Indecency in her to reply to what *Caliban* was last speaking of' (Theobald[1], 1.18), i.e. attempted rape. Yet there are other, less fastidious, reasons for assigning the speech to Prospero. Its verbal style, some argue, not only fits his character more closely than it does Miranda's but is congruous in tone and wording with his other speeches rather than with hers. Miranda's have far fewer polysyllables and never use the second person singular 'thee', as does the 'Abhorred slave' speech and many of Prospero's. The disputed passage, moreover, is a unique instance (if assigned to Miranda) of a speech of hers to which Prospero, when he is part of the dialogue, does not react (RP). And some critics doubted that young Miranda could have served, as the speech claims, as Caliban's tutor. Morton Luce, for one, contended in the first Arden edition that Miranda would not have 'had much to do with the monster's education' (Ard[1], 35–6).

Since the mid-twentieth century, editors have generally sided with the Folio's speech prefix on several grounds. Her outburst at Caliban admittedly deviates from her usual decorum, but in light of Caliban's sexual assault, which her father has just brought up and Caliban has mocked in reply, her anger is timely and appropriate. It is also, according to many modern critics, consonant with her character, which is more forceful and sexually aware than early editors seemed to prefer. And the argument that Miranda, only 3 years old when she arrived at the island, could not have been Caliban's teacher is countered by the likelihood that later on – by age 10 or so – she could have introduced him to European words and ideas that Prospero had recently taught her. Caliban admits as much when Stephano claims to have been 'the man i'th' moon when time was'. 'My mistress showed me thee', Caliban responds, 'and thy dog and thy bush' (2.2.135–8). Caliban's assault on Miranda presumably did not occur until she reached puberty at approximately 13, an age at which she would have recognized his intentions and heartily endorsed his enslavement and banishment to separate quarters; her emotional outburst against the savage who seems to be 'capable of all ill' (1.2.354) is wholly plausible.

The second and more vexing crux occurs after the masque, when Ferdinand exclaims:

> Let me live here ever!
> So rare a wondered father and a wise
> Makes this place paradise.
>
> (4.1.122–4)

Although the final word in the second line is probably 'wise' in all copies of F–F4, in 1709 Rowe substituted 'wife', on the tacit assumptions that it made better sense for Ferdinand to acknowledge Miranda's importance and that F's compositor had misread a long 's'. Most eighteenth-century editors accepted Rowe's emendation. Many nineteenth- and early twentieth-century editors returned to 'wise', but often with the assertion that a few copies of F (which they admittedly had not seen) had 'wife'. In 1978, Jeanne Addison Roberts persuaded most subsequent editors that the apparent long 's' was actually a broken 'f' which remained intact in the first few impressions but subsequently lost half of its crossbar (Roberts, 'Wife', 203–8). Feminists took comfort in the text's reference to Miranda's importance in a play so male-oriented (see Thompson), and several widely used editions accepted this reading. In an influential psychoanalytic interpretation in 1986, Stephen Orgel reflected on the conspicuous absence of Prospero's wife from the magician's language and Miranda's consciousness, and hailed the new reading of the problematic word (Orgel, 'Wife'). More recently, Valerie Wayne has documented the crux's erratic history, its relation to gender-based perspectives and its continuing instability (Wayne, 183–7).

However much one would like to read the word as 'wife' in some copies of the Folio, we have been counter-persuaded by Peter W.M. Blayney's exegesis of early seventeenth-century casting and printing techniques, supported by his magnification to the 200th power of all relevant instances of the key word in the Folger Shakespeare Library's extensive Folio collection. The letter in question appears to be 's' in all instances, including the few that Roberts identified with 'f'; blotted ink, not a broken crossbar, encouraged such readings.[1] Although the syntax with 'wise' appears awkward to the modern eye, the placing of an adjective after the noun, as in 4.1.123, was not unusual in Shakespeare's works. Moreover, 'wise' forms a rhymed couplet with the ensuing line's 'paradise', an effect which strikes some critics as poetically appealing, while a few others contend that it is poetically inelegant and uncharacteristic of Shakespearean verse and therefore impressive evidence against the 'wise' reading. But rhymed couplets were not, in fact, uncommon in Shakespeare's late plays.

There is, moreover, an alternative to the assumption that Ferdinand must include Miranda in his notion of paradise. Biblical definitions of heaven excluded marriage (Mark, 12.25; Luke, 20.35); rather, it can be argued, Ferdinand's image of paradise may have been (however implausible to modern sensibilities) inhabited exclusively by himself and his seemingly omnipotent, omniscient new father-in-law (Katherine Duncan-Jones, private communication). If Miranda was also in paradise – the text implicitly includes her in the place where Ferdinand wishes to live forever – she would not have been his, or anyone else's, wife.

Such arguments notwithstanding, Shakespeare may have intended 'wife' all along. Before 1623, it may have been the

---

1 Blayney (*Norton*, xxxi) offers a preliminary version of his findings.

spoken word in performances of *The Tempest* and the written word in all manuscript copies. If so, authorial intent was thwarted by Ralph Crane's inaccurate deciphering of the rough manuscript, or by compositor C's misreading of Crane's handwriting, or by an apprentice's misplacement of a long 's' in the type case's (probably) adjacent compartment for 'f',[1] a possibility made more likely by the uncommon similarity between lower-case 'f' and long 's' in the font employed by the Jaggards for the Folio. On all these grounds, feminist and psychoanalytic critics have a highly plausible case; their reading is syntactically and logically sound. We opt for the Folio's 'wise' because there is no compelling reason to alter a word that is as plausible as the alternative in syntax and logic, more feasible in rhyme and more compatible with the technology of Jacobean type-founding.

The 'wise / wife' conundrum fittingly concludes our introductory observations because it encapsulates several of the play's major issues: the role of the chaste female (daughter / wife) in Prospero's generative project; the magician's wisdom and control of events (or lack thereof); and, most centrally, the question of what it takes to turn a paradise into a 'brave new world' in a universe corrupted by greed and egoism. While *The Tempest* masterfully probes these concerns, it tenaciously resists solutions.

---

1 There is no way of knowing the precise layout of Jaggard's type cases, but the leading authority on early English printing asserts that standard lays 'were certainly established by the mid-seventeenth century and probably long before'. The standard English lay called for the two letters to be side by side. See Philip Gaskell, *A New Introduction to Bibliography* (Oxford, 1972), 34 and the diagram on 37.

ADDITIONS AND RECONSIDERATIONS

Prospero lost his dukedom, was banished from Milan, and landed on a remote island twelve years before *The Tempest* begins. As he recounts past events to Miranda in 1.2, Prospero recognizes his earlier sins of omission: failure to keep a wary eye on his brother Antonio and to perform diligently his responsibilities in Milan. As 1.2 continues, Prospero's confrontations with his minions Ariel and Caliban bring the audience up to date on what has happened on the island during those dozen years: Prospero's rescue of Ariel from a cloven pine, Miranda's efforts to teach Caliban language, Caliban's attempt to seduce Miranda and his consequent enslavement. What a difference twelve years can make!

It has been the same number of years since our Arden 3 edition of *The Tempest* was first published. During the interval, we, too, have recognized some omissions from our discussion of *The Tempest*'s genesis and, equally important, witnessed another chapter in the play's continuing afterlife. Enmeshed in increasingly international cultural exchanges, *The Tempest* has undergone some new theatrical sea-changes, most significantly in Julie Taymor's 2010 film adaptation. The year 2011, the 400th anniversary of *The Tempest*'s first recorded representation on stage, is an opportune time to offer some additions and reconsiderations to our initial introduction during 'Twelve year since', as Prospero said to Miranda, '. . . twelve year since' (1.2.53).

SHAKESPEARE'S SOURCES REVISITED

The search continues for texts and events that may have influenced *The Tempest*. One potential historical source has recently surfaced – or, more precisely, a new twist has appeared in an old cluster of probable sources: the several texts of 1609–10 that described the wreck of *Sea Venture* on the uninhabited Bermuda archipelago. Although those texts have long been credited with inspiring the hurricane of the opening scene and a number of themes that run through the rest of the play – the island's lush flora and fauna, its frequent storms and eerie sounds, and the multiple conspiracies against legitimate authorities, for example – their sparse allusions to Indians have caused students of *The Tempest* to look elsewhere for clues about Caliban. If that primitive man was, as has often been claimed, based wholly or partly on Shakespeare's familiarity with American natives in English and continental travel narratives or the scores of visiting Indians in London during the late sixteenth and early seventeenth centuries, the contribution of the Bermuda narratives must have been slight. (See above, 39–54, for our prior discussion of Caliban's Indian and European archetypes.)

But another source of information about Indians that Shakespeare almost certainly encountered in the autumn of 1610 has recently emerged: Sir Thomas Gates's unwritten account of two Powhatan men who had been to England (one of them twice) and were homeward bound on the *Sea Venture*. Evidence of their presence on Bermuda was readily available in Captain John Smith's report of 1624 (thirteen or fourteen years after the alleged event) that among the shipwrecked party 'were two Salvages also sent from *Virginia* by Captain *Smith*, the one called *Namuntack*, the other *Matchumps*, but some such differences fell betweene them, that *Matchumps* slew *Namuntack*, and having made a hole to bury him, because it was too short, he cut of[f] his legs and laid them by him, which murder he concealed until he was in *Virginia*' (Smith, J., *Gen. Hist.*, 174–5). In 1625 the clergyman–historian Samuel Purchas confirmed the murder, but not the details, in a marginal note to *Purchas His Pilgrimes* (4.1771), but Purchas presumably echoed Smith, whose veracity has often been doubted. Hence the reluctance of *Tempest* scholars to propose Matchumps as a possible Caliban prototype or even to acknowledge his presence on Bermuda.

Corroboration for Smith's and Purchas's addendum to the Bermuda story was available as early as 1614, when a Dutch chronicler reported that Sir Thomas Gates numbered among the few fatalities on Bermuda 'a "Casicke" or son of a king in Virginia [i.e., Namuntack] who had been in England and who had been killed by an Indian, his own servant' (Parker, 66–7).[1] If, as seems probable, Gates's account was widely repeated and perhaps embellished by other *Sea Venture* survivors, Shakespeare may have partly fashioned his treacherous Caliban on the assassin Matchumps. Shakespeare may also have partly adapted *The Tempest*'s gaberdine scene from Namuntack's incompletely buried and mutilated body with its apparent extra pair of legs: 'Do you put tricks upon's with savages and men of Ind?' asks Stephano; 'Ha! I have not 'scaped drowning to be afeard now of your four legs . . . This is some monster of the isle, with four legs' (2.2.56–9, 64–5).

This conjecture – and it is only that – further enhances the Bermuda episode's probable influence on *The Tempest*. In any case, the emergence of this long overlooked evidence is a vivid reminder of the salience of oral communication in Shakespeare's era, when a reliance on printed texts was rapidly emerging but word of mouth reportage remained vital. The Bermuda survivors' arrival in London in September 1610 made Gates's 'wracke, and redemption' the talk of the town, supplementing the written accounts, most notably Silvester Jourdain's tract of October and two manuscript versions of William Strachey's lengthy epistle that offer no hint of the two Powhatans' presence

---

1   John Parker's *Van Meteren's Virginia, 1607–1612* contains Parker's translation of portions of Emmanuel van Meteren's history of Dutch America (edition of 1614) in which van Meteren tells of overhearing Sir Thomas Gates, or perhaps someone quoting Gates, speak about two Virginia Indians on Bermuda. Hobson Woodward, in *A Brave Vessel: The True Tale of the Castaways Who Rescued Jamestown and Inspired Shakespeare's 'The Tempest'* (New York: Viking, 2009), connects the dots between van Meteren and the Bermuda episode and offers additional evidence of the Powhatans' presence on Bermuda in 1609–10.

on the ship or the islands. Before the Dutch publication of 1614 and John Smith's English publication of 1624, that intriguing ingredient of the Bermuda experience, and perhaps other details that may be reflected in *The Tempest*, had to be heard rather than read.[1]

No less important than Shakespeare's conversations about America in London were his interactions with his fellow players in the King's Men, England's premier acting company. As Stanley Wells observes, recent scholarship now sees 'Shakespeare not as a lone eminence but as a fully paid-up member of the theatrical community of his time'. He worked 'within the same intellectual and theatrical environment as his contemporaries, was subject to the same commercial and social pressures, and interacted with fellow dramatists and actors throughout his career' (Wells, ix and 3). As we noted twelve years ago, Shakespeare's Prospero might have been influenced by Ben Jonson's satiric portrait of Subtle in *The Alchemist* (see 63 above). But there were other King's Men's plays that might also have contributed to *The Tempest*'s design. Shakespeare would have been especially familiar with at least two plays in their repertoire performed at the Globe and the Blackfriars with Richard Burbage, Shakespeare's Prospero, in a leading role: John Marston's *The Malcontent* and Beaumont and Fletcher's *Philaster*. Both feature a deposed ruler from an Italian court that has become 'a venue for lurid criminal behaviour' and a setting for the 'personal abuse of power' (G. K. Hunter, 112). This was the Italy of the early sixteenth century as described in Francesco Guicciardini's *Storia d'Italia*, which was published in English as early as 1579. Jacobean dramatists disillusioned with the

1 Strachey in Purchas, 4.1734–58; Ivor Noël Hume, 'William Strachey's unrecorded first draft of his *Sea Venture* saga', *Avalon Chronicles* 6 (2001), 57–87; 'An account written circa 1616', in J.H. Lefroy, *Memorials of the Discovery and Early Settlement of the Bermudas or Somers Island, 1515–1685*, 2 vols. (London, 1877–79), 1.103–4; A.Vaughan, 256–9, 270–1.

cronyism and corruption of James I's court frequently set their plays in Guicciardini's dark corridors, making Italian dukes and cardinals a mirror of the decay they perceived at home.

The Malcontent, first printed in 1604, began as a vehicle for a children's company but was soon appropriated by the King's Men for performance at the Globe. The central figure is a court satirist, Malevole, the former Duke of Genoa, who has been deposed by the Duke of Florence's son-in-law and banished a year before the play begins. His wife, Maria, recognized by all as – to use Prospero's words – a 'piece of virtue', has been imprisoned ever since. Malevole explains that he lost his dukedom by placing too much trust in the members of his court. Akin to Prospero, who relied on his brother Antonio, Malevole lost his throne by being '[s]uspectless, too suspectless' (Marston, 33). In disguise, the banished Duke observes his enemies and comments satirically on the court's corruption, which is figured, as in many Jacobean plays, through sexual intrigue. Except for one confidant, Count Celso, an older man, like *The Tempest*'s Gonzalo, 'who loves virtue only for itself' (Marston, 33), Malevole is isolated from the Genoese court and as a disguised prince is caught, to use G.K. Hunter's words, 'between the desire to participate in the life of power, and the desire to condemn and withdraw' (120–1).

The main action of *The Malcontent* involves the Duchess's lover, Mendoza, who seeks to murder the current Duke and take the throne for himself. (As in *The Tempest*, history repeats itself as one usurpation leads to another.) After a series of assignations, attempted murders and mistaken identities, the play concludes with a court masque. Mendoza has taken over as Duke and in celebration is entertained by a pageant of illustrious former Genoan dukes who have come from Elysium to congratulate him on his accession. The play ends without revenge, without joyous reconciliation – without even suggestions that anything important has changed. Parallels to *The Tempest* are obviously incomplete.

The deposition of a rightful ruler also drives the plot of Francis Beaumont and John Fletcher's first major success for the King's Company, *Philaster*.[1] Particularly in the plot's reliance on a woman disguised as a young page who becomes embroiled in royal intrigue fuelled by jealousy, *Philaster* is closely related to *Cymbeline*, but some elements point to *The Tempest* as well. Like Shakespeare's Alonso, Beaumont and Fletcher's King has deposed a rightful monarch to become ruler of two kingdoms, in this case Calabria and Sicily. Hoping to keep his ill-gotten kingdoms intact, he plans the marriage of his daughter Arethusa to the Spanish prince Pharamond, but she secretly loves the true heir to Calabria, young Philaster. Because Philaster is so popular with the people, the King has allowed him life and liberty. Philaster loves Arethusa in turn, but before the tragicomedy can end happily with their marriage, the prince is beset with jealousy that the princess has been unfaithful with a youthful page. When the lovers are reconciled and their secret marriage announced in words that suggest a wedding masque, the angry King promises an anti-masque that will turn Hymen's 'saffron into a sullen coat / And sing sad requiems to your departing souls' (Beaumont & Fletcher, *Philaster*, 239). But after the page is revealed to be a young woman, the King repents his usurpation and makes Philaster and Arethusa his heirs to the two kingdoms. Although the knowing but chaste princess Arethusa is a far cry from the innocent Miranda, Shakespeare was surely familiar with *Philaster*, and it is possible that Beaumont and Fletcher's portrayal of a dynastic marriage uniting two kingdoms under the rule of one virtuous couple influenced his plot.

These King's Company's tragicomedies partake in a scathing critique of political ambition and court corruption. Set in

---

1   Suzanne Gossett argues that *Philaster* was probably written during 1609, when the theatres were closed due to plague, and was likely to have been first performed early in 1610. See Beaumont & Fletcher, *Philaster*, 4–7.

venal Italian city states, they showcase human crimes and misdemeanours fuelled by greed and ambition. At first glance, the world they depict seems wholly dissimilar to Prospero's enchanted island. But Prospero's origins are in Italy: before he was put to sea in a leaky boat twelve years before the play begins, Prospero was a learned Italian duke, and the coup that displaced him has all the trappings of Guicciardini's Italian shenanigans. Prospero tells Miranda that he lost his power gradually; step by step he turned over more authority to his brother Antonio so that he could indulge in his study of the liberal arts. Antonio used this power to bestow patronage and arrange a secret deal with the King of Naples, who conspired to depose Prospero in return for Milan's tribute payments. If this part of Prospero's story – an injured Italian prince robbed of his kingdom and seeking retribution – had been dramatized rather than narrated, it would have struck Jacobean audiences as thoroughly familiar.

Prospero's brother Antonio is a Machiavellian villain, albeit writ small. In a scene that has often been drastically cut in performance, Antonio talks Sebastian, brother to the King of Naples, into a conspiracy very similar to his own of twelve years earlier. Sebastian remembers, 'You did supplant your brother Prospero', and Antonio, agreeing, replies, 'And look how well my garments sit upon me' (2.1.272–3). Sebastian agrees to kill Alonso and volunteers that when he becomes King of Naples, he will free Antonio from the tribute to Naples – and the inherent dependency the tribute suggests. But Antonio never asks for a tangible reward when he proposes the assassination because, as a true Machiavellian, his pleasure and reward is in manipulating other people through wordplay and in creating havoc for its own sake.

Although he doesn't soliloquize like Malevole, Prospero relates to Miranda the story of what happened before the play begins, and like Malevole, he expresses pleasure in an aside to the audience at his success in manipulating his enemies. He

145

wrecks their ship (an ironic recompense for their sending him to sea in a leaky vessel), then traumatizes them. And while Prospero doesn't observe Alonso, Antonio and Sebastian from the court's dark corners, he instead sends his chief minion, Ariel, to spy on all the island's inhabitants. Prospero also threatens Ariel with confinement and Caliban with physical punishment if they do not do his bidding. He arranges for Ariel to appear as a harpy, a birdlike monster from classical mythology often associated with the Erinyes, or Furies, goddesses of revenge who snatched souls and took them off to the underworld. Prospero, in short, makes his enemies suffer, and given his status as a deposed Italian duke, it would not be surprising if he sought some grotesque revenge. Instead Shakespeare chooses a tragicomic mode, and Prospero finds the rarer action in virtue than in vengeance.

There are many obvious differences between *The Tempest* and the King's Company's other tragicomedies, most notably in space and time. Prospero describes the claustrophobic world of the Italianate court to Miranda, but the ensuing action is set on an uncharted island, where sea breezes, eerie sounds and exotic flora and fauna bring the natural world to bear on court intrigue. The island's early inhabitants, Ariel and Caliban, are unlike any other characters in Jacobean drama. Prospero's loss of power is not recent. A dozen years have passed since he was banished; the resulting expanse of time and space creates a new perspective. Moreover, Shakespeare's choice of name for his hero – Prospero as opposed to Malevole or Vindice – indicates a different dramatic trajectory.

Placing *The Tempest* in intertextual relationship to plays that Shakespeare must have known casts light on some of his choices. Consider, for example, what many have found to be Prospero's obsession with his daughter's chastity. He had enslaved Caliban in retaliation for sexual advances towards Miranda – 'seek[ing] to violate / The honour of my child' (1.2.348–9) – and in 1.2 he treats Ferdinand quite cruelly. Prospero's purpose, he tells us, is to test the lovers, to place obstacles in their way so that their love might not seem 'light'. But juxtaposed to the sexual corruption that rots the court in so many Jacobean dramas, Miranda's and Ferdinand's chaste love suggests that by contrast Milan and Naples will be well governed when the young lovers inherit the thrones.

The tragicomic endings of Marston and of Beaumont and Fletcher celebrate the rightful monarch's restoration to the throne, and in each play the usurper repents. Shakespeare follows this pattern with Alonso, but Antonio's future remains ambiguous. When Prospero threatens to expose Antonio and Sebastian as traitors if they do not cooperate, Antonio says nothing, and if he spends the play's final moments contemplating another coup, we shall never know. Although Prospero willingly gives up the instruments of his power – his magic book and staff, the services of Ariel – the knowledge he has gained of humanity's potential for evil will perhaps ensure the watchfulness that he lacked twelve years earlier, when he preferred his library to his government offices. Surely he will use that knowledge.

Another possible source that we neglected in 1999 is the anonymous sixteenth-century romance *Primaleon, Prince of Greece*, written originally in Spanish but translated frequently into other European languages and by the end of the century into English. Gary Schmidgall's essay on Shakespeare's possible borrowings from Anthony Munday's English translation of *Primaleon* (Schmidgall, *Primaleon*) should be added to our earlier discussion of *The Tempest*'s literary forerunners (see above, 54–6).

The case for *Primaleon* as a *Tempest* source rests partly on publishing history, partly on substantive affinity. Schmidgall persuasively demonstrates that although the standard publishing records list no English version of the essential Book III of *Primaleon* before 1619, which largely accounts for its being overlooked as a *Tempest* source by earlier scholars, other evidence reveals beyond reasonable doubt that Munday had published all three books before 1610–11. *Primaleon* was therefore available (including Book III, although no copy from that period now survives) when Shakespeare wrote his island play and, presumably, drew eclectically on one or more Renaissance romances as well as other classical and modern texts and events.

How much, if at all, Shakespeare borrowed from *Primaleon* is much harder to demonstrate. Schmidgall summarizes the affinities between *Primaleon* and *The Tempest*:

> [a] Mediterranean island where old wounds are healed, friendships reaffirmed, marriages arranged . . . ; the central and benevolent mage-*cum*-master of ceremonies; a central action devoted to the manipulation of groups of isolated mariners; and a story line that is ebulliently harmonizing and keenly attentive to patrimonial issues. Several details – notably the conveyance of entranced mariners and the mage 'more addicted' to studies than his brother – are especially suggestive. (430)

As Schmidgall's précis of the convoluted romance attests (Schmidgall, *Primaleon*, 425–9), while such narrative elements can indisputably be found in *Primaleon*, they are so intertwined with non-*Tempest* features (and of such imprecise affinity to Shakespeare's play) that to label *Primaleon* a *Tempest* 'source' is problematic. It may be true, as Schmigdall concludes, that 'No other Renaissance romance comes near to shadowing *The Tempest* as comprehensively as does *Primaleon*' (430), but because the shadows are so obfuscated by other events and characters (none of them cogent counterparts to Caliban or Ariel) in the story's 700-plus quarto pages, it remains, like *The Mirror of Knighthood* and *Die Schöne Sidea*, an unproven influence on Shakespeare's play.

As we observed twelve years ago, scholars will probably never be able to identify with much confidence the numerous narrative, psychological and thematic threads that Shakespeare wove into *The Tempest*. Whether he gleaned material from voracious reading in classical and contemporary texts, from travellers' tales, from conversations with friends and acquaintances in London and Stratford, from day-to-day work with his fellow actors and dramatists, or, most likely, some eclectic combination of most or all of these disparate sources, *The Tempest*'s precise origins remain elusive.

AFTERLIFE, AMENDED AND EXTENDED

In the second decade of the new century, it is no longer possible to speak of Shakespeare simply in terms of English-speaking countries. Like everything else, he has gone global. From England, Rupert Goold's Royal Shakespeare Company *Tempest* played at Ann Arbor, Michigan, in 2006; from Africa, Capetown's Baxter Theatre *Tempest* toured England in 2009; and from the United States, New York's Bridge *Tempest* moved to London's Old Vic in 2010. Nowadays, *The Tempest* is often on the move.

This is not only true of Anglophone acting companies. *The Tempest* is frequently produced in translation and preserved on DVDs and other media that circulate across national boundaries. And even when the actors speak Shakespeare's lines in a different language, innovative foreign productions can shape British and American views. Most notably, Giorgio Strehler's 1978 *La Tempesta* and Yukio Ninagawa's 1988 *Ninagawa's Tempest: A Rehearsal of a Noh Play on the Island of Sado* had powerful impacts on their original audiences and remain influential renditions of Shakespeare's *Tempest* to the present day, particularly in their focus on Prospero as a surrogate director.

After World War II Milanese directors Giorgio Strehler and Paolo Grassi co-founded a repertory company, the Piccolo Teatro di Milano. Under its auspices Strehler's first *Tempest* was performed for the Maggio Musicale Fiorentino in Florence's

Boboli Gardens, where the fountain, lake and garden statuary created the *mise en scène*. Strehler drew on traditional Italian theatre by making Stephano and Trinculo the *commedia dell'arte* figures of Brighella (the comic boss) and Pulcinella (the talkative clown), but for the most part the production featured spectacles, including fireworks as a display of Prospero's magical powers. When Strehler returned to *The Tempest* in 1978, he moved the play to an indoor venue, the Piccolo's Lirico Theatre, where it remained in repertory for several years. The production toured to the United States in 1984, and not long afterwards a video was made before a live audience for Italian television (and is now available on DVD).

Bertolt Brecht's influence on Strehler's 1978 *La Tempesta* is palpable. Throughout the performance the audience could see stagehands at work, orchestrating the island's music and manipulating Ariel's wire. The set, a circle of sand imprinted with the signs of the zodiac on a cyclorama, contained multiple trapdoors from which Prospero's robe and staff, as well as other useful articles, appeared. In what has since become standard practice, Prospero (Tino Carrero) could be seen in the storm's midst, much like the conductor of a great orchestra, with his upraised staff directing the stagehands who shook blue sheets to make the undulating waves. Strehler gave Prospero absolute authority over his island theatre, yet emphasized the magus's dependence on Ariel. Giulia Lazzerini's petite Ariel, dressed as the *commedia*'s Pierrot – all in white, including cap, face paint and baggy uniform – entered from the fly on the wire she wore until freed in Act 5. Her job was to be stage manager, to obtain props and wardrobe when needed and stow them away when they weren't. Whenever Lazzerini's Ariel felt unhappy or restless, she tugged at the wire that confined her but, when performing her tasks, she made playful acrobatic movements, as if in delight. As the instrument who crafted Prospero's playswithin-the play, Ariel was omnipresent. Indeed, the professional partnership between Carrero's Prospero and Lazzerini's

Ariel was more intimate and intense than the magician's paternal relationship to Miranda.

The Caliban of Massimo Fosch (who alternated the role with Michele Placido) was painted entirely black, and when he entered from a trapdoor, one leg and arm at a time, he resembled a giant spider. After he stood upright, however, he had the shape of a well-formed young man. Although Caliban's blackness suggested to some his colonized status, its greatest impact was to set up a visual contrast with Ariel's whiteness. Caliban appeared in the gaberdine scene with one side of his face painted in a white, circular design; carrying a shamanistic wand and wearing his gaberdine, he visually parodied Prospero's first appearance with cloak and wand. As in 1948, Stephano (Mimmo Craig) and Trinculo (Armando Mara) were performed as *commedia dell'arte*'s Brighella and Pulcinella, but this time they added bawdy jokes and comic business to Shakespeare's original.

Strehler's most striking effect came at the play's conclusion. After Ariel was freed from her harness and exited through the audience, Prospero removed his robe and crown, and dropped his book into the cloth-waters. As if she couldn't bear to leave her master, Ariel then returned to sit at his feet. Suddenly, the set, cyclorama and all, collapsed into pieces. After Prospero spoke the Epilogue and the audience applauded, the set slowly reassembled, as if by a miracle. The production's final moments thus underscored the audience's contribution to the theatrical illusion.

Yukio Ninagawa's *Tempest* was first staged by the Toho Company at Tokyo's Nissei Theatre, but toured to wide acclaim at the Edinburgh Festival in 1988 and at London's Barbican Theatre in 1992. Ninagawa set the play on the island of Sado, the home of Zeami, Noh theatre's founding father. Zeami had been exiled to this isolated island off the coast of the Sea of Japan in 1434, and more than thirty extant Noh theatres remain on the island, several still in operation. As the programme at the Barbican observed, 'Zeami himself can be seen as a Prospero figure – he was known as a magician, and as a singer, songwriter, playwright, actor and director [who] created a magical world.'

Using a 'rehearsal' of a Noh play as a framework, Ninagawa stressed its metatheatrical elements by using four levels of illusion. On the outermost level, the production was a rehearsal in a modern Japanese theatre with Yukio Ninagawa as the director. As the audience entered the theatre, they could see Ninagawa sitting in a director's chair, from which he ran the costumed actors through their paces, including vocal exercises and some Kabuki-style routines. Once the play began, Ninagawa left and Haruhiko Joh, the actor playing Prospero – surrogate to Ninagawa/Zeami – took the director's chair to supervise the action. This moved the drama to the next level: the performance was now a Noh rehearsal where Zeami himself gave instructions to the actors and directed wind machines and musical instruments to create the tempest. When Joh donned Prospero's black robe and picked up his wand, the production moved to the third level. The audience was now on Prospero's island, where he directed the action. Inside these performances was the masque, a microcosmic production also directed by Prospero. On all levels, the director was prime mover.

Ninagawa made his *Tempest* accessible to Japanese audiences by grafting elements of Noh drama on to Shakespeare's plot. He selected the style of Mugen-Noh, a genre in which the hero (the *Shite*) reveals his identity as a good or bad spirit, often appearing in the dreams of a bystander (the *Waki*) who relays this vision to the audience. Prospero became the *Shite*, Miranda the *Waki*. In contrast to Noh's stylized movements in the main plot, Caliban, Stephano and Trinculo's antics were performed in comic Kyogen style. While the production followed Shakespeare's plot, Ninagawa occasionally inserted stage business familiar to Japanese audiences, such as the slender white threads Prospero tossed in the air to subdue Ferdinand, like the threads demon-spiders spew in Noh. Caliban was portrayed as a monstrous dragon with a long fishlike body. Ariel, in contrast, wore white robes and sang from atop a Noh-style hut. In the masque, Ninagawa employed traditional Japanese *onnagata* (female impersonators) for Juno, Ceres and Iris, who directed the audience's attention to the back of the hut, where an artist's rendition of a Japanese wedding appeared.

Like Strehler, Ninagawa highlighted Prospero's directorial authority in a variety of ways. In the scenes in which Prospero has no lines, Joh, the director, observed from his chair in front of the stage, following the other characters' lines in his prompt book. At the end of Caliban, Stephano and Trinculo's first encounter, he clapped his hands to signal the beginning of the ensuing scene, as if this were indeed a run-through rather than a finished performance. Similarly, after Ariel alighted on the hut as 3.3's harpy and sang harshly in Noh style, Prospero signalled from his director's chair that it was time for the intermission. After he delivered the 'Ye elves' speech (5.1), however, Joh abandoned his post as director, leaving the actors to fend for themselves; they followed the newly freed Ariel off stage as Prospero delivered the Epilogue but returned to see him break his staff and tear his prompt book. The performance – whether contemporary Japanese, ancient Noh or Shakespearean – was over.

Giorgio Strehler's *La Tempesta* and Ninagawa's *Tempest* transformed Shakespeare's play for non-English-speaking audiences in Italy and Japan, and on tours to Britain and the United States their productions influenced English-speaking audiences as well. Both directors came to *The Tempest* with a coherent vision of what they wanted – a production that spoke eloquently to the nature of theatre itself. The resulting *Tempest*s were thus characteristic of late twentieth-century 'director's theatre', where a particular directorial concept shapes every element of the play. For both, Prospero was the centre of the play; however harsh his actions may have seemed, his control was never questioned.

In contrast to Strehler and Ninagawa's metatheatrical app-roach, many twenty-first century *Tempest*s have taken a negative view of Prospero's authority, particularly when they apply the colonial paradigm to his relationships with the other characters. To see *The Tempest* from a post-colonial perspective is not new, of course. Twelve years ago we discussed several *Tempest* pro-ductions that applied the colonial paradigm, beginning with Jonathan Miller's 1970 transformation of Prospero into a colonial governor, Ariel into his mulatto house servant, and Caliban into his darker field hand (see 114 above). Two recent Royal Shakespeare Company productions serve to illustrate where the colonial *Tempest* is today.

Rupert Goold's RSC *Tempest* of 2006 moved Prospero's enchanted island from the usual post-colonial venues of Africa, Latin America or the Caribbean to a frozen Arctic wasteland. After a shipping forecast announced the storm, the projected image of a sinking ship behind the court party, dressed in evening clothes and life jackets, suggested a scene from *The Titanic*. Prospero's cell was a primitive cabin, with bunk beds and oilcan stove. Patrick Stewart's Prospero first appeared in a reindeer headdress and bearskin cloak, while Mariah Gale's Miranda wore an embroidered Inuit costume. John Light's Caliban, clad in fringed leather, was the enslaved native. The exception to the Arctic/Inuit theme was Julian Bleach's Ariel, whose head slowly rose from the burning oilcan. With white face and spiked hair, Bleach's Ariel was more like a post-Apocalyptic cyborg than an Indian servant. Moving like an automaton, he crept around the stage holding an hourglass, obsessed with gaining his freedom.

On this frozen landscape, Prospero and his fellow Europeans encountered a frighteningly alien culture. Instead of a tasty dis-appearing banquet, Antonio, Alonso and Gonzalo confronted a mammoth seal, brought in on a sled while native drums sounded menacingly in the background. As the hungry courtiers sliced open the carcass, out of its belly roared Ariel's harpy, a bony raptor in the mode of Edward Scissorhands. The masque of 4.1was transformed into an Inuit fertility rite featuring fire and water; Ferdinand and Miranda were blindfolded, bathed in cold water and then anointed with soot while three Inuit women's atonal chanting crescendoed to the sound of drums. *The Tempest*'s most significant native, Caliban, occasionally injected an atonal chant into the Inuit mix, but otherwise he seemed more European than Indian.

Stewart's Arctic explorer Prospero was a somewhat nasty control freak. He kept Caliban on a leash, and even spat in the dog bowl containing his slave's supper. There were occasional tender moments when he touched Miranda, but for most of the performance he was disaffected and somewhat aloof, leaving Ariel to figure out the best tortures for Prospero's enemies. In a stunning final effect, after Ariel finally shuffled off the stage, Prospero turned to see his hut explode in a ball of flame, then threw his magic staff into the fire, and sadly delivered the Epilogue. In this production it seemed almost as if Prospero, the colonist, bored with his Arctic existence and tired of keeping the natives at bay, was ready to quit and go home.

In 2009 the RSC moved *The Tempest* to a warmer clime when it hosted Janice Honeyman's production, which originated at Capetown's Baxter Theatre Centre. Designed to evoke an African ambience, this *Tempest* was set in the jungle, where tree foliage framed three levels of performance space for humans and spirits alike. The latter, dressed in straw bodysuits, created the island's music with drums and chants, manipulated the serpentine puppet that substituted for Shakespeare's storm, and shaped the audience's responses by their facial expressions and exclamations in Bantu, Zulu and Swahili. The spirits also crafted the wedding masque with colourful marionettes, their ululations signalling communal approval of Ferdinand and Miranda's union, and when Prospero called on 'Ye elves' in Act 5, the spirits, wearing African masks and perched atop stilts, hovered over him. The spirits' interactions with audience and characters, as well as the puppetry, music and arboreal set, were intended to evoke the idea of Africa rather than South Africa as such. They also gave the impression that on Prospero's magical island all of nature was alive.

Antony Sher's dishevelled Prospero seemed uncomfortable in this animistic environment, but Tinarie Van Wyk Loots's Miranda, resembling Tarzan's Jane in her leather dress, seemed quite at home. Like a human orang-utang, she climbed trees with ease and, upon meeting Ferdinand, unselfconsciously touched his face and plucked nits from his hair. Prospero's rage was evident when he shook his staff at Ariel, when he knocked the sticks an infirm Caliban needed from under his battered body, and, in the final scene, when he grabbed a rifle as if to shoot his European enemies. Yet whenever Prospero addressed Miranda, he tenderly caressed her cheek, suggesting that she alone kept him sane.

South Africa's most illustrious black actor, John Kani, played an aged Caliban, hunched over on canes, bent in anger and bent on getting his country back. Kani's son, Atandwa Kani, made a handsome Ariel, naked from the waist up except for white body paint. Into this African community came the white Europeans, Alonso, Antonio and Sebastian, wearing the dress of nineteenth-century British naval officers. Accompanying them was Gonzalo (Ivan Abraham), a South Asian Sikh who served as a loyal subaltern. When Kani's dignified Caliban claimed, 'This island's mine', the connection Honeyman intended between *The Tempest* and South Africa's recent history was crystal clear. Prompted by Ariel's description of the Europeans' suffering, this Prospero still had a hard time forgiving. In some ways, he seemed to long for connection more than separation. Reaching frequently to touch Ariel's body, he always held back, until he finally washed the white paint off the younger Kani's torso, an act that perhaps signalled Prospero's cleansing as well as Ariel's freedom. Most poignant, dressed in his linen suit, suitcase in hand and ready to leave Africa, Sher's Prospero turned from the audience and delivered the last lines of the Epilogue to Kani's Caliban: 'As you from crimes would pardoned be, / Let your indulgence set me free.' After Prospero left the stage, Caliban stood upright and, letting the canes fall, raised his arms in the air in a gesture of 'Freedom'. The production's resonance with Nelson Mandela's South Africa struck some viewers as overly simplistic, but for many it was the most compelling post-colonial production since Jonathan Miller initiated the approach in 1970.

Twenty-first-century productions of *The Tempest* have also taken some liberties with the play's gender relations. Although it was customary during the eighteenth and nineteenth centuries for Ariel to be female, only recently has Prospero become a role for women actors. Vanessa Redgrave paved the way at Shakespeare's Globe in 2000 in a transvestite performance, but her soft-spoken country squire was overpowered by Jasper Britton's fish-eating Caliban, who stole the show. The Oregon Shakespeare Festival was more adventurous in 2001, when Demetra Pittman presented an overtly female Prospero, whose maternal care for her daughter Miranda (Linda Morris) conveyed an alternative emotional dynamic between parent and child.

Taking a third of the play's lines and dominating the action, Prospero is a plum role, so it is hardly surprising that talented female actors are interested in it, and that when film director Julie Taymor and actress Helen Mirren discussed working together, they agreed that she, too, would be a female Prospero. Julie Taymor's film adaptation of 2010, bringing together celebrated British and American actors, was calculated to appeal to a mass audience. To make Prospero into Prospera, Taymor enlisted playwright Glen Berger to insert some lines into Prospero's 1.2 explanation of the events of twelve years earlier. The original Duke of Milan had encouraged his wife in her study of the liberal arts, including magic, but when he died and left Milan to her, her brother Antonio spread rumours that she was a witch and had her banished. This intriguing shift makes Prospera, Duchess of Milan, more clearly an alter ego to Sycorax, and the danger that her magic may slip from the power to heal to the power to hurt became a key theme in Taymor's film. As a result of these changes, Shakespeare's emphasis on confinement broadened to include the patriarchal entrapment of women. Clad in a loose tunic, Mirren's Prospera enjoys the island's freedom, but when Ariel tightly laces her corset as she once again becomes the Duchess of Milan, she visibly winces. The film makes clear that returning to Milan brings her no joy; were it not for her daughter Miranda (Felicity Jones), she would not relinquish her island life. Despite occasional annoyance at her daughter's 'teenage' rebellion, Mirren shows Prospera's affection for Miranda with gentle caresses that might be troublesome from a male Prospero.

Taymor filmed her *Tempest* on Hawaii, where shots of the sea, the sky and the volcanic landscape shift between water, air, earth and fire. Prospera is identified with the volcano by her magic cloak made from shards of obsidian. In her cave, made of earth and volcanic rock, the magician spends her time blowing

23 Prospera (Helen Mirren) makes a ring of fire in Julie Taymor's 2010 *Tempest*.

glass. Ben Whishaw's naked Ariel is a creature of water and air. Painted entirely white (with his genitals airbrushed out), he floats in the waves, soars through the air, and frequently separates into several simultaneous Ariels. Caliban, played by Djimon Hounsou, is by contrast tied to the earth. With a face half black, half white, and one eye blue, the other brown, his mud-covered skin suggests the subterranean cave where he lives. Fire emanates from the island's volcanic fury, but it also burns in Prospera's anger. The black mastiffs she sets on Stephano, Trinculo and Caliban spew fire as they run, and the magic circle she makes for her enemies is a ring of fire.

Taymor's film adaptation often substitutes rich visual imagery for Shakespeare's language. She cut 2.1 into two, inserting the gaberdine scene between the opening badinage of Antonio's (Chris Cooper's) seduction of Sebastian (Alan Cumming). By dropping a single black feather into a glass of water, Prospera creates Ariel's harpy, a ferocious black bird raptor who waves his wings in slow motion. Like many twenty-first-century directors, Taymor concluded that Act 4's masque was unplayable. Instead Ferdinand (Reeve Carney) and Miranda are treated to a celestial panorama of stars moving in geometrical patterns that culminate in an androgynous image of Vitruvian man/woman as one being. Taymor also cut lines in Prospera and Caliban's final confrontation; instead of receiving pardon and seeking for grace, Mirren and Hounsou stare at each other for a moment in mutual respect (but not liking), before Hounsou walks slowly and with great dignity up the stairs, out of Prospera's cell, into a new life.

The joys of Taymor's *Tempest* – Hawaii's variegated landscape, Ariel's tricksy manoeuvres, Ferdinand and Miranda's youthful delight, and Trinculo's (Russell Brand's) antics – are interleaved with pain. While Trinculo does his best to be funny, Alfred Molina's menacing Stephano seems more thug than clown. Mirren's pleasure in her magic powers flashes instantaneously into fury at her enemies. Taymor had originally intended to end her film with the shattering of Prospera's glass wand and a shot of the ship, but later decided to use the Epilogue for the credits. Set by the film score's composer Elliot Goldenthal and sung by Beth Gibbons, the Epilogue's words exude pain rather than joy, as do visual images of Prospera's precious books sinking into the sea. Prospera's decision to forgive her enemies, break her staff, and drown her books symbolizes a woman's costly sacrifice for her child.

Whether Julie Taymor's *Tempest* will inspire other kinds of gender-bending productions remains to be seen. It is clear, however, that despite the twenty-first century's opening decade of terrorism, war and natural disasters, *The Tempest* still speaks profoundly to stage and film audiences. On its 400th anniversary, Shakespeare's vision of an enchanted island, where even the worst of us can find forgiveness, remains relevant.

THE TEMPEST

LIST OF ROLES

NAMES OF THE ACTORS

ALONSO	*King of Naples*	
SEBASTIAN	*his brother*	
PROSPERO	*the right Duke of Milan*	
ANTONIO	*his brother, the usurping Duke of Milan*	
FERDINAND	*son to the King of Naples*	5
GONZALO	*an honest old councillor*	
ADRIAN *and* FRANCISCO	*lords*	
CALIBAN	*a savage and deformed slave*	
TRINCULO	*a jester*	
STEPHANO	*a drunken butler*	10
MASTER	*of a ship*	
BOATSWAIN		
MARINERS		
MIRANDA	*daughter to Prospero*	
ARIEL	*an airy spirit*	15
IRIS		
CERES		
JUNO	*spirits*	
Nymphs		
Reapers		20

0] The Scene, an vn-inhabited Island   3+ *Milan*] *(Millaine)*   4+ ANTONIO] *(Anthonio)*   6 *councillor*] *(Councellor)*   8 *savage*] *(saluage)*   12 BOATSWAIN] *(Boate-Swaine)*   15 ARIEL] *(Ariell)*

162

0.1 NAMES OF THE ACTORS This list, originally appended to the text in F and recorded here verbatim, was probably compiled by the scrivener Ralph Crane; the descriptive terms may reflect his knowledge of contemporary stage practice and perhaps, too, his personal assessment of the characters as performed at the time. See Introduction, p. 127.

1 ALONSO a common Italian name used here for a fictional character. As *King of Naples* Alonso controls a large area of the Italian peninsula south of the Papal States. During Shakespeare's lifetime, Spain controlled that part of Italy.

2 SEBASTIAN a common Italian name used for Alonso's brother. Sebastian is second in line to the throne of Naples after Ferdinand, Alonso's son.

3 PROSPERO an Italian name taken from the adjective *prospero*: favourable, propitious, flourishing. A Prospero appears in the first version of Ben Jonson's *Every Man in his Humour*, performed by the Lord Chamberlain's Men (including Shakespeare) in 1598. See Introduction, pp. 23–4. *Tem*'s Prospero is the *right* (legitimate) *Duke of Milan*, pronounced Milan. Located in Lombardy, Milan was one of the most powerful states in Renaissance Italy; in the sixteenth century, however, it was first taken over by the French and then by the Spanish. In the fifteenth century, its ruler was indeed supplanted, but by his nephew, not his brother.

4 ANTONIO As Prospero explains in 1.2.66–120, twelve years earlier his brother Antonio had arranged a palace coup and usurped the dukedom of Milan. See Introduction p. 35.

5 FERDINAND another common name, here used for Alonso's son and heir, perhaps suggested to Shakespeare by Castiglione's *The Courtier*, translated into English in 1561 by Thomas Hoby, which refers to a King Ferdinand of Naples who 'tooke occasion verye well to stryppe hymselfe sometyme into his doblet: and that bicause he knewe he was verye well made and nymble

wythall' (sig. R1ᵛ); Ferdinand has the opportunity to demonstrate his physical attractiveness when he appears carrying logs in 3.1.

6 GONZALO Although *gonzo* in Italian means 'simpleton, blockhead, dolt', this honourable gentleman proves to be far more intelligent than Sebastian and Antonio think him, one of the many ways in which this play shows the deceptiveness of appearances. Gonzalo serves Alonso as *an honest . . . councillor*. F's '*Councellor*' combines two modern words: 'councillor', member of a council, and 'counsellor', one who gives advice. Dryden & Davenant use 'Counsellor' in the sense of an advisor ('you are a Counsellor, if you can advise these Elements to silence'), but we have chosen the alternative spelling to suggest his official position. In contrast to Alonso, Antonio and Sebastian, who also serve as councillors, Gonzalo is honest in today's sense of truthfulness. 'Honest' could also describe a person 'Having honourable motives or principles' (*OED a.* 3).

7 ADRIAN *and* FRANCISCO members of Alonso's court, of unspecified rank, with very brief lines in 2.1 and 3.3

8 CALIBAN For a discussion of the etymology of Caliban's name, see Introduction, pp. 31–2. Caliban is described here as (1) *savage*. F's '*saluage*' is an obsolete form of the modern 'savage' and means 'uncivilized; existing in lowest stage of culture' (*OED a.* and *sb.*¹ 5). See *LLL* 4.3.218, where Berowne compares Rosaline to 'a rude and savage man of Inde'. As the only native on the island, Caliban had been ignorant of European language, customs and values until Prospero's arrival twelve years earlier. He is also (2) *deformed*. In 5.1.291–2 Prospero says that Caliban 'is as disproportioned in his manners / As in his shape'; though he is in these senses *deformed*, he is nevertheless human. For a discussion of Caliban's physical appearance, see Vaughan, *Caliban*, 10–15, and Introduction, pp. 32–4. Finally, he is termed (3) *slave*. While Caliban assisted Prospero upon the latter's

arrival and showed him about the island, 1.2.337–49 indicates that Caliban was not enslaved until he made sexual advances towards Miranda. Thereafter he is an involuntary servant whom Prospero's sprites punish with pinches when he disobeys.

9 TRINCULO This name is perhaps taken from the Italian verb *trincare*, to drink greedily, to swill. The adjective *trincato* means drunk; a *trincone* is a heavy drinker. Trinculo is described as *a jester*, a buffoon or fool maintained in a royal or noble household to entertain, often distinguished by a motley costume.

10 STEPHANO pronounced Stèphano; the name of a messenger in *MV* 5.1.28 and also a character in Ben Jonson's *Every Man in his Humour* (1598), in which Shakespeare acted. *Tem*'s Stephano is Alonso's *butler*, the servant in charge of the wine cellar who dispensed liquor to the royal household.

11 MASTER the ship's captain. The master was traditionally in charge of all components of the ship, cargo and crew.

12 BOATSWAIN (pronounced bosun) the officer in charge of a ship's sails, rigging and anchors, who directs the other mariners in such matters. See J. Smith, *Sea Grammar*, 35. The Boatswain dominates the play's opening scene 'by his professionalism in translating the Master's signals into commands and ensuring these are carried out rapidly' (Mahood, 212).

13 MARINERS Mahood describes the popular image of seamen in Elizabethan culture: 'the sailor whose uninhibited behaviour could be a social problem on the London streets had a shipboard life, revealed in countless narratives, which demanded expertise, endurance, enterprise, and ceaseless adaptability. It was a life apart, outside the laws of normal society, yet sustained by the mutual trust on which survival depended, and calling constantly for the propitiation of stern powers' (209).

14 MIRANDA from the nominative singular feminine form of the gerundive of the Latin verb *miror*, to wonder, be astonished at. In Italian, *mirando* is an adjective meaning 'wondrous'. As Prospero's (presumably) only child, Miranda is next in line to the Milanese throne. See Introduction pp. 26–7.

15 ARIEL For discussion of the etymology of Ariel's name and the creation of his character, see Introduction, pp. 27–8. The position of this name in F's list (after Miranda, with the women's roles) suggests that the part was performed by a boy actor. Because Ariel's role calls for several songs, the actor must also have been a singer.

16 IRIS a figure in the masque of 4.1, the Greek goddess who served as the gods' messenger and whose presence was signified by the rainbow. See Introduction pp. 70–1.

17 CERES a figure in the masque of 4.1, goddess of the earth and protectress of the harvest (also known as Demeter), often symbolized by food or grain. This role was probably doubled by the actor playing Ariel (see 4.1.167). See Introduction pp. 70–2.

18 JUNO a figure in the masque of 4.1, the wife of Jupiter (or, in Greek, Zeus) and the goddess of marriage. See Introduction pp. 68–73.

19–20 **Nymphs, Reapers** Spirits appear in 1.2, where they sing the refrain to Ariel's song; in 3.3, where they assist with the disappearing banquet; in 4.1, where they are Nymphs and Reapers for the dance that concludes the masque; and in 5.1, where they are the dogs who chase Caliban, Stephano and Trinculo on to the stage. The same actors probably doubled as Mariners in 1.1 and assisted in providing music when the text called for it.

THE TEMPEST

1.1 *A tempestuous noise of thunder and lightning heard;*
enter a Shipmaster *and a* Boatswain.

MASTER   Boatswain!

BOATSWAIN   Here master. What cheer?

MASTER   Good, speak to th' mariners. Fall to't yarely or
we run ourselves aground. Bestir, bestir!   *Exit.*

1.1 We have maintained F's act and scene divisions, but the former may be Ralph Crane's rather than Shakespeare's.

0.1 Pope's additional SD 'On a ship at sea' suggests the location of the Mariners, Boatswain and court party. Presumably the ship is somewhere in the Mediterranean close to Prospero's island. At Whitehall and the Blackfriars, the ship was easily presented on a flat stage through dialogue and action. A sea machine (pebbles in a drum) could echo the ocean's sounds and a wind machine (a loose length of canvas turned on a wheel) could create gusts (see Sturgess, 81–2). According to Dessen & Thomson, the *noise of thunder* and the flash of *lightning* were probably originally created by the sound of a drum and squibs (fireworks) that could be hung from a rope across the rear of the stage. In the Prologue to the revised version of *Every Man in his Humour* (1598), however, Ben Jonson describes the stage technology used to create thunder; in his play, there is no 'roul'd bullet heard / To say, it thunders; nor tempestuous drumme / Rumbles, to tell you when the storme doth come' (3.303). Dessen & Thomson conclude

that thunder and lightning (which were invariably linked) were often associated with a supernatural figure such as a devil, spirit, witch or magician; even when the SD indicated a storm, divine or satanic agency was usually assumed (see entries for 'thunder' and 'lightning'). In a modern production, the storm can be staged minimally, with a waving blue cloth or a swinging lantern suggesting the motion of the ship, or more elaborately with a mechanized bow rising and falling.

0.2 **Shipmaster ... Boatswain** See List of Roles, nn. 11, 12 and 13.

2 **What cheer?** 'What is your state or mood?' (*OED sb.* 3b).

3 **Good** probably an abbreviation for the familiar 'goodman' (as in 15), or, perhaps, a perfunctory dismissal of the Boatswain's *What cheer?*, though it might simply be an acknowledgement of the Boatswain's presence. Some editors have read *Good* as an explicit answer to the Boatswain's question, but with the ship about to run aground, the Master would be unlikely to respond so genially.

yarely quickly (cited in *OED adv. arch.*); see also 6 and 33.

1.1] *Actus primus, Scena prima.*   Location] On a ship at sea *Pope*   3 to't] *(*too't*)*

Enter Mariners.

BOATSWAIN   Heigh, my hearts; cheerly, cheerly, my   5
hearts! Yare! Yare! Take in the topsail. Tend to the
master's whistle! [*to the storm*] Blow till thou burst thy
wind, if room enough.

Enter ALONSO, SEBASTIAN, ANTONIO, FERDINAND,
GONZALO *and others.*

ALONSO   Good boatswain, have care. Where's the master?
Play the men!   10

BOATSWAIN   I pray now, keep below!

ANTONIO   Where is the master, boatswain?

BOATSWAIN   Do you not hear him? You mar our labour.
Keep your cabins! You do assist the storm.

GONZALO   Nay, good, be patient.   15

---

5   **my hearts** my hearties; heart was a
'man of courage or spirit. Often in nautical language' (cited in *OED* heart *sb.*
15a)
   cheerly 'Heartily, with a will' – a
sailor's shout of encouragement (first
occurrence in *OED a.* and *adv.* B 1b)
6–7   **Tend . . . whistle!** 'Pay attention!'
Shipmasters often directed the crew
with blasts on a whistle; a gold whistle
was a sign of the naval commander's
rank (Var, 12).
7–8   **Blow . . . wind** is the Boatswain's
defiant challenge to the storm to blow
until it is out of wind, or, perhaps, a
challenge to the clouds to blow until
their cheeks burst. Also plausible is the
scatalogical notion of the storm blowing until it loses force by breaking
wind. In a similar situation in *Per* a
sailor cries to the storm, 'Blow, and
split thyself' (3.1.44).
8   **if room enough** suggests the ship's
dangerous proximity to the coast. On
nautical matters in this scene, see

Falconer, 36–40.
8.2   *others*   This part of the SD is consistent with the opening of 2.1 and 3.3
where SDs also suggest the presence of
extra people in the Neapolitan party.
The King's Men could have drawn on
a number of trained extras for performances of *Tem* (Sturgess, 77), but
modern productions seldom include
any supernumeraries. See List of
Roles, nn. 19–20.
10   **Play the men!** Act with spirit, be
manly. John Upton argued in *Critical
Observations on Shakespeare* (London,
1748) that 'Ply' rather than 'Play' –
'keep them to their business' – was
intended (249). In either case the pronunciation is very similar. Although
Alonso could be telling the Boatswain
to set the men to work (*OED v.* 1a), it
is more likely that he is speaking
directly to the Mariners, admonishing
them to act like men (cf. Halliwell,
Notes, 9–11).

---

5 Heigh] Hey *F3*   7 SD] *Oxf¹*   8.1 FERDINAND] *Rowe; Ferdinando F, Rowe**
12 boatswain] (Boson)   14 do] *om. Pope*

BOATSWAIN   When the sea is! Hence. What cares these
roarers for the name of king? To cabin! Silence!
Trouble us not.

GONZALO   Good, yet remember whom thou hast aboard.

BOATSWAIN   None that I more love than myself. You are   20
a councillor; if you can command these elements to
silence and work the peace of the present, we will not
hand a rope more. Use your authority! If you cannot,
give thanks you have lived so long and make yourself
ready in your cabin for the mischance of the hour, if it   25
so hap. – Cheerly, good hearts. – Out of our way, I say!

Exit.

GONZALO   I have great comfort from this fellow.
Methinks he hath no drowning mark upon him – his

---

16 **cares** The use of a singular verb
with a plural subject was common
n the early seventeenth century. Cf.
Per 4.1.59: 'Never was waves
nor wind more violent'. See Abbott,
§333.

17 **roarers** loud, violent waves; also a reference to people who are unruly, as in
Middleton's *The Roaring Girl* (*c.* 1608)

19 **Good** probably meant as in 3 and 15
above, but perhaps an acknowledgement of the Boatswain's sensible
admonition

21 **councillor** See List of Roles, n. 6.
these elements wind and water

22 **work . . . present** There is no sound
reason to change *present* to 'presence'
(cf. Ard², 5); the Boatswain challenges
Gonzalo to silence the elements and
'make the present moment peaceful'
(Folg²).

23 **hand . . . more** handle any more rope,
i.e. 'we could stop work'
authority The Boatswain introduces
the theme of the proper and improper

uses of authority, which resonates
throughout the play.

26 SD Presumably some, if not all, of the
Mariners exit with the Boatswain here,
to re-enter at 49.1.

28–9 **he . . . gallows** in accordance with
the proverb, 'He that is BORN to be
hanged (drowned) shall never be
drowned (hanged)' (Dent, B139),
Gonzalo relies on the Boatswain's rope
of destiny (i.e. the hangman's rope) to
be more useful than the ship's anchor
cable, which in the midst of a storm is
worthless. *OED sb.* 2b cites this as an
instance of 'to have the look of one predestined to or deserving the gallows'.
Cf. *TGV* 1.1.148–50, where Proteus
suggests that Speed's presence on
board will save the ship because he is
'destin'd to a drier death on shore'. In
LLL 5.2.12 Katherine refers to
Cupid as 'a shrowd unhappy gallows',
i.e. a scoundrel who deserves to be
hanged.

---

20 more love] love more *Dryden & Davenant*   21 councillor] *(Counsellor)*   28 him –] *Oxf¹*; him,
F; him; *F4*

complexion is perfect gallows. Stand fast, good fate, to
his hanging; make the rope of his destiny our cable, for   30
our own doth little advantage. If he be not born to
be hanged, our case is miserable.   *Exeunt*

Enter Boatswain.

BOATSWAIN   Down with the topmast! Yare! Lower,
lower! Bring her to try with main course. (*A cry
within.*) A plague upon this howling. They are louder   35
than the weather or our office.

Enter SEBASTIAN, ANTONIO *and* GONZALO.

Yet again? What do you here? Shall we give o'er and
drown? Have you a mind to sink?

29 **complexion** may refer to the Boatswain's hue or to his temperament, or, most likely, to the former as indicative of the latter
     perfect utter, unmitigated (first occurrence in *OED a.* B 5e)

31 **doth little advantage** scarcely benefits (*OED* advantage *v.* 4c)

33–4 **Down . . . course.** The Boatswain orders the main sail lowered in hope that the ship will thereby slacken its speed and avoid the land. *To try* meant to adjust certain sails and rigging so that the ship would ride out the storm. See J. Smith, *Sea Grammar*, 40: 'A storme, let us lie at Trie with our maine course' (cited in *OED*, trie *v.* 17 for 'Of a vessel: To lie to'); see also Whall, 98–9, and Falconer, 38–9. Some editors have inserted a comma or semicolon after *to*, thus making the commands 'bring her to; try with main course', which conforms to modern rather than Jacobean nautical terminology.

33 **Yare!** 'Be yare' or quick; see 3 and 6.

34–6 *The SDs follow *A plague* in F, but they are customarily separated, and the entry placed after *office* to fit better with the text. *Yet again* (37) almost certainly refers to the reappearance of the annoying passengers, whom the Boatswain accuses of ensuring, by their meddling presence on deck, that all hands will drown.

35 **plague** In F the word is followed by a long dash, perhaps to indicate oaths, possibly implied by Sebastian's characterization of the Boatswain in 39–40, although *blasphemous* may have meant 'abusive', as the Boatswain surely had been, rather than the modern 'irreverent' (Halliwell, *Notes*, 12). The latter form of blasphemy had been outlawed by the Act to Restrain Abuse of (i.e. by) Players (1606). In any event, the interjection of oaths at that point would disrupt the sentence's syntax. See also 39 below and 5.1.218.

35–6 **They . . . office.** The first word refers to the passengers, the last to the sailors' work.

33 SD] *Theobald; Exit.* F 34 her ... with] her to: try wi'th' *R.G. White*   34–5 SD, 36.1] *Ard¹; one line following plague... F*

SEBASTIAN   A pox o'your throat, you bawling, blasphemous, incharitable dog.   40

BOATSWAIN   Work you, then.

ANTONIO   Hang, cur! Hang, you whoreson, insolent
noise-maker! We are less afraid to be drowned than
thou art.

GONZALO   I'll warrant him for drowning, though the ship   45
were no stronger than a nutshell and as leaky as an
unstanched wench.

BOATSWAIN   Lay her a-hold, a-hold! Set her two courses
off to sea again! Lay her off!

Enter Mariners, *wet.*

MARINERS   All lost! To prayers, to prayers! All lost!   50
BOATSWAIN   What, must our mouths be cold?

---

39 **pox . . . throat** literally, 'may your
throat be wracked by disease', i.e. the
French pox (syphilis) or smallpox;
here used metaphorically

39–40 **blasphemous** Unless the Boatswain's blasphemy has been obscured
by the storm or the courtiers' wailing,
the charge is false (see Falconer, 153),
but Sebastian should not perhaps be
taken literally. The Boatswain has
been palpably disrespectful.

45–7 Gonzalo promises to *warrant* (guarantee immunity; cited in *OED v.* 8) the
Boatswain *for* (i.e. from) drowning, no
matter how unseaworthy the ship,
because – as he earlier proclaimed – the
man was born to hang. The term
unstanched wench probably refers to
menstrual bleeding, but *leaky* in collo-
quial speech sometimes implied sexual
incontinence.

48–9 The Boatswain, trying to keep the
ship from crashing on the shore, orders
it held as closely to the wind as possible, then calls for both major sails
(*courses*) to be set, so as to drive the ship

out to open sea again. J. Smith, *Sea
Grammar*, 44–5, described 'Offing' as
'the open Sea from the shore, or the
middest of any great streame' – hence
Lay her off is an order to get out to sea
again. Nautical authorities disagree on
some aspects of these directions. Allen
argues for an emendation to 'Lay her
a-hull'. See also Whall, 30, 99.

51 **must . . . cold** perhaps an allusion to
the proverbial expression 'To be cold
in the MOUTH (i.e. dead)' (Dent,
M1260.1). The Boatswain asks 'Must
we be dead?', presumably from drowning in the icy ocean waters. Cf. Francis
Beaumont's *The Scornful Lady* (1616):
'would I had been cold i'th' mouth
before this day, and neer have livd to
see this dissolution' (sig. D2ʳ). Alternatively, the Boatswain may be referring to the prayers which are 'cold in
the mouth'. In the storm scene that
opens Beaumont and Fletcher's *The
Sea Voyage*, the Master shouts at a
sailor who is praying: 'is this a time, /
To discourage our friends with your

---

40 incharitable] uncharitable *Dryden & Davenant, Rowe*   49 off!] off. *F*

GONZALO The King and prince at prayers, let's assist them, for our case is as theirs.

SEBASTIAN I'm out of patience.

ANTONIO We are merely cheated of our lives by 55 drunkards. This wide-chopped rascal – would thou mightst lie drowning the washing of ten tides!

GONZALO He'll be hanged yet, though every drop of water swear against it and gape at widest to glut him. *(A confused noise within)* Mercy on us! – We split, we split! 60 – Farewell my wife and children! – Farewell brother! – We split, we split, we split!

ANTONIO Let's all sink wi'th' King.

SEBASTIAN Let's take leave of him.   *Exit [with Antonio].*

GONZALO Now would I give a thousand furlongs of sea 65 for an acre of barren ground – long heath, brown furze,

cold orrizons?' (*Comedies and Tragedies* (London, 1647), Aaaaa1ʳ). Less likely is the suggestion that the prospect of drowning may divert him from his duties to the bottle (Mahood, 212). Some *Tem* editors have the Boatswain and Mariners exit here to join in the *confused noise* mentioned in 60, but there's no reason why some or all the Mariners cannot fall to their knees in prayer on deck.

52 **The . . . prayers** The verb 'are' is implied after *prince*.

55 **merely** altogether, wholly

56 **wide-chopped** big-mouthed (cited in *OED* wide *a.* 12)

57 **lie . . . tides** Courts of Admiralty sentenced pirates to be hanged at water's edge and their bodies to remain awash for three tides; Antonio's curse greatly exaggerates the second part of the penalty.

58–9 Gonzalo clings to his belief that despite the storm's fury, the Boatswain will survive to be hanged and thus

none aboard will drown, even if every drop of water tries to open its mouth to swallow him greedily (*glut him*). Strachey described 'the glut of water (as if throttling the wind erewhile)' that enveloped *Sea Venture* (1735).

60 SD The following exclamations (*confused noise*) come from several voices below the stage or from behind the discovery space.

60–2 **split** Literally, the ship splits apart and, figuratively, *we* are shipwrecked (first occurrence in *OED v.* 9b).

65–6 **furlongs . . . acre** Both terms are units of linear measurement; the former is now regularized at 220 yards, the latter (in its now obsolete sense) equalled a furlong. Cf. Hermione's description of women in *WT* 1.2.94–6: 'You may ride's / With one soft kiss a thousand furlongs ere / With spur we heat an acre'.

66 **long . . . furze** *Heath* is heather, *furze* is a low shrub, also known in Scotland

52 prince at prayers] *F4, Rowe*;* Prince, at prayers *F;* Prince are at prayers *Rowe*   54 I'm] *(I'am)*
56 wide-chopped rascal –] *Rowe;* wide-chopt-rascall, *F;* wide-chapp'd rascal, *Dyce*   63 wi'th']
Rowe*, R.G. White; with' *F;* with *F3;* with the *Rowe;* wi' the *Capell*   64 SD] *Signet*   66 ground –]
Dyce; ground: *F*   brown furze] *Rowe;* Browne firrs *F;* brown firs *F4, Rowe*;* Broom-furs *Dryden &
Davenant*

anything. The wills above be done, but I would fain die
a dry death.   *Exit.*

1.2   *Enter* PROSPERO *and* MIRANDA.

MIRANDA

If by your art, my dearest father, you have
Put the wild waters in this roar, allay them.
The sky, it seems, would pour down stinking pitch
But that the sea, mounting to th' welkin's cheek,
Dashes the fire out. O, I have suffered   5
With those that I saw suffer – a brave vessel

and northern England as 'gorse', a characteristic moorland plant. The other two words are arguable. Hanmer emended *long* to 'ling' (a type of heather (*OED sb.*[2] 1)), but it is clear from Henry Lyte's translation of Rembert Dodoens's *Niewe Herbal* (London, 1578) that *long heath* was a distinct plant: long heath 'beareth his flowers alongst the stemmes', as opposed to small heath that bears flowers in 'tuftes at the toppes of the branches' (677). Following Dryden & Davenant, Hanmer emended *brown* to 'broom', but *furze* and 'broom' were synonyms and *furze* was often *brown*. Because of F's apparently intentional adjective–noun pairings, we prefer F's *brown*. In any event, gorse, broom and *furze* were associated with *barren ground* (Gerard, 1139), and Gonzalo, accordingly, expresses his preference for dry land, however sterile.

67 **fain** gladly (cited in *OED* B)

1.2 Above the list of characters provided at the end of the text, F notes: 'The Scene, an vn-inhabited Island'. This island lies somewhere in the Mediterranean between Naples and Tunis. Presumably Prospero and Miranda are standing on a point, which could be anywhere on the Blackfriars stage,

where they can see the ship 'at sea'. Many editors have located this scene near Prospero's cell (20), though it need not be. Prospero seems to call Caliban forth from his cave (320–1), which at the Blackfriars could have been off the side of the stage or below the trap door. Just how close Caliban's den is to the magician's cell is up to the director and designer.

1 **art** in this context, magic. *Art* is consistently capitalized in F; some editors assume this implies Shakespeare's special emphasis on Prospero's powers, but it may well be the result of Ralph Crane's predilection.

2 **allay them** set them to rest

3 **stinking pitch** The blackness of the clouds suggests to Miranda that they might disgorge foul-smelling pitch, a common commodity of the time, especially in shipbuilding. Cf. Stephano in 2.2.51 and J. Smith's 'powre hot pitch upon it' (*Sea Grammar*, 13).

4 **welkin's cheek** the sky's, or cloud's, billowed edges. Dover Wilson suggests 'the side of a grate' (Cam[1], 112), but we agree with Oxf[1] (101) that this usage seems inappropriate here.

5 **fire** lightning; possibly dissyllabic (fi-er)

6 **brave** magnificent, splendid

1.2] Scena Secunda.   Location] The Inchanted Isle. *Pope*   1 art] *Pope;* Art *F*   6 suffer –] *this edn;* suffer: *F;* suffer! *Capell;* suffer. *Riv*

171

(Who had no doubt some noble creature in her)
Dashed all to pieces. O, the cry did knock
Against my very heart! Poor souls, they perished.
Had I been any god of power, I would   10
Have sunk the sea within the earth or ere
It should the good ship so have swallowed and
The fraughting souls within her.

PROSPERO   Be collected;
No more amazement. Tell your piteous heart
There's no harm done.

MIRANDA   O woe the day.

PROSPERO   No harm!   15
I have done nothing but in care of thee,
Of thee, my dear one, thee my daughter, who
Art ignorant of what thou art, naught knowing
Of whence I am, nor that I am more better
Than Prospero, master of a full poor cell,   20
And thy no greater father.

MIRANDA   More to know

8–9 **knock / Against** rap for attention

11 **or ere** Both words mean 'before'; here they are probably doubled for emphasis (see Abbott, §131).

13 **fraughting souls** cargo of souls (cited in *OED* fraught *vbl. sb.* 3b)
Be collected 'Compose yourself'; the opposite of 'distracted' (first occurrence in *OED* collected *ppl. a.* 2)

14 **amazement . . . piteous** Orgel links *amazement* (fear and wonder) along with *piteous* (full of pity) to the catharsis proposed by Aristotle as the effect of the best kind of tragedy (Oxf[1], 102).

16–17 **thee . . . thee . . . thee** Prospero's repetition emphasizes his concern for Miranda and her centrality to his plans.

19 **whence I am** where I came from
more better of more distinguished status. The use of a double comparative is fairly common in Shakespeare. See Abbott, §11.

20 **full poor cell** extremely humble dwelling; a hut or cottage, often the home of a hermit or monk (*OED sb.*[1] 3c), but usually a cave in stage and artistic renderings of *Tem.* Cf. Friar Lawrence's 'cell' in *RJ* 3.5.232. In the early seventeenth century, 'cell' did not yet carry implications of imprisonment.

21 **no greater father** no more important a father than his poor cell suggests

---

7 creature] creatures *Theobald*   13 fraughting] fraighted *Pope;* freighting *Bantam (Steevens)*
19 I . . . better] I am more or better *Rowe*, Rowe[3];* I'm more *Dryden & Davenant*

Did never meddle with my thoughts.

PROSPERO   'Tis time

I should inform thee further. Lend thy hand

And pluck my magic garment from me. So,

Lie there my art. Wipe thou thine eyes, have comfort;   25

The direful spectacle of the wreck which touched

The very virtue of compassion in thee,

I have with such provision in mine art

So safely ordered, that there is no soul –

No, not so much perdition as an hair,   30

Betid to any creature in the vessel

Which thou heard'st cry, which thou sawst sink. Sit
    down,

For thou must now know further.

MIRANDA   You have often

Begun to tell me what I am, but stopped

And left me to a bootless inquisition,   35

Concluding, 'Stay, not yet'.

PROSPERO   The hour's now come;

---

22 **meddle with** intrude upon
25 **Lie . . . art** addressed to his magician's
robe, which was probably covered
with cabalistic signs (Sturgess, 79).
Prospero distinguishes between his
identity as a man, his role as a magician
(signalled by this robe) and his role as
Duke (indicated by the garments he
dons in 5.1.84ff). He then again
addresses Miranda. Thomas Fuller
reported that Elizabeth's closest advisor, Sir William Cecil, Lord Burleigh,
'At night when he put off his gown,
. . . used to say, "Lie there, Lord
Treasurer!"' (*The Holy State and the
Profane State* (London, 1841), 253).
27 **virtue** essence (Ard²). Johnson
glossed it as 'the most efficacious part'

(Johnson & Steevens, 8).
28 **provision** 'the action of providing,
seeing to things beforehand' (cited in
OED sb. 2a)
29 **safely ordered** effectively arranged
that . . . soul An implied 'lost' com-
pletes this line.
30 **not . . . hair** a use of the proverb, 'To
hurt (or lose) a HAIR' (Dent, H26.1).
See also 217: 'Not a hair perished'.
perdition loss; Ariel uses this word
again in 3.3.77, but with the added
connotation of eternal damnation.
31 **Betid** happened, befell
32 **Which . . . which** The first clause
modifies *creature*, the second *vessel*
(31).
35 **bootless inquisition** fruitless inquiry

22 'Tis time] *F, Rowe*, Rowe³;* 'Tis true *F4, Rowe¹*   24 So,] So! *(Lays down his mantle) Pope*   26+
wreck] *(wracke)*   28 provision] compassion *F2*   29 soul –] *Rann;* soule *F;* soul, *F3;* soul lost,
Rowe; foyle, *Theobald;* loss, *Capell;* soil, *Cam¹*   35 a] the *F2*   36 'Stay . . . yet'] *Dyce; no quotation
marks F; ital. Theobald*   hour's] *(howr's)*

The very minute bids thee ope thine ear.
Obey and be attentive. Canst thou remember
A time before we came unto this cell?
I do not think thou canst, for then thou wast not   40
Out three years old.

MIRANDA   Certainly, sir, I can.

PROSPERO

By what? By any other house or person?
Of any thing the image, tell me, that
Hath kept with thy remembrance.

MIRANDA   'Tis far off,
And rather like a dream than an assurance   45
That my remembrance warrants. Had I not
Four or five women once, that tended me?

PROSPERO

Thou hadst, and more, Miranda. But how is it
That this lives in thy mind? What seest thou else
In the dark backward and abysm of time?   50
If thou rememb'rest aught ere thou cam'st here,
How thou cam'st here thou mayst.

MIRANDA   But that I do not.

PROSPERO

Twelve year since, Miranda, twelve year since,
Thy father was the Duke of Milan and

---

41 **Out** completely, quite; i.e. Miranda
  was not yet three years old (cited in
  OED adv. 7c).
44 **Hath ... remembrance** that you can
  recall; literally, kept within your memory
45 **assurance** certainty
46 **warrants** knows surely
47 **tended** cared for; in 3.1.48–50 Miranda claims she cannot remember any

woman's face, so her recollection of
her attendants must be vague, at
best.
50 **backward** 'the past portion (of time).'
  Shakespeare appears to have originated this rare usage (*OED sb.* C 2).
  abysm a variant of 'abyss', meaning
  'any deep immeasurable space, a profound chasm or gulf' (cited in *OED* 2)
54 **Milan** Milan; see List of Roles, n. 3.

---

38 thou] *om. Pope*   40 wast] *(was't)*   41 Out] full *Dryden & Davenant*   44 with] in *Dryden &
Davenant*   50 dark backward] *(dark-backward)*   abysm] *(Abisme)*   53 Twelve year ... year]
'Tis twelve years ... years *Pope*

A prince of power.

MIRANDA   Sir, are not you my father?   55

PROSPERO

Thy mother was a piece of virtue, and
She said thou wast my daughter; and thy father
Was Duke of Milan, and his only heir
And princess, no worse issued.

MIRANDA   O, the heavens!
What foul play had we that we came from   ence?   60
Or blessed wast we did?

PROSPERO   Both, both, my girl.
By foul play, as thou sayst, were we heaved thence,
But blessedly holp hither.

MIRANDA   O, my heart bleeds
To think o'th' teen that I have turned you to,
Which is from my remembrance. Please you, farther.   65

PROSPERO

My brother and thy uncle, called Antonio –
I pray thee mark me, that a brother should

---

56 **piece of virtue** masterpiece or model of chastity. Cf. Dent, P291.1 and M1193, which cite this line.
59 **And princess** Some editors, assuming a printer's error, have replaced *And* with 'A', which accords better with the comma after *heir* in F, thus making *A princess* appositive to *heir*. But F's semicolon after *princess* raises doubts about that reading.
    no worse issued of no lesser birth than a princess
61 **blessed** blessèd; fortunate, with a suggestion of divine intervention (*OED ppl. a.* 3a)
    Both, both Shakespeare uses this repetition to express great emotion when Bertram asks for pardon in *AW* 5.3.308.

63 **holp** helped
64 **teen** trouble, suffering. Cf. *R3* 4.1.96: 'And each hour's joy wrack'd with a week of teen'.
65 **from** absent from. Abbott, §158, notes that 'from' is frequently used as a shortened form for 'apart from' or 'away from'.
66–74 The difficult syntax of Prospero's speech may indicate the stress he feels at recalling his brother's treachery and the events of twelve years earlier. But according to Russ McDonald (*Shakespeare's Late Style* (Cambridge, 2006), pp. 77–107), complex syntax and elliptical expression are characteristic of Shakespeare's late style.

58 and his] and thou his *Hanmer*   59 And] A *Pope*   63 O] *om. Pope*   66 Antonio –] *Rowe³*; *Anthonio*: F

175

Be so perfidious – he, whom next thyself
Of all the world I loved, and to him put
The manage of my state, as at that time   70
Through all the signories it was the first,
And Prospero the prime Duke, being so reputed
In dignity, and for the liberal arts
Without a parallel; those being all my study,
The government I cast upon my brother   75
And to my state grew stranger, being transported
And rapt in secret studies. Thy false uncle –
Dost thou attend me?

MIRANDA   Sir, most heedfully.

PROSPERO

Being once perfected how to grant suits,
How to deny them, who t'advance and who   80

68–9 **whom . . . loved** Presumably,
Prospero's wife died giving birth to
Miranda or soon after, thus leaving
him with a daughter and brother as
closest kin; otherwise Prospero's omission of his wife here and elsewhere
would almost surely signify marital
disharmony. Miranda's recollection
only of 'Four or five women once, that
tended me' (47), also implies her
mother's early death.

70 **manage** management

71 **signories** 'A governing body, *esp*. that
of Venice or other medieval Italian
republic' (*OED* 4)

74 **those** the *liberal arts* (i.e the *trivium*:
grammar, logic and rhetoric; and the
quadrivium: arithmetic, geometry,
music and astronomy), to which
Prospero has just referred. Prospero's
syntax is slightly jumbled in this
emotional recounting of his fall from
power and eventual exile by Antonio.
Editors have variously punctuated

this and the next several passages in
efforts to clarify and impose gram-
matical order, but this speech defies
precise reconstruction. In general,
especially on stage, the message is
coherent.

76 **stranger** either substantive (*OED sb.*
1–2: an alien or outsider) or adjectival
form with the same meaning

76–7 **transported . . . studies** enraptured
by his studies, especially of magical
(*secret*) matters

78 **Dost . . . me?** Prospero's demands for
Miranda's attention here and later in
87 and 106 need not imply that she is
inattentive; they more likely indicate
Prospero's increasing agitation as he
recalls the circumstances of Antonio's
treachery.

79 having mastered the procedures for
granting favours to suitors; *pèrfected*
should have an accent on the first syllable.

---

68 perfidious –] *Johnson & Steevens;* perfidious: *F, Rowe**; perfidious! *Rowe*   77 rapt] wrap'd
Dryden & Davenant   uncle –] *Rowe³; vncle F;* uncle *Rowe**; Uncle, *Rowe¹*   78 me?] *om. F3*

To trash for overtopping, new created
The creatures that were mine, I say, or changed 'em,
Or else new formed 'em; having both the key
Of officer and office, set all hearts i'th' state
To what tune pleased his ear, that now he was   85
The ivy which had hid my princely trunk
And sucked my verdure out on't. Thou attend'st not!

MIRANDA

    O, good sir, I do.

PROSPERO   I pray thee, mark me.

I thus neglecting worldly ends, all dedicated
To closeness and the bettering of my mind   90
With that which, but by being so retired,
O'er-prized all popular rate, in my false brother
Awaked an evil nature, and my trust,

---

81 **trash for overtopping** put down for being overly ambitious. 'Trash' meant literally to rein in a dog (first occurrence in *OED v.*¹ 1). Steevens also suggested that to trash is to cut away superfluities: 'This word I have met with in books containing directions for gardeners, published in the time of Q. Elizabeth' (Johnson & Steevens, 11). In either case, the verb suggests the effort to keep matters in check. *Overtopping* (contra *OED*) here means to excel or surpass.

    new created Antonio won the loyalty of Prospero's followers by giving them new offices.

82 **creatures** officials appointed by Prospero – i.e. *his* men – but perhaps also meant pejoratively

    changed 'em substituted other people, who would be loyal to Antonio rather than Prospero

82–3 **or . . . Or** either . . . or

83 **new formed 'em** reconstituted the offices and those who held them (first

occurrence in *OED* new-form *v.* 'form or shape anew')

    key Metaphorically, the key both controls the officer and sets the tone of his administration.

86–7 **ivy . . . on't** Prospero employs the common emblem of a vine-covered tree, each plant nourishing the other, but in this instance the ivy extracted the tree's vitality (*verdure*: 'The fresh green colour characteristic of flourishing vegetation' (cited in *OED* 1a)).

88 **mark me** pay attention

90–2 **closeness . . . rate** Prospero's mind was bettered with studies much more valuable than they were estimated (*o'er-prized*, valued too highly, overrated) by the populace, but such studies led him into solitude or seclusion (*closeness*). In effect: 'I was busy with studies more valuable than people rate them, except that they kept me *retired* (away from the people)'. This difficult passage shows Prospero's continuing agitation.

---

81 trash] plash *Hanmer*   84 i'th' state] *om. Pope*   88 O] *om. Pope;* O yes *Capell*   91 that which,] *Pope;* that, which *F*   so] *om. F2*

Like a good parent, did beget of him
A falsehood in its contrary as great   95
As my trust was, which had indeed no limit,
A confidence sans bound. He being thus lorded,
Not only with what my revenue yielded
But what my power might else exact, like one
Who, having into truth by telling of it,   100
Made such a sinner of his memory
To credit his own lie, he did believe
He was indeed the duke, out o'th' substitution
And executing th'outward face of royalty
With all prerogative. Hence his ambition growing –   105
Dost thou hear?

MIRANDA   Your tale, sir, would cure deafness.

PROSPERO

To have no screen between this part he played
And him he played it for, he needs will be
Absolute Milan. Me, poor man, my library

---

96 **trust ... limit** Prospero contends that his boundless trust in his brother, like a parent's trust in a child, was perversely rewarded by a falseness of equal magnitude. Perhaps Shakespeare is alluding to the proverb: 'TRUST is the mother of deceit' (Dent, T555). As Miranda ruefully comments at 120, 'Good wombs have borne bad sons'.

97 **sans bound** without limit, a paraphrase of the previous line. Shakespeare used the French *sans* in *AYL* 2.7.166 and in *LLL* 5.2.415–16.
lorded made lord

98–9 **Not ... exact** having not only the revenue of the office but also the rewards elicited by power

98 **revenue** revènue

100 **having into truth** *Into* is used here in the sense of 'unto' (Warburton) or 'against'. Antonio has sinned against the truth.

100–2 **Who ... lie** By repeated tellings of the lie, Antonio has deluded his memory into believing it. See Var, 36–9.

103 **out o'th' substitution** by virtue of substituting

104 **executing . . . royalty** playing the part of (and giving the appearance of being) a legitimate ruler

105 **prerogative** rights and privileges of office

107–8 **To have . . . for** to eliminate any discrepancy between his role and that of the Duke himself (Prospero), whose part he is playing; or, to blend his own role with the person's for whose benefit he played it – i.e. himself

107 **screen** a means of securing from attack; anything which intervenes obstructively (cited in *OED sb.* 4a)

108–9 **he . . . Milan** He must be absolute sovereign of Milan.

---

95 its] *(it's)*   100 of it,] oft *Oxf (Warburton);* oft' *Hanmer*   103 out o'th'] from *Pope*   105 his] is *F2*   growing –] *Rowe³;* growing: *F, Rowe*;* growing; *Rowe¹*   107 screen] *(Schreene)*

Was dukedom large enough. Of temporal royalties   110
He thinks me now incapable; confederates,
So dry he was for sway, wi'th' King of Naples
To give him annual tribute, do him homage,
Subject his coronet to his crown, and bend
The dukedom yet unbowed (alas, poor Milan)   115
To most ignoble stooping.

MIRANDA   O, the heavens!

PROSPERO

Mark his condition and th'event, then tell me
If this might be a brother.

MIRANDA   I should sin
To think but nobly of my grandmother;
Good wombs have borne bad sons.

PROSPERO   Now the condition.   120
This King of Naples, being an enemy
To me inveterate, hearkens my brother's suit,
Which was that he, in lieu o'th' premises
Of homage, and I know not how much tribute,

---

110 **temporal royalties** secular, as distinct from spiritual, powers
111 **confederates** makes an alliance, conspires
112 **So...sway** so thirsty was he for power
114 **Subject ... crown** *Subject* is here a verb: subjèct. Antonio decided to make his previously independent dukedom (symbolized by a *coronet*) subordinate to the kingdom of Naples (a *crown*).
115 **yet** heretofore
117 **condition** Antonio's terms for confederation with Naples
    th'event the outcome
119 **but** other than
120 **Good . . . sons.** a common proverb: 'Many a good COW has an ill (evil) calf' (Dent, C761). Miranda rejects the possibility that her grandmother committed adultery and conceived Antonio by another man than Prospero's father; instead,

she concludes that good women can still produce bad children. Theobald[1] grudgingly allowed Miranda to keep this line, but in his notes he argued that Shakespeare originally intended it for Prospero: 'How could *Miranda*, that came into this *Desart Island* an Infant, that had never seen any other Creatures of the World, but her Father and *Caliban*, with any Propriety be furnish'd to make such an Observation from Life, that the Issue has often degenerated from the Parent?' (10). Hanmer agreed; in his 1744 edition, he gave this line to Prospero. Both forgot Prospero's efforts to educate his daughter and prepare her for her royal role.
122 **hearkens** hears with attention, pays heed to (cited in *OED v.* 4)
123–4 **in lieu . . . homage** in return for the obligations that homage and tribute carry

---

112 wi'th'] *Rowe;* with *F, Rowe**   116 most] much *F2*   119 but] not *Pope*   120 Good ... sons] *assigned to Prospero / Hanmer (Theobald)*

Should presently extirpate me and mine 125
Out of the dukedom and confer fair Milan,
With all the honours, on my brother. Whereon –
A treacherous army levied – one midnight
Fated to th' purpose did Antonio open
The gates of Milan and i'th' dead of darkness 130
The ministers for th' purpose hurried thence
Me and thy crying self.

MIRANDA   Alack, for pity.
I, not rememb'ring how I cried out then,
Will cry it o'er again. It is a hint
That wrings mine eyes to't.

PROSPERO   Hear a little further, 135
And then I'll bring thee to the present business
Which now's upon's, without the which this story
Were most impertinent.

MIRANDA   Wherefore did they not
That hour destroy us?

PROSPERO   Well demanded, wench:

125 **presently** immediately, without delay (*OED adv.* 3), or, shortly, soon, before long (*OED adv.* 4)
extirpate literally, to pull out by the roots and thus be incapable of regeneration; destroy
129 **Fated** destined by fate (cited in *OED v.* 2). Cf. Helena's observation: 'The fated sky / Gives us free scope, only doth backward pull / Our slow designs when we ourselves are dull' (*AW* 1.1.217–19). Cf. the different use of 'fate' in 180–4 below.
131 **ministers . . . purpose** the agents assigned to this task, which presumably included Gonzalo, coerced by Antonio. Whether Gonzalo was 'Master of this design' (163) from the beginning or only during the final stage – setting the prisoners adrift – depends on how one reads *then* (162).
134 **hint** 'indication intended to be caught by the intelligent; a suggestion or implication conveyed in an indirect or covert manner' (*OED sb.* 2a)
135 **wrings . . . to't** causes my eyes to weep at the tale
137 **upon's** upon us
138 **impertinent** not pertinent, irrelevant
Wherefore why
139 **demanded** asked, as in the French *demander*. It did not carry the modern coercive sense.
wench a young woman and, in Shakespeare's day, a term of endearment, especially for wives and daughters. Petruchio calls Kate a 'wench' in the final scene of *TS* (5.2.180), and Berowne addresses Rosaline the same

127 Whereon –] *this edn;* Whereon *F;* Whereon, *Capell* 128 levied –] *this edn;* leuied, *F* 131 ministers] minister *Rowe* 133 out] on't *Theobald²* 135 to't] (too't) 138 Wherefore] Why *Pope*

My tale provokes that question. Dear, they durst not,   140
So dear the love my people bore me, nor set
A mark so bloody on the business, but
With colours fairer painted their foul ends.
In few, they hurried us aboard a bark,
Bore us some leagues to sea, where they prepared   145
A rotten carcass of a butt, not rigged,
Nor tackle, sail, nor mast – the very rats
Instinctively have quit it. There they hoist us
To cry to th' sea that roared to us, to sigh
To th' winds, whose pity, sighing back again,   150
Did us but loving wrong.

MIRANDA   Alack, what trouble
Was I then to you?

PROSPERO   O, a cherubin
Thou wast that did preserve me. Thou didst smile,
Infused with a fortitude from heaven,

way in *LLL* (5.2.414). The word also
had the very different, pejorative
definition of lower-class or wanton
woman, which later became the standard usage. Most editors assume that
Prospero uses the word benignly. In
the next line he addresses her as *Dear*.
141–2 **set . . . business** A bloody mark
would reveal the treachery.
144 **In few** in a few words; briefly
   bark small sailing vessel. Presumably
   Prospero and Miranda were conveyed
   some miles down river from Milan and
   then put to sea, or the scene's imprecise geography may be akin to the location of a seaport at Verona in *TGV*.
146 **butt** clearly slang for a small, decrepit
   boat but not so recorded in *OED*
   (Dryden & Davenant use 'boat'); literally a tub or cask, usually for storing
   liquids or agricultural produce
147 **Nor . . . mast** neither tackle, nor sail,

nor mast
148 **have quit** had abandoned
   hoist probably used in the sense of
   'launched' (*OED* hoise *v.* 1)
151 **loving wrong** The winds did wrong
   in blowing the ship to sea, but they
   were also full of pity.
   Alack 'An exclamation originally of
   dissatisfaction, reprobation, or depre-
   cation', probably combining 'Ah' or
   'O' with 'lack' – failure, disgrace,
   shame (cited in *OED int.*)
152 **cherubin** obsolete form of cherub
   (angel); spoken to a beautiful or
   beloved woman (cited in *OED* 3b). Cf.
   Shakespeare, *LC* (Riv, 1986), 319:
   'Which like a cherubin above them
   hover'd'.
153 **preserve** Miranda saved him from
   spiritual despair and hence, presumably, from death at sea.
154 **Infused** infusèd

146 butt] boat *Dryden & Davenant*   147 sail] nor sail *F2*   mast –] *Oxf;* mast, *F*   148 have] had
Dryden & Davenant   152 cherubin] cherubim *F4*

When I have decked the sea with drops full salt,   155
Under my burden groaned, which raised in me
An undergoing stomach to bear up
Against what should ensue.

MIRANDA

How came we ashore?

PROSPERO   By providence divine.
Some food we had, and some fresh water, that   160
A noble Neapolitan, Gonzalo,
Out of his charity – who, being then appointed
Master of this design – did give us, with
Rich garments, linens, stuffs and necessaries,
Which since have steaded much; so of his gentleness,   165
Knowing I loved my books, he furnished me
From mine own library with volumes that
I prize above my dukedom.

MIRANDA   Would I might

155 **decked . . . salt** literally, 'adorned', but
equally plausible is 'covered with a deck';
in either case, the point is that Prospero
shed abundant tears. See 'deck' (*OED v.*
4) and 'decked' (*OED ppl. a.* 1). Johnson
suggested 'the original import of the
verb *deck* is, *to cover*; so in some parts
they yet say *deck the table*. This sense
may be borne, but perhaps the poet
wrote *fleck'd*, which I think is still used in
rustic language of drops falling upon
water' (Johnson & Steevens, 14). Malone
argued that 'To *deck*, I am told, signifies
in the North, to *sprinkle*', as one might
treat laundry before ironing (14).

156 **which** refers back to Miranda's smile

157 **An undergoing stomach** a staunch
determination or the courage to perse-
vere, as in 'he has a strong stomach for
such matters'

158 **what** probably used as 'whatever'

159 **divine**. Orgel argues for different

punctuation, stressing the ambiguity
of F's original 'diuine', (Oxf[1], 110), but
since it is incongruous to make *providence divine* responsible for Gonzalo's
generosity as well as Prospero and
Miranda's safe arrival on the island, we
opt for Pope's full stop after *divine*.

164 **stuffs** stores, equipment

165 **steaded much** been very helpful;
'stood us in good stead' (Ard[2], 19)
gentleness like 'gentleman', this word
implied more profound virtue than
does its modern derivative.

166–8 Prospero's love for his books indicates his clear preference for the con-
templative life over the active, a
preference that contributed to the loss
of his dukedom.

167 **volumes** presumably his books on
magic as well as on the liberal arts

168–9 **Would . . . man!** I only (*But*) wish
I might some day see that man.

155 decked] mock'd *Warburton;* brack'd *Hanmer;* fleck'd *Johnson & Steevens (Johnson)*   159
divine.] *Pope;* diuine, *F*   162 charity –] *Dyce;* Charity, *F*   who] *om. Pope*   163 design –] *Dyce;*
designe) *F*   165 much; so] *Ard²;* much, so *F;* much. So *Rowe*

But ever see that man!

PROSPERO   Now I arise.

Sit still and hear the last of our sea-sorrow.   170

Here in this island we arrived, and here

Have I, thy schoolmaster, made thee more profit

Than other princes can that have more time

For vainer hours, and tutors not so careful.

MIRANDA

Heavens thank you for't. And now I pray you, sir,   175

For still 'tis beating in my mind, your reason

For raising this sea-storm?

PROSPERO   Know thus far forth:

By accident most strange, bountiful fortune

(Now, my dear lady) hath mine enemies

Brought to this shore; and by my prescience   180

I find my zenith doth depend upon

A most auspicious star, whose influence

---

169 **Now I arise.** an implied SD, indicating that Prospero gets up from a sitting position, probably to retrieve his magic robe, while Miranda remains seated (170: *Sit still*). But, as Ard² (20) and Oxf¹ (101) point out, the words may also refer to Prospero's fortunes which, after plummeting twelve years earlier in Milan, are now about to rise.

170 **last** the last part, remainder
sea-sorrow Other compounds in the text as noted in Ard² (20) are *sea-change* (1.2.401), *sea-marge* (4.1.69), *sea-storm* (1.2.177), *sea-swallowed* (2.1.251).

172 **made . . . profit** provided a more valuable education

173 *****princes** F's 'Princesse' is a characteristic spelling of 'princes' in Ralph Crane manuscripts; the word is a 'generic term for royal children of either sex' (Oxf¹, 110).

174 **vainer hours** less serious uses of their time

175 **Heavens** pronounced 'Heav'ns'

176 **beating in** exercising the brain (*OED vbl. sb.* 1a), perhaps with a pulsating sensation (*OED vbl. sb.* 5); cf. Claudius' description of Hamlet: 'This something-settled matter in his heart, / Whereon his brains still beating' (*Ham* 3.1.173–4).

177 **thus far forth** to this extent

180 **prescience** prèscience

181 **zenith** highest point in Prospero's fortunes

181–4 **depend . . . droop** Prospero's reading of heavenly signs reflects the magician's reliance on astrology, much as other passages invoke his practice in alchemy.

182 **influence** Prospero must heed the astrological power of the star.

173 princes] *Rowe;* Princesse *F;* Princess, *Rowe*;* princess' *Ard² (Dyce)*   178 fortune] *(Fortune)*
181 zenith] *(Zenith)*

If now I court not, but omit, my fortunes
Will ever after droop. Here cease more questions.
Thou art inclined to sleep; 'tis a good dullness,   185
And give it way. I know thou canst not choose.
[*to Ariel*] Come away, servant, come; I am ready now.
Approach, my Ariel. Come.

Enter ARIEL.

ARIEL

All hail, great master; grave sir, hail! I come
To answer thy best pleasure, be't to fly,   190
To swim, to dive into the fire, to ride
On the curled clouds. To thy strong bidding, task
Ariel and all his quality.

PROSPERO   Hast thou, spirit,
Performed to point the tempest that I bade thee?

ARIEL

To every article.   195
I boarded the King's ship: now on the beak,

---

183 **but omit** and instead (*but*) leave disregarded, take no notice of (*OED* omit *v.* 2c)
185 **dullness** sleepiness
186 **give it way** succumb to it. In the following sentence, Prospero suggests that Miranda cannot choose but to sleep, either because she is so tired or because his magical powers are forcing her to sleep.
187 **Come away** come here
Many editions direct Miranda to sleep here. As Ariel approaches, Prospero slips his magic garment back on. Ariel may enter from aloft or from either side of the stage.
190–2 **fly . . . clouds** Ariel's travels associate him with three of the four classical elements: air, water and fire. Ariel is later associated with the fourth element, earth, in 255–6.
192 **task** set tasks for
193 **quality** skills; or, possibly, as some editions (Ard², 22; Oxf¹, 111) suggest, Ariel's subordinate Spirits who assist his work
194 **to point** 'To the smallest detail; exactly, completely' (cited in *OED* point *sb.*¹ D 6b as the second such use, after *FQ*)
195 **article** clause, item
196 **beak** bow; Johnson suggested that 'The beak was a strong pointed body at the head of the ancient gallies; it is used here for the forecastle, or the boltsprit' (Johnson & Steevens, 16).

184 Here] *(*Heare*)*   187 SD] *this edn*   188.1] *Enter Ariel. Miranda sleeps. / Theobald*   193 quality] qualities *Dryden & Davenant*

Now in the waist, the deck, in every cabin
I flamed amazement. Sometime I'd divide
And burn in many places – on the topmast,
The yards and bowsprit would I flame distinctly,   200
Then meet and join. Jove's lightning, the precursors
O'th' dreadful thunderclaps, more momentary
And sight-outrunning were not; the fire and cracks
Of sulphurous roaring, the most mighty Neptune
Seem to besiege and make his bold waves tremble,   205
Yea, his dread trident shake.

PROSPERO   My brave spirit,
Who was so firm, so constant, that this coil
Would not infect his reason?

ARIEL   Not a soul

197 **waist** middle of the ship or middle part of a ship's upper deck (cited in *OED* 3a)
deck the platform extending from side to side of the ship (*OED sb.*¹ 2a). J. Smith describes the variety of ships' decks in *Sea Grammar*, 5–7.

198 **flamed amazement** flashed causing amazement. Apparently a description of St Elmo's fire, perhaps based on Strachey, 1737. See Introduction, pp. 40–2.

200 **yards** the crossbars on masts to which sails are attached. See J. Smith, *Sea Grammar*, 17–24.
bowsprit F's 'Bore-spritt' is one of several obsolete spellings of this nautical term (J. Smith, *Sea Grammar*, 15–25, spelled it 'Bowle spret', 'Boultspret', 'Boule-spret', 'Boulspret' and 'Bolspret') for the pole that extends from the bow and holds the lower edge of a sail (jib).
distinctly obsolete word for 'In a distinct or separate manner; separately; individually' (cited in *OED adv.* 1)

201 **Jove's lightning** flashes of light, asso-

ciated with punishment or vengeance. Jove, the most powerful god in Roman mythology, cowed his enemies with bolts of lightning. Flashes of light also torture the sinners in 26.47–8 of Dante's *Inferno*: 'Dentro dai fuochi son li spirti; / catun si fascia di quel ch'elli e inceso' ('Within the fires are the spirits: each swathes himself with that which burns him' (vol. 1, 272–3)). Perhaps there is also a reference to the commonplace that we see lightning before we hear thunder (Dent, L281), used in *KJ* 1.1.24–6. Prospero declares that he has appropriated Jove's *own bolt* for his magic in 5.1.46.

203 **sight-outrunning** moving so fast as to disappear from sight

204 **sulphurous** Sulphur was often used in explosive devices; here the adjective suggests how Ariel 'staged' the storm.
Neptune god of the sea in Roman mythology

206 **dread trident** fearful three-pronged spear, Neptune's trademark weapon
brave fine

207 **coil** confusion

197 waist] *(Waste)*   198 Sometime] sometimes *F2*   199 places –] *this edn;* places; *F;* places. *Penguin*   200 bowsprit] *(Bore-spritt);* bolt-sprit *Rowe*   202 O'th'] Of *Pope*
205 Seem] Seem'd *Rowe³*   206 dread] dead *F2*

But felt a fever of the mad and played
Some tricks of desperation. All but mariners   210
Plunged in the foaming brine and quit the vessel;
Then all afire with me, the King's son Ferdinand,
With hair up-staring (then like reeds, not hair),
Was the first man that leapt, cried 'Hell is empty,
And all the devils are here'.

PROSPERO   Why, that's my spirit!   215
But was not this nigh shore?

ARIEL   Close by, my master.

PROSPERO
But are they, Ariel, safe?

ARIEL   Not a hair perished;
On their sustaining garments not a blemish,
But fresher than before; and, as thou bad'st me,
In troops I have dispersed them 'bout the isle.   220

209 **of the mad** of the kind suffered by mad people
209–10 **played . . . desperation** made gestures and performed wild actions expressing despair
210–15 Some productions have used the actions described here, especially Ferdinand's escape from the ship, in staging the conclusion of 1.1.
212 **Then . . . Ferdinand** F's punctuation indicates that Ferdinand is on fire along with the ship; editors since Rowe have argued that such a reading is implausible and insert a colon or semi-colon after *me* to break the clause. Thus *with hair up-staring* (hair standing on end) is unconnected to the fire in the rigging. Still, as Kermode suggests, 'the idea of Ferdinand leaping overboard with flaming hair and fingertips is very attractive' (Ard[2], 23).
215 **devils** pronounced dev'ls
    spirit pronounced as one syllable
218 **sustaining garments** Many editors suggest that 'sustain' is used in a now rare sense (*OED v.* 11a): 'to hold up, bear the weight of, to keep from falling by support from below'. If this is, indeed, what Shakespeare intended, the line suggests that the Neapolitans' garments filled with air and somehow served as life-preservers. See also *Ham* 4.7.175–83, where Ophelia's garments are said to bear her up for a while in the water, but eventually, 'heavy with their drink', they pull her down 'To muddy death'. But 'sustain' may also be taken in another sense (*OED v.* 6a): 'to support life'. The garments are *sustaining* on land in that they protect the Neapolitans from exposure to the sun and weather.
220 **troops** groups of (usually military) people. This should not be taken literally; when Ariel speaks this line, there is one group of survivors – the court party – and three scattered individuals: Ferdinand, Stephano and Trinculo. The last two join forces in 2.1.

209 mad] mind *Dryden & Davenant*   214–15 'Hell . . . here'] *Theobald; no quotation marks F*

The King's son have I landed by himself,
Whom I left cooling of the air with sighs,
In an odd angle of the isle, and sitting,
His arms in this sad knot.

PROSPERO   Of the King's ship,
The mariners, say how thou hast disposed,   225
And all the rest o'th' fleet?

ARIEL   Safely in harbour
Is the King's ship, in the deep nook where once
Thou called'st me up at midnight to fetch dew
From the still-vexed Bermudas; there she's hid,
The mariners all under hatches stowed,   230
Who, with a charm joined to their suffered labour,
I have left asleep. And for the rest o'th' fleet,
Which I dispersed, they all have met again,

---

223 **odd angle** out of the way (*odd*) corner or nook

224 **arms . . . knot** an implied SD for folded or crossed arms. Cf. *JC* 2.1.240, where Portia describes Brutus as 'musing and sighing, with your arms across'. This pose was also associated with the sighing lover: Valentine argues that Proteus must be a lover because he wreathes his 'arms, like a malcontent' in *TGV* 2.1.19–20, and Moth suggests in *LLL* 3.1.18–19 that Armado's position, 'with . . . arms cross'd . . . like a rabbit on a spit', indicates he is in love.

228 **midnight . . . dew** an ingredient for a magical potion; see also 322, *wicked dew*

229 **still-vexed Bermudas** The uninhabited Bermuda islands were first brought to Europe's attention by a Spaniard, Juan de Bermúdez, in 1515 but were dreaded for the hidden reefs and ferocious storms that, nearly a century later, *still vexed* the island. The 'Bermuda triangle' continues to sug-

gest mysterious losses at sea. Strachey, with a touch of hyperbole, called Bermuda 'the dangerous and dreaded . . . Ilands', notorious for 'tempests, thunders, and other fearefull objects . . . seene and heard about them', and known as 'the *Devil's Ilands*' (1737; see Appendix 1.1). After *Sea Venture*'s wreck in 1609, the islands remained virtually uninhabited until 1612. 'The Bermudas' (and variations of that spelling) was also a section of London notorious for harbouring thieves and prostitutes; Ben Jonson implied the Bermudas' nefarious character in *Bartholomew Fair* (6.57–8). The area was apparently named for the islands because they attracted fugitives from justice during the early years of English settlement.

230 **stowed** 'To fasten down (persons) under the hatches for confinement or safety' (cited in *OED v.* 4b)

231 **suffered labour** hard labours performed during the storm (only occurrence in *OED* suffered *ppl. a.*)

229 Bermudas] *Theobald; Bermoothes* F

187

And are upon the Mediterranean float,
Bound sadly home for Naples, 235
Supposing that they saw the King's ship wrecked
And his great person perish.

PROSPERO   Ariel, thy charge
Exactly is performed; but there's more work.
What is the time o'th' day?

ARIEL   Past the mid-season.

PROSPERO
At least two glasses. The time 'twixt six and now 240
Must by us both be spent most preciously.

ARIEL
Is there more toil? Since thou dost give me pains,
Let me remember thee what thou hast promised,
Which is not yet performed me.

PROSPERO   How now? Moody?
What is't thou canst demand?

ARIEL   My liberty. 245

PROSPERO
Before the time be out? No more!

---

234 **Mediterranean float** afloat upon
the Mediterranean or on the waves of
the Mediterranean Sea (*OED* float *sb*.
3a cites this for the second meaning),
but *OED* float *v*. 11a is also plausible:
'Of the tide, to lift up or support on its
surface', as opposed to the ships that
were sunk. A fourth possibility is in the
sense of the Spanish 'flotilla' – that the
ships were reunited into a small fleet.
Some editors have suggested an emendation to 'flood': 'a body of flowing
water' (*OED sb*. 2).

239 **mid-season** noon

240 **At . . . glasses** 2 p.m., i.e. two hour
glasses past midday, although sailors at
the time usually used half-hour glasses
(J. Smith, *Sea Grammar*, 38). Prospero
amplifies Ariel's *Past the mid-season*,
declaring that the time is now 2 p.m.,
and the action must end by 6 p.m.,

thereby maintaining the unity of time.
See Introduction, pp. 14–16, and the
reference to *glasses* at 5.1.223: 'three
glasses since we gave out split'.

241 **preciously** valuably, now obsolete
(cited in *OED adv*. 2)

243 **remember** remind

243–4 **promised . . . performed** This
may be an allusion to the proverbial
expression, 'Great PROMISE small
performance' (Dent, P602).

244 **Moody** angry, ill-humoured. Prospero's query suggests that Ariel is
palpably impatient to be free.

246 **time** Ariel is Prospero's indentured
servant, under an oral agreement to
work for a fixed period, though in the
following lines Ariel suggests that the
magician had offered him a one-year
reduction in return for services rendered.

ARIEL   I prithee

Remember I have done thee worthy service,
Told thee no lies, made thee no mistakings, served
Without or grudge or grumblings. Thou did promise
To bate me a full year.

PROSPERO   Dost thou forget   250
From what a torment I did free thee?

ARIEL   No.

PROSPERO

Thou dost, and think'st it much to tread the ooze
Of the salt deep,
To run upon the sharp wind of the north,
To do me business in the veins o'th' earth   255
When it is baked with frost.

ARIEL   I do not, sir.

PROSPERO

Thou liest, malignant thing; hast thou forgot
The foul witch Sycorax, who with age and envy
Was grown into a hoop? Hast thou forgot her?

ARIEL   No, sir.

PROSPERO

Thou hast! Where was she born? Speak; tell me.   260

---

250 **bate** reduce (abate) the length of his
  servitude
252–6 **tread . . . frost** Prospero accuses
  Ariel of exaggerating his chores: to
  walk on the muck of the ocean floor, to
  be buffeted by cold north winds, to
  labour in the frozen ground. These
  descriptions suggest Ariel's wide-
  ranging action in contrast to his earlier
  immobility in a pine tree (see 269–80
  below).
256 **baked with frost** hardened by the
  cold
258 **Sycorax** The origins of this name are
  uncertain. Unique to Shakespeare, it
  may be derived from the Greek words

for sow (*sus*) and raven (*korax*). Both
animals are associated with witchcraft;
Medea was known as the Scythian
raven, and Circe the sorceress turned
Odysseus' men into pigs. The witches
Circe and Medea were associated with
Colchis, home of the Coraxi tribe.
Prospero's contempt for Sycorax's
witchcraft may reflect his anxiety
about his own magical powers, which
he used to counteract her spells (see
291–3 below and n.).
envy malice
259 **hoop** a circular band or ring of metal
  (*OED sb.* 1a). Sycorax is bent over with
  age.

248 ²thee] *om. Rowe³*

189

ARIEL

Sir, in Algiers.

PROSPERO   O, was she so? I must

Once in a month recount what thou hast been,

Which thou forget'st. This damned witch Sycorax,

For mischiefs manifold and sorceries terrible

To enter human hearing, from Algiers,   265

Thou knowst, was banished. For one thing she did

They would not take her life; is not this true?

ARIEL   Ay, sir.

PROSPERO

This blue-eyed hag was hither brought with child,

And here was left by th' sailors. Thou, my slave,   270

---

261 **Algiers** In Shakespeare's era (and
therefore in F), the placename was
Argier, pronounced Argièr.
  O, was she so? Prospero is perhaps
being sarcastic here, but as Orgel
(Oxf[1], 115) notes, his knowledge of
Sycorax is not first-hand but derived
from Ariel's accounts.

265 **human** F's 'humane' suggests feelings of compassion in addition to the
fact of being human. In Shakespeare's
time these spellings and 'humain(e)'
were interchangeable.

266 **For ... did** Debate over the *one thing*
has flourished. Charles Lamb quoted
John Ogilby's 'accurate description of
Africa' (1670) to argue that Shakespeare was drawing on the legend of an
Algerian witch who saved the city
when it was besieged by Charles V's
navy in 1541; she put a curse on the
fleet, raising a furious storm that drove
the ships away (*Critical Essays* (London, 1903), 70–2). Most twentieth-
century editors acknowledge that
Sycorax's pregnancy (269 below), by
the laws and conventions of the time,
would have prevented her execution.
Cf. *1H6* 5.4.62–85, where Joan claims

to be pregnant in order to avoid execution. Older theories are set forth in
Var, 60–1.

269 **blue-eyed hag** witch with blue eyes.
Twentieth-century editors have traditionally argued that the eye colour is
meant pejoratively and probably refers
to blue eyelids (Ard[2], 27) or pregnancy, as in Webster's *The Duchess of
Malfi* (1623), 2.1.67, where the pregnant Duchess is described: 'The fins of
her eyelids look most teeming blue'.
Leah Marcus contends that the sobri-
quet is far more problematic. In the
aftermath of the nineteenth century's
racial Darwinism, blue eyes became
associated with people of Anglo-Saxon
heritage. As an Algerian witch,
Sycorax did not fit the stereotype, and
commentators accordingly found
alternative explanations for the colour
of her eyes (see Marcus, 5–17).
Despite the prejudices that may have
shaped earlier assumptions, the words
are Prospero's, and his angry speech
should probably be read in its most
negative sense.

270–1 **Thou ... thyself** Ariel's apparent
protest that he is Prospero's *slave*

261+ Algiers] *Oxf; Argier F*   264 terrible] too terrible *Dryden & Davenant*   265 human] *(humane)*

As thou report'st thyself, was then her servant,
And – for thou wast a spirit too delicate
To act her earthy and abhorred commands,
Refusing her grand hests – she did confine thee,
By help of her more potent ministers   275
And in her most unmitigable rage,
Into a cloven pine, within which rift
Imprisoned thou didst painfully remain
A dozen years, within which space she died
And left thee there, where thou didst vent thy groans   280
As fast as millwheels strike. Then was this island
(Save for the son that she did litter here,
A freckled whelp, hag-born) not honoured with
A human shape.

ARIEL   Yes, Caliban, her son.

echoes a common complaint of servants in Shakespeare's time; Prospero
mocks the contention.
272 **for** because
   spirit probably monosyllabic
   delicate fine or exquisite in quality or
   nature (cited in *OED a.* 6b)
273 **act** carry out, perform (first occurrence in *OED v.* 3)
   earthy bestial, as opposed to Ariel's
   spiritual quality
274 **hests** behests, requests
275 **ministers** agents; presumably,
   Sycorax's servants disappeared with
   her death, their potency no longer
   effective.
276 **unmitigable** with no possibility of
   softening or lessening (first occurrence
   in *OED*)
277 **cloven pine** See *FQ*, 1.2.33, where
   Fradubio is confined in a tree.
279 This line establishes much of the
   play's chronology. If Sycorax imprisoned Ariel for twelve years before
   Prospero and Miranda (then aged
   three) arrived, and assuming that
   Caliban was born soon after Sycorax
   came to the island (see 269–70), he was

at least twelve years old when they
landed and twenty-four when the play
takes place.
281 **millwheels strike** i.e. as frequently
   as each blade of a millwheel hits the
   water
281–4 This sentence establishes Caliban's
   human physique; see Vaughan,
   Caliban, 9–12.
282 *she . . . here** give birth to, using a
   term usually applied to animal births
   to demean Sycorax and Caliban, as
   does *freckled whelp* (i.e. puppy). F's
   'he' has, beginning with Dryden &
   Davenant, almost always been emended to *she* to be consistent with all
   other references to Sycorax. Jonathan
   Goldberg, however, suggests that F's
   'he' conveys intentional sexual ambiguity, a theme that Goldberg (105–28)
   also finds elsewhere in the play.
283 **whelp** 'the young of the dog', here
   applied 'deprecatingly to the offspring
   of a noxious creature'; 'son of a bitch'
   (cited in *OED sb.*[1] 3a)
284 **Yes . . . son.** Ariel confirms that
   Caliban was left on the island, 'A
   freckled whelp, hag-born'.

273 earthy] earthly *Rowe*[2]   274 hests –] *this edn;* hests, F   282 she] *Dryden & Davenant;* he F

PROSPERO

    Dull thing, I say so – he, that Caliban,   285

    Whom now I keep in service. Thou best knowst

    What torment I did find thee in: thy groans

    Did make wolves howl and penetrate the breasts

    Of ever-angry bears. It was a torment

    To lay upon the damned, which Sycorax   290

    Could not again undo. It was mine art,

    When I arrived and heard thee, that made gape

    The pine and let thee out.

ARIEL   I thank thee, master.

PROSPERO

    If thou more murmur'st, I will rend an oak

    And peg thee in his knotty entrails till   295

    Thou hast howled away twelve winters.

ARIEL   Pardon, master,

    I will be correspondent to command

    And do my spriting gently.

PROSPERO

    Do so, and after two days

    I will discharge thee.

ARIEL   That's my noble master.   300

---

285 **Dull . . . so** Prospero continues to chide Ariel for the spirit's impatience to be free, although the line might conceivably be read as a reference to Caliban: '*he*'s a dull thing, I say, that Caliban'. In either case, Prospero is annoyed at Ariel's interruption.

286 **in service** Prospero holds Caliban as a servant (cited in *OED* service *sb.*[1] 1), though in this case Caliban is an entirely unfree servant – i.e. a slave. See 2.1.152n.

287–9 **thy groans . . . bears** Ariel's agony aroused sympathy even in wolves and bears. In a similar scene in canto 13 of the *Inferno*, when the pilgrim Dante plucks a thornbush, the soul lost within it cries out in blood and anguish (Dante, 13.31–151).

291–3 **Could . . . out** Prospero contends (presumably on Ariel's testimony) that Sycorax, having imprisoned Ariel in the cloven pine, could not counteract the spell. Prospero asserts that his own superior magic did so.

295 **peg . . . entrails** fasten you with a peg in its (*his*) gnarled inner parts

297 **correspondent** responsive, compliant, submissive (cited in *OED a.* 3)

298 **gently** slowly, softly; in a quiet, moderate or subdued fashion (*OED adv.* 2)

---

285 so –] *this edn;* so: *F;* so; *Capell;* so! *Penguin*   295 peg thee] *(*peg-thee*)*

What shall I do? Say what? What shall I do?

PROSPERO

    Go make thyself like a nymph o'th' sea;

    Be subject to no sight but thine and mine, invisible

    To every eyeball else. Go take this shape

    And hither come in't. Go! Hence with diligence.   305

                                         Exit [Ariel].

    [*to Miranda*] Awake, dear heart, awake; thou hast slept

       well.

    Awake.

MIRANDA   The strangeness of your story put

    Heaviness in me.

PROSPERO   Shake it off. Come on,

    We'll visit Caliban, my slave, who never

    Yields us kind answer.

MIRANDA   'Tis a villain, sir,   310

    I do not love to look on.

PROSPERO   But as 'tis,

    We cannot miss him; he does make our fire,

    Fetch in our wood, and serves in offices

    That profit us. – What ho, slave! Caliban,

---

301 **shall** in the sense of 'must'

303 **invisible** Prospero hands Ariel some kind of robe or costume (*this shape*) that suggests a sea-nymph. *Henslowe's Diary* (Cambridge, 1961, 325) lists 'a robe for to goo invisibell' in the inventory of the Admiral's Men, but as Sturgess contends, Ariel's sea-nymph costume is somewhat different, making him/her blend in with the marine atmosphere of the play in performance (87). After this speech, the audience knows that whenever it sees Ariel in this garment, the spirit is meant to be invisible to all the characters on stage except Prospero.

308 **Heaviness** sleepiness

309 **visit Caliban** Ard[2] (29) and Oxf[1] (118) suggest that Caliban's cave was located at the rear of the stage in the discovery space. In many modern productions, he rises from a trap door down stage centre. Locating Caliban's cave below underscores his opposition to Ariel, who can enter from aloft, but it can also suggest his status as a slave who sleeps, as it were, below ground.

310 **villain** in the original sense of a low-born person or servant

312 **miss** do without

313 **serves in offices** performs duties

302 like] like to *F2*   303 thine and] *om. Rowe[3]*   305 Go!] *Signet;* goe: *F*   Hence . . . diligence] *Pope; F lines* hence / diligence.   SD] *Rowe; Exit. F*   306 SD] *Oxf[1]*   310–11 'Tis . . . on] *one line in F*   312 does] *(do's)*   313 serves in] serves *F2;* serve *Dryden & Davenant*

Thou earth, thou: speak!

CALIBAN [*within*]   There's wood enough within.   315

PROSPERO

Come forth I say, there's other business for thee.
Come, thou tortoise, when?

Enter ARIEL, *like a water nymph.*

Fine apparition, my quaint Ariel,
Hark in thine ear.

ARIEL   My lord, it shall be done.   *Exit.*

PROSPERO

Thou poisonous slave, got by the devil himself   320
Upon thy wicked dam; come forth!

Enter CALIBAN.

CALIBAN

As wicked dew as e'er my mother brushed

---

315 **Thou earth** Prospero again emphasizes Caliban's earthiness (cf. 274 and n.), in contrast to Ariel's spirituality. See Introduction, pp. 28–30.

317 **thou tortoise** This epithet has induced some editors, critics and artists to visualize Caliban as a giant turtle (see the discussion in Vaughan, *Caliban*, 13, 76, 223–4), but the epithet's context and the subsequent *when* leave no doubt that Prospero is responding to Caliban's dilatoriness.
when? 'When will you get here?' or, more imperatively, 'get a move on'. See *R2* 1.1.162: 'When, Harry? when?'

317.1 Ariel is wearing the costume Prospero had given him earlier, signifying to the audience that Ariel is invisible to Miranda.

318 **Fine** 'Exquisitely fashioned; delicately beautiful' (cited in *OED a.* 6a)
quaint clever, skilful. See *TS* 3.2.145–7: 'We'll overreach . . . / The quaint musician'.

320 **got . . . himself** In the Jacobean play, *The Birth of Merlin*, the devil (who is described as having 'a face like a Frying-Pan') claims Merlin for his son. Although Merlin does not seem to have inherited his father's blackness, the magician's resonance with Caliban (both are sons of the devil) may suggest a dark hue for Shakespeare's monster. See Udall, 50–5. Prospero's knowledge of Caliban's paternity could only have come from Ariel or Caliban, neither of whom had first-hand information. In any case, the line indicates Prospero's animus towards Caliban.

322–4 **As . . . both.** Prospero had earlier sent Ariel to Bermuda for dew to use in his magic; Caliban now wishes some for his bag of tricks, in this case *wicked* (offensive, foul: cited in *OED a.* 2b) dew from swampy ground. Ravens were commonly associated with witchcraft. See 258n.

With raven's feather from unwholesome fen
Drop on you both. A southwest blow on ye
And blister you all o'er.   325

PROSPERO

For this, be sure, tonight thou shalt have cramps,
Side-stitches, that shall pen thy breath up; urchins
Shall forth at vast of night that they may work
All exercise on thee; thou shalt be pinched
As thick as honeycomb, each pinch more stinging   330
Than bees that made 'em.

CALIBAN   I must eat my dinner.

This island's mine by Sycorax, my mother,
Which thou tak'st from me. When thou cam'st first
Thou strok'st me and made much of me; wouldst give
        me
Water with berries in't, and teach me how   335

324 **southwest** Winds from the south-west often brought warm, damp air, with implications of unhealthiness. Cf. *Cor.* 1.4.30: 'All the contagion of the south light on you'.
325 **blister** i.e. cause infectious lesions
327 **Side-stitches** pains between the shoulders and hips (first occurrence in *OED* side *sb.*[1] 22)
   pen ... up stop your breath
   urchins spirits assuming the shape of hedgehogs; cf. Mrs Page's call for children to dress 'Like urchins' in *MW* 4.4.50.
328 *****forth at** F's syntax is faulty here, but many editors leave it unremarked. Dryden & Davenant solve the problem by substituting 'Urchins shall prick thee 'till thou bleed'st'. Thomas White first emended the spacing to read 'forth at': '*Urchins ... shall ... go forth* [*at vast of night*] *and work all exercise on thee*' (Var, 70). Though this reading has been rejected by many twentieth-century editors, it nicely resolves an ambiguous line and is adopted in Oxf,

Bantam and Folg[2].
   vast of night 'The *vast of night* means the night which is naturally empty and deserted, without action' (Johnson & Steevens, 24).
329 **exercise** perform, practise (cited in *OED v.* 6b as obsolete)
329–30 **pinched ... honeycomb** pinched as densely as bee cells in a honeycomb, which are formed by a sort of pinching
330 **thick** frequently, as in 'thick and fast' (*OED adv.* 3)
332 Caliban here makes his claim to the island on the grounds of inheritance, which many editors and critics (e.g. Oxf[1], 119) have assumed would be invalid were Caliban illegitimate. Yet, as the only human on the island at the time of Sycorax's death, he perforce would possess it regardless of legitimacy.
334 **strok'st** properly 'strok'd'st', which is difficult to pronounce, although Rowe emended to it
335 **Water with berries** Some editors suggest that this line is adapted from Strachey's account of Bermuda (see

328 forth at] *Oxf (R.G. White)*; for that *F*   vast] waste *Rowe[1]*

To name the bigger light and how the less
That burn by day and night. And then I loved thee
And showed thee all the qualities o'th' isle:
The fresh springs, brine pits, barren place and fertile.
Cursed be I that did so! All the charms   340
Of Sycorax – toads, beetles, bats – light on you,
For I am all the subjects that you have,
Which first was mine own king; and here you sty me
In this hard rock, whiles you do keep from me
The rest o'th' island.

PROSPERO   Thou most lying slave,   345
Whom stripes may move, not kindness; I have used thee
(Filth as thou art) with humane care and lodged thee
In mine own cell, till thou didst seek to violate
The honour of my child.

Appendix 1.1), where the shipwrecked
Englishmen discovered that cedar
berries, 'seething, straining, and
letting stand some three or foure
daies, made a kind of pleasant drinke'
(1739). Another possibility is that
berries refers to 'grapes', a synonym for
berries, especially in Old English
(*OED sb.* 1a). If so, Prospero's wine
was apparently weaker and less intoxi-
cating than the sack in Stephano's
butt, unless the local drink was used up
many years earlier and Caliban only
dimly remembers its wonders (Bate,
Genius, 246).
336–7 **the bigger . . . night** Prospero
drew his elementary astronomy lesson
from Genesis, 1.16 (Geneva Bible),
which reports God's creation of
'greater' and 'lesser' lights – the sun
and moon.
338 **qualities** characteristics

340 **Cursed** Cursèd
charms spells or incantations
341 **you** Byrne explains the shift here
from 'thou' to 'you': 'Caliban uses
course, rough *thou* to Prospero, but *you*
in anger and cursing' (138).
343 **sty** confine or pen up, as in a pig sty
(first occurrence in *OED v.*[2] 1b)
346 **stripes** strokes of the whip
move influence, prompt
347 **humane** 'Human' and 'humane'
were interchangeable spellings in
Shakespeare's time (see 265n.). We
concur with several recent editions
(Oxf[1], Bantam, Folg[2]) which choose
F's 'humane' to stress Prospero's
compassionate care. Modernizing to
'human', as some editors do, emphasizes Prospero's humanity as opposed
to Caliban's bestiality, a reading
that privileges the magus over his
slave.

340 I . . . so] I that I did so *F2*   341 Sycorax –] *Signet; Sycorax: F; Sycorax; / Rowe; Sycorax, /*
Pope   bats –] *this edn;* Batts *F;* bats, *Pope*   343 Which] I *Dryden & Davenant;* Who *Pope*
mine] *(min)*   sty me] *(sty-me)*   347 humane] human *F4*   thee] *om. F4*   3

CALIBAN

    O ho, O ho! Would't had been done;   350

    Thou didst prevent me, I had peopled else

    This isle with Calibans.

MIRANDA   Abhorred slave,

    Which any print of goodness wilt not take,

    Being capable of all ill; I pitied thee,

    Took pains to make thee speak, taught thee each hour   355

    One thing or other. When thou didst not, savage,

    Know thine own meaning, but wouldst gabble like

    A thing most brutish, I endowed thy purposes

    With words that made them known. But thy vile race

    (Though thou didst learn) had that in't which good

       natures   360

    Could not abide to be with; therefore wast thou

    Deservedly confined into this rock,

---

350 **Would't . . . done** Although some critics have recently suggested that the attempted violation was Prospero's fabrication, Caliban here defiantly admits it.

351 'had you not prevented me, I would have populated'

352–63 From Dryden to the early twentieth century, editors generally reassigned this speech from Miranda to Prospero on the grounds of decorum. See Introduction, pp. 135–6.

352 **Abhorred** Abhorrèd

353 **print** imprint. One of the signs of barbarism in Shakespeare's day was thought to be the inability to absorb virtue as well as information. Miranda here consigns Caliban to the ranks of the morally ineducable.

356–9 Miranda implies that whatever Caliban's native language was, to her ears it was simply brutish gabbling that Caliban himself couldn't understand. For discussion of the role of language

in Europe's colonization of the New World, see Greenblatt, 16–39.

359 **thy vile race** in effect, creatures of your kind who share your diabolical nature. 'Race' had a wide range of meanings in the seventeenth century and did not necessarily connote systematic and legal categories as it would later. Steevens suggested '*Race*, in this place, seems to signify original disposition, inborn qualities' (Johnson & Steevens, 26, and *OED* race *sb.*² 7, which cites this occurrence as meaning 'natural or inherited disposition'); however, if we think of Caliban as African, the term resonates strongly with modern audiences who then see Miranda's contempt for a dark-hued slave as predictive of modern racism. See Introduction, pp. 48–51.

362 **rock** implies that Caliban lives in a cave. See 309n. In *The Birth of Merlin*, Merlin confines his devil-father in a rock (Udall, 176–7).

---

351 Would't] I wou'd it *Pope*   352 SP] PROSPERO *Dryden & Davenant, Theobald*   359 vile] *(vild):* wild *Dryden & Davenant*

Who hadst deserved more than a prison.

CALIBAN

You taught me language, and my profit on't
Is I know how to curse. The red plague rid you   365
For learning me your language.

PROSPERO   Hag-seed, hence:

Fetch us in fuel, and be quick – thou'rt best –
To answer other business. Shrug'st thou, malice?
If thou neglect'st, or dost unwillingly
What I command, I'll rack thee with old cramps,   370
Fill all thy bones with aches, make thee roar,
That beasts shall tremble at thy din.

CALIBAN   No, pray thee.

[*aside*] I must obey; his art is of such power
It would control my dam's god Setebos,   374
And make a vassal of him.

PROSPERO   So, slave, hence.   *Exit Caliban.*

---

363 **more . . . prison** i.e. a worse punishment than imprisonment
364–6 See 356–9 and n.
366 **red plague** *The General Practice of
Physic* (London, 1605) identified red,
black and yellow sores caused by
plague (675). 'Red' was applied to various diseases marked by 'evacuation of
blood or cutaneous eruptions' (cited in
OED 16b). Johnson suggested that
the red plague came 'from the red-
ness of the body universally inflamed'
(Johnson & Steevens, 27). See also
Var, 75.
366 **learning** teaching
   Hag-seed the offspring of a hag
367 **thou'rt best** you are advised to
368 **answer other business** do other
work

370 **rack** affect with severe pain, as by
torture
   old cramps either cramps of old age
or, perhaps, more of the same cramps
that Caliban has suffered already
371 **aches** originally pronounced with
two syllables, soft 'ch', and a soft 'e' –
'aitches'; cf. *AC* 4.7.7–8, where Scarus
puns: 'I had a wound here that was like
a T, / But now 'tis made an H'.
372 **That . . . din** so loudly that beasts will
tremble
374 **Setebos** a Patagonian god, mentioned in Antonio Pigafetta's narrative
of a voyage to Patagonia in 1519, published in 1526. It first appeared in
English in Eden, 219ᵛ. See Introduction, pp. 40–1.

---

363 Who . . . prison] *Theobald; F lines* hadst / prison.; *om. Pope*   367 quick –] *this edn;* quicke *F;*
quick, *F4*   thou'rt] thou wer't *Rowe*   best –] *this edn;* best *F;* best) *Pope;* best, *Capell*   373 SD]
Ard¹

Enter FERDINAND[,] *and* ARIEL, *invisible, playing*
and singing.

ARIEL [*Sings.*]

    Come unto these yellow sands,
      And then take hands;
    Curtsied when you have, and kissed
      The wild waves whist;
    Foot it featly here and there,   380
    And sweet sprites bear
      The burden.

                      (*burden dispersedly*)

SPIRITS   Hark, hark! Bow-wow,
             The watch dogs bark, bow-wow.
ARIEL   Hark hark, I hear,   385
             The strain of strutting chanticleer
             Cry cock a diddle dow.

375.1 *invisible* Prospero has already (301–4) told Ariel to be invisible to everyone else, thus informing the audience that Ferdinand will not see Ariel. The sea-nymph costume serves as a reminder of his invisibility. Cf. 302 and 317.1.

playing Oxf[1] (121) suggests that Ariel plays a lute.

376 **yellow sands** perhaps suggested by Virgil's *Aeneid*. In the Elysian fields Aeneas finds that 'Some disport their limbs on the grassy wrestling-ground, vie in sports, and grapple on the yellow sand' ('*fulva . . . harena*' (*Aeneid*, Bk 6, 640–4)). Cf. *MND* 2.1.126, where Titania recalls sitting 'on Neptune's yellow sands'.

378–9 **kissed . . . whist** The song tells the dancers to kiss each other until the waves grow silent or, perhaps, to kiss the waves to silence. It was customary at country dances for couples to kiss at certain measures. *OED a.* 1 uses this line to illustrate the archaic meaning of

whist: 'silent, quiet, still, hushed; making no sound; free from noise or disturbance'. See Var, 78–9, and Oxf[1] (122). Long concludes that this 'music calms the storm', which had continued in the background until this point (99).

380 **Foot it featly** dance skilfully, gracefully (*OED* 2b). Cf. *WT* 4.4.176: 'She dances featly'.

382 SD **burden dispersedly** a refrain or chorus that is sung from various positions around the stage, or perhaps from beneath, but not in unison. From Capell on, many editors have made the sounds of dogs barking the only chorus, but Noble argues persuasively that 383–4 form a refrain (105).

383 SP *Ariel is accompanied in the chorus by his fellow Spirits. Otherwise F's inclusion of the ARIEL SP – calling for Ariel to sing solo in 385 – makes no sense. See Noble, 105–6.

386 **strain . . . chanticleer** song of a rooster, as in Chaucer's *Nun's Priest's Tale*

376 SD] *Oxf[1]; Ariel* Song *F; Ariel's* Song *F3*   381–2 bear / The burden] *one line in* Pope   383–4]
this edn; F lines barke, / bowgh-wawgh. /   385–7] *Rowe[3]; F lines* Chanticlere / dowe. /

FERDINAND

    Where should this music be? I'th' air, or th'earth?

    It sounds no more, and sure it waits upon

    Some god o'th' island. Sitting on a bank,   390

    Weeping again the King my father's wreck,

    This music crept by me upon the waters,

    Allaying both their fury and my passion

    With its sweet air. Thence I have followed it

    (Or it hath drawn me, rather) but 'tis gone.   395

    No, it begins again.

ARIEL [*Sings.*]

        Full fathom five thy father lies,

        Of his bones are coral made;

        Those are pearls that were his eyes,

        Nothing of him that doth fade   400

        But doth suffer a sea–change

        Into something rich and strange.

        Sea nymphs hourly ring his knell.

SPIRITS   Ding dong.

ARIEL   Hark, now I hear them.

SPIRITS   Ding dong bell.   405

FERDINAND

    The ditty does remember my drowned father;

    This is no mortal business nor no sound

    That the earth owes. I hear it now above me.

389 **waits upon** attends
393 **passion** deeply felt grief; suffering
394 **air** tune
    Thence from that place
397 **Full fathom five** five fathoms (30 feet) by nautical measurement. The earliest setting of this song by Robert Johnson dates from 1613. See Introduction, p. 19 and Fig. 3.
400 **fade** decay, decompose (*OED v.* 2)

401 **suffer** undergo
404 SP *Ariel's fellow Spirits join in the chorus. See 383n.
406 **ditty does remember** song commemorates
407 **no . . . business** a supernatural event
408 **owes** owns
    I . . . me. Perhaps, as Orgel suggests, music comes from a consort in the upper gallery (Oxf[1], 123).

388 I'th . . . th'earth] in air, or earth *Pope;* i'th'air or the 'arth *Ard[2]* 390 island.] *Pope;* Iland, *F*
391 again] against *F3* 397 SD] *Oxf[1]; Ariell* Song *F; Ariel's* Song *F3* 404 SP] *Oxf; not in F*
Ding dong] *Oxf;* Burthen: ding dong *F; Burthen (within):* Ding-Dong *Riv* 405 Hark . . . / Ding
dong bell] *as Oxf; one line F* Ding dong bell] *(within)* Ding-dong bell. *Oxf*

PROSPERO [*to Miranda*]

    The fringèd curtains of thine eye advance,

    And say what thou seest yond.

MIRANDA   What is't, a spirit?   410

    Lord, how it looks about. Believe me, sir,

    It carries a brave form. But 'tis a spirit.

PROSPERO

    No, wench, it eats and sleeps and hath such senses

    As we have – such. This gallant which thou seest

    Was in the wreck, and but he's something stained   415

    With grief (that's beauty's canker) thou mightst call him

    A goodly person. He hath lost his fellows

    And strays about to find 'em.

MIRANDA   I might call him

    A thing divine, for nothing natural

    I ever saw so noble.

PROSPERO [*aside*]   It goes on, I see,   420

    As my soul prompts it. [*to Ariel*] Spirit, fine spirit,

      I'll free thee

    Within two days for this.

FERDINAND   Most sure the goddess

---

409 **fringèd . . . advance** (fringèd); eyes
with fringes (a metaphor for eyelashes)
that are raised or lifted up (cited in
OED advance *v.* 9)

410 **yond** over there, yonder

412 **carries . . . form** has a handsome
shape
But it has to be, alas

413 **wench** See 139n.

414 **gallant** pronounced gàllant; fine,
attractive gentleman, here meant playfully, perhaps ironically

415 **but** except that
something somewhat

416 **canker** The cankerworm feeds on
shrubs and trees, slowly destroying the
buds; a glancing reference to the
proverb, 'The CANKER soonest eats

the fairest rose' (Dent, C56). The
metaphor compares grief to a cancer
that eats away at a flower (*beauty*). Cf.
TN 2.4.110–15, where Viola reports
how concealed love destroys beauty
'like a worm i'th' bud'.

417 **goodly** handsome

421 **soul prompts** intellectual or spiritual power, distinguished from physical (*OED* soul *sb.* 3b), that inspires or
directs (*prompts*)
Spirit perhaps monosyllabic

422 **Most . . . goddess** a paraphrase of
Virgil's 'O dea certe' from the *Aeneid*,
where Aeneas encounters his mother
Venus. When he asks if she is a goddess, Venus replies, 'Nay, I claim not
such worship' (Bk 1, 328–35).

409 SD] *Oxf*   410 What . . . a] *Rowe;* What is't a *F;* What is't? *A Capell;* What, is't a *Riv*
420 SD] *Pope*   421 SD] *Oxf*

On whom these airs attend! – Vouchsafe my prayer
May know if you remain upon this island,
And that you will some good instruction give   425
How I may bear me here. My prime request,
Which I do last pronounce, is (O, you wonder!)
If you be maid or no?

MIRANDA   No wonder, sir,
But certainly a maid.

FERDINAND   My language? Heavens!
I am the best of them that speak this speech,   430
Were I but where 'tis spoken.

PROSPERO   How? The best?
What wert thou if the King of Naples heard thee?

FERDINAND
A single thing, as I am now, that wonders
To hear thee speak of Naples. He does hear me,
And that he does, I weep. Myself am Naples,   435
Who, with mine eyes, never since at ebb, beheld
The King my father wrecked.

MIRANDA   Alack, for mercy!

FERDINAND
Yes, faith, and all his lords – the Duke of Milan

423 **on . . . attend** for whom these songs
are played
Vouchsafe grant
424 **remain** dwell (*OED v.* 4b)
426 **bear me** comport myself, behave
(*OED v.*[1] 4)
427 **wonder** a play on Miranda's name
from the Latin verb *miror*: to wonder,
be astonished at. See List of Roles n.
14.
429 **maid** a human (not goddess); an
unmarried woman; a virgin. Shakespeare may have been alluding to *FQ*,
3.5.35–6, where Spenser records the
meeting between Timias and Bel-
phoebe: 'Angell, or Goddesse, do I call
thee right? . . . Therat she blushing

said, Ah! gentle Squire, / Nor
Goddesse I, nor Angell, but the Mayd,
/ And daughter of a woody Nymphe'.
430 **best** highest in rank. Ferdinand
assumes that his father drowned.
433 **single** one and the same person as the
King of Naples. The word also resonates with Ferdinand's bereavement:
he is 'Unaccompanied or unsupported
by others' (*OED a.* 1); 'standing alone'
as the unique ruler of Naples (*OED a.*
7); as well as a bachelor (*OED a.* 8a).
434 **He . . . me** 'I, being the King of
Naples, hear myself.'
436 **at ebb** at low tide; i.e. without tears
437 **for mercy** 'may God have mercy!'

428 maid] *F3*; (Mayd*); made *F4*   438 lords –] *Cam*[1]*; Lords, *F*; Lords; *Rowe*[3]*; lords: *Theobald*

And his brave son being twain.

PROSPERO [*aside*]   The Duke of Milan
And his more braver daughter could control thee   440
If now 'twere fit to do't. At the first sight
They have changed eyes. [*to Ariel*] Delicate Ariel,
I'll set thee free for this. [*to Ferdinand*] A word, good sir;
I fear you have done yourself some wrong. A word.

MIRANDA [*aside*]

Why speaks my father so ungently? This   445
Is the third man that e'er I saw, the first
That e'er I sighed for. Pity move my father
To be inclined my way.

FERDINAND   O, if a virgin,
And your affection not gone forth, I'll make you
The Queen of Naples.

PROSPERO   Soft, sir, one word more.   450

---

439 **his brave son** The Duke's (Antonio's) son is mentioned nowhere else in *Tem*; critics have variously explained this oddity, usually by assuming that Shakespeare originally intended to develop the character but later decided against it and neglected to adjust this line. Alonso makes clear in the next scene that he intended Ferdinand to inherit both Milan and Naples (2.1.112–13). Similarly, one of Prospero's central goals is to ensure that his grandchildren inherit the thrones of both Milan and Naples; in either case, Antonio's son is alienated from the succession (Kastan, 96). See also Var, 86–7.

twain two of them (cited in *OED adj.* B 2a)

440 **more braver** The adjective *more* is added to the comparative *braver* for greater emphasis (Abbott, §11).

control rebuke, reprove (*OED v.* 3a)

442 **They . . . eyes** Ferdinand and Miranda have exchanged affectionate

glances; perhaps a reference to falling in love at first sight. Cf. Dent, L426: 'Love not at the first LOOK', a proverb that warns against it, although Shakespeare's characters often succumb (cf. Rosalind and Orlando, Romeo and Juliet, as well as Ferdinand and Miranda).

444 **done . . . wrong** spoken falsely; made a serious error

445–7 Although Miranda speaks these words to herself in an aside, she may intend that her father overhear, with the final clause meant as an appeal for pity on Ferdinand.

447 **Pity move** let compassion sway

448 **if a virgin** As a prince (or, as he thinks, a king), Ferdinand must marry a virgin to ensure that any children born of the union are his legitimate descendants and thereby eligible to inherit his throne.

450 **Soft** a call for silence but meant kindly (*OED adv.* 8a)

---

439 SD] *Ard²* (*Dyce*)   442 SD] *Johnson & Steevens*   443 SD] *Ard¹*   445 SD] *Oxf* ungently] urgently] *F2*

203

> [*aside*] They are both in either's powers, but this swift
>   business
> I must uneasy make, lest too light winning
> Make the prize light. [*to Ferdinand*] One word more.
>   I charge thee
> That thou attend me. Thou dost here usurp
> The name thou ow'st not and hast put thyself   455
> Upon this island as a spy, to win it
> From me, the lord on't.

FERDINAND   No, as I am a man.

MIRANDA
> There's nothing ill can dwell in such a temple.
> If the ill spirit have so fair a house,
> Good things will strive to dwell with't.

PROSPERO [*to Ferdinand*]   Follow me. –   460
> Speak not you for him; he's a traitor. – Come,
> I'll manacle thy neck and feet together;
> Sea water shalt thou drink; thy food shall be
> The fresh-brook mussels, withered roots, and husks
> Wherein the acorn cradled. Follow!

FERDINAND   No,   465

---

452 **uneasy** hard, difficult
452–3 **light . . . light** easy . . . of little
    value, perhaps with a suggestion of
    unchastity
453 **charge** command
454 **attend** listen to, pay attention to
455 **ow'st** own. Prospero again accuses
    Ferdinand of falsely claiming to be
    King of Naples.
458 Miranda expresses a truism of
    Renaissance neo-Platonic discourse,
    that beauty is the physical signifier of a
    virtuous moral nature. Castiglione's
    The Courtier, the most widely circu-
    lated Renaissance courtesy book and
    translated into English by Thomas

Hoby in 1561, made the connection
explicit: 'beawtie commeth of God,
and is like a circle, the goodnesse
wherof is the Centre. And therefore, as
there can be no circle without a centre,
no more can beawty be without goodnesse' (sig. Tt4^v).
459–61 'If the evil spirit has such a handsome body, it will attract goodness to
live with it.'
460–1 Prospero begins by addressing
Ferdinand, then turns to Miranda, and
then back to Ferdinand.
464 **fresh-brook mussels** an inedible
variety

451 SD] *Ard²* (*Dyce*)   453 SD] *Ard¹*   One] Sir, one *Pope*   460 SP] *repeated in F* (*in first line of fol.*
A3ᵛ, which was the first page of F to be set): catchword on A3ᵛ is 'Pro.'   SD] *Johnson & Steevens*

I will resist such entertainment till
Mine enemy has more power.

> *He draws and is charmed from moving.*

MIRANDA   O dear father,
Make not too rash a trial of him, for
He's gentle and not fearful.

PROSPERO   What, I say,
My foot my tutor? Put thy sword up, traitor,   470
Who mak'st a show but dar'st not strike, thy conscience
Is so possessed with guilt. Come from thy ward,
For I can here disarm thee with this stick
And make thy weapon drop.

MIRANDA   Beseech you, father –

PROSPERO
Hence; hang not on my garments.

MIRANDA   Sir, have pity;   475
I'll be his surety.

PROSPERO   Silence! One word more
Shall make me chide thee, if not hate thee. What,
An advocate for an impostor? Hush.
Thou think'st there is no more such shapes as he,

---

466 **entertainment** in the now obsolete sense of 'treatment' (*OED* 5)

468 **rash** hasty, impetuous, reckless (*OED a.* 2a)

469 **gentle** noble, but also tame, easily managed (*OED a.* 4b)
fearful causing fear, inspiring terror (*OED a.* 1). Kermode, stressing Ferdinand's noble birth, takes this to mean 'not a coward' (Ard², 40), but since Miranda's intent is to soften Prospero's anger, she is more likely to be emphasizing Ferdinand's mildness than his courage.

470 **My . . . tutor?** Prospero borrows from the proverb 'Do not make the FOOT the head' (Dent, F562), asserting his patriarchal authority over his daughter.

472 **ward** defensive posture (Oxf¹, 127) or position (Folg², 46); Johnson glossed 'come from thy ward' as 'Desist from any hope of awing me by that posture of defence' (Johnson & Steevens, 29).

473 **stick** presumably Prospero's magic staff

474 **make . . . drop** This line hints at Prospero's symbolic emasculation of Ferdinand.

475 **hang . . . garments** Miranda grabs Prospero and tries to stop him.

479 **such . . . he** human males who are shaped like him

471 mak'st] makes *F2*   472 Is so] Is *F2;* Is all *Pope*   474 father –] *Oxf¹;* Father. *F;* father! *Capell*

Having seen but him and Caliban. Foolish wench,   480
To th' most of men, this is a Caliban,
And they to him are angels.

MIRANDA   My affections
Are then most humble. I have no ambition
To see a goodlier man.

PROSPERO [*to Ferdinand*]   Come on, obey:
Thy nerves are in their infancy again   485
And have no vigour in them.

FERDINAND   So they are!
My spirits, as in a dream, are all bound up.
My father's loss, the weakness which I feel,
The wreck of all my friends, nor this man's threats
(To whom I am subdued) are but light to me,   490
Might I but through my prison once a day
Behold this maid. All corners else o'th' earth
Let liberty make use of; space enough
Have I in such a prison.

PROSPERO [*aside*]   It works. [*to Ferdinand*]   Come on. –
Thou hast done well, fine Ariel. – Follow me; –   495
Hark what thou else shalt do me.

MIRANDA [*to Ferdinand*]   Be of comfort;
My father's of a better nature, sir,
Than he appears by speech. This is unwonted

481–2 **To . . . to** in comparison to
485 **nerves** sinews or tendons (*OED sb.* 1), or the parts that constitute strength, vigour (*OED sb.* 2)
489 **nor** an unusual use of the word; it here means 'and'. See Abbott, §408.
490 **light** minor burdens
491 **through** from
492 **all . . . earth** everywhere else
493 **liberty** i.e. people who have liberty
494 SD2 Although it is possible to read this speech differently, it appears most likely that Prospero commands Ferdinand to 'come on', before turning to Ariel, then back to Ferdinand. He next whispers further instructions to Ariel, and Miranda then tries to comfort Ferdinand in 496–8.
496 **do me** do for me
498 **unwonted** unusual, infrequent (*OED ppl. a.* 1)

---

484 SD] *Johnson & Steevens*   485 again] *Riv;* againe. *F;* again, *F3*   489 nor] *and Dryden & Davenant;* or *Capell*   494 SD1] *Dyce*   SD2] *Ard² (Cam¹)*   496 SD] *Oxf*

Which now came from him.

PROSPERO [*to Ariel*]   Thou shalt be as free

As mountain winds, but then exactly do   500

All points of my command.

ARIEL   To th' syllable.

PROSPERO [*to Ferdinand*]

Come, follow; – speak not for him.   *Exeunt.*

2.1   *Enter* ALONSO, SEBASTIAN, ANTONIO,
              GONZALO, ADRIAN, FRANCISCO *and others.*

GONZALO

Beseech you, sir, be merry. You have cause

(So have we all) of joy, for our escape

Is much beyond our loss. Our hint of woe

Is common: every day some sailor's wife,

The masters of some merchant, and the merchant,   5

Have just our theme of woe. But for the miracle,

I mean our preservation, few in millions

Can speak like us. Then wisely, good sir, weigh

Our sorrow with our comfort.

499–500 **free . . . winds** a proverbial expression: 'As free as the AIR (wind)' (Dent, A88). In *AYL* 2.7.48 Jaques calls for liberty, 'as large a charter as the wind', and in *Cor* 1.9.88–9 Cominius offers to release a prisoner: 'he should / Be free as is the wind'.

500 **then** implies 'if so, then you must'

501 **To th' syllable.** in every detail

2.1.0.2 **and others** Orgel omits this part of F's SD (as does Bell's eighteenth-century acting edition), noting that when the courtiers reassemble in the final scene no others are included. Perhaps, as Orgel suggests, 'the supernumerary characters were erroneously included in Crane's text' (Oxf[1], 128), but we prefer to leave open to readers and directors the possibility of extra Neapolitans on stage. See similar SDs in 1.1.8.2 and 3.3.0.2.

3 **beyond** greater than
hint occasion (*OED sb.* 1a)

5 **masters . . . [2]merchant** This obscure line has puzzled editors but seems to indicate the officers or the owners of a merchant vessel (*OED* merchant *sb.* A 4) and the merchant who owns the cargo. In either case, Gonzalo is referring to the woes caused by shipwreck. For a roughly analogous usage, see *H5* 4.1.147–54.

6 **theme** topic, subject

8–9 **weigh . . . comfort** 'Consider not only the shipwreck but also our remarkable survival.'

499 SD] *Hanmer* 502 SD] *Johnson & Steevens* 2.1] *Actus Secundus. Scoena Prima.* Location] Another Part of the Island *Pope* 0.2 *and others*] om. *Oxf*

ALONSO   Prithee, peace.

SEBASTIAN [*to Antonio*]   He receives comfort like cold   10
     porridge.

ANTONIO [*to Sebastian*]   The visitor will not give him
     o'er so.

SEBASTIAN   Look, he's winding up the watch of his wit;
     by and by it will strike –   15

GONZALO [*to Alonso*]   Sir –

SEBASTIAN   One. Tell.

GONZALO   When every grief is entertained that's offered,
     comes to th'entertainer –

SEBASTIAN   A dollar.   20

GONZALO   Dolour comes to him, indeed. You have

9–10 **peace . . . porridge** a pun on 'pease-porridge hot, pease-porridge cold'. Pease-porridge is made from peas.

10 Here Shakespeare shifts from blank verse to prose; the latter is more appropriate for Sebastian and Antonio's sarcastic badinage. Although their punning wordplay is spoken to each other, after 13 they clearly mean to be overheard. Pope found their dialogue distasteful and suggested that it might have been interpolated by the players, but the discourse shows Sebastian and Antonio to be insensitive and cynical, if not downright cruel. And, as Theobald pointed out, the dialogue does provide important background about Claribel's marriage. Bell's acting edition, however, omitted this badinage as 'not worth either utterance or perusal' (Bell, 24). The text returns to blank verse from line 107, when Alonso expresses his despair at Ferdinand's loss. Gonzalo then describes his ideal commonwealth in verse, only to be interrupted by more prose wordplay. The scene reverts to verse from line 191 until the end for Antonio's seduction of Sebastian. The shifts back and forth seem to have caused some lineation problems in F; major changes are listed in the t.n.

12–13 A visitor is 'One who visits from charitable motives or with a view of doing good' (*OED* 2a); i.e. Gonzalo, as comforter, will not readily abandon his efforts to console Alonso.

14 **winding . . . wit** 'Striking or "repeating" watches were invented about the year 1510' (Ard², 44).

17 **One. Tell.** Sebastian imitates the clock striking one and suggests that they continue to count aloud (*Tell*) (*OED v.* B 1). T.W. Craik suggests that *Tell* may have been an SD in Shakespeare's manuscript; the imperative verb instructed the actor in Sebastian's role to 'count the clock' with his hand as he says *One* (*N&Q*, 244 (1997), 514).

18–19 'when the recipient of grief embraces every grief that comes his way'

20 **dollar** 'The English name for the German thaler, a large silver coin' (*OED* 1). Sebastian puns on Gonzalo's *entertainer*, as if the word were used in the sense of paid performer.

21 **Dolour** sorrow. Gonzalo can play with words, too.

10 SD] *Oxf*   12 SD] *Bantam*   15 strike –] *this edn;* strike. F   16 SD] *Oxf* Sir – 1 *Signet;* Sir. F
17 One] On *F2*   18 – 19] *Folg²; F lines* entertaind, / 19 th'entertainer –] th'entertainer. *F*

spoken truer than you purposed.

SEBASTIAN   You have taken it wiselier than I meant you
should.

GONZALO   Therefore, my lord –   25

ANTONIO   Fie, what a spendthrift is he of his tongue!

ALONSO   I prithee, spare.

GONZALO   Well, I have done; but yet –

SEBASTIAN   He will be talking.

ANTONIO   Which, of he or Adrian, for a good wager, first   30
begins to crow?

SEBASTIAN   The old cock.

ANTONIO   The cockerel.

SEBASTIAN   Done! The wager?

ANTONIO   A laughter.   35

SEBASTIAN   A match!

ADRIAN   Though this island seem to be desert –

ANTONIO   Ha, ha, ha.

SEBASTIAN   So, you're paid.

22 **purposed** intended (*OED ppl. a.*)

27 **spare** refrain, desist (cited in *OED v.*[1] 6d)

29 proverbial – 'The greatest TALKERS . . . are the least . . . doers' (Dent, T64 and T64.1). Cf. *MA* 3.5.33, where Dogberry describes Verges as a man who 'will be talking'. Sebastian expresses impatience with Gonzalo's garrulity. Cf. 26 above.

31–3 **crow . . . cock . . . cockerel** Antonio and Sebastian engage in a series of puns comparing Gonzalo to an old rooster and Adrian to a younger fowl. Cf. Dent, C491: 'The young COCK crows as he the old hears'. *Cockerel* was sometimes applied figuratively to a young man (*OED* 2).

35 a pun on two senses of laughter: the act of laughing and 'The whole number of eggs laid by a fowl before she is ready to sit' (*OED*, *sb.*[2]), whereby Antonio picks up on the previous references to cocks. Antonio wins the bet and laughs at Adrian and, implicitly, at Sebastian, who accepts that *laughter* as completion of the *wager* (34).

37 **desert** 'deserted' (*OED a.* 1)

38, 39 SPs * R.G. White was the first editor to reverse the Folio's speech headings, giving 38 to Antonio rather than Sebastian and 39 to Sebastian rather than Antonio. Sebastian has lost the bet on who would speak first; since the agreed stakes were a *laughter* (a winner's laugh, as in Dent, L93: 'He LAUGHS that wins'), the *Ha, ha, ha* should come from Antonio. But as Bevington notes, 'The Folio assignment can work in the theater . . . if Sebastian pays for losing with a sardonic laugh of concession' (Bantam, 27). An alternative solution would be to assume that the loser is to pay with a laugh, retain F's SPs, and emend 39 to 'you've paid'. Theobald combined the two lines into one remark and assigned it to Sebastian.

25 lord –] *Theobald*; Lord. F   28 yet –] *Rowe*; yet F   30 – 1] *Ard*[1]; F lines wager, / 37 desert –] *Rowe*: desert. F   38 SP] *R.G. White*; Seb. F   38 – 9] *Seb. . . . paid. Theobald*   39 SP] *R.G. White*; Ant. F

ADRIAN   Uninhabitable and almost inaccessible –   40

SEBASTIAN   Yet –

ADRIAN   Yet –

ANTONIO   He could not miss't.

ADRIAN   It must needs be of subtle, tender and delicate
temperance.   45

ANTONIO   Temperance was a delicate wench.

SEBASTIAN   Ay, and a subtle, as he most learnedly
delivered.

ADRIAN   The air breathes upon us here most sweetly.

SEBASTIAN   As if it had lungs, and rotten ones.   50

ANTONIO   Or, as 'twere perfumed by a fen.

GONZALO   Here is everything advantageous to life.

ANTONIO   True, save means to live.

SEBASTIAN   Of that there's none, or little.

GONZALO   How lush and lusty the grass looks! How green!   55

ANTONIO   The ground indeed is tawny.

SEBASTIAN   With an eye of green in't.

ANTONIO   He misses not much.

SEBASTIAN   No; he doth but mistake the truth totally.

GONZALO   But the rarity of it is, which is indeed almost   60
beyond credit –

43 'Adrian could not avoid talking about it (the island).'

44 **subtle** 'refined' (*OED a.* 9)

46 **Temperance** Antonio puns on Adrian's use of 'temperance' to describe the island, using it instead as a proper name for a woman (or *wench*) who is *delicate*, or, in a bawdier sense, given to pleasure.

47 **subtle** Sebastian puns on Adrian's description of the island as *subtle* or *delicate* (*OED a.* 2) by applying the term to a person (*Temperance*) who is crafty or insidious (*OED a.* 10). Sebastian and Antonio are determined to undercut Adrian's idealistic image of the island.

47–8 **learnedly delivered** lectured with authority (sarcastic)

51 **fen** smelly marshland

52 **advantageous** useful, beneficial (cited in *OED a.* 1b)

55 **lush** 'succulent and luxuriant in growth, of plants' (cited in *OED a.* 2a), which Orgel doubts (Oxf[1], 130), in favour of 'soft, tender'

56 **tawny** of a yellowish brown colour

57 **eye of green** *OED sb.*[1] 9a credits the first application of 'eye' as 'Slight shade, tinge' to this line.

61 **credit** belief, credence (cited in *OED sb.* 1)

40 inaccessible –] *Rowe*; inaccessible. F   41 Yet –] *Theobald*; Yet F   42 Yet –] *Rowe*; Yet F   61 credit –] *Rowe*; credit. F

SEBASTIAN   As many vouched rarities are.

GONZALO   That our garments being, as they were,
drenched in the sea, hold notwithstanding their
freshness and gloss, being rather new-dyed than   65
stained with salt water.

ANTONIO   If but one of his pockets could speak, would it
not say he lies?

SEBASTIAN   Ay, or very falsely pocket up his report.

GONZALO   Methinks our garments are now as fresh as   70
when we put them on first in Africa, at the marriage of
the King's fair daughter Claribel to the King of Tunis.

SEBASTIAN   'Twas a sweet marriage, and we prosper well
in our return.

ADRIAN   Tunis was never graced before with such a   75
paragon to their queen.

GONZALO   Not since widow Dido's time.

62 **vouched rarities** unusual events that
are guaranteed (*vouched*) to be true

65 ***freshness . . . new-dyed** 'Our garments look brand new.' *Freshness*: 'Not
faded or worn' (cited in *OED* A 8);
'Superficial lustre' (cited in *OED sb.*²
1a). Orgel argues that F's 'glosses' is a
misreading of 'glosse' (Oxf¹, 131).

67 **his pockets** Antonio suggests that the
pockets, if not the outer surfaces of
their garments, are not as fresh as
Gonzalo claims.

69 **falsely pocket up** a pun on pocket:
the pocket will conceal (hide)
Gonzalo's lying report; from the
proverbial expression, 'To pocket up
an INJURY' (Dent, I70). See also *KJ*
3.1.200, *1H4* 3.3.162–3 and *H5* 3.2.51,
where the wording is similar.

71 ***Africa** Unlike previous editors, we
have modernized F's 'Affricke' to be
consistent with our treatment of other
placenames. The extra syllable does
not affect this prose passage.

72 **Tunis** a city in northern Africa, now
the capital of Tunisia. The reference

here is to Tunis as a city-state, as
Carthage was earlier.

73 **prosper** Sebastian's inadvertent pun
suggests Prospero's hand in the
Neapolitans' fate.

76 **to** as

77 **widow Dido** Dido was the widow of
Sychaeus, and Aeneas was a widower
when he met her. *Aeneid* (Bks 1–4)
describes how Dido, the Queen of
Carthage, killed herself when her lover
Aeneas abandoned her to travel to
Italy, where he founded the city of
Rome. Gonzalo's comment, and
Sebastian and Antonio's feeble jokes
which follow, have puzzled editors,
but as Paster contends, Shakespeare
may be referring indirectly to
Montaigne's essay 'Of Diverting and
Diversions' which twice mentions
Dido in connection with the themes of
shipwreck, loss and consolation.
Gonzalo tries to divert the King's
attention from his lost son, while the
hard-hearted Sebastian and Antonio
make jokes. 'At this moment', Paster

65 gloss] *Cam¹*; glosses F   71 Africa] *this edn;* Affricke F

ANTONIO   Widow? A pox o'that. How came that widow
in? Widow Dido!

SEBASTIAN   What if he had said widower Aeneas too?   80
Good lord, how you take it!

ADRIAN   Widow Dido, said you? You make me study of
that. She was of Carthage, not of Tunis.

GONZALO   This Tunis, sir, was Carthage.

ADRIAN   Carthage?   85

GONZALO   I assure you, Carthage.

ANTONIO   His word is more than the miraculous harp.

SEBASTIAN   He hath raised the wall, and houses too.

ANTONIO   What impossible matter will he make easy
next?   90

SEBASTIAN   I think he will carry this island home in his
pocket and give it his son for an apple.

ANTONIO   And sowing the kernels of it in the sea, bring
forth more islands!

GONZALO   I –   95

ANTONIO   Why, in good time.

GONZALO   Sir, we were talking that our garments seem
now as fresh as when we were at Tunis at the marriage
of your daughter, who is now Queen.

concludes, 'two of Shakespeare's
sources – the French essayist and the
Roman poet – seem to come together'
in the unusual juxtaposition of 'consolation and revenge, of Dido and hard-
ness of heart' (94).

82   **study of** 'to think intently; to meditate' (cited in *OED v.* 2a)

84   Carthage and Tunis were not physically the same city, but 'after the
destruction of Carthage Tunis took its
place as the political and commercial
centre of the region' (Oxf[1], 132).

87–8   **miraculous . . . wall** In Greek
mythology, Amphion used a harp to
raise the walls of Thebes. Sebastian
suggests that Gonzalo rebuilt all of
Carthage by conflating it with Tunis.

91–2   Cf. Cleopatra's description of
Antony: 'realms and islands were / As
plates dropp'd from his pocket' (*AC*
5.2.91–2).

93   **kernels** seeds, presumably from the
apple in Gonzalo's pocket (91–2)

95   Although most editors have emended
Gonzalo's *I* to 'Ay', we have retained
F's reading because it suggests that
Gonzalo begins to make another pro-
nouncement but is rudely interrupted
by Antonio. 'Ay', as a term of assent,
seems inappropriate in this conversation. For an interesting discussion of
this editorial point, see Warren, 33. Cf.
Hartwig, 147.

95   I –] I. *F;* Ay. *Rowe;* Ay? *Capell*

ANTONIO   And the rarest that e'er came there.   100

SEBASTIAN   Bate, I beseech you, widow Dido.

ANTONIO   O, widow Dido? Ay, widow Dido.

GONZALO   Is not, sir, my doublet as fresh as the first day
    I wore it? I mean, in a sort.

ANTONIO   That sort was well fished for.   105

GONZALO   When I wore it at your daughter's marriage.

ALONSO

    You cram these words into mine ears, against
    The stomach of my sense. Would I had never
    Married my daughter there, for coming thence
    My son is lost and (in my rate) she too,   110
    Who is so far from Italy removed
    I ne'er again shall see her. O thou mine heir
    Of Naples and of Milan, what strange fish
    Hath made his meal on thee?

FRANCISCO   Sir, he may live.
    I saw him beat the surges under him   115
    And ride upon their backs. He trod the water,
    Whose enmity he flung aside, and breasted
    The surge most swoll'n that met him. His bold head
    'Bove the contentious waves he kept and oared

---

101 **Bate** 'To omit, leave out of count, except' (*OED v.*[2] 7). Sebastian playfully posits that Claribel would be the fairest queen except for widow Dido.

104–5 **sort . . . sort** used differently, with a play on words. Where Gonzalo's *in a sort* (104) means 'in a way' or manner (*OED sb.*[2] 21d), Antonio's response in 105 uses *sort* in the sense of kind, variety (*OED sb.*[2] 12a).

107–8 **You . . . sense.** a metaphor of forced feeding. Alonso is in no mood to listen to their chatter.

108 **sense** temper, disposition, state of feeling (*OED sb.* 7a)

110 **in my rate** 'in my estimation' (first occurrence in *OED sb.*[1])

113 **Naples . . . Milan** Alonso had intended that Ferdinand inherit control of Milan as well as the kingdom of Naples, a sentiment that may further motivate Antonio to seduce Sebastian into a conspiracy to assassinate the King. Alonso's statement negates the rights of Antonio's *brave son* of 1.2.439 (see Kastan, 96).

115–22 Francisco's description may derive from Virgil's report of serpents 'breasting the sea . . . Their bosoms rise amid the surge, and their crests, blood-red, overtop the waves' (*Aeneid*, Bk 2, 203–8).

115 **beat . . . him** push the waves down

119 **oared** oar: 'to propel with or as with oars' (cited in *OED v.* 1)

---

103 sir, my doublet] my doublet, sir *F2*   107–8] *F4; prose in F*

Himself with his good arms in lusty stroke   120
To th' shore, that o'er his wave-worn basis bowed,
As stooping to relieve him. I not doubt
He came alive to land.

ALONSO   No, no, he's gone.

SEBASTIAN

Sir, you may thank yourself for this great loss,
That would not bless our Europe with your daughter   125
But rather loose her to an African,
Where she at least is banished from your eye,
Who hath cause to wet the grief on't.

ALONSO   Prithee, peace.

SEBASTIAN

You were kneeled to and importuned otherwise
By all of us, and the fair soul herself   130
Weighed between loathness and obedience, at
Which end o'th' beam should bow. We have lost your
    son,
I fear, for ever. Milan and Naples have
More widows in them of this business' making
Than we bring men to comfort them.   135

---

121 **his wave-worn basis** the base of the
cliffs rising from the shore. Francisco
suggests that the shore itself bent over
as if (*As*) to relieve Ferdinand (122).
124 **yourself** This reflexive pronoun
emphasizes that Alonso is to blame for
his son's presumed death.
126 **loose ... African** Many editors modernize F's 'loose' to 'lose', removing
any sexual connotations in Claribel's
being 'loosed' or pandered by her
father to a potential customer (and
thus suggesting a subtle criticism of a
patriarchally arranged interracial marriage). For comparison, see Dover
Wilson's discussion of Polonius'
promise to 'loose' his daughter to
Hamlet in 2.2.162 (J.D. Wilson,

Hamlet, 103–4).
128 **wet ... on't** weep for the sorrow of it
(i.e. her loss and absence)
129 **importuned** importunèd
131 **Weighed ... obedience** Balanced
(as on a scale) between repulsion
(*loathness*) at marrying the King of
Tunis and obedience to her father's
will. *Weigh* is similarly used in 2.1.8.
See 126 above and n.
132 **end ... bow** continuing the scale image
used in 131: whether *loathness* or *obedience* would prove heavier, causing one
end of the scale to become lower (*bow*)
134–5 **this ... them** Sebastian refers to
the wedding and subsequent shipwreck and the presumed paucity of
survivors.

120 stroke] strokes *F4, Rowe*   126 loose] lose *F2, Rowe*   134 More] *Rowe;* Mo *F*

The fault's your own.

ALONSO

So is the dear'st o'th' loss.

GONZALO   My lord Sebastian,
The truth you speak doth lack some gentleness,
And time to speak it in. You rub the sore
When you should bring the plaster.   140

SEBASTIAN

Very well.

ANTONIO   And most chirurgeonly!

GONZALO

It is foul weather in us all, good sir,
When you are cloudy.

SEBASTIAN   Foul weather?

ANTONIO   Very foul.

GONZALO

Had I plantation of this isle, my lord –

ANTONIO

He'd sow't with nettle-seed.

---

137 **dear'st** referring to Ferdinand, a 'dear' loss

139 **time . . . it** the right timing for such a harsh sentiment
rub the sore irritate, annoy. Perhaps proverbial, as in Dent, S649: 'to rip up (rub) old SORES'.

140 **plaster** originally 'an external curative application' of some medicines 'spread upon a piece of muslin, skin, or some similar material' (*OED sb.* 1a). Gonzalo tells Sebastian he should administer to the wound rather than exacerbate it.

141 **chirurgeonly** Although 'chirurgeon' was a common sixteenth-century spelling of the word that gradually evolved into 'surgeon', the adverb *chirurgeonly* was so rare that *OED* cites only this example. It has four syllables.

143 ***Foul weather?*** F's 'Fowle' suggests that perhaps Sebastian is making another feeble attempt at a pun, picking up on the earlier jokes about cocks (31–3), but Antonio doesn't take the bait. See *AW* 5.3.32–6 for a similar metaphor relating weather to the mood of a king.

144 **plantation** a term for a colonial settlement that originated in England's efforts to subdue Ireland (*OED* 1c). Gonzalo here begins an extended allusion to Montaigne's essay 'Of the Caniballes', which contrasts the culture of Brazilian Indians to, more corrupted European ways. In the following line, Antonio and Sebastian teasingly apply instead the word's agricultural meaning. See Appendix 1.2.

---

141 SEBASTIAN . . . chirurgeonly] *R.G. White*   143 Foul] *(Fowle)*   144 plantation] the plantation *Rowe;* the planting *Hanmer*   lord –] *Pope;* Lord. *F*

SEBASTIAN   Or docks, or mallows.   145

GONZALO

And were the king on't, what would I do?

SEBASTIAN

'Scape being drunk, for want of wine.

GONZALO

I'th' commonwealth I would by contraries
Execute all things, for no kind of traffic
Would I admit; no name of magistrate;   150
Letters should not be known; riches, poverty
And use of service, none; contract, succession,
Bourn, bound of land, tilth, vineyard – none;
No use of metal, corn, or wine or oil;

145 **nettle-seed** seed of the plant *Urtica*, a prickly weed that grows on waste ground (*OED sb.* 1a)

docks a coarse weedy herb that is used as an antidote for nettle stings (*OED sb.*[1] 1)

mallows a wild plant with hairy stems and leaves and deeply cleft reddish purple flowers (cited in *OED* 1). Cf. Gerard, 782, for a discussion of garden mallows, which are similar to hollyhocks.

148–57 Gonzalo's description of his ideal commonwealth borrows heavily from John Florio's translation of Montaigne's 'Of the Caniballes'. See Introduction, pp. 60–2.

148 **commonwealth** a nation or self-governing community; a body politic. Antonio may use the term sarcastically in 158. The word appears frequently and variously in Tudor and Stuart writings, including twenty-seven times in Shakespeare's plays (Spevack, 224).

148 **by contraries** contrary to usual customs

149 **traffic** business, commerce

150 **admit** 'to consent to the performance, doing, realization, or existence of' (*OED v.* 2a). Cf. *TN* 1.2.45–6: 'she will admit no kind of suit, / No, not the Duke's'.

151 **Letters** sophisticated learning. Gonzalo, in keeping with this passage's hyperbole, perhaps means *Letters* in the more general sense of 'writings, written records' (*OED sb.*[1] 3).

152 **use of service** custom of masters employing (and often abusing) servants, i.e. a system of masters and hired subordinates (*OED* service *sb.*[1] 1). Cf. 1.2.247 and 286 and 4.1.35.

succession 'The process by which one person succeeds another in the occupation or possession of an estate, a throne, or the like' (*OED* 5a)

153 **Bourn . . . land** both mean boundaries; i.e. Gonzalo wants no private landholdings or, at least, no rigid boundaries between them. Cf. *WT* 1.2.133–4: 'one that fixes / No bourn 'twixt his and mine'.

tilth farming labour, husbandry (*OED sb.* 2); the labour's produce (*OED sb.* 3); or tilled land (*OED sb.* 4)

154 **use of metal** Gonzalo may mean any metal or, more specifically, precious metal (*OED sb.* 1d), as in *CE* 4.1.81–2:

153 Bourn] *Rowe*[3]*;* Borne *F*   vineyard –] *Cam*[1]*;* Vineyard *F*

No occupation, all men idle, all;   155
And women, too, but innocent and pure;
No sovereignty —
SEBASTIAN   Yet he would be king on't.
ANTONIO   The latter end of his commonwealth forgets
the beginning.
GONZALO

All things in common nature should produce   160
Without sweat or endeavour; treason, felony,
Sword, pike, knife, gun, or need of any engine
Would I not have; but nature should bring forth
Of its own kind all foison, all abundance,
To feed my innocent people.   165
SEBASTIAN   No marrying 'mong his subjects?
ANTONIO   None, man, all idle – whores and knaves.
GONZALO

I would with such perfection govern, sir,

'you shall buy this sport as dear / As all the metal in your shop will answer'. Gonzalo's context also suggests the banning of usury.

155 **occupation** 'Employment' seems to be the principal meaning intended here, but because 'occupy' was also a slang term for 'cohabit with', Gonzalo may be inadvertently punning.

155–6 **idle . . . pure** Gonzalo claims that in contrast to the proverbial expression 'IDLENESS begets Lust' (Dent, I9), his islanders will remain *innocent* and *pure*. *Idle* connotes lack of employment (*OED a.* A 4a) and also lazy, indolent, useless (*OED a.* A 6).

157 **sovereignty** All four syllables are pronounced. Gonzalo calls for a class-less society with rule vested in the community.

158–9 Antonio sarcastically notes the inconsistency in Gonzalo's wanting to be *king* of a society that he has decreed

will have no *sovereignty*.

160–1 Gonzalo proposes a prelapsarian society in which all inhabitants share all products, perhaps in contrast to Genesis, 3.19: 'In the sweat of thy brow shalt thou eat bread' (Geneva Bible).

162 **engine** a machine or instrument, especially one used in warfare (*OED sb.* 5a), but also for other uses, including torture. Cf. *KL* 1.4.268–9: 'like an engine, wrench'd my frame of nature / From the fixed place'.

164 **Of . . . kind** i.e. natural to each separate crop; by its own nature (cited in *OED* kind *sb.* 3b). Cf. 5.1.23.
foison plenty, abundance

167 **idle** Antonio refutes Gonzalo's claim that the islanders will be *idle* and *pure* simultaneously (155–6) by here using *idle* in the sense of frivolous or wanton.

157 sovereignty –] *Cam¹; Soueraignty. F*   164 its] *F4;* it *F;* it's *F3*   167 idle –] *Signet;* idle; *F*

217

T'excel the Golden Age.

SEBASTIAN

'Save his majesty!

ANTONIO   Long live Gonzalo!   170

GONZALO

And – do you mark me, sir? –

ALONSO   Prithee, no more.

Thou dost talk nothing to me.

GONZALO   I do well believe your highness, and did it to
minister occasion to these gentlemen, who are of such
sensible and nimble lungs that they always use to laugh   175
at nothing.

ANTONIO   'Twas you we laughed at.

GONZALO   Who, in this kind of merry fooling, am nothing
to you, so you may continue and laugh at nothing still.

ANTONIO   What a blow was there given!   180

SEBASTIAN   An it had not fallen flat-long.

GONZALO   You are gentlemen of brave mettle. You would

---

169 **Golden Age** a reference to the first
'age of man' described in Ovid
1.91–128. Like the biblical Garden of
Eden, the age of gold was a prelapsarian world without discord, war or disease; it was followed by progressively
degenerate ages of silver, bronze and
lead.

170 **'Save** abbreviation of 'God save'

171 **mark** take notice of, pay attention to
(*OED v.* 16)

174 **minister occasion** furnish an
opportunity (for laughter)

175–6 **sensible . . . nothing** lungs ready
for laughter; i.e. they habitually laugh
with little provocation. *Sensible* here
has the obsolete meaning of 'Having
(more or less) acute power of sensation; sensitive' (cited in *OED* 8a).

179 **nothing** Gonzalo engages in wordplay here on the multiple senses of
nothing: the absence of any material
object as well as lack of importance or
significance, 'A thing (or person) not
worth reckoning, considering, or men-
tioning' (*OED sb.* 3a).

181 **An** 'If' (see Abbott, §105).
flat-long with the flat side of a sword,
not the sharp edge, and therefore relatively harmless

182 **mettle** 'Metal' (in F, 'mettal') and
'mettle' were interchangeable spellings in the early seventeenth century.
Perhaps Gonzalo is punning on 'metal'
in response to the previous references
to swords. The overriding sense, however, is *mettle* – spirit or courage.

---

171 And – do] *Signet*; And do *F*; Do *Cam¹*   181 An] *Pope*; And *F*   182 brave] a brave *F4, Rowe*
mettle] *(*mettal)*

lift the moon out of her sphere, if she would continue
in it five weeks without changing.

Enter ARIEL *playing solemn music.*

SEBASTIAN   We would so, and then go a bat-fowling.   185
ANTONIO   Nay, good my lord, be not angry.
GONZALO   No, I warrant you, I will not adventure my
   discretion so weakly. Will you laugh me asleep, for
   I am very heavy.
ANTONIO   Go sleep, and hear us.   190
   [*All sleep except Alonso, Sebastian and Antonio.*]
ALONSO

What, all so soon asleep? I wish mine eyes
Would, with themselves, shut up my thoughts. I find
They are inclined to do so.
SEBASTIAN   Please you, sir,
Do not omit the heavy offer of it.
It seldom visits sorrow; when it doth,   195
It is a comforter.
ANTONIO   We two, my lord,

183–4 **lift ... weeks** Gonzalo charges that
Sebastian and Antonio would lift the
moon out of its orbit round the earth if
it would stay still for five weeks – an
obvious impossibility; i.e. although
they talk a good game, one should not
expect any action from them.
184.1 Ariel is presumably wearing the
invisible costume Prospero provided in
1.2.304 and so cannot be seen by the
characters on stage.
185 **bat-fowling** 'the catching of birds at
night when at roost' (cited in *OED vbl.
sb.* 1) by hitting them with a club; the
birds are especially vulnerable when
blinded by sudden light on a moonless
night (see Strachey, 31). The term was
also used metaphorically for 'swind-
ling, victimizing the simple' (*OED*

vbl. sb. 2), an intriguing *double entendre*
from Sebastian, given Gonzalo's references to the moon's being lifted from
its sphere and the action that follows.
187–8 **adventure ... weakly** 'risk losing
my composure so lightly' (*OED*
adventure *v.* 2: risk, imperil)
188 **discretion** prudence, sound judgement (*OED* 6)
   laugh me asleep 'put me to sleep
with your (tedious) laughter'; or, 'tire
me to sleep from laughing'
189 **heavy** sleepy, drowsy
190 **and hear us** i.e. hear us laugh
194 **omit ... offer** disregard the invitation to drowsiness
195 **It ... sorrow** 'Sleep rarely comes to
one who grieves.'

190 SD] *Oxf¹*; GON. ADR. FRA. *and Train sleep.* / Capell   192–3] *Pope; F lines* thoughts, / so. /
Sir, /   195–6 It ... comforter] *R.G. White; one line F*   196–8 *Rowe³; F lines* person, / safety. /

Will guard your person while you take your rest,
And watch your safety.

ALONSO   Thank you. Wondrous heavy.
                          [*Alonso sleeps. Exit Ariel.*]

SEBASTIAN
What a strange drowsiness possesses them!

ANTONIO
It is the quality o'th' climate.

SEBASTIAN   Why   200
Doth it not then our eyelids sink? I find not
Myself disposed to sleep.

ANTONIO   Nor I. My spirits are nimble.
They fell together all, as by consent;
They dropped, as by a thunderstroke. What might,
Worthy Sebastian, O, what might – ? No more;   205
And yet, methinks I see it in thy face
What thou shouldst be. Th'occasion speaks thee, and
My strong imagination sees a crown
Dropping upon thy head.

SEBASTIAN   What, art thou waking?

ANTONIO
Do you not hear me speak?

SEBASTIAN   I do, and surely   210
It is a sleepy language, and thou speak'st
Out of thy sleep. What is it thou didst say?
This is a strange repose, to be asleep
With eyes wide open – standing, speaking, moving,

---

204 **as** as if
205 **No more** Antonio hesitates, as if
afraid to articulate what he is thinking.
The following dialogue has a striking
similarity to Lady Macbeth's conversation with her husband in *Mac*
1.7.28–82.
207 **Th'occasion ... thee** 'The opportu-

nity confronts (speaks to) you.'
208 **strong** intense, fervent (cited in *OED*
a. 13i)
209 **art thou waking?** Are you awake?
211 **sleepy language** incoherent or
dreamlike speech. Sebastian is not sure
he has heard Antonio correctly.

198 SD] *Dyce*   200–1] *F lines* Clymate. / Why / finde /   205 might – ?] *Riv*   214 open –]
Bantam; open: *F;* open; *Capell*

And yet so fast asleep.

ANTONIO   Noble Sebastian,   215

Thou let'st thy fortune sleep – die rather; wink'st

Whiles thou art waking.

SEBASTIAN   Thou dost snore distinctly.

There's meaning in thy snores.

ANTONIO

I am more serious than my custom. You

Must be so too, if heed me, which to do   220

Trebles thee o'er.

SEBASTIAN   Well, I am standing water.

ANTONIO

I'll teach you how to flow.

SEBASTIAN   Do so. To ebb

Hereditary sloth instructs me.

ANTONIO   O,

If you but knew how you the purpose cherish

Whiles thus you mock it, how in stripping it   225

You more invest it. Ebbing men, indeed,

216–17 **wink'st . . . waking** 'You close your eyes while you are awake'; i.e. you are perversely refusing to see.

217 **distinctly** 'In a distinct or clear manner; without confusion or obscurity: so as to be clearly perceived or understood' (*OED adv.* 2)

220 **if heed me** sometimes (unnecessarily) emended to 'if you heed me', which is the sense here

221 **Trebles thee o'er** makes you three times greater. Cf. Portia's desire to 'be trebled twenty times myself' (*MV* 3.2.153).

221–2 **standing water . . . flow . . . ebb** Sebastian and Antonio play with the concept of tides that can *flow* (grow higher), stand still or *ebb* (recede). Sebastian replies that his natural laziness – or perhaps his position as a younger brother – has kept him from

improving his position. Latham glosses the metaphor with reference to Joseph Hall's *Characters of Vertues and Vices* (London, 1608), which describes the slothful: 'this man is a standing Poole, and cannot chuse but gather corruption . . . as nothing but a colder earth molded with standing water'.

224–5 **If . . . mock it** '*if* you realized how truly you cherish the prospect while you *mock* it in this way'

226 **invest** clothe it (after having stripped it). Antonio uses the metaphor of ceremonial robing to imply Sebastian's secret desire for the throne. ,

226–8 **Ebbing . . . sloth.** 'Men who are *ebbing* (losing power) stay near the bottom (of the ocean) because of their own fear or *sloth*.' Cf. *AC* 1.4.43–7 and *KL* 5.3.17–19 for other uses of tidal imagery for political power.

216 sleep –] *Johnson & Steevens¹*; sleepe: F   221 Trebles . . . o'er] Troubles . . . o'er *Rowe³*; Troubles . . . not *Hanmer*; Trembles . . . o'er *Johnson*

Most often do so near the bottom run
By their own fear or sloth.

SEBASTIAN   Prithee, say on;
The setting of thine eye and cheek proclaim
A matter from thee, and a birth, indeed,   230
Which throes thee much to yield.

ANTONIO   Thus, sir:
Although this lord of weak remembrance – this
Who shall be of as little memory
When he is earthed – hath here almost persuaded
(For he's a spirit of persuasion, only   235
Professes to persuade) the King his son's alive,
'Tis as impossible that he's undrowned
As he that sleeps here swims.

SEBASTIAN   I have no hope
That he's undrowned.

ANTONIO   O, out of that 'no hope',

229 **setting** 'the manner or position in which anything is set, fixed, or placed' (*OED vbl. sb.* 2a)

230 **matter** reason or cause (*OED sb.* 13). Cf. *TC* 2.1.8–9: 'Then would come some matter from him; I see none now'.

231 **throes** We change F's spelling to *throes* (see t.n.), as do most editors, to continue Sebastian's metaphor of childbirth with a reference to labour pains. Sebastian observes that Antonio is having difficulty giving birth to (talking about) the matter. Cited in *OED* throe (throw) *v.* 1: 'to agonize as if in child birth'.
    yield probably means 'produce', 'generate' or 'give birth to' (*OED* 8a) – an extension of the *birth . . . throes* metaphor. Cf. *Per* 5.3.47–8: 'Thy burden at the sea, and call'd Marina / For she was yielded here'. Other plau-

sible meanings include 'declare', 'communicate' (*OED* 12), as in *AW* 3.1.10: 'The reasons of our state I cannot yield'; and 'grant', 'allow', as in *WT* 4.4.410–11: 'I yield all this; / But for some other reasons'.

232–4 **weak . . . earthed** 'This lord who being now in his dotage has outlived his faculty of remembring, and who once laid in the Ground shall be as little remembered himself, as he can now remember other things' (Johnson, 38).

235 **spirit of persuasion** The *spirit* ('essential principle or power' (*OED sb.* 7a)) of *persuasion* ('presenting inducements or winning arguments' (*OED* 1)). Gonzalo is an expert at *persuasion*.

235–6 **only . . . persuade** Because he is a councillor, Gonzalo's sole profession is to persuade and give opinions.

239–40 **'no hope' . . . great hope**

231 throes] *Pope;* throwes *F*   232 remembrance –] *this edn;* remembrance; *F*   234 earthed –] *this edn;* earth'd, *F*

What great hope have you! No hope that way is 240
Another way so high a hope that even
Ambition cannot pierce a wink beyond,
But doubt discovery there. Will you grant with me
That Ferdinand is drowned?

SEBASTIAN He's gone.

ANTONIO Then tell me,
Who's the next heir of Naples?

SEBASTIAN Claribel. 245

ANTONIO

She that is Queen of Tunis; she that dwells
Ten leagues beyond man's life; she that from Naples
Can have no note unless the sun were post –
The man i'th' moon's too slow – till newborn chins

Antonio picks up on Sebastian's double negative to make a positive: *great hope* or expectation.

242-3 **Ambition . . . there** '*Ambition* cannot go (*pierce*: penetrate) the least bit higher (*wink beyond*; cited in *OED* wink *sb.*[1] 3b) than the kingship without fear of discovery.' Sebastian's *great hope* is the crown, and circumstances have just presented him with a unique opportunity to attain it without being discovered. As Orgel notes, the exact sense of Antonio's words seems to contradict what he has just said (Oxf[1], 139–40), though the confused syntax may also reflect the excitement of the moment or Antonio's deliberate obfuscation of the murder he is suggesting. Antonio seems to realize that Sebastian does not understand him, so he tries a more straightforward approach in the following lines. See Furness for a summary of earlier editorial conjectures about this obscure passage (Var, 115–16).

247 **Ten . . . life** A league was about three miles, but the term was most often used metaphorically, as it is here. Antonio claims that Tunis is far away from Naples – 30 miles *beyond* a *man's life*, or, perhaps, beyond human (or civilized) habitation – and that consequently Claribel will never make any claim to the crown.

248 **no note . . . post** no communication, unless the sun were to serve as messenger

249 **The . . . slow** The moon takes a month to circle the earth, in contrast to the sun's (presumed) circumnavigation, which only requires twenty-four hours. Cf. 2.2.135–7, where Stephano claims to have been 'the man i'th' moon when time was', and Caliban has 'seen thee in her'.

249-50 **newborn . . . razorable** until *newborn* male children mature to the age when they can shave. Antonio exaggerates the amount of time it would take for news to travel from Naples to Tunis, a distance of only about 300 miles. He seems to have a

244-5 Then . . . Naples] *Theobald; one line F* 248 post –] *Penguin;* post: *F* 249 slow –] *Signet;* slow, *F*

Be rough and razorable; she that from whom   250
We all were sea-swallowed, though some cast again,
And by that destiny to perform an act
Whereof what's past is prologue, what to come
In yours and my discharge!

SEBASTIAN

What stuff is this? How say you?   255
'Tis true my brother's daughter's Queen of Tunis,
So is she heir of Naples, 'twixt which regions
There is some space.

ANTONIO   A space whose every cubit
Seems to cry out, 'How shall that Claribel
Measure us back to Naples? Keep in Tunis,   260
And let Sebastian wake.' Say this were death
That now hath seized them; why, they were no worse
Than now they are. There be that can rule Naples
As well as he that sleeps; lords that can prate
As amply and unnecessarily   265

Eurocentric notion that even the
northernmost cities of Africa were off
the end of the earth, as suggested also
in 256–60.

250 **from whom** coming away from
Claribel's wedding; as Kermode notes,
from functions as a verb of motion
(Ard², 56).

251 **sea-swallowed . . . cast** As far as
Claribel will know, we were all swallowed by the sea, with only a few survivors cast up (or vomited) on shore.
Some editors suggest that *cast* also has
theatrical connotations that are echoed
in the next lines.

253 **past is prologue** Sebastian's previous life is only a *prologue* to what
Macbeth would call the 'swelling act /
Of the imperial theme' (*Mac*
1.3.128–9) – to becoming king.

253–4 **what . . . discharge** What's to

come is up to us.

254 **discharge** 'Fulfilment, performance,
execution (of an obligation, duty, function, etc.)' (first occurrence in *OED sb.*
6)

255 **stuff** 'nonsense, rubbish' (*OED sb.*
8b)

258 **cubit** a measure of distance, about 20
inches, roughly the length of a forearm

260 **Measure us** 'retrace (one's steps, the
road)' (cited in *OED v.* 11b). The
cubits ask how Claribel can traverse
the distance back to Naples.
Keep keep yourself, stay

261 **death** Sleep was often described as a
mirror of death. See for example
Hamlet's conflation of sleep and death
in his 'To be or not to be' soliloquy
(*Ham* 3.1.59–66). See also Dent, S527.

263 **There be** 'there are other men'

252 And by that] May by that *Pope;* And that by *Ard² (Johnson)*   253 past is] past in *F2, Rowe*
259–61 'How . . . wake.'] *Ard²; no quotation marks F*   260 to] by *F2, Rowe*

As this Gonzalo. I myself could make
A chough of as deep chat. O that you bore
The mind that I do! What a sleep were this
For your advancement! Do you understand me?

SEBASTIAN

Methinks I do.

ANTONIO   And how does your content   270
Tender your own good fortune?

SEBASTIAN   I remember
You did supplant your brother Prospero.

ANTONIO   True:
And look how well my garments sit upon me
Much feater than before. My brother's servants
Were then my fellows; now they are my men.   275

SEBASTIAN

But for your conscience?

ANTONIO

Ay, sir, where lies that? If 'twere a kibe
'Twould put me to my slipper, but I feel not
This deity in my bosom. Twenty consciences
That stand 'twixt me and Milan, candied be they   280

266–7 **I . . . chat.** Antonio claims he could teach a prating bird (jackdaw) to speak as profoundly as the chatty Gonzalo. *OED* uses this line to illustrate both *chough* (1b *fig.*), a chatterer; and *chat* (*sb.* 1), idle or frivolous talk. See also *AW* 4.1.19–20, where the gibberish used to expose Parolles is called 'choughs' language, gabble enough'.

267–8 **bore . . . do** shared my resolution or, perhaps, my awareness of the opportunity

270–1 **And . . . fortune?** 'How does your contentment (at what I've just said) translate into (*Tender*) your good fortune?'

270 **content** (1) satisfaction, contentment (*OED sb.* 2); (2) tenor, purport (*OED sb.²* 3)

273 **garments** royal robes. Cf. *Mac* 5.2.20–2: 'Now does he feel his title / Hang loose about him, like a giant's robe / Upon a dwarfish thief', and 1.7.32–6, for extended metaphors of clothing.

274 **feater** with a better fit (cited in *OED* feat *a.* 3)

275 **fellows** companions (*OED sb.* 2a), or, perhaps, accomplices (*OED sb.* 1b) **men** servants

277 **kibe** a sore on the heel, usually caused by exposure to cold weather; chilblain

278 **put me to** force me to wear

279 **deity** conscience, as in 276

280 **candied** formed into crystals, congealed. Kermode argues for 'sugared' as the meaning, linking *candied* to Shakespeare's characteristic associa-

279 Twenty] (*'Twentie*)

225

And melt ere they molest! Here lies your brother,
No better than the earth he lies upon.
If he were that which now he's like (that's dead)
Whom I with this obedient steel – three inches of it –
Can lay to bed forever (whiles you, doing thus,   285
To the perpetual wink for aye might put
This ancient morsel, this Sir Prudence, who
Should not upbraid our course) – for all the rest
They'll take suggestion as a cat laps milk;
They'll tell the clock to any business that   290
We say befits the hour.

SEBASTIAN   Thy case, dear friend,
Shall be my precedent. As thou got'st Milan,
I'll come by Naples. Draw thy sword! One stroke
Shall free thee from the tribute which thou payest,
And I the king shall love thee.

ANTONIO   Draw together,   295
And when I rear my hand, do you the like

tion among candy, dogs and flattery
(Ard², 58). However, 'congealed' fits
more clearly with the ensuing verb,
melt. Malone glosses 279–81: 'Let
twenty consciences be first congealed,
and then dissolved, ere they molest
me, or prevent me from executing my
purposes' (45).
281 **molest** 'vex, annoy' (*OED v.* 1)
284 **steel** sword, or, perhaps, dagger
285 **doing thus** stabbing (perhaps spoken
with an appropriate gesture)
286 **perpetual . . . aye** closing of his
(Gonzalo's) eyes forever. The redun-
dancy (*perpetual, for aye*) reinforces
the point.
287 **morsel** piece of food or flesh. Cf.
Antony's 'I found thee as a morsel,
cold upon / Dead Caesar's trencher'
(*AC* 3.13.116–17) and Lucio's reference to Mistress Overdone as 'my dear

morsel' (*MM* 3.2.54).
288 **Should not** must not be allowed to
289 **take suggestion** They'll accept as
true our suggestions.
    cat . . . milk proverbial; see Dent,
C167: 'That CAT is out of kind that
sweet milk (cream) will not lap'. In
1H4 4.2.58–9 Falstaff exults that he is
'as vigilant as a cat to steal cream'.
290–1 **tell . . . hour** The court party will
say whatever Antonio and Sebastian
want; literally, they'll report the time
(*clock*) to accord with Antonio and
Sebastian's wishes. Cf. 17 and n.
290 **business** probably trisyllabic
292 **precedent** F's 'president' was the
common spelling at the time.
294 **tribute** Alonso agreed to Prospero's
deposition provided Antonio paid annual tribute to Naples. See 1.2.112–15.
296 **rear** raise, lift up

284 steel –. . . it –] *R.G. White;* steele (. . . it) *F*   288 course) –] *this edn;* course: *F*
292 precedent] (*president*)

To fall it on Gonzalo.

SEBASTIAN   O, but one word –

Enter ARIEL *with music and song.*

ARIEL

My master through his art foresees the danger

That you, his friend, are in, and sends me forth

(For else his project dies) to keep them living.   300

                                   Sings in Gonzalo's ear.

          While you here do snoring lie,

          Open-eyed conspiracy

          His time doth take.

          If of life you keep a care,

          Shake off slumber and beware.   305

          Awake, awake!

ANTONIO

Then let us both be sudden.

GONZALO [*Wakes.*]

Now, good angels preserve the King!

ALONSO [*Wakes.*]

Why, how now, ho! Awake! Why are you drawn?

Wherefore this ghastly looking?

GONZALO   What's the matter?   310

---

297 **fall it** let it fall

  O . . . word a common late Shakespearean theatrical contrivance to
  intercept the action, as in *WT* 4.4.594:
  ' – one word', and 661: 'Pray you a
  word'

297.1 Once again Ariel is invisible, and
  neither Sebastian nor Antonio can see
  or hear him.

299 **his friend** Ariel refers to the sleeping
  Gonzalo.

300 **project** Prospero's plan for Miranda's marriage to Ferdinand and

the couple's inheritance of both
Naples and Milan. *Project* was also an
alchemical term for the adept's experiment.

them Ariel turns to the audience and
here refers to both Gonzalo and
Alonso, who must be kept alive if
Prospero's plan is to succeed.

309 **Why . . . drawn?** Why have you
  drawn your swords?

310 **ghastly** 'full of fear, inspired by fear'
  (cited in *OED a.* 3)

297 word –] *Theobald;* word. F   308 SD] *Ard²; Ard¹ lines* angels / King! /   309 SD] *Signet*

SEBASTIAN

    Whiles we stood here securing your repose,

    Even now we heard a hollow burst of bellowing,

    Like bulls, or rather lions. Did't not wake you?

    It struck mine ear most terribly.

ALONSO   I heard nothing.

ANTONIO

    O, 'twas a din to fright a monster's ear –   315

    To make an earthquake! Sure it was the roar

    Of a whole herd of lions.

ALONSO   Heard you this, Gonzalo?

GONZALO

    Upon mine honour, sir, I heard a humming,

    And that a strange one too, which did awake me.

    I shaked you, sir, and cried. As mine eyes opened,   320

    I saw their weapons drawn. There was a noise,

    That's verily. 'Tis best we stand upon our guard,

    Or that we quit this place. Let's draw our weapons.

ALONSO

    Lead off this ground, and let's make further search

    For my poor son.

GONZALO   Heavens keep him from these beasts, 325

    For he is, sure, i'th' island.

ALONSO   Lead away.

ARIEL

    Prospero, my lord, shall know what I have done;

    So, King, go safely on to seek thy son.   *Exeunt.*

---

311 **securing** watching over, guarding

312–13 **burst . . . bellowing . . . bulls** Sebastian's mendacity may be indicated by the forced alliteration.

315 **monster's ear** Presumably a monster is less easily frightened than a human, because of its monstrous size or, perhaps, stupidity.

318 **humming** Gonzalo refers to Ariel's song, which he dimly heard.

322 **That's verily** 'That's true.' This unusual construction, in which *That's* is combined with an adverb is found also in *Cor* 4.1.53: 'That's worthily'. Pope emended to 'That's verity'. (Abbott, §78, cites this.)

315 ear –] *this edn;* eare; *F*   322 verily] verity *Pope*

2.2   *Enter* CALIBAN, *with a burden of wood;*
           a noise of thunder heard.

CALIBAN

All the infections that the sun sucks up
From bogs, fens, flats, on Prosper fall, and make him
By inchmeal a disease! His spirits hear me,
And yet I needs must curse. But they'll nor pinch,
Fright me with urchin-shows, pitch me i'th' mire,   5
Nor lead me, like a firebrand in the dark,
Out of my way unless he bid 'em. But
For every trifle are they set upon me:
Sometime like apes that mow and chatter at me
And after bite me, then like hedgehogs which   10
Lie tumbling in my barefoot way and mount
Their pricks at my footfall. Sometime am I
All wound with adders, who with cloven tongues
Do hiss me into madness. Lo now, lo,

2.2.0.2 *noise of thunder* However the
sound of thunder was created in performances of *Tem* (see 1.1.0.1. and n.),
it was repeated appropriately throughout the scene.
1   **infections** 'morbific influences, principles or germs' (cited in *OED* 3b).
Caliban 'alludes to the Renaissance
view that infection-carrying fogs were
drawn out of the earth by the sun'
(Everyman, 78).
2   **bogs . . . flats** spongy grounds,
marshes and swamps
3   **By inchmeal** inch by inch
4   **nor** neither
5   **urchin-shows** apparitions of goblins
or elves, perhaps in the shape of hedgehogs (*OED sb.* 1a, 1c)

6   **firebrand** an ephemeral light, perhaps
like a 'phosphorescent light that hovers over swampy ground at night'
(Folg², 76)
9   **mow** grimace
10–12 Prospero's spirits appear like
hedgehogs, covered with spiny quills
that hurt Caliban's bare feet.
13 **adders** viperous snakes. Eighteenth-
and nineteenth-century engravings
often depict Caliban at the mouth of a
cave with snakes twisted about his
body. Cf. Vaughan, *Caliban*, 231.
cloven tongues bifurcated, split;
probably intended to connote an evil or
Satanic connection. Cf. 1.2.277, where
Prospero asserts that Sycorax imprisoned Ariel in *a cloven pine*.

2.2] *Scoena Secunda.*   Location] Changes to another part of the island. *Pope*   4 nor] not *F3,*
Dryden & Davenant, Rowe   9, 12 Sometime] Sometimes *Dryden & Davenant*

Enter TRINCULO.

Here comes a spirit of his, and to torment me   15
For bringing wood in slowly. I'll fall flat;
Perchance he will not mind me.

TRINCULO   Here's neither bush nor shrub to bear off any
weather at all, and another storm brewing; I hear it sing
i'th' wind. Yond same black cloud, yond huge one, looks   20
like a foul bombard that would shed his liquor. If it
should thunder as it did before, I know not where to hide
my head. Yond same cloud cannot choose but fall by
pailfuls. [*Sees Caliban.*] What have we here, a man or a
fish? Dead or alive? A fish: he smells like a fish, a very   25
ancient and fish-like smell, a kind of – not of the newest
– poor-John. A strange fish! Were I in England now (as
once I was) and had but this fish painted, not a holiday
fool there but would give a piece of silver. There would
this monster make a man; any strange beast there makes   30
a man. When they will not give a doit to relieve a lame
beggar, they will lay out ten to see a dead Indian. Legged

15 **spirit** Caliban mistakes Trinculo for
one of Prospero's Spirits. Probably
monosyllabic.

16 **fall flat** In his effort to hide from
Trinculo, Caliban mostly covers himself under the *gaberdine* (37).

17 **Perchance** perhaps

18 **bear off** keep away, ward off

21 **bombard** a leather jug or bottle for
liquor (cited in *OED sb.* 3a). In *1H4*
2.4.451 Hal describes Falstaff as a
'huge bombard of sack'.

27 **poor-John** dried fish. Caliban smells
like a long-dead fish.

28 **painted** painted on a sign to attract the
notice of passers-by

28–9 **holiday fool** someone on holiday

and therefore likely to spend money on
souvenirs and sideshows, as in *WT*
4.4.231–314. See also the mindless
spending of Bartholomew Cokes in
Jonson's *Bartholomew Fair*, 6.67–72.

30–1 **any . . . man** (1) make a man's fortune, as in *MND*, where the mechani-
cals hoped their play would be selected
for the courtly revels and 'we had all
been made men' (4.2.17–18); or (2)
pass for human. Both senses may be
intended.

31 **doit** half an English farthing, a trifling
sum (cited in *OED* 1)

32 **dead Indian** Especially after Martin
Frobisher's expedition to North
America in 1576, native Americans

14.1 *Rowe; Enter / Trinculo. opp. 14–15*   15 and] sent *Dryden & Davenant; now Pope*
20 Yond . . . yond] Yon . . . yon *Oxf*   21 bombard] *(bumbard)*   23 Yond] Yon *Oxf*
24 SD] *this edn*   26 of –] *this edn;* of, *F*   26–7 newest –] *this edn;* newest *F*   28 this] his *F2*
28–9 a holiday fool] *(a holiday-foole);* an holy-day fool *F4*

like a man and his fins like arms! Warm, o'my troth! I do
now let loose my opinion, hold it no longer: this is no
fish, but an islander that hath lately suffered by a   35
thunderbolt. Alas, the storm is come again. My best
way is to creep under his gaberdine; there is no other
shelter hereabout. Misery acquaints a man with
strange bedfellows! I will here shroud till the dregs of the
storm be past.   40

Enter STEPHANO *singing.*

STEPHANO

> I shall no more to sea, to sea,
> Here shall I die ashore.

This is a very scurvy tune to sing at a man's funeral.
Well, here's my comfort.   *Drinks [and then] sings.*

> The master, the swabber, the boatswain and I;   45
>   The gunner and his mate,
> Loved Mall, Meg, and Marian, and Margery,
>   But none of us cared for Kate.

were occasionally brought back to
England and, for a fee, displayed by
their masters to a public audience. See
Var, 128–9, and Introduction, pp.
43–4.
Legged Caliban has human legs; he is
not a fish.
35 **islander** Trinculo concludes that this
strange creature is an inhabitant of the
island.
37 **gaberdine** a long, loose cloak for men
made of coarse cloth. Its simplicity
contrasts with Prospero's and the
court party's finery. Cf. Shylock's
'Jewish gaberdine' (*MV* 1.3.112).
38–9 **Misery . . . bedfellows** proverbial;
see Dent, B197.1: 'Misery (Adversity)
makes (acquaints men with) strange
BEDFELLOWS'. In Shakespeare's era,

travellers often shared beds with
strangers.
39–40 **I . . . past.** Trinculo crawls under
Caliban's gaberdine. Usually the two
lie on the stage, facing each other (or
with one on top), with pairs of legs pro-
truding from opposite sides of the gaberdine and Caliban's head partly or
wholly visible – hence Stephano's perception of a strange, four-legged beast.
39 **shroud** take shelter
dregs continues the metaphor of *bombard* (21)
40.1 As Capell first noted, Stephano
enters with a bottle in his hand. Since
he has already been drinking, most
actors play him as tipsy.
43 **scurvy** contemptible, despicable
45 **swabber** the sailor who mops the deck

40.1] *singing [a bottle in his hand] / Capell*   41–2] *Capell; one line F*   43–4] *Pope; as verse F, lined*
mans / comfort. /   44 SD *and then] this edn*

231

> For she had a tongue with a tang,
> Would cry to a sailor, 'Go hang!'   50
> She loved not the savour of tar nor of pitch,
> Yet a tailor might scratch her where'er she did itch.
> Then to sea, boys, and let her go hang!
> This is a scurvy tune too, but here's my comfort.

Drinks.

CALIBAN   Do not torment me! O!   55

STEPHANO   What's the matter? Have we devils here? Do
you put tricks upon's with savages and men of Ind? Ha!
I have not 'scaped drowning to be afeard now of your
four legs; for it hath been said, 'As proper a man as ever
went on four legs cannot make him give ground'. And   60

---

49 **tang** 'A pungent or stinging effect' (cited in *OED sb.*[1] 5c), a usage that may have begun with *Tem.*

50 **Go hang** proverbial; see Dent, H130.1: 'Farewell . . . and be HANGED'. Often meant figuratively: 'Go to the devil'. Cf. *TS* 3.2.226, where Petruchio tells the wedding guests to 'go hang yourselves'.

52 **tailor . . . itch** Kate would let a tailor scratch her anywhere; i.e. she would sleep with a tailor but not with a sailor. But, as H. Hulme notes, *tailor* could also mean 'penis' (100–1).

55–9 Caliban fears *torment* by Prospero's spirits, heralded by Stephano's singing or Trinculo's wriggling; Stephano, in turn, is startled by the unexpected voice and his first sight of the gaberdine-covered quadruped. See Introduction, p. 44.

57 **tricks** proverbial; see Dent, PP18: 'To PUT a trick upon one'. See also *AW* 4.5.60, where the Clown threatens: 'If I put any tricks upon 'em, sir, they shall be jades' tricks'.
*savages . . . Ind *Savages* ('Saluages' in F, a common spelling at the time)

suggests only that Stephano perceives the mostly concealed creature to be an uncivilized being, perhaps an Indian, though whether from West (more likely, given their topicality) or East India is uncertain. Cf. *LLL* 4.3.218: 'like a rude and savage man of Inde', which almost certainly refers to an East Indian, in light of the play's subsequent lines. Some early English Bibles (e.g. Coverdale (1535), Bishops' (1568)) tell in Jeremiah, 13.23, that 'the man of Inde' could not change his skin, but subsequent and more widely used English Bibles substituted other terms, e.g. 'blacke More' (Geneva, 1560) or 'Ethiopian' (King James, 1611). Like Oxf, we change F's 'Inde' to *Ind* to indicate its probable pronunciation, as in *AYL* 3.2.88, where it rhymes with Rosalind.

60 **four legs** proverbial: 'as good a MAN as . . . (ever went on legs)' (Dent, M66). Here, of course, the tipsy Stephano is indulging in a fanciful paraphrase of the proverb because he sees four legs. See also 64–5.

---

50 'Go hang!'] *Signet; no quotation marks F*   54] *Pope; F lines* too: / comfort. /   56] *Pope; as verse F, lined* matter? / here? /   57 savages] *Capell;* Saluages *F*   58 afeard] afraid *F4, Rowe*   59–60 'As . . . ground'] *Signet; no quotation marks F*

it shall be said so again while Stephano breathes at'
nostrils.

CALIBAN   The spirit torments me! O!

STEPHANO   This is some monster of the isle, with four
legs, who hath got, as I take it, an ague. Where the devil   65
should he learn our language? I will give him some
relief, if it be but for that. If I can recover him and keep
him tame, and get to Naples with him, he's a present
for any emperor that ever trod on neat's leather.

CALIBAN   Do not torment me, prithee. I'll bring my wood   70
home faster.

STEPHANO   He's in his fit now and does not talk after the
wisest. He shall taste of my bottle; if he have never
drunk wine afore, it will go near to remove his fit. If I
can recover him and keep him tame, I will not take too   75
much for him! He shall pay for him that hath him, and
that soundly.

61–2 **at' nostrils** at (through) his, i.e.
Stephano's, nostrils. For this gram-
matical construction, see Abbott, §143.

63 **spirit torments** As above (55), Caliban
is distraught by Stephano's voice, which
he assumes to be a spirit's, or by
Trinculo's trembling (79), or both.

64 **monster** 'An imaginary animal . . .
having a form either partly brute and
partly human or compounded of elements from two or more animal forms'
(cited in *OED sb.* and *a.* A 3a)

65 **ague** fever or chill that causes shivers.
The creature (Caliban/Trinculo) is
shaking.

66 **language** assuming the four-legged
creature to be an indigenous monster,
Stephano is surprised to hear it speak
his language (ostensibly Neapolitan,
actually English).

67 **recover** revive

68–9 **he's . . . leather** proverbial; see
Dent, M66: 'As good a MAN as ever
trod on shoe (neat's) leather (as ever

went on legs)'. See also the cobbler's
comment in *JC* 1.1.25–6 that 'As
proper men as ever trod upon neat's-
leather have gone upon my handiwork',
and 59–60 above. *Neat's leather*:
cowhide.

72–3 **does . . . wisest** does not speak sen-
sibly. See also Dent, W534.1: 'To be
none of the WISEST'.

74 **remove** take away, relieve (cited in
OED v. 4a)

75–6 **I . . . him** No price is too high for
him. '[I]t is impossible for me to sell
him too dear' (Malone, 50). Stephano
shares Trinculo's earlier observation
(27–32) that the monster is marketable
as an oddity, or, as Stephano has suggested (67–9), as a gift to an *emperor*.

76 **that hath him** who will have (i.e buy)
him

77 **soundly** 'Dearly, heavily, in respect of
payment' (first occurrence in *OED
adv.* 3c)

61–2 at' nostrils] at his nostrils *Rowe³*; at 's nostrils *R.G. White*

CALIBAN   Thou dost me yet but little hurt. Thou wilt anon, I know it by thy trembling. Now Prosper works upon thee.   80

STEPHANO   Come on your ways; open your mouth. Here is that which will give language to you, cat. Open your mouth! This will shake your shaking, I can tell you, and that soundly. [*Pours into Caliban's mouth.*] You cannot tell who's your friend. Open your chaps again.   85

TRINCULO   I should know that voice. It should be – but he is drowned, and these are devils. O, defend me!

STEPHANO   Four legs and two voices – a most delicate monster! His forward voice now is to speak well of his friend; his backward voice is to utter foul speeches and   90 to detract. If all the wine in my bottle will recover him, I will help his ague. Come. Amen! I will pour some in thy other mouth.

TRINCULO   Stephano!

STEPHANO   Doth thy other mouth call me? Mercy,   95 mercy! This is a devil and no monster. I will leave him; I have no long spoon.

TRINCULO   Stephano? If thou be'st Stephano, touch me and speak to me, for I am Trinculo! Be not afeard – thy good friend Trinculo.   100

---

79 **thy trembling** i.e. Trinculo's fearful shaking, as Caliban hinted earlier (55, 63), which suggests possession by spirits of the devil

81–2 **Here ... cat.** proverbial; Dent, A99: 'ALE (Liquor) that would make a cat speak'

84–5 **You ... friend.** 'You don't know what's good for you' – i.e. I'm your friend because I have the bottle.

85 **chaps** jaws, chops

88–91 Stephano notes that words are coming out of both ends of the strange monster.

88 **delicate** in the now obsolete sense of 'pleasant' or 'delightful' (*OED a.* 1) rather than the modern 'fragile'

92–3 **Amen ... mouth.** Stephano stops pouring liquor into Caliban's mouth and moves to the opposite side of the gaberdine where Trinculo's head is hidden. *Amen* implies that Caliban has imbibed heartily on his second draught.

97 **long spoon** proverbial: 'He must have a long SPOON that will eat with the devil' (Dent, S771). See also *CE* 4.3.63–4, where Dromio of Syracuse makes an almost identical statement.

---

78 dost] *F3;* do'st *F;* does *Bantam*   84 SD] *this edn*   86 I ... be] *Pope; as verse F, lined* voyce: / I ... be, / be –] *Rowe;* be, *F*   88 voices –] *Signet;* voyces; *F;* voices! *R.G. White*   89 speak well of] speak of *F2*   99 afeard –] *Signet;* afeard, *F;* afraid, *Rowe*

STEPHANO   If thou be'st Trinculo, come forth. I'll pull
thee by the lesser legs. If any be Trinculo's legs, these
are they. [*Pulls him from under the cloak.*] Thou art
very Trinculo indeed! How cam'st thou to be the siege
of this mooncalf? Can he vent Trinculos?   105

TRINCULO   I took him to be killed with a thunderstroke.
But art thou not drowned, Stephano? I hope now thou
art not drowned. Is the storm overblown? I hid me
under the dead mooncalf's gaberdine for fear of the
storm. And art thou living, Stephano? O Stephano, two   110
Neapolitans 'scaped?

STEPHANO   Prithee, do not turn me about; my stomach is
not constant.

CALIBAN
These be fine things, an if they be not sprites;
That's a brave god and bears celestial liquor.   115
I will kneel to him.

STEPHANO   How didst thou scape? How cam'st thou
hither? Swear by this bottle how thou cam'st hither. I

---

102 **lesser legs** Presumably Trinculo's
legs are shorter, thinner or more abundantly clad than Caliban's, if the latter
are clad at all.
104 **very true, real**
siege literally, 'shit' (*OED sb.* 3c:
'Excrement, ordure'). Stephano has
pulled Trinculo from between
Caliban's legs. *Siege* is also an obsolete
word for 'seat', which has encouraged
some editors to argue that Trinculo
crept underneath Caliban.
105 **mooncalf** a misshapen birth, a monstrosity (cited in *OED* 2b), presumably
caused by the full moon. Warburton
notes: 'It was imagined that the Moon
had an ill influence on the infant's
understanding. Hence Idiots were
called *Moon calves*' (45). Steevens's

observation that 'A *moon-calf* is an
inanimate shapeless mass, supposed by
Pliny to be engendered of woman only'
(Malone, 52) fits with Caliban's mysterious parentage but not with most of
the play's references to his physique.
vent excrete: *OED v.*[2] 2b, 'to evacuate
(urine, etc.)'
112–13 Stephano has trouble keeping his
balance because he is so drunk or, as
Orgel notes (and stage productions
often demonstrate), Trinculo might be
swinging Stephano in joy (Oxf[1], 148).
114 **an . . . sprites** Kermode notes that
'Caliban's brave new world, unlike
Miranda's, can only be if the people are
not spirits' (Ard[2], 66). Orgel points out
the connection between *sprites* (spirits)
and celestial liquor (Oxf[1], 148–9).

103 SD] *Oxf*[1]   114 an if] *Pope;* and if *F*   114 – 16] *Ard*[1]*; prose F*   117 – 18 How ...hither] *Pope; F
lines* scape? / hither?/

escaped upon a butt of sack, which the sailors heaved
o'erbord – by this bottle, which I made of the bark of 120
a tree with mine own hands since I was cast ashore.

CALIBAN I'll swear upon that bottle to be thy true subject,
for the liquor is not earthly.

STEPHANO Here, swear then how thou escaped'st.

TRINCULO Swum ashore, man, like a duck. I can swim 125
like a duck, I'll be sworn.

STEPHANO Here, kiss the book.   [*Trinculo drinks.*]
Though thou canst swim like a duck, thou art made like
a goose.

TRINCULO O Stephano, hast any more of this?   130

STEPHANO The whole butt, man. My cellar is in a rock
by th' seaside, where my wine is hid. How now, mooncalf, how does thine ague?

CALIBAN Hast thou not dropped from heaven?

STEPHANO Out o'th' moon, I do assure thee. I was the 135
man i'th' moon when time was.

---

119 butt of sack a cask of white wine.
Sack was a general name for a class of
white wines imported from Spain and
the Canaries (*OED sb.*³ 1a). Its strength
varied greatly; Stephano seems to dis-
pense a potent vintage.

122 thy As with subsequent *thou* (e.g.
134) and *thee* (e.g. 137), Caliban may
signify awe of Stephano, but elsewhere
Stephano uses *thou* to Trinculo (128)
and *thee* to Caliban (135).

125 duck proverbial; see Dent, F328: 'To
swim like a FISH (duck)'.

127 kiss the book a sign of fealty, akin to
kissing the Bible when swearing an
oath. Here, a metaphor for taking
another swig. Stephano realizes his
control of the wine cask determines his
authority, a parallel to Prospero's control of a different sort of 'spirits'.

128–9 made . . . goose Perhaps Trinculo
is shaped like a goose, or perhaps the
liquor makes him waddle.

134–5 The notion that deities inhabit the
sky was, of course, compatible with
classical mythology as well as Christian
popular   theology.   Additionally,
natives along the Virginia Coast were
reputed to believe that 'all the gods
are of humane shape' and initially
suspected, as did natives elsewhere,
that Europeans were supernatural
(Hakluyt, vol. 8, 376–8).

136 man i'th' moon Stephano claims to
be the man whose face appears in a full
moon.
time was proverbial; see Dent,
T341.1: 'When TIME was (i.e. once
upon a time)'.

---

120 o'erbord –] *Cam¹*; o'reboord, *F*   127] *Pope; as verse line F*   SD] *Folg²*
132–3] *Pope; as verse F, lined* hid: / Ague? /

CALIBAN

I have seen thee in her, and I do adore thee!
My mistress showed me thee, and thy dog and thy
    bush.

STEPHANO   Come, swear to that. Kiss the book. I will
furnish it anon with new contents. Swear!   140

[*Caliban drinks.*]

TRINCULO   By this good light, this is a very shallow
monster. I afeard of him? A very weak monster. The
man i'th' moon? A most poor credulous monster! Well
drawn, monster, in good sooth.

CALIBAN

I'll show thee every fertile inch o'th' island,   145
And I will kiss thy foot. I prithee, be my god.

TRINCULO   By this light, a most perfidious and drunken
monster; when's god's asleep, he'll rob his bottle.

CALIBAN

I'll kiss thy foot. I'll swear myself thy subject.

STEPHANO   Come on, then, down and swear.   150

---

138 This line appears to corroborate
Miranda's claim that she taught
Caliban 'each hour / One thing or
other' (1.2.355–6) and thus to support
F's original assignment of 1.2.352–63
to her.
    dog . . . bush The man in the moon
was accompanied by his dog and his
thorn bush, because, according to folk
legend, he had disobeyed the Sabbath
regulations by gathering firewood on a
Sunday; thereupon, the man, still carrying the brush he had gathered, and
his dog were banished to the moon. Cf.
the representation of Moonshine with
thorn bush and dog in *MND*
5.1.238–59.
140 **furnish** provide, supply
141 **By . . . light** probably a paraphrase of

the mild oath 'by God's light'
    shallow lacking in depth of mind,
feeling, or character (*OED a.* 6c). The
fool Trinculo exults in what he sees as
Caliban's credulity.
143–4 **Well drawn** Trinculo praises
Caliban for taking a deep drink.
144 **in good sooth** a mild oath meaning
'truly', 'indeed'
145 **I'll . . . island** Caliban promises to do
for Stephano what he did for Prospero
twelve years earlier, thus underscoring
the parallel between Stephano's liquor
and Prospero's magic.
148 **when's . . . bottle** Trinculo worries
that when Stephano (Caliban's new
god) is asleep, Caliban will steal the
bottle.

---

140 SD] *Penguin*   142 weak] shallow *F2, Rowe*   142–4 The . . . sooth] *Pope; F lines* Moone? /
Monster: / sooth. /   145–6] *Bantam; prose F*   145 island] isle *F2, Rowe*

TRINCULO I shall laugh myself to death at this puppy-
headed monster. A most scurvy monster. I could find
in my heart to beat him –

STEPHANO Come, kiss.

TRINCULO But that the poor monster's in drink. An   155
abominable monster!

CALIBAN

I'll show thee the best springs; I'll pluck thee berries;

I'll fish for thee, and get thee wood enough.

A plague upon the tyrant that I serve!

I'll bear him no more sticks but follow thee,   160

Thou wondrous man.

TRINCULO A most ridiculous monster – to make a
wonder of a poor drunkard!

CALIBAN

I prithee, let me bring thee where crabs grow,

---

151 **laugh . . . death** proverbial; see
Dent, L94.1: 'To die LAUGHING'.

151–2 **puppy-headed** As a result of this
remark, Caliban is sometimes portrayed with floppy ears (cf. John
Mortimer's engraving of 1775; Fig.
15), but there is no reason to assume he
looks especially doglike. Trinculo more
likely means that Caliban is stupid-
looking. Cited in *OED* puppy *sb.* 6 for
'puppy-headed' meaning 'stupid'.

154 **kiss** take another drink, as in 127

157–61 F prints Caliban's speech largely
as prose but, from Pope on, editors
have divided it into iambic pentameter
lines. Caliban speaks the only verse in
this scene when he describes the wonders of his island in speeches that set
him apart from Stephano and
Trinculo. Because Miranda and Prospero were members of the nobility and
taught him their language, Caliban's

poetic idiom reflects their characteristic speech rather than the lower-class
prose of Trinculo and Stephano.
Dryden noted that 'his language is as
hobgoblin as his person; in all things he
is distinguished from other mortals'
(53), a theme that was echoed in Rowe:
'Shakespear *had not only found out a
new Character in his* Caliban, *but had
also devis'd and adapted a new manner of
Language for that Character*' (Rowe[1],
xxiv).

164–9 Like 157–61, this passage was
printed as prose in F, but, since Pope,
editors have divided it into blank verse.
Caliban is describing the island delica-
cies that only he knows how to procure.

164 **crabs** crabapples from trees, or, more
likely, shellfish that breed in rockpools
along the beach

---

153 him –] *Pope;* him. *F*   155 – 6] *Ard[1]; F lines* drinke: /   157 – 8] *Pope; prose F*   160 – 1] *Pope;
prose F*   162 monster –] *this edn; Monster. F*   164 – 9] *Pope; prose F*

And I with my long nails will dig thee pignuts,   165
Show thee a jay's nest, and instruct thee how
To snare the nimble marmoset. I'll bring thee
To clust'ring filberts, and sometimes I'll get thee
Young scamels from the rock. Wilt thou go with me?

STEPHANO   I prithee, now, lead the way without any more   170
talking. Trinculo, the King and all our company else
being drowned, we will inherit here. Here, bear my
bottle. Fellow Trinculo, we'll fill him by and by again.

CALIBAN (*Sings drunkenly.*)

        Farewell, master; farewell, farewell!

TRINCULO   A howling monster, a drunken monster!   175

CALIBAN

        No more dams I'll make for fish,

---

165 **pignuts** a type of edible tuber (*bunium flexuosum*). The nutty root is only obtained by digging; it cannot be pulled up. See Var, 138.

166 **jay's nest** Orgel notes that jays 'were prized for their plumage', but because Caliban seems to be listing things to eat, 'he may be offering Stephano the eggs' (Oxf[1], 150).

167 **marmoset** a small monkey to be captured for a pet or for eating

168 **filberts** hazelnuts

169 **scamels** Theobald suggested a printer's error for 'shamois' or 'sea-mews'; the latter is a sea bird that feeds on fish and is the reading adopted in Oxf. As Orgel notes, the 'context requires, a crustacean, bird, or a fish of the sort frequenting rocks' (Oxf[1], 151). Theobald also suggested a bird called a 'stannel', a kind of hawk (39). Other possibilities come from explorers' descriptions of Patagonian man-eating small fish, *fort scameux* ('very scaly'), or from the French word *squamelle* ('having small scales') that appeared, with variant spellings, in several dictionaries (Frey, 33), from Thomas Hariot's report of

'Seekanauk, a kinde of crusty shel-fish . . . found in shallowes of waters, and sometimes on the shore' in Raleigh's Virginia (Hakluyt, vol. 8, 370–1), or from the Irish *scallachan* (Callaghan). We imagine scamels as shellfish, perhaps like mussels, but the exact meaning remains a mystery. See the long discussion in Var, 138–40. First occurrence in *OED* 'scamel', its 'meaning uncertain'.

172 **inherit** 'to succeed as an heir; to take possession of an inheritance' (cited in *OED v.* 5)

173 **him** Ostensibly Stephano refers to the empty bottle, but the use of this pronoun suggests Caliban as well.
    by and by immediately (*OED* 3), or, soon (*OED* 4)

176 **dams** Caliban refers to a method of catching fish by damming streams so that they can be easily caught in fish weirs. Although some commentators have claimed this as evidence of American Indian influence on the play, catching fish in weirs on dammed streams had long been common in England and was perhaps a universal fishing technique.

---

169 scamels] *om. Dryden & Davenant*; shamois *Theobald*; sea-malls *Hanmer*; seamews *Oxf*

Nor fetch in firing at requiring,
Nor scrape trenchering, nor wash dish.
    Ban' ban' Ca-caliban,
    Has a new master, get a new man.   180
Freedom, high-day; high-day freedom; freedom high-
day, freedom.

STEPHANO   O brave monster, lead the way.   *Exeunt.*

3.1   *Enter* FERDINAND, *bearing a log.*

FERDINAND
There be some sports are painful, and their labour
Delight in them sets off. Some kinds of baseness
Are nobly undergone; and most poor matters
Point to rich ends. This my mean task

---

177 **firing . . . requiring** firewood on
demand
178 **trenchering** wooden or earthenware
plates (only occurrence in *OED* 2:
'Trenchers collectively'), perhaps
invented as a progressive verb to
extend the pattern of 177
179 **Ca-caliban** Caliban's syncopation
may be a sign of intoxication or simply
a rhythmic embellishment to his song.
180 proverbial; see Dent, M723: 'Like
(Such a) MASTER like (such a) man
(servant)'. Stephano will replace Prospero as Caliban's master; Prospero will
have to *get* a new servant.
181–2 **high-day** day of celebration, holiday
183 **brave** Stephano uses the word sarcastically, in mockery of Caliban's
bravado in declaring his independence
from Prospero (176–80). Cf. *AYL*
3.4.40–1: 'O, that's a brave man! he
writes brave verse, speaks brave words,
swears brave oaths'.
3.1 Early editors located this scene in
front of Prospero's cave, but it could

also occur elsewhere on the island. In a
visual parallel to Caliban's entrance in
2.1, Ferdinand enters bearing wood
that Prospero has ordered him to move
from one unspecified place to another,
presumably for heating or cooking, or
perhaps for creating an alchemical boil
(Simonds, 'Charms', 543).
1 **sports** exercises or athletic pastimes.
Ferdinand alludes to the mixture of
satisfaction taken in exercise and the
physical effort required by such pastimes; the effort and the delight, in
effect, compensate for the pain. See
Mac 2.3.50: 'The labour we delight in
physics pain'.
painful 'causing pain or suffering'
(*OED a.* 1), or, more likely, 'toilsome,
laborious' (*OED a.* 3)
2–3 **Some . . . undergone** One may perform base acts (manual labour) and still
retain a noble character.
2 **baseness** a reference to the low status
of manual labour
4 **ends** results
mean humble

181–2 high-day] Heigh-day *Dryden & Davenant*; Hey-day *Rowe*   3.1] *Actus Tertius. Scoena Prima.*
Location] Prospero's Cave *Pope*; Before Prospero's Cell *Theobald*   1 and] *(&)*; but *Pope*   2 sets]
Rowe; set *F*

Would be as heavy to me as odious, but   5
The mistress which I serve quickens what's dead,
And makes my labours pleasures. O, she is
Ten times more gentle than her father's crabbed,
And he's composed of harshness. I must remove
Some thousands of these logs and pile them up,   10
Upon a sore injunction. My sweet mistress
Weeps when she sees me work and says such baseness
Had never like executor. I forget;
But these sweet thoughts do even refresh my labours
Most busilest when I do it.

Enter MIRANDA[,] *and* PROSPERO
[at a distance, unseen].

MIRANDA   Alas now, pray you,   15
Work not so hard. I would the lightning had

---

5   **heavy** sorrowful, grievous (*OED a.* 25)
6   **quickens** makes alive
8   **crabbed** irritable, churlish (cited in *OED a.* 1b)
9   **harshness** severity, rigour
11   **sore injunction** harsh command
13   **executor** exècutor; agent, performer, one who carries out a purpose (cited in *OED* 1)
     I forget After these reveries, Ferdinand reminds himself to get back to work. He is working when Miranda addresses him in 15.
15   *****busilest** a heavily debated textual crux, generating twelve pages of commentary in Furness (*Var*, 144–55). We adopt this reading from Kermode (Ard², 71–3), who argues to our satisfaction that F's 'busie lest' is a corruption entered by the compositor for Shakespeare's *busilest*, the rarely used superlative form of the adverb 'busily',

modifying the verb *refresh*. Other commentators have emended to the adjective 'busiest'. In either case, Ferdinand is reflecting on the pleasure that thoughts of Miranda have for him and how they lighten the onerous task (*it*) that Prospero has assigned him. Kermode concludes that such thoughts 'attend him [Ferdinand] even more assiduously when he works'.

15.2 Rowe's addition to F's SD (see t.n.) clarifies the actors' stage positions. Prospero enters separately from Miranda and places himself in a position to overhear her conversation with Ferdinand. He might have appeared on the upper stage at the Globe or the Blackfriars, though he could eavesdrop equally well from behind a pillar on the main stage. Bell omits Prospero altogether from this scene in his 1773 acting edition.

---

5 as] as 'tis *Pope*   9 remove] move *Pope*   15 busilest] *Ard²;* busie lest *F;* busie least *F2;* least busy *Pope;* busie-less *Theobald;* busiest *R.G. White;* busil'est *Riv*   15.2] *Rowe*

241

Burnt up those logs that you are enjoined to pile!
Pray set it down and rest you. When this burns,
'Twill weep for having wearied you. My father
Is hard at study; pray now, rest yourself.   20
He's safe for these three hours.

FERDINAND   O most dear mistress,
The sun will set before I shall discharge
What I must strive to do.

MIRANDA   If you'll sit down,
I'll bear your logs the while. Pray give me that;
I'll carry it to the pile.

FERDINAND   No, precious creature,   25
I had rather crack my sinews, break my back,
Than you should such dishonour undergo
While I sit lazy by.

MIRANDA   It would become me
As well as it does you, and I should do it
With much more ease, for my good will is to it,   30
And yours it is against.

PROSPERO [*aside*]   Poor worm, thou art infected!
This visitation shows it.

MIRANDA   You look wearily.

19 **'Twill weep** Resin will seep from the log when it burns. Miranda personifies the log, attributing to it tears of sympathy for Ferdinand's enforced labour.

21 **He's ... hours.** 'He will remain safely in his study, away from us, for the next three hours.'

22 **discharge** 'fulfill, execute' (*OED v.* 11). Cf. *MND* 5.1.204: 'Thus have I, Wall, my part discharged so'.

23 **strive** 'endeavour vigorously' (*OED v.* 9)

26 **crack my sinews** sprain my tendons (or muscles)

28–31 Cf. 2–3. Like Ferdinand, Miranda does not find manual labour beneath her dignity.

31 **worm** 'A human being likened to a worm' (*OED sb.* 10a) with a 'qualification expressing tenderness, playfulness, or commiseration' (cited in *OED sb.* 10c). Prospero affectionately compares Miranda to a *worm* who is infected with disease, in this case, love and desire for Ferdinand.

32 **visitation** Miranda's visit to Ferdinand, but Prospero – following up on the previous line's *infected* – may also be punning on *visitation* as 'the onset of plague'.
wearily Use of an adverb in lieu of an adjective is not unusual in Shakespeare. Cf. 2.1.322 and n.

17 you are] thou art *F2, Rowe¹*; thou'rt *Rowe³*; you're *Hanmer*   31 SD] *Signet (Capell)*

FERDINAND

    No, noble mistress, 'tis fresh morning with me
    When you are by at night. I do beseech you –
    Chiefly that I might set it in my prayers –   35
    What is your name?

MIRANDA   Miranda. – O my father,
    I have broke your hest to say so!

FERDINAND   Admired Miranda!
    Indeed the top of admiration, worth
    What's dearest to the world! Full many a lady
    I have eyed with best regard, and many a time   40
    Th' harmony of their tongues hath into bondage
    Brought my too diligent ear. For several virtues
    Have I liked several women; never any
    With so full soul but some defect in her
    Did quarrel with the noblest grace she owed   45
    And put it to the foil. But you, O you,
    So perfect and so peerless, are created
    Of every creature's best.

MIRANDA   I do not know

---

34 **by** near, nearby
37 **hest** behest, command
    Admired Miranda See List of Roles, n. 14. She is literally 'worthy of wonder'.
38 **top of admiration** epitome of wonder, the most admired
39 **dearest . . . world** the most valued in the world
40 **regard** look, glance (*OED sb.* 2a); or, esteem, affection (*OED sb.* 10a)
42 **diligent** 'attentive', 'heedful' (*OED a.* 3)
44–6 **but . . . foil** A *foil* is a rapier used in fencing. Ferdinand reports that the ladies he has known always had some defect that overwhelmed or defeated their virtues (as in a swordfight or

quarrel). Or, he may use *foil* in the sense of 'thwart' – i.e. the lady's defect foiled the otherwise successful effects of her *noblest grace*.
45 **owed** owned, possessed
47 **perfect** complete (*OED a.* B 3a); or, 'free from any flaw' (*OED a.* B 4a)
48 **Of . . . best** Johnson suggested an allusion here to Apelles' painting of Venus, which 'was a synthesis of the most perfect features of the most beautiful women the painter could find' (Oxf[1], 154). Steevens disagreed and cited instead a fable from Sidney's *Arcadia* (1598), Bk 3, 384–7, where the animals ask Jupiter to create a king to rule over them. Jove combines every creature's 'best' feature to make 'Man'.

---

34 you –] *Cam[1]*; you *F*   35 prayers –] *Cam[1]*; prayers, *F*   37 I have] I've *Pope*   47 peerless] *F2*; peetlesse *F*

One of my sex, no woman's face remember –
Save, from my glass, mine own. Nor have I seen   50
More that I may call men than you, good friend,
And my dear father. How features are abroad
I am skilless of, but by my modesty
(The jewel in my dower), I would not wish
Any companion in the world but you,   55
Nor can imagination form a shape,
Besides yourself, to like of. But I prattle
Something too wildly, and my father's precepts
I therein do forget.

FERDINAND   I am, in my condition,
A prince, Miranda; I do think a king   60
(I would not so!) and would no more endure
This wooden slavery than to suffer
The flesh-fly blow my mouth! Hear my soul speak:
The very instant that I saw you did
My heart fly to your service, there resides   65

Miranda, Ferdinand implies, combines all the *best* features of women without their defects. Cf. Orlando's description of the composite Rosalind in *AYL* 3.2.141–50.

50 **glass** mirror

51–2 In 1.2.446 Miranda states that Ferdinand is the *third man* she ever saw, thus including Prospero and Caliban in the trio. Here she omits Caliban and compares Ferdinand only with her father.

52 **features** bodily shapes, proportions
abroad elsewhere, in the world at large

53 **skilless** ignorant
modesty 'Womanly propriety of behaviour; scrupulous chastity of thought, speech, and conduct' (cited in *OED* 3a)

54 **jewel . . . dower** Miranda refers to her

virginity, the most precious gift she will bring as a dowry to her husband when she marries.

57 **like of** admire, derive pleasure from

58 **Something** somewhat, a little (cited in *OED adv.* B 2e)

59 **condition** 'social position, rank' (cited in *OED sb.* 10)

61 **I . . . so** I wish it were not so.

62 **wooden slavery** an implied comparison with Caliban. Ferdinand alludes to his forced log-carrying and his virtual enslavement by Prospero.
suffer allow

63 **flesh-fly** a fly that lays its eggs in carrion
blow 'to deposit eggs on or in (a place)' (cited in *OED v.* 28c). Cf. *LLL* 5.2.408–9: 'these summer flies / Have blown me full of maggot ostentation'.

49 remember –] *this edn;* remember, *F*   59 therein] *om. Pope*   62 wooden] *F2, Rowe;* wodden *F*
to] I would *Pope*

To make me slave to it, and for your sake
Am I this patient log-man.

MIRANDA   Do you love me?

FERDINAND

O heaven, O earth, bear witness to this sound,
And crown what I profess with kind event
If I speak true; if hollowly, invert   70
What best is boded me to mischief! I,
Beyond all limit of what else i'th' world,
Do love, prize, honour you.

MIRANDA   I am a fool
To weep at what I am glad of.

PROSPERO [*aside*]   Fair encounter
Of two most rare affections! Heavens rain grace   75
On that which breeds between 'em.

FERDINAND   Wherefore weep you?

MIRANDA

At mine unworthiness that dare not offer
What I desire to give, and much less take
What I shall die to want. But this is trifling,
And all the more it seeks to hide itself,   80
The bigger bulk it shows. Hence, bashful cunning,
And prompt me, plain and holy innocence!
I am your wife, if you will marry me;

---

66 **it** i.e. *your service* (stress probably on
    your, and similarly in 65)
69 **kind event** good fortune, happy out-
    come
70–1 **invert . . . mischief** turn any
    promised good fortune into bad; *mis-*
    chief, misfortune, distress (*OED sb.* 1)
72 **what** whatever
75–6 **Heavens . . . 'em.** a reminder of
    Prospero's awareness of the dynastic
    implications in Ferdinand and Mir-
    anda's union; the child they breed

will become heir to both Naples and
Milan.
79 **die to want** die for lack of. Miranda
    fears she will *die* (metaphorically) for
    not having Ferdinand's love.
80–1 **it . . . itself . . . it** Miranda's desire.
    Barton suggests a metaphor of preg-
    nancy (Penguin, 162).
81–2 **Hence . . . innocence!** Away with
    coyness; may candid and pure inno-
    cence guide me.

74 SD] *Signet (Capell)*

If not, I'll die your maid. To be your fellow
You may deny me, but I'll be your servant   85
Whether you will or no.

FERDINAND   My mistress, dearest,
And I thus humble ever.

MIRANDA
My husband, then?

FERDINAND   Ay, with a heart as willing
As bondage e'er of freedom. Here's my hand.

MIRANDA
And mine, with my heart in't. And now farewell   90
Till half an hour hence.

FERDINAND   A thousand thousand!
                    Exeunt [Miranda and Ferdinand].

PROSPERO
So glad of this as they I cannot be,
Who are surprised withal, but my rejoicing
At nothing can be more. I'll to my book,
For yet ere suppertime must I perform   95
Much business appertaining.   *Exit.*

---

84 **die your maid** Even though Miranda
has confessed her desire, she rejects
sexual relations outside marriage.
Maid is thus used in the double sense
of 'virgin' and 'servant'.
fellow spouse (cited in *OED sb.* 4a)

86 **Whether ... no.** proverbial; see Dent,
W400.1: 'Whether one WILL or no'.
mistress the feminized form of 'master', with no suggestion of illicit sex;
Ferdinand declares that Miranda is the
ruler of his heart.

89 **As . . . freedom** Ferdinand pledges
himself to Miranda as eagerly as a person in bondage embraces freedom.

89–90 Miranda and Ferdinand's pledge of

betrothal is signified by the taking of
hands.

91 **A thousand thousand!** a million
(farewells). Cf. *TN* 2.4.63: 'A thousand, thousand sighs'.

93 **withal** by it

93–4 **my . . . more** 'Nothing could make
me rejoice more.'

96 **business appertaining** appropriate
tasks; *business* refers to Prospero's
plans for the union of Miranda and
Ferdinand and, more generally, to
Prospero's agenda in raising the tempest. Placing the adjective after the
noun was a fairly common Shakespearean sequence (Abbott, §419, 420).

88 as] so *F2, Rowe*   91 SD] *Capell (Exeunt* FER. *and* MIR. *severally.)*   93 withal] *Theobald;* with
all *F*

3.2 *Enter* CALIBAN, STEPHANO *and* TRINCULO.

STEPHANO   Tell not me. When the butt is out, we will
drink water; not a drop before. Therefore bear up and
board 'em. Servant monster, drink to me.

TRINCULO   Servant monster? The folly of this island!
They say there's but five upon this isle; we are three of   5
them. If th'other two be brained like us, the state totters.

STEPHANO   Drink, servant monster, when I bid thee. Thy
eyes are almost set in thy head.

TRINCULO   Where should they be set else? He were a
brave monster, indeed, if they were set in his tail.   10

STEPHANO   My man-monster hath drowned his tongue
in sack. For my part, the sea cannot drown me. I swam,
ere I could recover the shore, five and thirty leagues off

3.2.1. **Tell not me.** Trinculo has perhaps
asked Stephano to stop drinking, but he
refuses; or, Trinculo may have pointed
out that the bottle is getting low, even if
Stephano replenished it after 2.2.
2   **bear up** stay up, do not fall
3   **board 'em** a naval command used figuratively here to mean 'Drink up!'
3, 4 **Servant monster** Ben Jonson derided Shakespeare's '*Servant-monster*'
in the Induction to *Bartholomew Fair*,
6. 16. In 4, Trinculo perhaps questions
how the drunken monster can be a servant when the master is as drunk as he
is. If the rest of the island's population
is equally pickled, *the state totters* (6).
4   **folly** Kermode suggests that Trinculo
means 'freak' rather than generalized
foolishness, perhaps in a reference to
the freaks and monsters who inhabit
Bartholomew Fair and thus to Caliban
(Ard[2], 78). But the term could equally
apply to Stephano's foolery or to the
general absurdity of the island, in
Stephano's drunken perception.
5   **They say** Although Trinculo suggests
that he is reporting general knowledge
– i.e. 'everyone knows' – the text gives
no hint that he has communicated with

anyone on the island but Stephano and
Caliban, and only the latter can have
known the number of people on the
island. Even Caliban, of course, is
unaware of the court party and
Ferdinand.
6   **brained . . . us** as addle-brained as we
are
7–8 **Thy . . . head.** slang expression for
'You're drunk'. See Eric Partridge, 1.
261.
10 **brave** probably in the sense of famous
or worthy (*OED a.* 3), though other definitions are possible. Cf. 2.2.183 and n.
tail Richard Farmer refers to a story
from Stowe's *Survey*: 'It seems, in the
year 1574, a whale was thrown a shore
near *Ramsgate*. "A *monstrous fish . . .*
but not so *monstrous* as some reported,
– for his eyes were in his *head*, and not
in his *back*"' (Malone, 60).
13 **five . . . leagues** A league was a measure of distance of approximately three
miles, so the total distance described
here would be about 100 miles.
Stephano's drunken boast is inconsis-
tent with his earlier claim that he
floated to shore on 'a butt of sack'
(2.2.118–19).

3.2] *Scoena Secunda.*   Location] The other part of the Island *Pope*

and on. By this light, thou shalt be my lieutenant,
monster, or my standard.   15

TRINCULO   Your lieutenant, if you list; he's no standard.

STEPHANO   We'll not run, Monsieur Monster.

TRINCULO   Nor go, neither; but you'll lie like dogs and
yet say nothing, neither.

STEPHANO   Mooncalf, speak once in thy life, if thou be'st   20
a good mooncalf.

CALIBAN   How does thy honour? Let me lick thy shoe. I'll
not serve him; he is not valiant.

TRINCULO   Thou liest, most ignorant monster. I am in
case to jostle a constable. Why thou deboshed fish,   25
thou, was there ever man a coward that hath drunk so
much sack as I today? Wilt thou tell a monstrous lie,
being but half a fish and half a monster?

CALIBAN   Lo, how he mocks me. Wilt thou let him, my lord?

TRINCULO   'Lord', quoth he? That a monster should be   30
such a natural!

CALIBAN   Lo, lo again! Bite him to death, I prithee.

STEPHANO   Trinculo, keep a good tongue in your head. If
you prove a mutineer – the next tree! The poor monster's my subject, and he shall not suffer indignity.   35

15, 16 **standard** ensign or flagbearer; the
standard could also be the pole that
bears the flag. Trinculo's retort 'is a
reminder that none of these characters
can now do much valiant standing'
(Everyman, 104).

16 **list** like

17 **run** run away from battle; perhaps
with the suggestion that, like a good
ensign, he'll hold the *standard* high

18 **go** walk; proverbial from 'He may ill
RUN that cannot go' (Dent, R208)
lie like dogs proverbial; see Dent,
D510.2: 'To lie (in field, etc.) like a

DOG (hound)', but also with the sense
of not telling the truth.

24–5 **in case** ready, or valiant enough

25 **deboshed** a variant of debauched. We
retain the original spelling (modernized) because it may suggest the
slurred quality of Trinculo's drunken
speech.

31 **natural** fool, idiot

33 **keep . . . head** proverbial for 'be careful what you say'; see Dent, T402: 'to
keep a good TONGUE in one's head'.

33–4 **If . . . tree!** 'You'll be hanged like a
mutineer from the *next tree*.'

14 on. By] *Johnson & Stevens;* on, by *F;* on; by *Rowe* light, thou] *Theobald;* light thou *F;* light. –
Thou *Capell* 25 deboshed] debauch'd *Dryden & Davenant;* debauched *Oxf¹* 27 tell] tell me *F2,*
Rowe 34 mutineer –] *Signet;* mutineere, *F*

CALIBAN   I thank my noble lord. Wilt thou be pleased to
   hearken once again to the suit I made to thee?
STEPHANO   Marry, will I. Kneel and repeat it; I will
   stand, and so shall Trinculo.

Enter ARIEL, *invisible.*

CALIBAN
   As I told thee before, I am subject to a tyrant,   40
   A sorcerer, that by his cunning hath
   Cheated me of the island.
ARIEL [*in Trinculo's voice*]
   Thou liest.
CALIBAN   Thou liest, thou jesting monkey, thou.
   I would my valiant master would destroy thee.
   I do not lie.   45
STEPHANO   Trinculo, if you trouble him any more in's
   tale, by this hand, I will supplant some of your teeth.
TRINCULO   Why, I said nothing.
STEPHANO   Mum, then, and no more. Proceed.
CALIBAN
   I say, by sorcery he got this isle.   50
   From me he got it. If thy greatness will
   Revenge it on him – for I know thou dar'st,

---

38 **Marry** a mild oath abbreviated from
  'by the Virgin Mary'
41 **sorcerer** Caliban equates Prospero's
  magic with the black magic practised
  by his mother Sycorax.
43 ¹**Thou liest.** Cf. *MND* 3.2.360–1,
  where Oberon commands Puck to imi-
  tate the voices of Lysander and
  Demetrius.
47 **supplant** an interesting word choice

given the play's emphasis on usurpation; cf. Antonio's language in 2.1.270
and the harpy's speech, 3.3.70.
48–9 **I . . . nothing. / Mum** proverbial:
'I will (etc.) say NOTHING (nought)
but mum' (Dent, N279).
51 **thy greatness** Caliban's honorific
attests to his infatuation with Stephano's authority and his *celestial liquor*
(2.2.115).

36 – 7 to . . . again] *F, Rowe³; once again to hearken F3, Rowe¹*   38 – 9] Pope; *as verse F, lined* it, /
Trinculo. /   40 – 2] *this edn; prose F*   43 SD] *Folg²*   43 – 5] *prose Folg²*   46 – 7] *Pope; as verse F,*
lined tale, / teeth. /   50 isle.] *this edn;* Isle *F;* Isle, *F4;* isle; *Ard²*   52 him –] *Signet (Capell);* him, *F*

But this thing dare not –
STEPHANO   That's most certain.
CALIBAN

Thou shalt be lord of it, and I'll serve thee.   55
STEPHANO   How now shall this be compassed? Canst
thou bring me to the party?
CALIBAN

Yea, yea, my lord, I'll yield him thee asleep,
Where thou mayst knock a nail into his head.
ARIEL [*in Trinculo's voice*]   Thou liest, thou canst not.   60
CALIBAN

What a pied ninny's this? Thou scurvy patch!
I do beseech thy greatness, give him blows,
And take his bottle from him. When that's gone,
He shall drink nought but brine, for I'll not show him
Where the quick freshes are.   65
STEPHANO   Trinculo, run into no further danger.
Interrupt the monster one word further, and by this
hand I'll turn my mercy out o'doors and make a
stockfish of thee.

---

53 **this thing** Trinculo
56 **compassed** accomplished
59 **knock . . . head** Cf. Judges, 4.21,
   where Jael hammered a nail into
   Sisera's temples.
61 **pied ninny** a reference to the jester and
   his costume; *pied* describes the parti-
   coloured garment and *ninny* is the simpleton who wears it. This passage, in
   accord with Crane's 'Names of the
   Actors' listing Trinculo as *a jester*, lends
   credence to those who personate
   Trinculo as an official court fool dressed
   in motley. He was represented in the
   harlequin's colourful costume in the
   RSC 1994 and A.R.T. 1995 productions, but some directors choose instead
   to costume him in a serviceable uni-

form similar to Stephano's steward's
garb (see Introduction, pp. 12–13).
patch another term for fool or jester.
According to *OED sb.²*, 'Patch' was the
name of Cardinal Wolsey's domestic
fool.
64 **brine** sea water
65 **quick freshes** flowing (*quick*) streams
   of fresh water. Caliban reported showing these to Prospero in 1.2.339.
68 **turn . . . doors** 'banish any merciful
   feelings I might have'
68–9 **make a stockfish** *stockfish*, dried
   cod or other fish. *OED* 1b cites this as
   an example of a 'jocular expression'
   referring to the 'beating of the fish
   before cooking'. See Dent, S867: 'To
   beat one like a STOCKFISH'.

---

53 not –] *Johnson & Steevens¹*; not. *F*   56 now] *om. Pope*   56–7] *Pope; as verse F, lined* compast? /
party? /   60 SD] *Folg²*   66] *prose Pope; as verse F*

TRINCULO   Why, what did I? I did nothing. I'll go farther   70
off.

STEPHANO   Didst thou not say he lied?

ARIEL [*in Trinculo's voice*]   Thou liest.

STEPHANO   Do I so? Take thou that! [*Hits Trinculo.*] As
you like this, give me the lie another time!   75

TRINCULO   I did not give thee the lie. Out o'your wits and
hearing too? A pox o'your bottle! This can sack and
drinking do. A murrain on your monster, and the devil
take your fingers.

CALIBAN   Ha, ha, ha!   80

STEPHANO   Now, forward with your tale. [*to Trinculo*]
Prithee, stand farther off.

CALIBAN

Beat him enough; after a little time,
I'll beat him too.

STEPHANO [*to Trinculo*]   Stand farther. [*to Caliban*] Come,   85
proceed.

CALIBAN

Why, as I told thee, 'tis a custom with him
I'th' afternoon to sleep. There thou mayst brain him,
Having first seized his books, or with a log
Batter his skull, or paunch him with a stake,   90
Or cut his wezand with thy knife. Remember

75 **give . . . lie** accuse me of lying
77 **pox** a standard seventeenth-century
curse, meaning may you be diseased.
'Pox' was often shorthand for 'the
French pox' or syphilis, though it
could be used less specifically.
78 **murrain** a plague or pestilence
82 **stand farther off** almost certainly
addressed to Trinculo, but see Var,
167, where Furness opines that
Stephano is telling the ill-smelling
Caliban to move farther away

87–8 **'tis . . . him** Cf. *Ham* 1.5.59–70,
where the ghost of Hamlet's father
describes how he was murdered during his customary nap.
89 **seized his books** Caliban knows that
Prospero's books are an important
source of his magical powers.
90 **paunch** 'to stab or wound in the
paunch' (i.e. stomach) (cited in *OED*
$v.^1$ 1)
91 **wezand** windpipe

70-1] *Pope; as verse F, lined* nothing: / off. /   70 go] *F*; go no *F²*, *Rowe*   73 SD] *Folg²*   74 thou] you *F3*   SD]
this edn; Beats him / Rowe; strikes him / Malone   74 – 5] *Ard¹*; *F lines* that, /   76 thee the] *F4*; the *F*
77 – 8 A Pox . . . do] *prose Pope; as verse F*   81 SD] *Signet*   85 SD1] *Riv*   SD2] *Oxf*

251

First to possess his books, for without them
He's but a sot, as I am, nor hath not
One spirit to command. They all do hate him
As rootedly as I. Burn but his books. 95
He has brave utensils (for so he calls them)
Which, when he has a house, he'll deck withal.
And that most deeply to consider is
The beauty of his daughter; he himself
Calls her a nonpareil. I never saw a woman 100
But only Sycorax, my dam, and she;
But she as far surpasseth Sycorax
As great'st does least.

STEPHANO   Is it so brave a lass?

CALIBAN

Ay, lord, she will become thy bed, I warrant,
And bring thee forth brave brood. 105

STEPHANO   Monster, I will kill this man. His daughter
and I will be king and queen – save our graces – and
Trinculo and thyself shall be viceroys. Dost thou like
the plot, Trinculo?

93 **sot** fool, but with the added connotation of 'drunkard'. *OED sb.*[1] A 2 defines a sot as 'One who dulls or stupefies himself with drinking'.
95 **rootedly** in a 'firmly grounded manner' (first occurrence in *OED adv.*)
but especially or only
96 **brave utensils** (ùtensils) impressive implements, perhaps for magic or alchemy, perhaps merely household goods with which Caliban would presumably be unfamiliar
97 **deck** decorate, furnish
100 **nonpareil** a person having no equal. Capt. John Smith described Pocahontas as 'the only *Nonpareil*' of Powhatan's chiefdom (J. Smith, *Relation*, E3ᵛ). Shakespeare had previously used the word in *AC*, *Cym*, *Mac* and *TN*.

100–1 **I . . . she** Caliban is in a situation analogous to Miranda; raised and educated by Prospero on the island, he has never seen any women besides her and his own mother, while until now she had never seen any men but Caliban and her father.
101 **dam** mother
103 **brave** splendid
104 **become** grace, adorn (cited in *OED v.* 9c)
105 **brood** Like Prospero, Caliban speculates about Miranda's children; as the offspring of Stephano and Miranda, they would inherit the island.
108 **viceroys** those appointed to rule in place of the monarch or as deputies
109 **plot** plan or scheme; but Kermode also suggests the Elizabethan sense of

93 nor] and *Pope*   100 ²a] *om. Pope*   103 least] the least *Rowe*   108–9] *Pope; as verse F, lined* Vice-royes: / Trinculo? /

TRINCULO   Excellent.   110

STEPHANO   Give me thy hand. I am sorry I beat thee, but
   while thou livest, keep a good tongue in thy head.

CALIBAN

   Within this half hour will he be asleep.

   Wilt thou destroy him then?

STEPHANO   Ay, on mine honour.

ARIEL [*aside*]   This will I tell my master.   115

CALIBAN

   Thou mak'st me merry; I am full of pleasure.

   Let us be jocund. Will you troll the catch

   You taught me but whilere?

STEPHANO   At thy request, monster. I will do reason, any
   reason. Come on, Trinculo, let us sing.   120
   Sings.

          Flout 'em and scout 'em,

          And scout 'em and flout 'em,

          Thought is free.

CALIBAN   That's not the tune.

               Ariel plays the tune on a tabor and pipe.

STEPHANO   What is this same?   125

---

a 'skeleton programme giving a synop-
sis of a masque or entertainment'
(Ard², 82).

117 **jocund** cheerful, merry
   troll the catch sing the song in a full,
   rolling voice (cited in *OED* troll *v.*
   10a). A catch, like a modern round (e.g.
   'Three Blind Mice'), begins with one
   voice singing the opening line and then
   proceeding to the next line while a second voice sings the first line, and so
   forth until at least three are singing different parts of the song at once.

118 **whilere** a short time ago; the only use
   of the word in Shakespeare (cited in
   OED adv. arch.)

119 **do reason** do anything reasonable

121 ***scout** 'mock' or 'deride'. F's reading, 'cout', is emended here to match
   skowt in 122, but, as Orgel implies
   (Oxf¹, 161), the original reading of
   'cout' (colt, gibe) also could have connoted an obscenity, such as 'cut' or
   'cunt'.

123 Cf. *TN* 1.3.68, where Maria says the
   same thing, in the sense of 'I can think
   whatever I like'.

124 SD *tabor* small drum used to accompany a tubular wind instrument (*pipe*)
   which, in this case, was played with
   one hand

111–12] *Pope; as verse F, lined* thee: / head. /   115 SD] *Oxf (Capell)*   119–20] *Pope; as verse F,
lined* reason, / sing. /   119 any] And *F2*   121–2] *Ard¹; one line F*   121 scout] *Capell; cout F;*
skout *Pope*   122 scout] *(skowt)*

TRINCULO   This is the tune of our catch, played by the
   picture of Nobody.

STEPHANO   If thou be'st a man, show thyself in thy
   likeness. If thou be'st a devil, take't as thou list.

TRINCULO   O, forgive me my sins!   130

STEPHANO   He that dies pays all debts. I defy thee. Mercy
   upon us!

CALIBAN   Art thou afeard?

STEPHANO   No, monster, not I.

CALIBAN

   Be not afeard. The isle is full of noises,   135
   Sounds and sweet airs that give delight and hurt not.
   Sometimes a thousand twangling instruments
   Will hum about mine ears; and sometimes voices,
   That if I then had waked after long sleep,
   Will make me sleep again; and then in dreaming,   140
   The clouds, methought, would open and show riches
   Ready to drop upon me, that when I waked
   I cried to dream again.

STEPHANO   This will prove a brave kingdom to me, where
   I shall have my music for nothing.   145

127 **picture of Nobody** Kermode suggests a topical allusion here to a picture of a man all head, legs and arms, with no trunk (body), which appeared on the title-page of the comedy *No-body and Some-body* (1606). John Trundle, a London bookseller who in 1603 helped to publish the first quarto of *Hamlet*, used the sign of Nobody (Ard², 83–4; Var, 171). Whether this was a topical joke or not, Trinculo is responding to Ariel's music, which seems to come from nowhere and be performed by *Nobody*.

129 **If . . . list** proverbial; see Dent, T27: 'TAKE as you will (list, please)' – in effect, 'if you're a devil, do what you will; we can't stop you'.

131 **He . . . debts.** proverbial; see Dent, D148: 'DEATH pays all debts'; i.e. the dead are free of debts. The jailor tells Posthumus in *Cym* 5.4.158–9 that 'the comfort' of his impending execution 'is, you shall be call'd to no more payments, fear no more tavern-bills'.

137 **twangling instruments** Pope emended to 'twanging', but F's reading (cited in *OED ppl. a*) connotes more clearly the sounds of stringed instruments. Hortensio complains that after Kate brained him with the lute, she called him a 'twangling Jack' (*TS* 2.1.158).

131 – 2] Ard²; F lines thee; / 137 twangling] twanging *Pope* 138 sometimes] *F2*; sometime *F* 142 that] then *Johnson*; om. *Pope* 144 – 5] *Pope*; as verse F, lined me, / nothing. /

CALIBAN   When Prospero is destroyed.

STEPHANO   That shall be by and by. I remember the
story.

TRINCULO   The sound is going away. Let's follow it, and
after do our work.   150

STEPHANO   Lead, monster, we'll follow. I would I could
see this taborer; he lays it on.

TRINCULO   [*to Caliban*]   Wilt come? I'll follow Stephano.

Exeunt.

3.3   *Enter* ALONSO, SEBASTIAN, ANTONIO,
GONZALO, ADRIAN, FRANCISCO *and others.*

GONZALO

By'r lakin, I can go no further, sir;
My old bones aches. Here's a maze trod, indeed,

147 **by and by** immediately (*OED adv.
phr.* 3); or, soon (*OED adv. phr.* 4)
152 **this taborer** Ariel, who plays the
tabor while invisible
153 Some editors assign *Wilt come?* to
Stephano (see Var, 173, and Folg²,
109); others (e.g. Ard², 85) place a
comma after *follow.* We see no persuasive reason to change F's assignment
and punctuation. The lines occur at
the end of a column in F and were
probably separated simply to fill out
the extra space caused by an under-
estimate of cast-off copy for the page.
Malone suggests that when Stephano
lingers in hopes of seeing the invisible
taborer, Trinculo enquires, 'Will you
come, or not? . . . If you will not, *I'll
follow* Caliban without you' (Malone,
65). It seems more likely that Trinculo
is addressing Caliban here, announc-

ing his own intention to follow
Stephano.
3.3.0.2 *F's SD lists '&c.'* along with the
Neapolitans and Antonio. Most editors simply record F's reading, but Oxf
and Oxf¹ omit it. We emend '&c.' to
and others to be consistent with the initial SD of 2.1. Directors can decide
whether to include supernumeraries
in the court party; presumably
Shakespeare did, or the '&c.' would
probably not have been recorded.
1   **lakin** an abbreviation for 'ladykin', an
obsolete shortening of 'by our
Ladykin' (the Virgin Mary) (cited in
OED lakin²)
2   **aches** A singular verb follows a plural
object. Cited in Abbott, §333.
Here's . . . trod 'We're lost!' Mazes
constructed of hedges were popular in
English gardens of the period.

147–8] *Pope; as verse F, lined* by: / storie. /   149–50] *Pope; as verse F, lined* away, / worke. /
151–2] *Pope; as verse F, lined* Monster, / Taborer, / on. /   152 this] his *F3*   153] *Pope; F lines*
come? / Stephano. /   SP] *om. Folg²*   I'll] STE. I'll follow. *Capell;* TRINCULO I'll follow *Folg²*
3.3] *Scena Tertia.*   Location] Changes again to another part of the Island *Pope*   0.2 *and others*]
Malone; &c. F; om. Oxf

Through forthrights and meanders! By your patience,
I needs must rest me.

ALONSO   Old lord, I cannot blame thee,
    Who am myself attached with weariness   5
    To th' dulling of my spirits. Sit down and rest.
    Even here I will put off my hope and keep it
    No longer for my flatterer. He is drowned
    Whom thus we stray to find, and the sea mocks
    Our frustrate search on land. Well, let him go.   10

ANTONIO [*aside to Sebastian*]
    I am right glad that he's so out of hope.
    Do not, for one repulse, forgo the purpose
    That you resolved t'effect.

SEBASTIAN [*aside to Antonio*]   The next advantage
    Will we take throughly.

ANTONIO   Let it be tonight,
    For now they are oppressed with travail; they   15
    Will not, nor cannot, use such vigilance
    As when they are fresh.

SEBASTIAN   I say tonight. No more.

---

3 **forthrights and meanders** paths
   that are straight and paths that are
   crooked

5 **attached with** seized by

7 **Even here** now, at this point in time.
   Cf. *AC* 4.12.19–20, where Antony
   motions to his men: 'even here / Do we
   shake hands'.

8 **flatterer** Like a court flatterer, *hope*
   has been telling Alonso what he wants
   to hear rather than the truth.

10 **frustrate** unsuccessful, thwarted

14 **throughly** thoroughly. We retain F's
    archaic spelling so that Shakespeare's
    metre will not be disturbed.

15 **travail** Many editors modernize F's
    'trauaile' to 'travel'. The words were
    interchangeable in 1611, when travel-
    ling was extremely arduous. We have
    retained the original word with its sug-
    gestions of exhaustion because it fits
    more closely with the royal party's
    experience and with Antonio's plan.

11 SD] *Hanmer*   13 SD] *Ard¹ (Capell)*   13–14 The . . . throughly] *Pope; one line F*   15 travail]
(trauaile)

Solemn and strange music, and PROSPERO *on the top (invisible).*
Enter several strange shapes, bringing in a banquet, and dance
about it with gentle actions of salutations, and inviting the
King etc. to eat, they depart.

ALONSO

What harmony is this? My good friends, hark!

GONZALO

Marvellous sweet music!

ALONSO

Give us kind keepers, heavens! What were these?   20

SEBASTIAN

A living drollery! Now I will believe
That there are unicorns; that in Arabia
There is one tree, the phoenix' throne, one phoenix
At this hour reigning there.

ANTONIO   I'll believe both;
And what does else want credit, come to me   25

17.1 *the top (invisible)* As Orgel notes, the top was 'a technical term for the level above the upper stage gallery, within which the musicians sat' (Oxf[1], 164). From this, the highest vista of the theatre, Prospero can view the ensuing action without being seen by the court party.

20 **keepers** protecting spirits, guardian angels

were F's use of the past tense here suggests that Prospero's Spirits do exactly what the SD directs – bring in a banquet, invite the court party to eat, and depart. Hence we see no merit in moving F's 17.4 ('*they depart*') to later in the scene as some editions do.

21 **living drollery** a comic puppet show enacted by living beings

22 **unicorns** mythological four-footed beasts with horns in the centre of their foreheads; when ground into powder, the horn was believed to be an aphro-

disiac. Pliny described a 'Licorne or monoceros: his bodie resembleth an horse, his head a stagge, his feet an Elephant, his taile a bore; he loweth after an hideous manner; one blacke horn he hath in the mids of his forehead, bearing out two cubits in length: by report, this wild beast cannot possibly be caught alive' (106). Sometimes the unicorn was confused with the rhinoceros, which explorers had encountered in Africa.

23–4 **phoenix' . . . there** The phoenix was a mythological Arabian bird which was miraculously reborn from the ashes of its own funeral pyre (*throne*) every 500 years; only one bird existed at any given time. Shakespeare's enigmatic 'The Phoenix and Turtle' appeared in a 1601 collection of poems appended to Robert Chester's *Love's Martyr*.

25 **want credit** lack credibility

17.1] *Pope; after* fresh *F*   PROSPERO] *Rowe; Prosper F*   17.3 *salutations*] salutation *Rowe²*   20
heavens] *(heaues); heauen Pope*   were] are *F4, Rowe*

257

And I'll be sworn 'tis true. Travellers ne'er did lie,
Though fools at home condemn 'em.

GONZALO   If in Naples

I should report this now, would they believe me?
If I should say I saw such islanders
(For certes, these are people of the island),   30
Who, though they are of monstrous shape, yet note
Their manners are more gentle, kind, than of
Our human generation you shall find
Many – nay, almost any.

PROSPERO [*aside*]   Honest lord,

Thou hast said well, for some of you there present   35
Are worse than devils.

ALONSO   I cannot too much muse

Such shapes, such gesture and such sound, expressing
(Although they want the use of tongue) a kind
Of excellent dumb discourse.

PROSPERO [*aside*]   Praise in departing.

---

26 **Travellers ... lie** Antonio inverts the
proverbial expression, 'A TRAVELER
may lie with authority' (Dent, T476).
In 21–4 Sebastian refers to the im-
probable stories brought home by travellers such as John Mandeville, whose
fourteenth-century travelogue, first
published in English in 1503, included
numerous woodcuts. It was published
several more times and circulated
widely in sixteenth-century England.
30 **certes** certainly
31–4 These lines seem to echo Montaigne's discussion of the comparative
merits of Brazilian Indian culture and
European ways in 'Of the Caniballes'.
See Appendix 1.2.
33 **Our human generation** (1) our
nation, (2) our 'race', or, more likely,
(3) our species – i.e. humankind.
Although Gonzalo calls them *people*

(30), he implies that the creatures are
not human, which comports with
other evidence, e.g. 3.2.4–5.
36 **muse** wonder at
39 **Praise in departing.** Prospero ruefully responds to Alonso's praise of the
vanishing figures with a proverbial
expression (Dent, P83) that advises
guests to reserve their praise for the
host's entertainment until they depart,
lest they prematurely praise something
that will prove unsatisfactory. This
should not be taken, as some editors
suggest, as a reference to the Spirits'
departure, which occurred some
twenty lines earlier, but as Prospero's
ironic aside. He knows what other
entertainment is in store for the
Neapolitans and that it won't be nearly
as pleasant as the spectacle they have
just experienced.

---

29 islanders] *F2, Rowe; Islands F*   34 Many –] *Signet;* Many, *F*   SD] *Johnson & Steevens*
(Capell)   35 present] *Rowe;* present; *F;* present, *F2*   39 SD] *Johnson & Steevens (Capell)*

FRANCISCO

They vanished strangely!

SEBASTIAN   No matter, since   40
They have left their viands behind, for we have
    stomachs.
Will't please you taste of what is here?

ALONSO   Not I.

GONZALO

Faith, sir, you need not fear. When we were boys,
Who would believe that there were mountaineers
Dewlapped like bulls, whose throats had hanging at 'em   45
Wallets of flesh? Or that there were such men
Whose heads stood in their breasts, which now we find
Each putter-out of five for one will bring us
Good warrant of?

ALONSO   I will stand to and feed,
Although my last; no matter, since I feel   50

---

41 **viands** dishes of food
   stomachs appetites
44–6 **mountaineers . . . flesh** exotic people dwelling in the mountains whose
   necks have a dewlap or fold of skin
   hanging down. *Wallets* are wattles, or
   protuberant nodules of flesh (cited in
   OED sb. 2).
46–7 **men . . . breasts** Travellers' tales
   reported the existence of strange 'men
   whose heads do grow beneath their
   shoulders' (*Oth* 1.3.144–5). See Pliny,
   96, where Blemmyi are described with
   'no heads, but mouth and eies both in
   their breast'.
48 **putter-out . . . one** English travellers
   often insured their trips with London
   brokers. Before leaving, they
   deposited a specified sum; if they
   returned with proof they had reached
   their destination, the broker owed
   them five times the amount. Given the
   difficulties of travel in that period, the

odds were in favour of the broker.
Theobald first clarified the passage
with a reference to Ben Jonson's *Every
Man out of his Humour*, in which
Puntarvolo, '*A Vaine-glorious Knight*',
declares: 'I doe intend this yeere of
Jubile . . . to travaile: and (because I will
not altogether goe upon expence) I am
determined to put forth some five
thousand pound, to be paid me, five for
one, upon the returne of my selfe, my
wife, and my dog, from the *Turkes*
court in *Constantinople*. If all, or either
of us miscarry in the journey, 'tis gone:
if we be successfull, why, there will be
five and twenty thousand pound, to
entertaine time withall' (3.423, 477).
In Shakespeare's passage, as Orgel
notes, the *putter-out* is either the traveller or the broker; either would be in
a position to give *Good warrant* of the
traveller's veracity (Oxf[1], 166).
49 **stand to** come forward; set to work

42 SP] *Ant. / Hanmer*

The best is past. Brother, my lord the Duke,
Stand to and do as we.

Thunder and lightning. Enter ARIEL, *like a harpy, claps
his wings upon the table, and with a quaint device the
banquet vanishes.*

ARIEL

    You are three men of sin, whom destiny,
That hath to instrument this lower world
And what is in't, the never-surfeited sea   55
Hath caused to belch up you, and on this island
Where man doth not inhabit – you 'mongst men
Being most unfit to live – I have made you mad;
And even with such-like valour, men hang and drown
Their proper selves.
       [Alonso, Sebastian and Antonio draw their swords.]
       You fools! I and my fellows   60

52.1 *harpy* a mythical predatory bird with a woman's head, talons for hands and the body of a vulture, associated with divine retribution. The spectacle that follows visually alludes to the *Aeneid*. After landing on the Strophades, Aeneas and his men are twice accosted by a band of harpies who disturb their attempts to dine. When the men draw their swords on the birds, Celaeno (their leader) predicts that Aeneas will find Italy: 'ye shall not gird with walls your promised city until dread hunger and the wrong of violence towards us force you to gnaw with your teeth and devour your very tables!' (Bk 3, 209–77).

52.2 *quaint device* an example of Crane's descriptive SD. A prompter would have specified the mechanism to be used; instead, Crane describes what the spectator would have seen. See Introduction, pp. 129–30.

52.3 *banquet vanishes* Some mechanical

device was probably used to make the banquet disappear; in many productions the table top is quickly overturned or swivelled to reveal a bare surface where the food had been. Mowat notes that this sort of magical disappearance was a common juggler's trick ('Hocus', 301).

53–4 destiny...world 'Destiny uses the lower, material world to enact its plans.'

53 destiny supernatural or preordained outcome (cited in *OED sb.* 4)

54 to instrument as its instrument

55–6 the...you The object precedes the verb; '*destiny* has caused the sea to *belch* you up'.

59 such-like valour 'the quality of mind which enables a person to face danger with boldness or firmness'(*OED* valour 3); the context here suggests excessive or misguided courage.

60 Their proper selves their own (as property) selves

52.1 *harpy*] *(Harpey)* 56 up you] you up *F4, Rowe;* up *Theobald* 57 inhabit –] *Riv;* inhabit, *F*
58 live –] *this edn;* liue: *F* 60 SD] *Bantam*

Are ministers of fate. The elements
Of whom your swords are tempered may as well
Wound the loud winds, or with bemocked-at stabs
Kill the still-closing waters, as diminish
One dowl that's in my plume. My fellow ministers   65
Are like invulnerable. If you could hurt,
Your swords are now too massy for your strengths
And will not be uplifted. But remember
(For that's my business to you) that you three
From Milan did supplant good Prospero,   70
Exposed unto the sea, which hath requit it,
Him and his innocent child; for which foul deed,
The powers delaying, not forgetting, have
Incensed the seas and shores – yea, all the creatures –
Against your peace. Thee of thy son, Alonso,   75
They have bereft, and do pronounce by me
Ling'ring perdition, worse than any death
Can be at once, shall step by step attend

61 **ministers** agents, servants
61–2 **elements . . . tempered** raw materials with which (*whom*) *your swords*
have been hardened
63 **bemocked-at** scorned
64 **still-closing waters** waters that close
again after the *bemocked-at stabs*
attempt to *Kill* them
65 **dowl . . . plume** *OED* dowl, which
cites this line, defines it as 'One of the
filaments or fibres of a feather; . . .
down'. Antonio and the Neapolitans
cannot touch a strand in Ariel's feath-
ery tail, which is either 'displayed in
pride' or 'ruffled in excitement'.
66 **like** similarly
    could This word should be stressed to
imply that they cannot hurt at all.
67 **massy** heavy, massive
69 **business** mission

71 **requit it** repaid. The attempt to
drown Prospero and Miranda has been
avenged by the tempest and the supposed drowning of Ferdinand.
73 **powers** deities
77 **Ling'ring perdition** This substantive serves both as the object of the
verb *pronounce* (76) and the subject of
the verb *shall . . . attend* (78). The con-
fusing syntax is perhaps symptomatic
of Ariel's (and Prospero's) agitation.
The phrase also connotes the continuous pain suffered under everlasting
damnation. *Perdition* here means 'utter
destruction, complete ruin' (*OED* 1a).
78 **attend** probably meant in the sense of
'To follow closely upon, to accompany', although the earliest example in
OED is from 1615 (*v.* 10)

63 bemocked-at stabs] *(*bemockt-at-Stabs*)*   64 still-closing] *(*still closing*)*   65 dowl] down *Pope*
plume] *Rowe;* plumbe *F*   74 shores –] *Cam¹;* Shores; *F*   creatures –] *this edn;* Creatures *F*

You and your ways, whose wraths to guard you from –
Which here, in this most desolate isle, else falls   80
Upon your heads – is nothing but heart's sorrow
And a clear life ensuing.

He vanishes in thunder. Then, to soft music, enter the
shapes again and dance with mocks and mows, and
carry out the table.

PROSPERO

Bravely the figure of this harpy hast thou
Performed, my Ariel; a grace it had, devouring.
Of my instruction hast thou nothing bated   85
In what thou hadst to say. So, with good life
And observation strange, my meaner ministers
Their several kinds have done. My high charms work,
And these, mine enemies, are all knit up
In their distractions. They now are in my power;   90
And in these fits I leave them while I visit

79 **whose wraths** the anger of *The pow-*
ers (73)
81–2 **is . . . ensuing** 'There is no means
but heartfelt repentance and a pure life
hereafter.'
82.1 *He vanishes* Dessen argues that in
this case, *vanishes* simply indicates
Ariel's sudden disappearance, not the
use of a special stage mechanism (213).
82.2 *mocks and mows* This descriptive
SD draws on the traditional association between two terms for grimacing
facial expressions. See Dent, M1030:
'To MOCK (mop) and mow'. Cf. *KL*
4.1.61–2, where Poor Tom raves about
'Flibbertigibbet, of mopping and
mowing'.
83 **Bravely** admirably, splendidly
figure in the obsolete sense of 'art
enacted' (cited in *OED sb.* 11a)
84 **devouring** could mean that (1) Ariel's

impersonation gracefully devoured
(consumed) the banquet, or (2) Ariel's
impersonation displayed a 'ravishing
grace'. Both senses may be in play at
once.
85 **bated** omitted, neglected
86–7 **good . . . strange** energy or vivacity
and attention to detail
87 **observation** 'observant care, heed'
(cited in *OED* 4)
meaner ministers the (lesser) Spirits
who assisted Ariel
88 **several kinds** according to their specific natures
high charms Prospero thinks his
magic (*charms*) are of the most elevated
(*high*) or superior kind, perhaps in contrast to the low charms of the witch
Sycorax.
89–90 **knit . . . distractions** entangled by
their temporary madness

79 from –] *Cam¹;* from, *F*   81 heads –] *Cam¹;* heads, *F*   heart's sorrow] *(*hearts-sorrow*)*   82.3
carry] *Capell; carrying F*   83 harpy] *(Harpie)*

Young Ferdinand (whom they suppose is drowned)
And his, and mine, loved darling.   *[Exit.]*

GONZALO

     I'th' name of something holy, sir, why stand you
     In this strange stare?

ALONSO   O, it is monstrous, monstrous!   95

     Methought the billows spoke and told me of it;
     The winds did sing it to me, and the thunder –
     That deep and dreadful organpipe – pronounced
     The name of Prosper. It did bass my trespass.
     Therefore my son i'th' ooze is bedded, and   100
     I'll seek him deeper than e'er plummet sounded,
     And with him there lie mudded.   *Exit.*

SEBASTIAN

     But one fiend at a time,
     I'll fight their legions o'er.

ANTONIO   I'll be thy second.
                      Exeunt [Sebastian and Antonio].

GONZALO

     All three of them are desperate: their great guilt,   105
     Like poison given to work a great time after,
     Now 'gins to bite the spirits. I do beseech you

---

92 **whom** who; see Abbott, §410.

96 **it** Alonso's *trespass* (99)

98 **deep** 'Low in pitch, grave' (cited in *OED a.* 14)

99 **bass my trespass** *OED* (bass *v.*²) uses this as its only example of 'To utter or proclaim with bass voice or sound'. *Bass* is a pun as well on the baseness of Alonso's actions.

101 **plummet** a weight-based mechanism used to determine vertical distances, especially in navigation. This line is echoed in 5.1.56.

103–4 **But . . . o'er.** 'If they come one by one, I'll battle whole legions of devilish spirits.'

second 'one who renders aid or support' (cited in *OED a.* 9), and – with a first recorded occurrence in 1613 – a term from duelling or boxing for the back-up combatant

106 **poison** *Leicester's Commonwealth*, a scurrilous tract attacking the Earl of Leicester and originally published as *The Copie of a Leter . . .* , refers to a poison that 'might so be tempered and given as it should not apeare presentlie, and yet should kill the partie afterward at what time should be appointed' (London, 1584, 29).

107 **bite the spirits** erode their vitality

93 mine] my *Rowe*   97–8 thunder – / That] *this edn;* Thunder / (That *F*   98 organpipe –] *this edn;* Organ-Pipe) *F*   99 bass] *Johnson;* base, *F*   104 SD *Sebastian and Antonio*] *Malone*   107 do] *om. Pope*

That are of suppler joints, follow them swiftly,
And hinder them from what this ecstasy
May now provoke them to.

ADRIAN   Follow, I pray you.   110

Exeunt omnes.

4.1   *Enter* PROSPERO, FERDINAND *and* MIRANDA.

PROSPERO [*to Ferdinand*]

If I have too austerely punished you,
Your compensation makes amends, for I
Have given you here a third of mine own life,
Or that for which I live, who once again
I tender to thy hand. All thy vexations   5
Were but my trials of thy love, and thou
Hast strangely stood the test. Here, afore heaven,
I ratify this my rich gift. O Ferdinand,
Do not smile at me that I boast her off,

---

108 **suppler joints** more flexible and physically fit
109–10 **hinder . . . to** prevent their madness (*ecstasy*) from inducing *desperate* (105) actions, possibly suicide
4.1.3 **third . . . life** Several explanations are plausible: (1) that 15-year-old Miranda has been with, and was raised by, Prospero for one-third of his life (thus making him 45, in the play's most important clue to his age); or (2) that his daughter is one of his three greatest riches, along with his dukedom and his art, or, alternatively, his wife and himself; or, less literally, (3) that Miranda is a major ingredient of his happiness, expressed imprecisely as one-third, much as Prospero later uses *Every third thought* as a rough estimate (5.1.312). Theobald argued that *third* was an insult to Miranda and

emended to 'thread', a reading rejected by later editors. Bacon contends that the explanation based on Prospero's age makes the most sense, and we agree. For an extended discussion see Var, 187–9.

7 **strangely** exceptionally, admirably
9 ***her off** Although F has 'of', F2–4 emend to 'off', as does Rowe. *Boast her off* suggests that Prospero is singing Miranda's praises, which he insists she *will outstrip*. Some editions since Cam[1] have argued that the compositor of F reversed the words and therefore invert the sequence to 'of her'. The second 'f' was often omitted from 'off' in the Jacobean era, though seldom in Shakespeare. See Var, 189. J.D. Wilson's suggestion of 'hereof' (i.e. the gift of Miranda) is also plausible (Cam[1], 101–2).

4.1] *Actus Quartus. Scena Prima.*   Location] Prospero's Cave *Pope*   3 third] thread *Theobald*
5 tender] render *Rowe[1]*   7 test] rest *F2*   9 her off] *F2, Rowe;* her of *F;* hereof *Cam[1];* of her *Oxf,*
Oxf[1], Folg[2]

For thou shalt find she will outstrip all praise   10
And make it halt behind her.

FERDINAND   I do believe it

Against an oracle.

PROSPERO

Then as my gift and thine own acquisition
Worthily purchased, take my daughter. But
If thou dost break her virgin-knot before   15
All sanctimonious ceremonies may
With full and holy rite be ministered,
No sweet aspersion shall the heavens let fall
To make this contract grow; but barren hate,
Sour-eyed disdain and discord shall bestrew   20
The union of your bed with weeds so loathly
That you shall hate it both. Therefore take heed,
As Hymen's lamps shall light you.

FERDINAND   As I hope

11 **halt** limp (*OED v.*[1] 1). Miranda is so far beyond *praise* that *praise* itself limps *behind her*.

12 i.e. in defiance of an oracle's testimony

13 *****gift** Modern editors have accepted Rowe's emendation of F's 'guest' to 'gift' on the basis of Crane's characteristic spelling, 'guift', which the compositor may have misread as 'guest'. *Gift* suggests the cultural practice in which men exchange a woman to consolidate their relationship. Prospero's *gift* of Miranda to Ferdinand establishes a kinship tie between the men (Singh, 199).

15 **virgin-knot** maidenhead. Prospero warns of the dangers of taking Miranda's virginity before marriage, in what could be an allusion to the Latin expression *zonam solvere* – to untie the girdle, a euphemism for loss of virginity. Shakespeare might also have had in mind Catullus' poem to Hymen (LXI, 52–3): '*tibi virgines zonula soluunt sinus*' – 'for thee the virgins loose their garments from their

girdle' (Loeb trans., Cambridge, Mass., 1988), an allusion that only makes sense if the girdle is knotted.

16 **sanctimonious** holy, sacred

17 *****rite** F's 'right' is not implausible, but the context of *sanctimonious ceremonies* (holy in character) suggests that the modern *rite* was intended, although either or both meanings could apply. Cf. *Oth* 1.3.257, where Desdemona's 'rites' (F) conflates the sense of sexual rights (as a wife) with the sense of ceremonial rites (marriage rituals).

18 **sweet aspersion** sprinkling or shower of, presumably, holy water (cited in *OED* aspersion 2). Prospero suggests that the marriage will be barren and miserable if the couple engages in premarital sex.

20–1 **bestrew . . . weeds** cóver the marriage bed (and the marriage) with *weeds* rather than the customary flowers

23 **Hymen's lamps** Hymen, god of marriage in Greek and Roman mythology, carried a torch that shone brightly on a

11 do] *om. Pope*   13 gift] *Rowe;* guest *F*   14 But] *om. F2, Rowe*   17 rite] *(right)*   20 Sour-eyed] *(Sower-ey'd)*

For quiet days, fair issue and long life,
With such love as 'tis now, the murkiest den,   25
The most opportune place, the strong'st suggestion
Our worser genius can, shall never melt
Mine honour into lust to take away
The edge of that day's celebration,
When I shall think or Phoebus' steeds are foundered   30
Or night kept chained below.

PROSPERO   Fairly spoke.
Sit then and talk with her; she is thine own.
What, Ariel! My industrious servant Ariel!

Enter ARIEL.

ARIEL
What would my potent master? Here I am.

PROSPERO
Thou and thy meaner fellows your last service   35
Did worthily perform, and I must use you
In such another trick. Go bring the rabble
(O'er whom I give thee power) here to this place.

happy union, smokily on a marriage that was ill-fated. See 97 (*Hymen's torch*), which suggests that *lamps* here should perhaps be singular.

25 **murkiest den** dark and concealed cave or hideaway, perhaps suggestive of the cave where Dido and Aeneas had sexual relations

26-7 **strong'st . . . can** greatest temptation that our most evil spirit (*worser genius*) can propose (first occurrence in *OED* genius 1c)

29 **edge** keenness, enjoyment (cited in *OED sb.* 2a), with implications too of anticipated sexual excitement when the marriage is consummated
  that . . . celebration the wedding-day festivities

30-1 **Phoebus' . . . below** Ferdinand will

not 'take away / The edge' of the forthcoming marriage when, to him, the sun will seem never to set (as if the sun god's horses have foundered, i.e. gone lame) nor the wedding night ever to arrive (as if night has been imprisoned beneath the Antipodes). The lengthiness of the wedding day and the anticipation of the wedding night were common themes in hymeneal songs and epithalamia.

33 **What** an exclamation used to 'summon, or call the attention of a person' (cited in *OED* B 3)

35 **meaner fellows** lesser Spirits; Ariel's subordinates

37 **such another** another such
  rabble Ariel's minions; apparently meant pejoratively (*OED sb.*[1] A 1–2)

27 genius] *(Genius)*

Incite them to quick motion, for I must
Bestow upon the eyes of this young couple   40
Some vanity of mine art. It is my promise,
And they expect it from me.

ARIEL   Presently?

PROSPERO
Ay, with a twink.

ARIEL
                    Before you can say 'come' and 'go',
                    And breathe twice and cry 'so, so',   45
                    Each one tripping on his toe,
                    Will be here with mop and mow.
                    Do you love me, master? No?

PROSPERO
Dearly, my delicate Ariel. Do not approach   49
Till thou dost hear me call.

ARIEL   Well, I conceive.   *Exit.*

PROSPERO [*to Ferdinand*]
Look thou be true. Do not give dalliance
Too much the rein. The strongest oaths are straw

---

39 **quick motion** rapid, swift (cited in *OED* quick *a.* 24)

41 **vanity . . . art** light-hearted display of magic, a pleasing illusion; perhaps an allusion to Cornelius Agrippa's *De vanitate et incertitudine artium et scientiarum*, translated into English by J. Sanford as *Of the Vanity of arts and sciences* (1569)

42 **Presently?** right away, immediately?

43 **twink** 'A winking of the eye', or 'the time taken by this' (*OED sb.*[1] 1). Cf. *TS* 2.1.308–10: 'kiss on kiss / She vied so fast . . . / That in a twink she won me to her love'.

46 **tripping** moving quickly, nimbly

47 **mop and mow** grimace (*OED sb.* 3) and pout (*OED sb.* 2). See also 3.3.82.2.

49 **delicate** 'fine or exquisite in quality or nature' (*OED a.* 6b); or, delightful, charming (*OED a.* 1)

50 **conceive** understand

51 **dalliance** amorous conversation and, perhaps, gestures. While Prospero addressed Ariel, Ferdinand and Miranda were no doubt demonstrating their mutual affection.

52 **Too . . . rein** undue liberty, perhaps from the proverbial expression, 'To give one the BRIDLE (reins)' (Dent, B671)

52–3 **strongest . . . blood** Blood was assumed to be the seat of strong passions, including sexual. Prospero warns that even the lovers' oaths of abstinence could melt in the heat of their *dalliance*.

51 SD] *Cam*[1]   52 rein] *(*raigne*)*

To th' fire i'th' blood. Be more abstemious
Or else good night your vow!

FERDINAND   I warrant you, sir,

    The white cold virgin snow upon my heart   55
    Abates the ardour of my liver.

PROSPERO   Well! –

    Now come, my Ariel; bring a corollary
    Rather than want a spirit. Appear, and pertly.   *Soft music.*
    No tongue, all eyes. Be silent!

Enter IRIS.

IRIS

    Ceres, most bounteous lady, thy rich leas   60
    Of wheat, rye, barley, vetches, oats and peas;
    Thy turfy mountains where live nibbling sheep,
    And flat meads thatched with stover them to keep;

54 **good night** farewell to
  warrant guarantee, assure
55–6 **The . . . liver** Ferdinand, his heart 'as chaste (pure) as ICE' (Dent, I1, from *Ham* 3.1.135), combats his liver's passions. The liver, according to humoural theory, was the seat of physical passion and desire.
57–8 **bring . . . spirit** i.e. bring an extra spirit (*meaner fellow*) rather than have too few for the task. *Corollary* is an obsolete word for 'something additional', or 'supernumerary' (cited in *OED* 4).
58 **want** lack
  pertly smartly, quickly (cited in *OED adv.* 3)
59 **No tongue** In some modern performances, Ferdinand and Miranda are caught 'French-kissing' here, but it is far more likely that Prospero simply

asks them to be quiet. Cf. Faustus's request to the emperor and his court to remain in 'dumb silence' while he presents the shapes of Alexander and his paramour (Marlowe, B text (1616), 4.1.96).
59.1 **IRIS** See List of Roles, n. 16; Introduction, pp. 70–1.
60 **Ceres** See List of Roles, n. 17; Introduction, pp. 70–2.
  leas fields, meadows
61 **vetches** coarse crops often used for fodder, tares; sometimes spelled 'fetches' before the late seventeenth century but almost always *vetches* thereafter. See Gerard, 1052–4.
62 **turfy** covered with grass (*OED a.*)
63 **meads . . . keep** meadows covered with growth of fodder for sheep. *Stover* is any type of grass that is stored to make fodder.

53 abstemious] *(abstenious)* 61 vetches] *(Fetches)* peas] *(Pease)* 62 turfy mountains]
(Turphie-Mountaines) 63 thatched with] *(thetchd with)*; with thatched *Hanmer*

Thy banks with pioned and twilled brims,
Which spongy April at thy hest betrims   65
To make cold nymphs chaste crowns; and thy
        broomgroves
Whose shadow the dismissed bachelor loves,
Being lass-lorn; thy pole-clipped vineyard,
And thy sea-marge, sterile and rocky-hard,
Where thou thyself dost air – the queen o'th' sky,   70
Whose watery arch and messenger am I,
Bids thee leave these, and with her sovereign grace,

64 **pioned and twilled** pionèd, twillèd.
OED pioned and *OED* twilled cite this
as the first occurrence and indicate that
the meanings are uncertain. The most
persuasive explanation of this long-
debated phrase seems to be that the
meadow's banks are lacerated or
trenched (*pioned*) by the currents of
streams or drainage ditches and tan-
gled with exposed roots, but whether
the phrase describes natural erosion or
human efforts to prevent further dam-
age (i.e. *twilled* or woven with sticks)
has no consensus. Early editors offered
horticultural substitutes, such as
'peonied' and 'tulip'd', and *twilled* was
sometimes changed to 'lilied' or 'wil-
low'd'. See Var, 195–201 for an
exhaustive account of early emendations. For more recent explanations,
see Harrison, who glosses the terms
using the 1936 *Handbook of Erosion-
Control Engineering on the National
Forests*, and Fox, who relates the terms
to ditching and hedging in Warwick-
shire.

65 **spongy** rainy
   hest behest, command
66 **cold nymphs** The nymphs are cold
   because of their restraint from sexual
   activity.
   chaste crowns coronets of flowers,
   symbols of virginity

broomgroves areas of terrain covered
with yellow-flowered shrubs. Although editors have debated whether
broom, which Gerard defines as 'a bush
or shrubbie plant' (Gerard, 1130), can
be described as growing in a grove,
which usually consists of trees (Var,
201–2), we agree with Orgel that the
passage should be taken as Shakespeare's invention. Orgel also notes
that 'broom figures significantly in
magic spells designed to ensure the
success of love affairs', which explains
why the *dismissed bachelor* loves it
(Oxf[1], 174).

67 **dismissed** dismissèd; rejected (first
   occurrence in *OED v.* 6)
68 **lass-lorn** bereft of lasses
   pole-clipped cited in *OED sb.*[1] 5 for
   hyphenated variant of *pole* – 'pertain-
   ing to or made of a pole or poles', but
   equally plausible is the sense of hedged
   in by tall stakes (*OED sb.*[1] 5c), or the
   modern 'poll', in which case the meaning is 'pruned short' (pollarded; *OED
   sb.*[1] 3)
69 **sea-marge** margin of the sea, sea-
   coast
70 **queen o'th' sky** Juno; see List of
   Roles, n. 18; Introduction, pp. 68–73.
71 **watery arch** rainbow, Iris' sign
72 **these** the terrain described above

64 pioned] peonied *Oxf;* pionied *Theobald²*   twilled] tulip'd *Rowe;* tilled *Capell;* lilied *R.G. White*
68 pole-clipped] poll-clipt *Ard²;* pale-clipt *Hanmer*   70 air –] *Cam¹;* ayre, *F*   71 I,] *F2; I. F*

JUNO *descends.*

Here on this grass-plot, in this very place,
To come and sport. Her peacocks fly amain.
Approach, rich Ceres, her to entertain.   75

Enter CERES.

CERES

Hail, many-coloured messenger, that ne'er
Dost disobey the wife of Jupiter;
Who, with thy saffron wings, upon my flowers
Diffusest honey-drops, refreshing showers,
And with each end of thy blue bow dost crown   80
My bosky acres and my unshrubbed down,
Rich scarf to my proud earth. Why hath thy queen
Summoned me hither to this short-grassed green?

72.1 Eighteenth-century editors usually moved F's SD to 102, arguing that Juno's appearance is not noted until Ceres announces, *Great Juno comes*. But, as Jowett contends, '*descends*' may refer to the 'convention of the floating deity' whereby 'the deity would be expected, upon appearing from the heavens, to remain suspended in the air rather than to come down to the stage'. Ceres' announcement of Juno's arrival at 102 marks the 'second stage of the descent to earth'. See Jowett, 115–17.

74 **peacocks fly amain** Peacocks, Juno's sacred birds, draw her carriage speedily. In many stage productions Juno appears in a chariot drawn by actors dressed as peacocks, but she may also descend astride a single giant bird.

75 **to entertain** 'to show hospitality to' (*OED v.* 13)

76 **many-coloured messenger** addressed to Iris, the gods' messenger,

who probably wears a costume suggesting her sign, the rainbow

77 **wife of Jupiter** Juno; Jupiter was the king of gods.

78 **saffron wings** yellow-coloured wings, perhaps reflecting the sun

79 **Diffusest honey-drops** shed sweet drops of rain

81 **bosky . . . down** cited in *OED* bosky *a.*[1] to illustrate 'Consisting of or covered with bushes or underwood; full of thickets, bushy' – hence, shrub-covered fields and bare undulating hills (*unshrubbed down*)

82 **Rich scarf** Iris, the rainbow or *many-coloured messenger*, forms a colourful *scarf* that covers Ceres' earth (first occurrence in *OED* scarf *sb.*[1] 3c as a figurative use).

83 **short-grassed green** the lawn on which the masque is imagined to take place, which was probably mowed short and thus made suitable for dancing. As Orgel contends, this phrase

72.1] *F; opp. 102 Ard¹, Bantam, Folg²*   74 Her] *Rowe;* here *F*   75.1] *enter [Ariel as] Ceres Oxf, Oxf¹*   83 short-grassed] *Rowe¹;* short gras'd *F;* short-grass *Rowe³, Pope;* short-grazed *(RP)*

IRIS

A contract of true love to celebrate,
And some donation freely to estate 85
On the blessed lovers.

CERES   Tell me, heavenly bow,
If Venus or her son, as thou dost know,
Do now attend the queen? Since they did plot
The means that dusky Dis my daughter got,
Her and her blind boy's scandaled company 90
I have forsworn.

IRIS   Of her society
Be not afraid. I met her deity
Cutting the clouds towards Paphos, and her son
Dove-drawn with her. Here thought they to have done
Some wanton charm upon this man and maid, 95

may also refer to the 'green cloth that carpeted the dancing area when the Banqueting House was set up for a masque' or to green rushes that covered the stages in public theatres (Oxf[1], 175).

85 **donation . . . estate** gift generously to bestow

86 **blessed** blessèd
bow rainbow, Iris' sign

87 **Venus . . . son** the goddess of love and her son Cupid. Both were associated with sexual desire. See Introduction, pp. 70–1.
as as far as

89 **dusky Dis** dark Pluto. Shakespeare uses a Roman name for the god of the underworld: 'dis', a contraction of *dius*, *divus* or *deus*, all of which mean 'divine'; since the number of his subjects increased exponentially, Dis was considered the richest of all gods. In a myth that explains the changing seasons, Pluto, aided by Venus and Cupid, kidnaps Ceres' (Demeter's) daughter Proserpina and continues to keep her in the underworld half of every year. While Proserpina lives

with Pluto in the underworld, it is winter and the earth is barren; when she returns, the earth bears fruit in spring, summer and early autumn. Cf. Perdita's reference to Dis and Proserpina in *WT* 4.4.116–18.

90 **blind boy's** Cupid's. He was often portrayed with a blindfold ('LOVE is blind', Dent, L506).
scandaled 'disgraceful, shameful' (first occurrence in *OED ppl. a. obs.*). Cupid's companionship is to be avoided because of his complicity with Venus, according to Ovid, in causing Pluto to abduct Ceres' daughter Proserpina. See Introduction, pp. 71–2.

93 **Paphos** Venus' sacred home on the island of Cyprus; cf. *VA* 1189–94, which describes Venus' journey to Paphos.

94 **Dove-drawn** Venus' chariot was pulled by doves, the birds of love (Dent, D573).

94–5 **done . . . charm** When Cupid's arrows strike the eyes, the recipient of the wound is overcome with sexual desire. Venus and Cupid intended to charm Ferdinand and Miranda into lust.

90 blind boy's] *(blind-Boyes)*

271

Whose vows are that no bed-right shall be paid
Till Hymen's torch be lighted, but in vain.
Mars's hot minion is returned again;
Her waspish-headed son has broke his arrows,
Swears he will shoot no more, but play with sparrows   100
And be a boy right out.

CERES   Highest queen of state,
Great Juno comes; I know her by her gait.

JUNO

How does my bounteous sister? Go with me
To bless this twain that they may prosperous be,
And honoured in their issue.   105

They sing.

JUNO

Honour, riches, marriage-blessing,
Long continuance and increasing,
Hourly joys be still upon you;
Juno sings her blessings on you.

96 **bed-right** consummation of the marriage
97 **Hymen's torch** as in 23. Prospero has asked Ferdinand and Miranda to postpone the consummation of their marriage until the wedding rites are complete and *Hymen's torch* (or lamp) is lit. See also 23n.
98 **Mars's hot minion** Mars, god of war, had an adulterous affair with Venus, his *hot minion*. Venus has returned to Paphos and is no longer a threat.
99 **waspish-headed son** the stingingly (with arrows instead of bees' stings) mischievous Cupid, who may also have broken his arrows in anger (cited in *OED* waspish *a.*[1] 2 for the meaning 'irascible, petulantly spiteful'). Silvius in *AYL* (4.3.9–11) observes that Phebe's 'waspish action' in writing a letter suggests its 'angry' message.
broke his arrows Cupid can no longer cast his spell on the lovers because he has broken his arrows.
100 **sparrows** appropriate playmates for Cupid, in accordance with the proverb 'As lustful as SPARROWS' (Dent, S715)
101 **right out** outright (first occurrence in *OED adv.* 4); i.e. behave properly, or (perhaps) behave like a human child instead of a god
102 **Great . . . comes** See 72.1. Juno's chariot arrives at centre stage, sometimes by descending from where it has been suspended aloft, or, in modern productions, sometimes from doors at the rear of the stage.
gait manner of walking or general bearing. Cf. *Aeneid*, Bk 1, 404–5, where Aeneas recognizes his mother by her gait. Ceres does not necessarily mean that Juno is walking along the stage, although she often does so in modern productions.
104 **twain** pair, couple (cited in *OED sb.* 2)

98 Mars's] *(Marses)*   101 Highest] High *Pope;* High'st *Capell*   102 gait] *(gate)*

CERES	Earth's increase, foison plenty,	110
	Barns and garners never empty.	
	Vines with clustering bunches growing,	
	Plants with goodly burden bowing;	
	Spring come to you at the farthest,	
	In the very end of harvest.	115
	Scarcity and want shall shun you,	
	Ceres' blessing so is on you.	

FERDINAND

This is a most majestic vision, and
Harmonious charmingly. May I be bold
To think these spirits?

PROSPERO   Spirits, which by mine art   120
I have from their confines called to enact
My present fancies.

FERDINAND   Let me live here ever!
So rare a wondered father and a wise
Makes this place paradise.

Juno and Ceres whisper, and send Iris on employment.

PROSPERO   Sweet now, silence!
Juno and Ceres whisper seriously.   125

---

110 SP *Theobald first added this SP: in
the light of the reference to *Ceres' blessing* at 117, Ceres must here take over
the speech.
    foison abundance (also in 2.1.164)
111 **garners** granaries
113 **bowing** bending
114–15 **Spring ... harvest** May spring
follow immediately after the autumn
harvest – meaning there will be no
winter but, instead, constant fair
weather and abundance. See Introduction, pp. 70–2.
119 **charmingly** enchantingly, delight-
fully (first occurrence in *OED adv.*)
121 **confines** confines; presumably
where the Spirits lurk when they are

not performing Prospero's bidding
    enact perform
123 **wondered** performing such rare
wonders (cited in *OED ppl. a.* 2), with
play on Miranda's name. See Abbott,
§294.
    wise See Introduction, pp. 136–8.
124 **Sweet ... silence!** Prospero appears
to be addressing Ferdinand, although
some editors have suggested that
Miranda is about to speak when her
father intercedes; other editors have
assigned this phrase and the subsequent line to Miranda. Elsewhere (e.g.
3H6 2.5.137: 'good sweet Exeter')
Shakespeare's male characters apply
sweet to each other.

---

110 SP] *Theobald; not in F*   121 from their] from all their *F2, Rowe*   123 wise] wife *Rowe*   124
Makes] Make *Pope*   124 SD] *Capell; opp. 127 F*

There's something else to do. Hush and be mute,
Or else our spell is marred.

IRIS

You nymphs, called naiads, of the windring brooks,
With your sedged crowns and ever-harmless looks,
Leave your crisp channels, and on this green land   130
Answer your summons; Juno does command.
Come, temperate nymphs, and help to celebrate
A contract of true love. Be not too late.

Enter certain Nymphs.

You sunburned sicklemen, of August weary,
Come hither from the furrow and be merry;   135
Make holiday! Your rye-straw hats put on,
And these fresh nymphs encounter every one
In country footing.

128 **naiads** water nymphs. Samuel Daniel's *Tethys' Festival*, a masque performed in 1610 for Prince Henry's investiture as Prince of Wales, describes 'Naydes' as 'attired in light robes adorned with flowers, their haire hanging downe, and waving with Garlands of water ornaments on their heads' (sig. E3ᵛ).
windring This word is not found elsewhere (*OED* cites this line only and suggests a misprint for winding). Shakespeare may have conflated 'winding' and 'wandering'. Whatever its origin, the word evokes the brooks' curving paths.

129 **sedged crowns** crowns or coronets woven from a rush-like river plant (first occurrence in *OED* sedged)
ever-harmless guiltless, innocent (*OED a.* 3); or, causing no harm (*OED*

a. 4)

130 **crisp channels** rippling waterways
green land grassy lawn; see 83 and n.

132 **temperate** abstemious (*OED a.* 1b). *Temperate nymphs* (*fresh nymphs* in 137) are appropriate for a marriage of chaste lovers.

134 **sicklemen** harvesters with sickles
of August weary tired from harvest labours

136 **rye-straw** straw made from rye, a cereal grain (and therefore appropriate to Ceres' pageant)

137 **encounter** stand opposite. The Nymphs and Reapers line up in pairs for the dance.

138 **country footing** The dance of Nymphs and Reapers that immediately follows should be rustic rather than courtly.

128 naiads] *(Nayades)* windring] winding *Rowe;* wand'ring *Malone (Steevens)*   130 green land] (greene-Land)

Enter certain Reapers, properly habited. They join with the
Nymphs in a graceful dance, towards the end whereof Prospero
starts suddenly and speaks; after which, to a strange hollow
and confused noise, they heavily vanish.

PROSPERO [*aside*]
  I had forgot that foul conspiracy
  Of the beast Caliban and his confederates   140
  Against my life. The minute of their plot
  Is almost come. [*to the Spirits*] Well done. Avoid, no
        more!   [*Spirits depart.*]
FERDINAND [*to Miranda*]
  This is strange. Your father's in some passion
  That works him strongly.
MIRANDA   Never till this day
  Saw I him touched with anger so distempered!   145
PROSPERO
  You do look, my son, in a moved sort,
  As if you were dismayed. Be cheerful, sir.
  Our revels now are ended. These our actors,
  As I foretold you, were all spirits and

138.4 *heavily vanish* Although some editors take *heavily* to mean 'reluctantly'
  or 'sadly', the adverb may indicate that
  the Nymphs and Reapers all exit
  quickly or, possibly, that they disappear through a trap door or other
  device. See Dessen, 209–15.
140 **beast** Because Caliban is generally
  described as human in 1.2.281–4 and
  elsewhere, this comment probably
  refers to his behaviour rather than his
  shape. See Introduction, pp. 33–4.
142 **Avoid** depart
143 **passion** excitement
144 **works** affects, stirs (cited in *OED v.*
  14b)
145 **distempered** out of humour, vexed,

troubled (*OED ppl. a.* 2)
146 **in . . . sort** upset, agitated
148 **revels** courtly entertainment. The
  term was used for 'the final dance
  between masquers and spectators' in
  the court masque (Oxf[1], 180).
148–58 This passage is often extracted
  from its context and treated as
  Shakespeare's farewell to his art; Al
  Pacino recited it, e.g., as Shakespeare's
  own words in his 1996 film *Looking for*
  Richard. The vanishing spectacle was a
  recurrent feature in Jacobean court
  masques, however. In Samuel Daniel's
  Tethys' Festival, Tethys sings that
  'Pleasures onely shadowes bee / Cast
  by bodies we conceive, / And are made

138.4 *heavily*] *om. Pope*   139 SD] *Johnson*   142 SD1] *Malone*   SD2] *this edn*   143 SD] *Oxf,*
Bantam, Folg[2]   146 You do look] You look *Pope;* Why, you do look *Hanmer*

Are melted into air, into thin air;   150
And – like the baseless fabric of this vision –
The cloud-capped towers, the gorgeous palaces,
The solemn temples, the great globe itself,
Yea, all which it inherit, shall dissolve,
And like this insubstantial pageant faded,   155
Leave not a rack behind. We are such stuff
As dreams are made on, and our little life
Is rounded with a sleep. Sir, I am vexed;
Bear with my weakness; my old brain is troubled.
Be not disturbed with my infirmity.   160
If you be pleased, retire into my cell
And there repose. A turn or two I'll walk
To still my beating mind.

FERDINAND, MIRANDA   We wish your peace.   *Exeunt.*

---

the things we deeme, / In those figures which they seeme. / But these pleasures vanish fast, . . . Glory is most bright and gay / In a flash, and so away' (italics removed). Daniel added a third spectacle after the vanishing sea nymphs 'to avoid the confusion which usually attendeth the desolve of these shewes' (sig. F3ᵛ); perhaps Prospero was not alone in finding such sudden disappearances disconcerting.

149 **foretold you** told you before

151 **baseless . . . vision** i.e. this spectacle, having no foundation in reality

152 **cloud-capped towers** towers so tall that they are 'Capped with heavy clouds about [their] summit[s]' (first occurrence in *OED a.*)

153 **great globe** the world, though probably with a simultaneous reference to the Globe playhouse for which Shakespeare wrote plays after 1599

154 **all . . . inherit** i.e. all people who will subsequently live on the earth and,

perhaps also, all who will perform in or attend (and possibly own) the Globe

156 **rack** 'driving mist or fog' (cited in *OED sb.*[1] 2b), which like the *pageant . . . Leave*(s) scarcely a trace *behind*

157 **on** of

158 **rounded with** finished by, completed by (cited in *OED v.*[1] 4a). Cf. Orgel, who argues against this usage and in favour of 'surrounded' (Oxf[1], 181).

162–3 **A . . . mind.** 'A short walk will calm my agitated mind'; see 1.2.176: 'still, 'tis beating in my mind'. Cf. *2H6* 1.3.152–3: 'my choler being overblown / With walking once about the quadrangle'.

163 **your** We follow F here, although many editors have preferred 'you', which appears in F4 and Rowe. We see no justification for the change but recognize the plausibility of a scribe's or compositor's misreading of the manuscript.

---

151 And –] *this edn;* And *F*   this] their *F2, Rowe;* th'air *Warburton*   vision –] *this edn;* vision *F*
163 your] you *F4, Rowe*

PROSPERO

Come with a thought, I thank thee, Ariel. Come!

Enter ARIEL.

ARIEL

Thy thoughts I cleave to. What's thy pleasure? 165

PROSPERO

Spirit, we must prepare to meet with Caliban.

ARIEL

Ay, my commander. When I presented Ceres,
I thought to have told thee of it, but I feared
Lest I might anger thee.

PROSPERO

Say again, where didst thou leave these varlets? 170

ARIEL

I told you, sir, they were red-hot with drinking,
So full of valour that they smote the air
For breathing in their faces, beat the ground
For kissing of their feet, yet always bending

---

164 **with a thought** as quickly as a thought; as soon as I think of you. Cf. Dent, T240: 'As swift as THOUGHT'.
I thank thee In *Riv* Prospero addresses these words to Miranda and Ferdinand, which is certainly plausible, but the previous and subsequent words, as well as the singular *thee*, make Ariel the more likely addressee. Prospero's appreciation of Ariel's alacrity contrasts with his impatience in 1.2 and suggests a closer relationship between master and servant.

165 **cleave to** adhere to; obey

167 **presented Ceres** This phrase is generally taken to mean that the actor who performs Ariel also doubles in Ceres' role, though Ariel might be using *presented* in the sense of serving as a stage manager. Prospero's meditation in

148–63 allows the actor playing Ariel / Ceres plenty of time to change costumes.

170 **varlets** scoundrels

171 **red-hot** literally red-faced and figuratively highly inflamed or excited, though it may also mean fired with false courage, as the next line suggests

172 3 **So . . . faces** 'They were so quarrelsome that they picked a fight with the air for surrounding their faces.'

173–4 **beat . . . feet** 'They beat the ground for being under (*kissing*) their feet', i.e. they walked ·(staggered?) heavily.

174 **bending** proceeding, turning (*OED* bend *v.* 20). Cf. *AW* 3.2.53–5: 'for thence we came; / And after some dispatch in hand at court, / Thither we bend again'.

169 Lest] *(Least)*

277

Towards their project. Then I beat my tabor,   175
At which like unbacked colts they pricked their ears,
Advanced their eyelids, lifted up their noses
As they smelt music; so I charmed their ears
That calf-like they my lowing followed, through
Toothed briars, sharp furzes, pricking gorse and thorns,   180
Which entered their frail shins. At last I left them
I'th' filthy-mantled pool beyond your cell,
There dancing up to th' chins, that the foul lake
O'erstunk their feet.

PROSPERO   This was well done, my bird.
Thy shape invisible retain thou still.   185
The trumpery in my house: go bring it hither,
For stale to catch these thieves.

ARIEL   I go, I go.   *Exit.*

PROSPERO
A devil, a born devil, on whose nature

175–9 **Then . . . followed** For a similar image of music's effect on wild horses, see *MV* 5.1.71–9.
175 **tabor** drum. See 3.2.124 SD and n.
176 **unbacked colts** unbroken young horses
177 **Advanced** raised, lifted
178 **As . . . music** as if they could smell music
179 **calf-like** as docile as a calf
    lowing mooing; making the sound of cattle
180 **sharp . . . gorse** prickly shrubs
182 **filthy-mantled** covered with slime or scum
184 **O'erstunk their feet** stank even worse than, or drowned the stench of, *their feet* (only occurrence in *OED* overstink *v.*)
    my bird This epithet suggests (1) Ariel's ability to fly, and (2) Prospero's affection for a faithful pet.
186 **trumpery** fancy garments; worthless

finery (first occurrence in *OED sb.* 2d), referred to in 193.1 as *glistering apparel*
187 **stale** Several uses of the word may apply here: (1) decoy, almost certainly, and perhaps also (2) prostitute, (3) cover for sinister designs and (4) playing on the *horse piss* of 199, horse's urine.
188–9 **nature/Nurture** In Shakespeare's day, as in ours, the respective roles of nature and nurture in the formation of human character were debated. If, as Prospero charges, Caliban is the son of a witch and the devil, he is immune to the benefits of nurture. But not quite: Prospero and Miranda taught him language and, they claim (1.2.308–63), much else. Prospero's emphasis here is probably on moral nature, to which Caliban (in Prospero's and Miranda's eyes, at least) appears wholly resistant.

180 gorse] *(gosse)*

Nurture can never stick; on whom my pains
Humanely taken – all, all lost, quite lost!   190
And, as with age his body uglier grows,
So his mind cankers. I will plague them all,
Even to roaring. Come, hang them on this line.

Enter ARIEL, *loaden with glistering apparel, etc.*
Enter CALIBAN, STEPHANO *and* TRINCULO, *all wet.*

CALIBAN

Pray you tread softly, that the blind mole may
Not hear a footfall. We now are near his cell.   195

STEPHANO   Monster, your fairy, which you say is a
harmless fairy, has done little better than played the
jack with us.

TRINCULO   Monster, I do smell all horse piss, at which
my nose is in great indignation.   200

STEPHANO   So is mine. Do you hear, monster? If I should

189–90 **pains . . . taken** Prospero earlier
   claimed to have *used* Caliban *with*
   humane care (1.2.346–7).
192 **cankers** grows malignant, decays
   plague afflict, torment
193 **line** For theatrical purposes, *line* is
   often interpreted as clothes line, but
   the subsequent reference to *line grove*
   (5.1.10) argues for a botanical meaning: the line, lime or linden tree.
   Clothes can, of course, be hung from
   a tree, but if ropes were used in the
   staging of 1.1, they could here be used
   equally well for a clothes line.
194 **blind mole** Moles, in their dark tun-
   nels, could hear but not see footfalls.
   Topsell explained in *The Historie of*
   Foure-footed Beasts (London, 1607):
   'These Moles have no eares, and yet
   they heare in the earth more nimbly
   and perfectly then men can above the
   same, for at every step or small noise
   and almost breathing, they are terrified

and run away' (499). Caliban asks
Stephano and Trinculo to tread so
softly that even the mole will not notice
them.
196 **your fairy** This may suggest that
   Caliban has told the conspirators about
   Ariel; many postwar appropriations
   expand on the relationship between
   Ariel and Caliban, but this line is one
   of the few indications that Caliban
   knew of the sprite. Yet they must have
   been acquainted before Prospero and
   Miranda arrived on the island, and
   Sycorax would presumably (if she
   lived until Caliban reached the age of
   understanding) have informed her son
   about the recalcitrant spirit–servant
   she confined for twelve 'years in *a*
   cloven pine (1.2.274–7).
198 **jack** trickster (cited in *OED sb.*[1] 2b)
199 **horse piss** All three conspirators
   must reek from the *filthy-mantled pool*
   (182).

190 taken –] *this edn;* taken, *F*   193 them on] *Rowe¹;* on them *F, Rowe³*   194–5] *Pope; prose F*
196–202] *Pope; as verse F, lined* Fairy, / vs. / which / indignation. / should / you. /

take a displeasure against you, look you!

TRINCULO   Thou wert but a lost monster.

CALIBAN

Good my lord, give me thy favour still.

Be patient, for the prize I'll bring thee to   205

Shall hoodwink this mischance. Therefore speak softly;

All's hushed as midnight yet.

TRINCULO   Ay, but to lose our bottles in the pool –

STEPHANO   There is not only disgrace and dishonour in

that, monster, but an infinite loss.   210

TRINCULO   That's more to me than my wetting, yet this

is your harmless fairy, monster.

STEPHANO   I will fetch off my bottle, though I be o'er ears

for my labour.

CALIBAN

Prithee, my king, be quiet. Seest thou here;   215

This is the mouth o'th' cell. No noise, and enter.

Do that good mischief which may make this island

Thine own forever, and I, thy Caliban,

For aye thy foot-licker.

STEPHANO   Give me thy hand. I do begin to have bloody   220

thoughts.

TRINCULO [*Sees the clothes.*]   O King Stephano! O peer!

O worthy Stephano! Look what a wardrobe here is for

thee!

203 **lost** ruined; probably meant in the
sense of 'as good as dead'
206 **hoodwink this mischance** cover up
this mistake
207 **hushed as midnight** 'As still as
MIDNIGHT' (Dent, M919.1)
212 **harmless fairy** See 196n.
213 **fetch off** retrieve
o'er ears over my ears in the *filthy-
mantled* horse pond (182)
217 **good mischief** This oxymoron fits
the purpose of the three conspirators:

harm, evil (*OED* mischief *sb.* 2), that
could serve them well.
219 **aye** ever
foot-licker Although Caliban resents
being treated as a slave earlier in the
play, here he seems willing to submit
to Stephano's authority.
222 **King . . . peer** a reference to the old
ballad 'King Stephen was a worthy
peer', which links clothing with social
status. Iago sings it in *Oth* 2.3.89–96.

208 pool –] *Hanmer*; Poole. *F*   211–14] *Pope; as verse F, lined* wetting: / Monster. / bottle, / labour./
220–4] *Pope; as verse F, lined* hand, / thoughts. / worthy *Stephano*, / thee. /   222 SD] *this edn*

CALIBAN

    Let it alone, thou fool; it is but trash.   225

TRINCULO   O ho, monster; we know what belongs to a
    frippery! O King Stephano!   *[Puts on a garment.]*

STEPHANO   Put off that gown, Trinculo. By this hand, I'll
    have that gown.

TRINCULO   Thy grace shall have it.   230

CALIBAN

    The dropsy drown this fool! What do you mean

    To dote thus on such luggage? Let't alone

    And do the murder first. If he awake,

    From toe to crown he'll fill our skins with pinches,

    Make us strange stuff.   235

STEPHANO   Be you quiet, monster. Mistress Line, is not
this my jerkin? Now is the jerkin under the line! Now jerkin you are like to lose your hair and prove a bald jerkin.

227 **frippery** old-clothing shop; Trinculo denies that the garments before
them are, as Caliban contends, *trash*.
228 **gown** Trinculo has apparently
donned a gown that reflects, because of
its finery or insignia, more rank or ele-
gance than 'King' Stephano can toler-
ate.
230 **grace** a courtesy title that in Shakespeare's day was reserved for the
monarch, although its application was
spreading to high ranks in church and
state. Here it is appropriate for 'King'
Stephano.
231 **dropsy** a disease in which the body
retains fluids
232 **luggage** meant in a general sense of
goods, in this case worthless garments
236 **Mistress Line** Stephano begins a
series of puns that has defied satisfac-
tory explanation, largely because 'line'
has a remarkable range of meanings,
several of which may be invoked here.
The initial reference (*Mistress Line*) is
to the line (linden) tree, or to a rope; in

either case it holds the *wardrobe* (223;
see also 193n.).
237 ¹**jerkin** jacket of leather (usually) and
fur, often sleeveless (*OED* a)
    under the line may mean only that
the jerkin is now under, rather than on,
the tree (or rope), but most editors take
line in this instance to be the equator,
where seafarers were believed to go
bald from tropical fevers or, in a parody of that possibility, sailors sometimes shaved the heads of those
crossing the equator for the first time.
A more persuasive explanation is
offered by R. Levin, who modifies and
extends Steevens's attribution of hair
loss to venereal disease: *under the line*
should be read anatomically, with
Stephano tucking the jerkin into his
trousers and associating it with the
body's lower and hotter regions, where
it may lose the hair from the head
(or, we suggest, from the pubic region)
from syphilis.

227 SD] *this edn*   232 Let't alone] *Rann;* let's alone *F;* Let's along *Theobald;* Let it alone *Hanmer*
236 Line] lime *Oxf*

TRINCULO   Do, do. We steal by line and level, an't like
    your grace.   240

STEPHANO   I thank thee for that jest; here's a garment
    for't. Wit shall not go unrewarded while I am king of
    this country. 'Steal by line and level' is an excellent pass
    of pate. There's another garment for't.

TRINCULO   Monster, come put some lime upon your   245
    fingers and away with the rest.

CALIBAN

    I will have none on't. We shall lose our time,

    And all be turned to barnacles, or to apes

    With foreheads villainous low.

STEPHANO   Monster, lay to your fingers. Help to bear this   250
    away where my hogshead of wine is, or I'll turn you out
    of my kingdom! Go to; carry this.

TRINCULO   And this.

STEPHANO   Ay, and this.

---

239 **Do, do.** yes; bravo
  line and level literally, a plumb
line and a carpenter's level, but also
a proverbial expression, 'To work
by LINE and level (measure)' (Dent,
L305), or, more loosely, to work
with craftsmanly precision – i.e. 'we're
skilful thieves'. Trinculo thus adds a
third meaning to the pun on *line* (see
236n.).

239–40 **an't . . . grace** if your grace
pleases

243–4 **pass of pate** witty jab or stroke
(first occurrence in *OED* pass *sb.*[2] 9b).
A *pass* is a thrust in fencing, while *pate*
refers to the head. Stephano makes his
own pun while praising Trinculo's
foray into clever wordplay.

245 **lime** probably birdlime, a sticky substance used to catch birds; it would
cause clothing to stick to the fingers.

See Dent, F236: 'His FINGERS are
lime twigs'.

247 **on't** of it

248 **barnacles** either the hardshelled sea
creatures that fasten onto rocks and
ship bottoms or, more likely, the bar-
nacle goose, which was widely believed
at the time to originate in such sea life
and thereby to signify a strange or stupid creature
  apes Caliban's recognition that, in
contrast to him and the others,
apes have low foreheads suggests
that – post-Darwinian interpretations
notwithstanding – he should not be
portrayed as apelike.

249 **villainous** vilely (cited in *OED a.* 5b)

250 **lay to** 'to put or bring into action'
(cited in *OED v.*[1] 58b)

252 **Go to** Get moving.

---

239 an't] (and't)   247 none] done *F2*   lose] (loose)   248 [2]to] *om. Pope*

A noise of hunters heard. Enter diverse Spirits in shape of
dogs and hounds, hunting them about, Prospero and Ariel
setting them on.

PROSPERO   Hey, Mountain, hey!   255
ARIEL   Silver! There it goes, Silver!
PROSPERO

Fury, Fury! There, Tyrant, there! Hark, hark!
[*The Spirits chase Caliban, Stephano and Trinculo off stage.*]
Go, charge my goblins that they grind their joints
With dry convulsions, shorten up their sinews
With aged cramps, and more pinch-spotted make them   260
Than pard or cat o'mountain.

ARIEL   Hark, they roar!

PROSPERO

Let them be hunted soundly. At this hour
Lies at my mercy all mine enemies.
Shortly shall all my labours end, and thou
Shalt have the air at freedom. For a little,   265
Follow and do me service.   *Exeunt.*

254.1 *diverse* (1) several in kind or quality
(*OED a.* 1); (2) varied, multiform
(*OED a.* 2); (3) perverse, 'opposed to
what is right' (*OED a.* 3)
254.3 *setting . . . on* urging the dogs to
attack (cited in *OED* set *v.*¹ 148c)
255–7 **Mountain . . . Silver . . . Fury . . .
Tyrant** These names for '*Spirits in
shape of dogs and hounds*' have no clear
origin. Silver appears in *TS* 1.1.19;
both Silver and Mountain are in
Ayrer's *Die Schöne Sidea*, a play
thought by some commentators to
have been *Tem*'s principal source. See
Introduction, pp. 55–6.
258 **charge** order
goblins mischievous demons
grind torment

259 **convulsions** cramps, contractions
(cited in *OED sb.* 2a)
shorten contract, draw together (cited
in *OED v.* 1d)
sinews tendons; nerves
260 **aged** agèd
pinch-spotted bruised from pinches
261 **pard . . . mountain** *Pard* was a leop-
ard or panther; *cat o'mountain* (cata-
mount) could be the same or any
wildcat.
262 **soundly** severely
263 **Lies** (1) is (are) in subjection; (2) is
(are) in a state of inactivity. F here uses
a singular verb with a plural subject.
265 **have . . . freedom** 'take to the air
when I (soon) set you free'
For a little for a while longer

254.2 *dogs and* | om. *Rowe, Pope*   257 SD] *this edn*

5.1   *Enter* PROSPERO, *in his magic robes, and* ARIEL.

PROSPERO

Now does my project gather to a head.

My charms crack not; my spirits obey; and time

Goes upright with his carriage. How's the day?

ARIEL

On the sixth hour, at which time, my lord,

You said our work should cease.

PROSPERO   I did say so,   5

When first I raised the tempest. Say, my spirit,

How fares the King and's followers?

ARIEL   Confined together

In the same fashion as you gave in charge,

Just as you left them; all prisoners, sir,

5.1 Although Prospero and Ariel were on stage at the end of 4.1, they normally go off stage so that Prospero can put on the *magic robes* called for at the beginning of Act 5 in F's SD. If the magus merely donned a cloak, the quick change would not have disrupted continuous staging at the Globe. At the Blackfriars a musical interval could have allowed the actor time to exit and change his costume.

1   **project** Prospero's plan, whether to wreak vengeance on his enemies or to arrange Miranda's marriage, with the added connotation of an alchemist's experiment, wherein 'projection' is the 'casting of the powder of philosopher's stone . . . upon a metal in fusion to effect its transmutation into gold or silver' (*OED sb.* 2a)
gather . . . head a reference to the alchemical boil, in which the ingredients of the experiment are heated to boiling point. At this crucial moment, the experiment succeeds or fails (Simonds, 'Charms', 553).

2   **crack** another alchemical reference, to

the breaking of the alembic if it is boiled over too high a heat. Since Prospero's charms *crack not*, his *project* seems to be a success (Simonds, 'Charms', 555–6).

3   **Goes . . . carriage** travels 'without stooping because his burden (*carriage*, what he carries) is no longer heavy' (Oxf[1], 187). In contrast to his anxiety in 4.1.139–42, Prospero declares that at this time his work is coming to a successful conclusion.
How's the day? What time is it?

4   **On** approaching
sixth hour In 1.2.239 Ariel told Prospero that it was 'Past the midseason'; three hours, more or less, have passed since the storm that began the play and it is almost six, the hour by which Prospero said his project would be finished. Repeated references to the hours create a sense of urgency and remind the audience that the unity of time has been observed.

7   **How fares** Here again, F has a singular verb with a plural subject.

8   'exactly as you ordered'

5.1] *Actus quintus: Scoena Prima.*   Location] Before the Cell *Theobald*   4 sixth hour] *(*sixt hower)*
7 together] *om. Pope*   9 all] all your *Pope*

In the line grove which weather-fends your cell.   10
They cannot budge till your release. The King,
His brother and yours abide all three distracted,
And the remainder mourning over them,
Brimful of sorrow and dismay; but chiefly
Him that you termed, sir, the good old Lord Gonzalo.   15
His tears run down his beard like winter's drops
From eaves of reeds. Your charm so strongly works 'em
That, if you now beheld them, your affections
Would become tender.

PROSPERO   Dost thou think so, spirit?
ARIEL

Mine would, sir, were I human.
PROSPERO   And mine shall.   20

Hast thou, which art but air, a touch, a feeling
Of their afflictions, and shall not myself
(One of their kind, that relish all as sharply,

---

10 **line grove** a grove of trees of the linden genus *Tilia*, sometimes referred to
as the European lime. Though these
trees are ornamental and do not bear
fruit, editions from Dryden &
Davenant to Oxf have emended to
'lime grove', but Oxf[1] and others
retain F's original. See 4.1.236 n. and
193.
   weather-fends defends from the
weather, shelters (first occurrence in
OED v.) – i.e. the trees serve as a wind-
break for Prospero's *cell* (see 1.2.20 and
n.).
11 **till your release** i.e. until you release
them
12 **abide** remain, stay
16 **winter's drops** drips of cold rain
17 **eaves of reeds** thatched roofs; possibly a metaphor for Gonzalo's beard
18 **affections** passions. Ariel may refer to
Prospero's anger and vindictiveness.

20 **human** Editors since Rowe have modernized F's 'humane' to *human*; as a
spirit Ariel is not human, but if he
were, Ariel would be filled with compassion for the Neapolitans. See
1.2.346–7.
   shall must (*OED v.* B 3b)
21 **touch** influence, sense (*OED sb.* 13)
23 **kind** 'A race, or a natural group of animals or plants having a common ori-
gin' (cited in *OED sb.* 10a)
23–4 **relish . . . Passion** F's punctuation
establishes two complementary
phrases: (1) *relish . . . sharply* means to
feel experiences as deeply (cited in
OED v.[1] 2b); (2) *Passion* (here used as
a verb) means 'to be affected by deep
passion', or perhaps 'to sorrow' (cited
in *OED v.*[1] 3). Prospero exclaims that
as 'One of their kind', he is deeply
affected by the Neapolitans' suffering.

---

10 line grove] *(Line-grove); lime-grove / Dryden & Davenant, Rowe, Oxf*   11 your] you *F3*
15 Him that you] Him you *Ard² (Cam¹);* He that you *Hanmer;* him, / that you *Malone*   sir] *om.
Pope*   16 run] *F2;* runs *F*   winter's] *F2;* winter *F4, Rowe*   20 human] *(humane);* human *Rowe*
23 sharply,] sharply *F3*

Passion as they) be kindlier moved than thou art?
Though with their high wrongs I am struck to th' quick,   25
Yet with my nobler reason 'gainst my fury
Do I take part. The rarer action is
In virtue than in vengeance. They being penitent,
The sole drift of my purpose doth extend
Not a frown further. Go, release them, Ariel.   30
My charms I'll break; their senses I'll restore;
And they shall be themselves.

ARIEL   I'll fetch them, sir.   *Exit.*

PROSPERO [*Traces a circle.*]
Ye elves of hills, brooks, standing lakes and groves,

---

24 **kindlier moved** more compassion-
ately affected, but also more in accord
with humankind
25–8 **Though . . . vengeance.** These
lines may derive from a similar passage
in Montaigne's essay, 'Of Crueltie', in
which the sage reflects that 'He that
through a naturall facilitie, & genuine
mildness, should neglect or contemne
injuries received, should no doubt performe a rare action. . . . But he who
being toucht & stung to the quicke . . .
should arme himselfe with reason
against this furiously-blinde desire of
revenge' (Montaigne, 243). But the
proverbial expression, 'To be able to
do HARM and not to do it is noble'
(Dent, H170), had wide currency;
Shakespeare reiterated the sentiment
in Sonnet 94: 'They that have pow'r
to hurt, and will do none'; and in
LLL 2.1.58, where Katherine describes Dumaine as possessing 'Most
power to do most harm, least knowing
ill'.
25 **high wrongs** *High* suggests the crimes
of treason and attempted murder.
struck . . . quick figurative: hit in a
tender, vital part, causing mental pain
or irritation (*OED sb.*[1] B 4b). 'To touch
one to the QUICK' was a proverbial

expression used to describe one person's emotional effect upon another
(Dent, Q13).
27 **rarer** unusual, exceptional (*OED a.*[1]
5a); or, finer, of uncommon excellence
(*OED a.*[1] 6a)
28 **virtue** Prospero no doubt uses *virtue*
to stand for forgiveness and mercy.
They being penitent Orgel asserts
that 'These conditions are not met'
(Oxf[1], 189), but we think the case is
less certain. While Antonio and
Sebastian remain silent on the issue,
Alonso meets Prospero's condition
and asks for pardon in 118–9.
Sebastian and Antonio may indicate
repentance by body language or, con-
versely, their silence can be taken as
defiance.
29 **drift** tendency (*OED sb.* 3); or, object,
intention (*OED sb.* 4)
33 SD *F's SD at 57.3–4 directs the
Neapolitans and Antonio to *enter the
circle* Prospero *had made.* At 33 many
editors direct the magician to make the
circle with his staff, but since an actor
might instead use his hand or foot, we
have kept the SD here to its essentials.
33–50 This speech is a rough paraphrase
of Medea's incantation from Ovid,
7.263–89. For a full analysis of

---

26 'gainst] against *F3*   28 They] *Rowe;* they, *F*   33 SD] *this edn*

And ye that on the sands with printless foot
Do chase the ebbing Neptune, and do fly him   35
When he comes back; you demi-puppets that
By moonshine do the green sour ringlets make,
Whereof the ewe not bites; and you whose pastime
Is to make midnight-mushrooms, that rejoice
To hear the solemn curfew, by whose aid –   40
Weak masters though ye be – I have bedimmed
The noontide sun, called forth the mutinous winds,
And 'twixt the green sea and the azured vault
Set roaring war; to the dread-rattling thunder
Have I given fire and rifted Jove's stout oak   45
With his own bolt: the strong-based promontory

Shakespeare's borrowing from Ovid's original, Golding's translation, and other sources, see Bate, *Ovid*, 251–5.

34 **printless foot** leaving no print or trace (first occurrence in *OED a*.). Because the elves are not corporeal, they leave no footprints. Cf. *VA* 147–8, where nymphs dance on the sands without leaving footprints.

35 **ebbing Neptune** As the god of the sea, Neptune appears in the ebb and flow of the waves.
fly run away from

36 **demi-puppets** half-sized or dwarf puppets (only occurrence in *OED*), i.e. fairy, elf

37 **green sour ringlets** rings that appear in the grass at the base of toadstools, supposedly caused by dancing fairies

38 **ewe not bites** Sheep won't eat the *sour* grass that circles the toadstools.

39 **midnight-mushrooms** mushrooms that spring up during the night
that who

40 **solemn curfew** the evening bell, rung at nine o'clock. After curfew, spirits were thought to be free to roam the earth until sunrise.

41 **Weak masters** The *elves* and *demi-puppets* who assist Prospero are subject to the magician, yet they are also *masters* in their own supernatural domains.

41–2 **bedimmed . . . sun** caused eclipses of the sun (cited in *OED* bedim *v*.: 'make dim, cover with dimness, becloud')

42 **mutinous winds** Perhaps a reference to an episode in the *Odyssey*, where Odysseus, driven by curiosity, untied the sack given to him by Aeolus that contained the contrary winds which later impeded his journey.

43 **azured vault** the sky

44 **roaring war** the tumult of tempests, such as was manifest in 1.1

45 **fire** i.e. lightning. Cf. 1.2.191 and 203.
rifted split
Jove's . . . oak As king of the gods, Jove demonstrated his power by hurling a thunderbolt. The oak, known for its hard wood, was sacred to him.

46 *__strong-based promontory__ Rowe's emendation of F's 'strong bass'd' better suits *promontory*, suggesting a mountain peak with a broad or sturdy base. 'Bass'd', however, could refer to the 'bass' sound made by the *promontory* as it shakes.

41 bedimmed] *(*bedymn'd*)*   44 dread-rattling] *RP;* dread ratling *F*   46 strong-based] *(*strong bass'd*)*

Have I made shake, and by the spurs plucked up
The pine and cedar; graves at my command
Have waked their sleepers, ope'd and let 'em forth
By my so potent art. But this rough magic   50
I here abjure; and when I have required
Some heavenly music (which even now I do)
To work mine end upon their senses that
This airy charm is for, I'll break my staff,
Bury it certain fathoms in the earth,   55
And deeper than did ever plummet sound
I'll drown my book.   *Solemn music.*

47 **spurs** the principal roots of the trees (cited in *OED sb.*[1] 9)

48–9 **graves ... forth** A loose translation of Ovid's *'manesque exire sepulcris'*, which Golding rendered as 'I call up dead men from their graves'. If these lines are taken literally, Prospero must be referring to events that occurred before he came to the island; more likely, Shakespeare includes the passage from Ovid as a rhetorical climax to Prospero's recitation of his magical powers (Ovid, Bk 7, 275). The ability to raise the dead was associated with black magic. As Bate contends, Medea's speech, here paraphrased, 'was viewed in the Renaissance as witch-craft's great set-piece'; Shakespeare's audience would have realized at this point that Prospero's magic must be rejected because it was the 'selfsame black magic as that of Medea' (Bate, *Ovid*, 252).

50 **rough magic** *OED* rough *a.* 5a describes 'rough' actions as 'marked by violence towards, or harsh treatment of others'. In this sense, Prospero hereby relinquishes his power to wreak physical harm on his former enemies – Alonso, Sebastian and Antonio – as well as on his servants Caliban and Ariel. *Rough* can also be taken in a more benign sense, meaning 'rudely sufficient', as in the Poet's reference to his 'rough work' in *Tim* 1.1.43 (*OED a.*

17a). Prospero could be self-deprecating here, referring to the imperfect nature of his craft (see also *OED a.* 13: unpolished, rugged). The interpretation of *rough*, therefore, depends upon Prospero's present mood and on the nature of his magic. Despite critical claims that Prospero is really a 'white magician' (see Introduction, pp. 62–6), the preceding allusions to Medea's incantation suggest to us that the adjective *rough* here indicates the underlying danger of the magus's power.

51 **abjure** renounce, recant (cited in *OED v.* 1)

required demanded. Cf. 132.

52 **heavenly ... do** In neo-Platonic discourse, music was thought to be an earthly embodiment of heavenly harmony; it soothes and heals the troubled mind. Prospero's line calls for *Solemn music* to sound in the background.

54 **airy charm** the *heavenly music*

break my staff Prospero will break and bury his magic staff so that it can never be used again.

55 **fathoms** A fathom was a distance of 6 feet (see 1.2.397n.); now (and usually in this play) used primarily for nautical depth but in the seventeenth century often applied to other contexts.

56 **plummet** a device used to measure the vertical, in this case to sound the depth of the ocean. See 3.3.101.

54 airy charm] (Ayrie-charme)

Here enters ARIEL *before; then* ALONSO *with a frantic gesture,*
attended by GONZALO; SEBASTIAN *and* ANTONIO *in like*
manner, attended by ADRIAN *and* FRANCISCO. *They all enter the*
circle which Prospero had made and there stand charmed, which
Prospero observing, speaks:

A solemn air and the best comforter
To an unsettled fancy, cure thy brains
(Now useless) boiled within thy skull. There stand,   60
For you are spell-stopped. –
Holy Gonzalo, honourable man,
Mine eyes, ev'n sociable to the show of thine,
Fall fellowly drops. [*aside*] The charm dissolves apace,
And as the morning steals upon the night,   65
Melting the darkness, so their rising senses
Begin to chase the ignorant fumes that mantle
Their clearer reason. – O good Gonzalo,
My true preserver and a loyal sir
To him thou follow'st, I will pay thy graces   70

57.4 *circle* See 33 SD and n.
57.5 *Prospero observing* Prospero stands outside the circle and addresses the Neapolitans, who cannot see or hear him until 106.
58–60 These lines are probably addressed to Alonso; then Prospero turns to the court party.
59 **unsettled fancy** troubled imagination
60 *****boiled** another alchemical reference; the 'boil' is a crucial step before base metal can be transformed to gold. See Simonds, 'Charms', 543.
61 **spell-stopped** put under a spell (first occurrence in *OED sb.*[1] 4)
64 **Fall fellowly drops** emit 'companionable, sympathetic' tears (cited in *OED* fellowly *a.* 2). At the sight of Gonzalo's tears, Prospero sheds tears in fellowship.
SD *****Prospero** may be speaking to

Ariel or mostly to himself.
apace speedily (*OED adv.* c); or, at once, immediately (*OED adv.* d)
66 **rising** Continuing the metaphor of sunrise, their senses emerge clear or (figuratively) emerge above the horizon (first occurrence in *OED ppl. a.* 3).
66–8 **their . . . reason** The courtiers' returning *senses* dispel the *fumes* that had blocked their ability to think clearly.
67 **ignorant . . . mantle** ignorance-causing *fumes* (vapours) *mantle* ('cover or conceal') the Neapolitans' understanding (cited in *OED* mantle *v.* 2). *Fumes* is perhaps another reference to the alchemist's boil.
69 **sir** gentleman
70 **him** Alonso
70–1 **pay . . . Home** a proverbial expression meaning to repay a debt completely (Dent, H535.1). Compare to

60 boiled] *Ard²* (*Rowe³*); boil F   64 fellowly] fellowy *Rowe³*; fellow *Pope*   SD]*Bantam (Capell)*
68 good] my good *Pope*

Home, both in word and deed. – Most cruelly
Didst thou, Alonso, use me and my daughter.
Thy brother was a furtherer in the act. –
Thou art pinched for't now, Sebastian! – Flesh and blood,
You, brother mine, that entertained ambition,   75
Expelled remorse and nature, whom with Sebastian
(Whose inward pinches therefore are most strong)
Would here have killed your king, I do forgive thee,
Unnatural though thou art. [*aside*] Their understanding
Begins to swell, and the approaching tide   80
Will shortly fill the reasonable shore
That now lies foul and muddy. Not one of them
That yet looks on me or would know me. – Ariel,
Fetch me the hat and rapier in my cell;
                   [*Exit Ariel and returns immediately.*]
I will discase me and myself present   85
As I was sometime Milan. Quickly, spirit,
Thou shalt ere long be free.

1H4 1.3.287–8, where Worcester maintains that the King believes the rebels should 'think ourselves unsatisfied, / Till he hath found a time to pay us home'.

72 **Didst* Although F's compositor printed 'Did', *Didst* appears as the catchword at the bottom of the previous page and is more likely the manuscript's original reading.

74 **pinched** hurt, tormented (*OED v.* 5 *obs.*). Cf. 1.2.329, where Prospero threatens Caliban: 'thou shalt be pinched'.

75 **entertained* harboured, cherished (*OED v.* 14c)

76 **Expelled . . . nature** 'rejected pity and natural feelings'
whom sometimes emended to 'who' (Abbott, §274)

77 **inward pinches** inner torment,

anguish. See 74 and n.

79–81 **Their . . . shore** Like a wave of the sea, their understanding grows and approaches the shore of their reason (*reasonable*).

79–83 Like 64–8, Prospero may be speaking to Ariel or to himself.

84 **hat and rapier** part of a Renaissance gentleman's costume. Ariel may bring a cloak and other fashionable items of dress, or Prospero may already wear courtier's clothing beneath his robe, as suggested in 85–6.
*SD Theobald was the first to supply this SD so that Ariel can comply with Prospero's command to fetch his hat and rapier.

85 **discase** undress (cited in *OED v. arch.*)

86 **As . . . Milan** the way I appeared when I was Duke of Milan

72 Didst] *catchword on B2ᵛ*, Did *on B3*   74 Thou art] Thou'rt *Rowe*   75 entertained] *Rowe*; entertaine *F*   76 whom] who *Rowe*   79 SD] *Oxf*   82 lies] *F3*; ly *F*   84 SD] *Theobald*

ARIEL (*Sings and helps to attire him.*)

> Where the bee sucks, there suck I,
> In a cowslip's bell I lie;
> There I couch when owls do cry.   90
> On the bat's back I do fly
> After summer merrily.
> Merrily, merrily, shall I live now,
> Under the blossom that hangs on the bough.

PROSPERO

> Why, that's my dainty Ariel! I shall miss thee,   95
> But yet thou shalt have freedom. – So, so, so. –
> To the King's ship, invisible as thou art;
> There shalt thou find the mariners asleep
> Under the hatches. The master and the boatswain
> Being awake, enforce them to this place,   100
> And presently, I prithee.

ARIEL

> I drink the air before me and return
> Or ere your pulse twice beat.   *Exit.*

88–94 For Robert Johnson's musical setting of Ariel's song, see Fig. 4.
89 **cowslip's bell** Gerard discusses seven
types of cowslips, primroses and oxlips
in chap. 118, and notes that the terms
were often confused. All flowered early
in the spring. Gerard's drawing of the
field cowslips show bell-shaped blos-
soms, and it is to these that Ariel probably refers.
90 **couch** crouch or lie close (*OED v.*[1] 2).
F3 and F4's 'crowch' works equally
well here, though most modern editors
prefer F's reading. In either case,
Ariel's ability to lie or hide inside a
cowslip's bell suggests his diminutive
fairy nature.
92 **After summer** 'following summer
from clime to clime' (Folg[2], 150)
96 **So, so, so.** Prospero has donned his

hat and rapier and is probably adjust-
ing an item of clothing to indicate his
readiness.
99 **Under the hatches** below the deck,
inside the ship
99–100 **The . . . awake** 'when you have
awakened them'
101 **presently** immediately, at once
102 **I . . . me** The Latin phrase *viam
vorare* – to devour the way – meant to
travel quickly. Thus in *2H4* 1.1.47, a
gentleman fleeing from battle is
described: 'He seem'd in running to
devour the way'. As an airy spirit, Ariel
moves through the air, and the
metaphor of drinking seems more
appropriate than devouring to his spiritual nature.
103 **Or ere** before. Cf. 1.2.11n.

88 SP, SD ARIEL (*Sings*] *Oxf; Ariell sings F*   90 couch] *(cowch); crowch F3*   95–6] *F2, Rowe; F
lines* misse / so. /

GONZALO

    All torment, trouble, wonder and amazement

    Inhabits here. Some heavenly power guide us   105

    Out of this fearful country.

PROSPERO   Behold, sir King,

    The wronged Duke of Milan, Prospero!

    For more assurance that a living prince

    Does now speak to thee, I embrace thy body,

    And to thee and thy company I bid   110

    A hearty welcome.

ALONSO   Whe'er thou be'st he or no,

    Or some enchanted trifle to abuse me

    (As late I have been), I not know. Thy pulse

    Beats as of flesh and blood; and since I saw thee,

    Th'affliction of my mind amends, with which   115

    I fear a madness held me. This must crave –

    An if this be at all – a most strange story.

    Thy dukedom I resign and do entreat

    Thou pardon me my wrongs. But how should Prospero

    Be living, and be here?

PROSPERO [*to Gonzalo*]   First, noble friend,   120

    Let me embrace thine age, whose honour cannot

---

105 **Inhabits** The singular verb may indicate a conflation of the compound
noun – *torment . . . amazement* – into a
single subject, but the use of singular
verbs with plural subjects is common
in F (Abbott, §333).

107 **wronged** wrongèd

111 ***Whe'er** F's 'Where' is a variant of
'whether'.

112 **enchanted trifle** a ghostly apparition caused by magic
abuse deceive and mistreat

115 **amends** heals, cures (cited in *OED v.*
6b)

116 **crave** require or demand (*OED v.* 6)

117 **An if** As Abbott notes, 'and if' (or 'an
if') can mean either 'even if' or 'if
indeed' (§105).
be at all is truly happening

118 **Thy . . . resign** The duchy of Milan
has become a tributary to Naples; even
though Antonio is now its Duke, as
King of Naples Alonso has the power
to revoke his title and restore it to
Prospero.

119 **how should** 'how is it possible that'

121 **thine age** Prospero addresses the
elderly Gonzalo.

---

106 Behold] Lo *Pope*   111 Whe'er] *Capell;* Where *F;* Whether *Ard² (Cam¹)*   thou be'st] Be'st
thou *Pope*   116 crave –] *Dyce;* craue *F*   117 An] *(And)*   all –] *Dyce;* all) *F*   120 SD] *Cam¹*

Be measured or confined.

GONZALO   Whether this be

Or be not, I'll not swear.

PROSPERO   You do yet taste

Some subtleties o'th' isle that will not let you

Believe things certain. Welcome, my friends all;   125

[*aside to Sebastian and Antonio*] But you, my brace of
    lords, were I so minded,

I here could pluck his highness' frown upon you

And justify you traitors! At this time

I will tell no tales.

SEBASTIAN   The devil speaks in him.

PROSPERO   No.

For you, most wicked sir, whom to call brother   130

Would even infect my mouth, I do forgive

Thy rankest fault – all of them; and require

My dukedom of thee, which perforce I know

Thou must restore.

ALONSO   If thou be'st Prospero,

---

124 **subtleties** Prospero puns here on
two senses of the word: (1) the inge-
nious contrivances of his magic and
(2), in conjunction with the verb *taste*,
the ornamental sugar desserts used in
elaborate Renaissance banquets that,
in this case, might cloud one's judgement. See Var, 245–6, and *OED*
subtleties 4, 5.

125 **my friends all** probably meant in a
loose sense of goodwill, not necessarily
implying fondness for or forgiveness of
Antonio and Sebastian (*OED* friends
sb. 2)

126 **brace** pair, couple. The term was
originally applied to dogs or certain
kinds of game and here is used with 'a
touch of humour or contempt' (*OED*
sb.[2] 15d).

127 **pluck** 'bring down' (*OED v.* 3b)

128 **justify** prove

129 **I will** elided in speaking to 'I'll'
devil The metre requires an elision
here to 'dev'l'.
No Prospero overhears Sebastian's
comment, emphatically denies that it
is the devil that speaks, and then
directly addresses Antonio; or, perhaps, Prospero reiterates that he will
tell no tales.

131 **even** probably elided to 'e'en'

132 **fault** F4 and Rowe emended to
'faults' but *all of them* may be an after-
thought to Antonio's *rankest fault*.
require demand as a right (cited in
OED v. 5a)

133 **perforce** by necessity. Antonio has
no choice.

---

124 not] *F3;* nor *F*   126 SD] *Johnson*   129 I will] I'll *Pope*   132 fault –] *R.G. White;* fault; *F;*
faults *F4*

Give us particulars of thy preservation,   135
How thou hast met us here, whom three hours since
Were wrecked upon this shore, where I have lost
(How sharp the point of this remembrance is!)
My dear son Ferdinand.

PROSPERO   I am woe for't, sir.

ALONSO

Irreparable is the loss, and patience   140
Says it is past her cure.

PROSPERO   I rather think

You have not sought her help, of whose soft grace
For the like loss I have her sovereign aid
And rest myself content.

ALONSO   You the like loss?

PROSPERO

As great to me as late; and supportable   145
To make the dear loss have I means much weaker
Than you may call to comfort you, for I

---

135 **particulars** the details
136 **whom** emended by F2 and Rowe to
'who', but cf. 76 and n.
  since ago
139 **I . . . for't** 'I am sorry (grieved, miserable (*OED* C 1a)) for it.' Cf. *Cym*
5.5.297, where the King declares, 'I am
sorrow for thee'. Shakespeare occasionally used *woe* as an adjective
(Abbott, §230).
141 **past her cure** beyond her ability to
cure
142 **her help** the help of patience
  soft compassionate, kind (*OED a.* 8a)
143–4 **her . . . content** With the aid of
patience, Prospero has accepted the
loss of his daughter (*sovereign*, efficacious, potent).
145 **late** recent
145–7 **supportable . . . you** The difficult

syntax of this passage probably
inspired F3, F4 and Rowe's emendation to 'insupportable'. Prospero
claims to lack the compensations that
Alonso has for the (presumed) death of
Ferdinand to make the loss of his
daughter *supportable* ('bearable, toler-
able, endurable' (cited in *OED* supportable *a.* 2)). Some editors have
speculated that Claribel, Alonso's
daughter, is the compensation Prospero has in mind, but the magician
could also be referring to Alonso's
royal power and prerogatives. More
likely, Prospero simply considers the
loss of his daughter through marriage
as a dear loss, dearer than Alonso could
comprehend (Melchiori, 69).
146 **dear** severe, grievous (*OED a.*[2] 2)
147 **comfort** console, solace

136 whom] who *F2*   139 I am] I'm *Pope*   145 supportable] insupportable *F3*

Have lost my daughter.

ALONSO   A daughter?

O heavens, that they were living both in Naples,

The king and queen there! That they were, I wish   150

Myself were mudded in that oozy bed

Where my son lies. When did you lose your daughter?

PROSPERO

In this last tempest. – I perceive these lords

At this encounter do so much admire

That they devour their reason and scarce think   155

Their eyes do offices of truth, their words

Are natural breath. – But howsoe'er you have

Been jostled from your senses, know for certain

That I am Prospero and that very duke

Which was thrust forth of Milan, who most strangely   160

Upon this shore where you were wrecked, was landed

To be the lord on't. No more yet of this,

For 'tis a chronicle of day by day,

---

148 **daughter . . . daughter** The implication of this exchange is that Alonso did not know that Prospero had a daughter, which seems implausible but not impossible – either because he had never been told of Miranda's birth or because during the twelve years since their exile, he had forgotten. It is even less plausible that Alonso knew of Miranda's birth but not that she had been exiled with her father.

151 **mudded** buried in the mud. Cf. 3.3.102 (these are the only occurrences cited in *OED v.*[1] 3a).

oozy bed the ocean's floor

154–5 **so . . . reason** 'their reason is swallowed up in amazement' (Oxf[1], 196). They may also be open-mouthed in astonishment. *Admire*, wonder, marvel.

156 **do . . . truth** perform the duties of truth; i.e. they think their eyes are deceiving them.

their Capell's emendation to 'these', adopted in Oxf, on the assumption that the compositor misread 'theis', changes F's sense, making Prospero refer to his own words. But since the point is to stress the Neapolitans' astonishment, there is no reason why they couldn't have trouble believing their own words and responses to what they are hearing. See Var, 248.

157 **natural breath** 'ordinary speech'; the Neapolitans are so amazed they can hardly believe the words they are saying.

160 **of** from

strangely in a most unusual way (*OED adv.* 3)

162 **on't** of it

163 **chronicle** narrative account

day by day 'to be told over many days' (Oxf[1], 196), or 'of daily events, over many years'

156 their] these *Oxf (Capell)*

Not a relation for a breakfast, nor
Befitting this first meeting. – Welcome, sir.   165
This cell's my court; here have I few attendants,
And subjects none abroad. Pray you, look in.
My dukedom since you have given me again,
I will requite you with as good a thing,
At least bring forth a wonder to content ye   170
As much as me my dukedom.

Here Prospero discovers Ferdinand and Miranda, playing at chess.

MIRANDA

Sweet lord, you play me false.

FERDINAND   No, my dearest love,

I would not for the world.

MIRANDA

Yes, for a score of kingdoms you should wrangle,
And I would call it fair play.

ALONSO   If this prove   175

164 **relation** report
167 **abroad** elsewhere
168 **you have** The metre requires an elision to 'you've'.
170 **wonder** Prospero deliberately puns on his daughter's name.
171.1 Furness contends that chess was associated with royalty in Jacobean England; it was 'a deeply intellectual pastime, above the reach of the vulgar, confined to royal and princely personages'. Moreover, Naples was known as a centre of chess-playing (Var, 250–1). Chess was featured in many courtly-love allegories and is found in Renaissance discourses on government. See Loughrey & Taylor.
discovers Dessen defines the theatrical term 'discover': 'to part a curtain or otherwise reveal to the playgoer (and often to onstage figures) something hitherto unseen' (42), in this instance, the seemingly miraculous existence of

Ferdinand and Miranda; the former had perished, the court party believes, in the tempest and the latter is no longer an infant but a lovely young woman. Alonso wonders if it is another 'vision of the island' (176), but this is the only spectacle Prospero produces without the aid of magic.
172 **play me false** Miranda claims that Ferdinand is cheating.
174 **a score of** twenty. Miranda checks Ferdinand with twenty kingdoms, as opposed to the *world*.
   wrangle dispute, take opposition
175 **And** Oxf interprets as 'An' (meaning 'If'), making Ferdinand's wrangling conditional upon Miranda's approval. F's *And* seems preferable; Miranda approves no matter what Ferdinand does.
   fair play Miranda would call Ferdinand's cheating fair play (because she loves him).

168 you have] you've *Pope*   172 dearest] dear *Pope:* dear'st *Capell*   175 And] An *Oxf*

A vision of the island, one dear son
Shall I twice lose.

SEBASTIAN   A most high miracle!

FERDINAND [*Sees Alonso and the others.*]
Though the seas threaten, they are merciful.
I have cursed them without cause.   [*He kneels.*]

ALONSO   Now all the blessings
Of a glad father compass thee about!   180
Arise and say how thou cam'st here.

MIRANDA   O wonder!
How many goodly creatures are there here!
How beauteous mankind is! O brave new world
That has such people in't.

PROSPERO   'Tis new to thee.

ALONSO
What is this maid with whom thou wast at play?   185
Your eld'st acquaintance cannot be three hours.
Is she the goddess that hath severed us
And brought us thus together?

FERDINAND   Sir, she is mortal,
But by immortal providence she's mine;
I chose her when I could not ask my father   190
For his advice, nor thought I had one. She
Is daughter to this famous Duke of Milan –

176 **vision** Alonso wonders whether the image of Ferdinand is just another of the island's illusions. See 171.ln. (*discovers*).

177 **A . . . miracle!** This line can be spoken with reverent wonder or sarcasm, depending on the actor's interpretation of Sebastian's emotional state.

183 **mankind** humans in general, though the people Miranda now admires are all male

186 **eld'st** oldest, longest

187 **goddess** Like Ferdinand in 1.2.422–3, Alonso assumes Miranda is a goddess. He may also think that his reunion with his son is providential.

190–1 **father . . . advice** Ferdinand would not normally be allowed to marry without his father's permission. Cf. *WT* 4.4.391–417, where Polixenes flies into a rage because his son Florizel plans to marry a shepherdess without consulting him.

191 **one** a living father

178 SD] *this edn*   179 I have] I've *Pope*   SD] *Theobald*   188 she is] she's *Pope*   192 Milan –] *this edn; Millaine, F*

Of whom so often I have heard renown
But never saw before – of whom I have
Received a second life; and second father　　　　　195
This lady makes him to me.

ALONSO　　　　　　　　　　I am hers.
But O, how oddly will it sound that I
Must ask my child forgiveness.

PROSPERO　　　　　　　　　　There, sir, stop.
Let us not burden our remembrances with
A heaviness that's gone.

GONZALO　　　　　　　　　I have inly wept,　　　200
Or should have spoke ere this. Look down, you gods,
And on this couple drop a blessed crown,
For it is you that have chalked forth the way
Which brought us hither.

ALONSO　　　　　　　　　I say 'amen', Gonzalo.

GONZALO
Was Milan thrust from Milan that his issue　　　　205

---

194 **of whom** from whom
　　renown report, rumour (with the
　　implication of being widely celebrated
　　(cited in *OED sb.* 3))
195 **second life** Ferdinand acknowledges
　　Prospero's role in his new life (after
　　nearly losing his life in the shipwreck)
　　on the island.
　　second father Prospero will be
　　Ferdinand's father-in-law, a term
　　rarely used in Shakespeare's time. The
　　spouse's parents were referred to as
　　'father' and 'mother'.
196 **I am hers.** 'I am *her* father (in law)';
　　i.e. Alonso consents to the marriage.
198 **forgiveness** This line shows that
　　Alonso repents his involvement in
　　Prospero's usurpation.
　　There, sir, stop. In some perfor-
　　mances, Alonso tries to kneel before
　　Miranda while asking forgiveness but

is prevented by Prospero who raises
him back up with this line.
200 **heaviness** sadness, grief (cited in
　　OED e)
　　inly 'Inwardly'; or 'thoroughly,
　　extremely' (*OED adv.*)
202 **blessed** blessèd
　　crown the combined crowns of Naples
　　and Milan
203 **chalked forth** marked out, as if with
　　chalk, 'as a course to be followed' (cited
　　in *OED* chalk *v.* 4c *fig.*). Cf. *H8*
　　1.1.59–60: 'ancestry, whose grace /
　　Chalks successors their way'.
205 [1]**Milan** the Duke of Milan. Shake-
　　speare and his contemporaries fre-
　　quently conflated the names of
　　countries with their rulers. Cf. *AC*
　　4.15.41, where Antony refers to
　　Cleopatra as 'Egypt'.

194 before –] *this edn;* before: *F*　199 remembrances] remembrance *Ard² (Rowe³)*　200 I have]
I've *Pope*

298

Should become kings of Naples? O, rejoice
Beyond a common joy, and set it down
With gold on lasting pillars: in one voyage
Did Claribel her husband find at Tunis;
And Ferdinand, her brother, found a wife   210
Where he himself was lost; Prospero his dukedom
In a poor isle; and all of us ourselves,
When no man was his own.
ALONSO [*to Ferdinand and Miranda*]
                                    Give me your hands.
Let grief and sorrow still embrace his heart
That doth not wish you joy.
GONZALO   Be it so; amen.   215

Enter ARIEL, *with the* Master *and* Boatswain
amazedly following.

O look, sir, look, sir; here is more of us!
I prophesied, if a gallows were on land
This fellow could not drown. [*to Boatswain*] Now,
    blasphemy,
That swear'st grace o'erboard, not an oath on shore?

206 **Naples** Prospero's descendants will
inherit both Naples and Milan by
virtue of Ferdinand and Miranda's
marriage.
208 **lasting pillars** Kay describes the *pillars*' 'recognized iconographic significance': after Charles V combined the
pillars of Hercules with the motto *plus
ultra* (greater than the greatest), European monarchs, including Elizabeth,
adopted the emblem to signify their
imperial ambitions. 'Gonzalo's pillars',
Kay concludes, 'would derive their status as an emblem of rule, ambition,
dynastic continuity, and the operation
of Providence' and resonate with the
play's political concerns.
214 **still** ever, always

his heart the heart of anyone
215 **That** who
    Be it probably elided to 'Be't' to fit the
    metre
216 **here is** Pope emended to 'here are'
    but, as Abbott indicates, a singular
    verb preceding a plural subject is com-
    mon in Shakespeare (§335).
218 **blasphemy** one who blasphemes.
    Sebastian had called the Boatswain a
    'bawling, blasphemous, incharitable
    dog' in 1.1.39–40, though we never
    actually heard the Boatswain say any-
    thing blasphemous.
219 **swear'st grace o'erboard** Gonzalo
    charges that the Boatswain's swearing
    will send *grace* overboard.

213 SD] *Capell*   215 Be it] Be't *Pope*   216 ²sir] *om. F3*   is] are *Pope*   218 SD] *Oxf*

Hast thou no mouth by land? What is the news?   220

BOATSWAIN

The best news is that we have safely found

Our King and company. The next: our ship,

Which but three glasses since we gave out split,

Is tight and yare and bravely rigged as when

We first put out to sea.

ARIEL [*to Prospero*]   Sir, all this service   225

Have I done since I went.

PROSPERO   My tricksy spirit!

ALONSO

These are not natural events; they strengthen

From strange to stranger. Say, how came you hither?

BOATSWAIN

If I did think, sir, I were well awake,

I'd strive to tell you. We were dead of sleep   230

And – how we know not – all clapped under hatches,

Where but even now with strange and several noises

Of roaring, shrieking, howling, jingling chains

And more diversity of sounds, all horrible,

We were awaked; straightway at liberty,   235

Where we, in all our trim, freshly beheld

---

220 **Hast . . . land?** Can't you speak on land?

223 **three glasses** three hours, each hour consuming one hourglass
gave out reported

224 **tight and yare** shipshape, seaworthy, easily manageable (cited in *OED* yare *a. arch.* 2b)
bravely finely, handsomely

226 **tricksy** 'full of or given to tricks, or pranks; playful, sportive; mischievous, capricious, whimsical' (cited in *OED a.* 2)

227 **strengthen** 'become strong or stronger, grow in strength or intensity' (first occurrence in *OED v.* 10)

228 **strange to stranger** curiouser and curiouser

230 **dead of sleep** deeply asleep

231 **clapped under hatches** confined under the deck

232 **even** The metre suggests an elision to 'e'en'.

236 **our trim** Assuming that the Boatswain referred to the ship, Theobald emended to 'her trim', and some modern editors have followed suit. Even without the emendation, the

---

220] *Pope; F lines* land? / newes? /   221 safely] safe *F3*   225 SD] *Malone*   227 events] *Fc* (euents); euens *Fu*   230 of sleep] a-sleep *Pope*   231 And – how] *Dyce;* And (how *F*   not –] *Dyce;* not) *F*   234 more] *Rowe;* mo *F*   236 our] her *Theobald*

Our royal, good and gallant ship; our master
Cap'ring to eye her. On a trice, so please you,
Even in a dream, were we divided from them
And were brought moping hither.

ARIEL [*to Prospero*]   Was't well done?   240

PROSPERO
Bravely, my diligence. Thou shalt be free.

ALONSO
This is as strange a maze as e'er men trod,
And there is in this business more than nature
Was ever conduct of. Some oracle
Must rectify our knowledge.

PROSPERO   Sir, my liege,   245
Do not infest your mind with beating on
The strangeness of this business. At picked leisure,
Which shall be shortly, single I'll resolve you
(Which to you shall seem probable) of every

---

reference (however oddly placed) may
be to the ship: '*our* trim on *our* ship'.
But the Boatswain more likely refers to
himself and his fellow sailors, the *trim*
being their garments or perhaps their
personal equipment.
freshly recently, lately (cited in *OED*
adv. 1)
237 **gallant** stately, noble; 'often used as
an admiring epithet for a ship' (*OED* A
4b)
238 **Cap'ring** dancing with joy
On a trice instantly, without delay
(Dent, T517)
239 **them** the other crew members
240 **moping** confused, bewildered
241 **Bravely, my diligence** i.e. well
done, my diligent one
242 **maze** Gonzalo compared the winding path the Neapolitans have travelled
to a maze in 3.3.2, and Alonso here
echoes the same theme.
244 **conduct** director. Alonso finds this

business beyond or outside nature's
usual guidance.
246 **infest . . . on** Emended to 'infect' in
F4 and Rowe, F's 'infest' – 'to attack,
assail, annoy, or trouble in a persistent
manner' (*OED v.*² 1) – accords better
with *beating on*, defined by Orgel as
'hammering, insistently thinking'
(Oxf¹, 201).
247 **picked leisure** a time that is deliberately selected
248 ***shortly, single** Since Rowe, editors
have added a comma after *shortly*, making *single* an adverb that modifies the
verb *resolve*. Prospero wants to talk to
Alonso privately, in single company,
without Sebastian and Antonio present.
resolve you explain to you, make you
understand
249 **probable** 'capable of being proved;
demonstrable, provable' (*OED a.* 1);
or, 'likely' (*OED a.* 3a)

240 SD] *Malone*   246 infest] infect *F4, Rowe¹*   248 shortly, single] *Rowe³;* shortly single *F*

These happened accidents. Till when, be cheerful   250
And think of each thing well.
[aside to Ariel]   Come hither, spirit.
Set Caliban and his companions free;
Untie the spell.   *[Exit Ariel.]*
[to Alonso]   How fares my gracious sir?
There are yet missing of your company
Some few odd lads that you remember not.   255

Enter ARIEL, *driving in* CALIBAN, STEPHANO *and*
TRINCULO *in their stolen apparel.*

STEPHANO   Every man shift for all the rest, and let no
man take care for himself, for all is but fortune.
Coraggio, bully monster, *coraggio*.

TRINCULO   If these be true spies which I wear in my head,
here's a goodly sight.   260

CALIBAN

O Setebos, these be brave spirits indeed!
How fine my master is! I am afraid
He will chastise me.

SEBASTIAN   Ha, ha!
What things are these, my lord Antonio?
Will money buy 'em?

ANTONIO   Very like. One of them   265

250 **accidents** unforeseen events
256–7 Drunken Stephano inverts the
sense of what he surely intended or at
least what custom called for: 'Let each
man shift for himself and not bother
with the others, for only chance (*fortune*) can save us from this predicament', i.e. 'Every man for himself'.
258 *Coraggio . . . coraggio* the Italian
exclamation for 'Have courage!'(cited
in *OED int.*). Cf. *AW* 2.5.92: 'Bravely,
coraggio!' Andrews suggests that F's

'*Coragio . . . Corasio*' was the playwright's way of conveying Stephano's
inebriation (Everyman, 172), but it
may have been a compositorial error.
bully gallant
259 'If I can believe my eyes'
261 **Setebos** Caliban's god. See 1.2.374
and n.
brave splendid, wonderful
262 **fine** finely dressed. Caliban had not,
presumably, ever seen Prospero in his
ducal attire.

251 SD] *Johnson*   253 SD1] *Capell*   SD2] *Oxf*   256–8] *Pope; as verse F, lined* let / is / Bully-
monster *Corasio*.   258 coraggio] *F2; Corasio F*

Is a plain fish and no doubt marketable.

PROSPERO

Mark but the badges of these men, my lords,
Then say if they be true. This misshapen knave,
His mother was a witch, and one so strong
That could control the moon, make flows and ebbs,   270
And deal in her command without her power.
These three have robbed me, and this demi-devil
(For he's a bastard one) had plotted with them
To take my life. Two of these fellows you
Must know and own; this thing of darkness I   275
Acknowledge mine.

CALIBAN   I shall be pinched to death.

---

266 **fish** perhaps a reference, probably not literal, to Caliban's appearance, or, more likely, to his smell (see 4.1.183–4 and 199–200). Cf. Trinculo's reaction in 2.2.25–35.

267 **badges** signs of employment. In Renaissance great houses, servants wore livery that identified their employer.

268 **true** genuine, legitimate; i.e. Prospero challenges the Neapolitans to certify that the servants are their own.

misshapen knave another elusive reference to Caliban's appearance, suggesting some sort of physical deformity

269 **mother** Sycorax. Cf 1.2.263–9 and 266n.

270 **control the moon** Ovid's Medea claims to control the moon in *Metamorphoses*, 7.207.

flows and ebbs By controlling the moon, Sycorax could also control the tides.

271 **deal . . . power** Sycorax could usurp some of the moon's authority but not all her power, although *without her power* might also mean 'beyond the limits of the moon's power', or 'without need to rely on the moon's power'.

272 **demi-devil** In 1.2.320–1 Prospero claimed that Caliban's sire was a devil.

Cf. Othello's charge that Iago is a 'demi-devil' (*Oth* 5.2.301).

273 **bastard one** Prospero could mean that Caliban was illegitimate or that he was a 'mongrel hybrid of inferior breed' (*OED* bastard B 2a).

275 **thing of darkness** Caliban's *darkness* has traditionally been interpreted as a sign of his moral depravity, or at least Prospero's conviction that he is morally depraved. Recently it has sometimes been taken as an epithet implying Caliban's African or Native American ancestry. See, e.g. two scholarly works: Hall, *Things of Darkness*, and Brown, '"This thing of darkness"'.

276 **Acknowledge mine** Prospero may be merely acknowledging Caliban as his servant (as opposed to Stephano and Trinculo who are Alonso's responsibility), but this line has often been taken as Prospero's 'anagnorisis', a recognition of his own part in the darker side of humanity or, more particularly, in Caliban's lust for Miranda. See, e.g., Bate, *Ovid*, 254–7, and Melchiori, 71–2.

pinched Caliban expressed his fear of the pinches inflicted by Prospero's Spirits in 2.2.4–6.

268 misshapen] mis-shap'd *Pope*

ALONSO

    Is not this Stephano, my drunken butler?

SEBASTIAN

    He is drunk now. Where had he wine?

ALONSO

    And Trinculo is reeling ripe! Where should they

    Find this grand liquor that hath gilded 'em?   280

    How cam'st thou in this pickle?

TRINCULO   I have been in such a pickle since I saw you

    last, that I fear me will never out of my bones. I shall

    not fear fly-blowing.

SEBASTIAN   Why, how now, Stephano?   285

STEPHANO   O touch me not; I am not Stephano, but a

    cramp!

PROSPERO   You'd be king o'the isle, sirrah?

STEPHANO   I should have been a sore one then.

ALONSO

    This is a strange thing as e'er I looked on.   290

---

279 **reeling ripe** so drunk that he 'reels', staggering or perhaps losing his balance

280 **liquor . . . 'em** Theobald first noted that this line is an alchemical reference and emended *liquor* to 'lixir' to make the connection clearer (73). Liquor has *boiled* their brains (see 60 above and n.), turning their base metal into gold; liquor may also have flushed their faces and thereby *gilded* them. There could also be a resonance of gild / guilt, as in *Mac* 2.2.52–4: 'If he do bleed, / I'll gild the faces of the grooms withal, / For it must seem their guilt'.

281 **pickle** (1) The liquor, as a preservative, has turned Trinculo into a *pickle*; (2) Trinculo has got himself into a sad predicament (Dent, P276). Both meanings are probably intended. Cf.

AC 2.5.65–6, where Cleopatra threatens the messenger: 'Thou shalt be whipt with wire, and stew'd in brine, / Smarting in ling'ring pickle'.

284 **fly-blowing** Because he is 'pickled', Trinculo will not worry about flies which otherwise would deposit their eggs on him as on raw meat.

286–7 **I . . . cramp** 'I've been so tormented by cramps (inflicted by Ariel's minions) that I've turned into one.'

288 **sirrah** 'a term of address used to men or boys expressing contempt, reprimand, or assumption of authority on the part of the speaker' (*OED* 1)

289 **sore** painful, aching (*OED a.*[1] 1), playing on *cramp* (287); or, 'distressed' (*OED a.*[1] 11)

278] *Pope; F lines* now; / wine? /   282–4] *Pope; as verse F, lined* last, / bones: / fly-blowing. /
290 This . . . as] 'Tis a strange thing as *F3, F4, Rowe;* This is as strange a thing as *Folg*[2] *(Capell)*

PROSPERO

He is as disproportioned in his manners
As in his shape. Go, sirrah, to my cell;
Take with you your companions. As you look
To have my pardon, trim it handsomely.

CALIBAN

Ay, that I will; and I'll be wise hereafter   295
And seek for grace. What a thrice-double ass
Was I to take this drunkard for a god,
And worship this dull fool!

PROSPERO   Go to, away.

ALONSO [*to Stephano and Trinculo*]

Hence, and bestow your luggage where you found it.

SEBASTIAN   Or stole it, rather.   300

[*Exeunt Caliban, Stephano and Trinculo.*]

PROSPERO

Sir, I invite your highness and your train
To my poor cell, where you shall take your rest
For this one night, which (part of it) I'll waste
With such discourse as, I not doubt, shall make it

291–2 **He . . . shape.** Another suggestion
that Caliban is somehow deformed,
reflecting the common view that the
physical body is a true reflector of the
moral condition.

291 **manners** in the now obsolete sense of
'conduct in its moral aspect' (*OED sb.*[1]
4b); and, perhaps, 'customary rules of
behaviour' (*OED sb.*[1] 4c)

293 **look** expect, hope

294 **trim it handsomely** decorate the
cell admirably, beautifully

296 **seek for grace** This line is often
taken to indicate Caliban's repentance
and promise of reform. *Grace* can be
read as either 'mercy' (forgiveness) or
'favour' in that Caliban will now seek
Prospero's goodwill. In either case,

Caliban now realizes how stupid he
was to involve himself with Stephano
and Trinculo.
thrice-double three times two – six
times over

298 **worship** intended in the general
sense of 'honour' or 'treat with respect'
(*OED v.* 2b) as well as 'revere as a
supernatural' (*OED v.* 1a)

299 **luggage** the stolen apparel; cf.
4.1.232.

300 SD *F does not provide an exit for
Stephano, Trinculo and Caliban here,
but it is common stage practice for
them to comply with Prospero's *Go to,
away*.

301 **train** entourage

303 **waste** pass away the time

299 SD] *this edn*   300 SD] *Capell*   303 which (part of it)] *Pope;* which part of it, *F*

Go quick away – the story of my life,   305
And the particular accidents gone by
Since I came to this isle – and in the morn
I'll bring you to your ship, and so to Naples,
Where I have hope to see the nuptial
Of these our dear-beloved solemnized;   310
And thence retire me to my Milan, where
Every third thought shall be my grave.

ALONSO   I long
To hear the story of your life, which must
Take the ear strangely.

PROSPERO   I'll deliver all,
And promise you calm seas, auspicious gales   315
And sail so expeditious that shall catch
Your royal fleet far off. [*aside to Ariel*] My Ariel, chick,
That is thy charge. Then to the elements
Be free, and fare thou well!

[*to the others*]   Please you, draw near.

Exeunt omnes.

---

305 **quick** used here as an adverb; quickly
306 **accidents** events, occurrences
310 **dear-beloved** dear-belovèd. F's 'belou'd' may be the result of Crane's habit of elision; we take instead Rowe's reading ('dear-beloved solemnized'), which makes the line metrical, with the extra accent on belovèd (not on solemnized), and suggests the Anglican marriage ceremony's 'dearly belovèd'.
312 **third thought** Prospero's plan to meditate on his own death is sometimes taken as an indication that he is quite old and near death. Since the *memento mori*, a meditation on death, was a widespread religious convention, this resolve need not imply Prospero's imminent mortality. We prefer to think of Prospero as a middle-aged man who looks forward to regaining his dukedom and watching his grand-

children grow up (see Introduction, pp. 24–5). Orgel contends that Prospero's meditation may also be a form of gloating over Antonio's loss of the throne to Ferdinand and Miranda (*Oxf*[1], 55).
314 **Take the ear** affect the listener; 'captivate, delight, charm' (*OED* take *v*. B 10)
    deliver all tell everything
316 **shall catch** They will catch up with the rest of the fleet, which was reported somewhere on *the Mediterranean float* (1.2.234).
317 **chick** literally, a young chicken but also a term of endearment (cited in *OED sb.*[1] 3). In 4.1.184 Prospero called Ariel *my bird*; both epithets suggest the spirit's avian qualities.
319 **Be . . . well!** In Ron Daniels's 1984–5 RSC production, Prospero (Derek

---

305 away –] *Penguin;* away: F   307 isle –] *this edn;* Isle: F   309 nuptial] nuptials *F2*   310 dear-beloved] *(*deere-belou'd*)*   317 SD] *Malone*   319 SD] *Signet*

EPILOGUE
spoken by PROSPERO

Now my charms are all o'erthrown,
And what strength I have's mine own,
Which is most faint. Now, 'tis true
I must be here confined by you,
Or sent to Naples. Let me not,   5
Since I have my dukedom got
And pardoned the deceiver, dwell
In this bare island by your spell;
But release me from my bands

Jacobi) addressed these words to empty space. More melodramatically, in some performances of the 1993-4 RSC production, Simon Russell Beale's Ariel spat at Prospero at this moment and then disappeared. As Dessen argues, Ariel's departure here, rather than after Prospero's last words, can call attention to his role as the agent of Prospero's magical powers and suggest the magus's loss and new-found vulnerability (214-15).

Please . . . near. This line is usually delivered as Prospero draws the court party into his cell, off stage. If Prospero remains on stage for the Epilogue, the line can be delivered to the audience as he moves forward.

EPILOGUE The Epilogue is not required for a coherent reading or production because the play's action is complete. Shakespeare may have added it for special performances, perhaps at court. However, the Epilogue, like 4.1.148–56, relates Prospero's art to the dramatist's skill, and the conventional request for applause also relates to the play's themes of reconciliation and forgiveness. The octosyllabic couplets used in the Epilogue are similar to some of Gower's choric speeches in *Per*; compare also Puck's epilogue in *MND*.

1   **charms . . . o'erthrown** a reference to the magic Prospero has relinquished or to the role of the actor. In George C. Wolfe's 1995 production for the New York Shakespeare Festival, Patrick Stewart gave up the microphone he had used throughout the outdoor performance and here addressed the audience without the aid of amplification. If Prospero has exited and returned, he may have doffed some of his ducal trappings and appear in a simple shirt or gown. Such theatrical choices can indicate Prospero's loss of power or the actor's loss of his role.

4   **you** the audience. As Orgel notes, 'Prospero puts himself in the position of Ariel, Caliban, Ferdinand and the other shipwreck victims throughout the play, threatened with confinement, pleading for release from bondage' (Oxf[1], 204).

8   **this bare island** presumably the stage as well as its imaginary setting

9   **bands** bonds, confinement. Prospero is confined to the island, the actor to his role, until the audience releases him.

EPILOGUE]   1 Now] Now, now *F3*   2 own,] *F2* (owne,); *owne. F;* own; *Pope*   3 Now] and
now *Pope*

With the help of your good hands.   10
Gentle breath of yours my sails
Must fill, or else my project fails,
Which was to please. Now I want
Spirits to enforce, art to enchant;
And my ending is despair,   15
Unless I be relieved by prayer,
Which pierces so that it assaults
Mercy itself, and frees all faults.
    As you from crimes would pardoned be,   19
    Let your indulgence set me free.   *Exit.*

10 **good hands** applause. It was thought that the sound of hands clapping could break a charm. Cf. Puck's similar request in *MND*: 'Give me your hands, if we be friends' (5.1.437).

11 **Gentle breath** from the audience's cheers or perhaps, as Orgel suggests, from their kind words about the performance (Oxf[1], 205)

12 **my project** perhaps the alchemist's experiment, though Prospero might also mean his project to regain his dukedom. The actor's project is, of course, to please his audience. See 5.1.1.

13 **please** implying *please* you, the audience
    want lack

15–6 **ending . . . prayer** Warburton contended that these lines allude 'to the old Stories told of the despair of Necromancers in their last moments;

and of the efficacy of the prayers of their friends for them' (89). But taken in context, the passage suggests that without his art – like the actor without his role – Prospero is simply human, in need of mercy and forgiveness like others.

17–18 **pierces . . . faults** Prayer is able to penetrate the heart of *Mercy* (a personification of divine grace) and attain pardon for all faults, in both the play and the performance.

19 **crimes** sins, offences

19–20 Cf. Matthew, 6.14 (Geneva Bible): 'For if ye do forgive men their trespaces, your heavenlie Father wil also forgive you'.

20 **indulgence** favour; but perhaps also an irreverent pun on the Roman Catholic practice of offering remission of the punishment due to a sin in return for a donation to the Church

13 Now] For now *Pope*   14 art] Arts *F3*

APPENDIX 1
SOURCES

Unlike most of Shakespeare's plays, *The Tempest* has no principal source for its plot nor even a cluster of sources for its central themes. It does, however, have several unquestionable general sources, such as Virgil's *Aeneid* and Ovid's *Metamorphoses*, for many of its minor themes, some of its characterizations and some of its language, as we discuss briefly in our Introduction and as books by Donna Hamilton and Jonathan Bate explain more fully. There are also two documents on which Shakespeare surely drew for specific passages: William Strachey's 'True Reportory', for the opening scene and perhaps for a few later references to dissensions, conspiracies, and retributions; and Michel de Montaigne's 'Of the Caniballes', for Gonzalo's utopian musings and perhaps for some observations about cultural differences. For other sources and analogues that may underly *The Tempest*, see our Introduction and Bullough's *Narrative and Dramatic Sources*, vol. VIII.

The following extracts from Strachey and Montaigne are here reproduced as first published in England (1625 and 1603 respectively), with minor modifications as set forth in our Preface, and with the omission of extraneous marginalia.

1 *Strachey, 'A True Reportory'*

William Strachey (1572–1621) attended Emmanuel College, Cambridge, and was later a resident of the Blackfriars area of London, where he was an acquaintance of Ben Jonson and a member of the Virginia Company. In 1609 Strachey was aboard the *Sea Venture* when she was wrecked on the coast of Bermuda;

after he and the other survivors reached Jamestown ten months later, Strachey composed his long narrative letter to a 'noble Lady' (probably Dame Sara Smith, wife of Sir Thomas Smith of the Virginia Company), which he sent to England that summer. It was first published by Samuel Purchas in *Purchas His Pilgrimes* in 1625, along with a portion of the Virginia Company's *True declaration of the estate of the colony* of 1610 (published several months after Strachey's letter arrived in England) and possibly with changes to the original manuscript. That manuscript was among Hakluyt's papers, acquired by Purchas on the former's death in 1616, but it has since disappeared. The following selection is from Purchas's version, vol. 4, pp. 1734–58.

A true reportory of the wracke, and redemption of Sir THOMAS GATES *Knight; upon, and from the Ilands of the* Bermudas: *his comming to* Virginia, *and the estate of that Colonie then, and after, under the government of the Lord* LA WARRE, *July* 15. 1610. *written by* WILLIAM STRACHY, *Esquire.*

I

A most dreadfull Tempest (the manifold deaths whereof are here to the life described[1]) their wracke on Bermuda, *and the description of those Ilands.*

Excellent Lady, know that upon Friday late in the evening, we brake ground out of the Sound of *Plymouth,* our whole Fleete then consisting of seven good Ships, and two Pinnaces, all of which from the said second of June, unto the twenty three of July, kept in friendly consort together not a whole watch at any time, loosing the sight of each other. . . . [W]e were within seven or eight dayes at the most, by Cap. *Newports*[2] reckoning of making Cape *Henry* upon the coast of *Virginia*: When on S. *James* his day, July 24. being Monday (preparing for no lesse all the blacke night before) the cloudes gathering thicke upon us, and the windes singing, and whistling most unusually, which made us

---

1 No lives were lost in the storm, but Strachey mentions the deaths of several people in Bermuda and others in Virginia.

2 Christopher Newport (*c.* 1565–1617) commanded the first expedition to Virginia in 1606–7; the ill-fated voyage of 1609 was his third of five trips to the English colony.

to cast off our Pinnace towing the same untill then asterne, a dreadfull storme and hideous began to blow from out the North-east, which swelling, and roaring as it were by fits, some houres with more violence then others, at length did beate all light from heaven; which like an hell of darkenesse turned blacke upon us, so much the more fuller of horror, as in such cases horror and feare use to overrunne the troubled, and overmastered sences of all, which (taken up with amazement) the eares lay so sensible to the terrible cries, and murmurs of the windes, and distraction of our Company, as who was most armed, and best prepared, was not a little shaken. For surely (Noble Lady) as death comes not so sodaine nor apparant, so he comes not so elvish and painfull (to men especially even then in health and perfect habitudes of body) as at Sea; who comes at no time so welcome, but our frailty (so weake is the hold of hope in miserable demonstrations of danger) it makes guilty of many contrary changes, and conflicts: For indeede death is accompanied at no time, nor place with circumstances every way so uncapable of particularities of goodnesse and inward comforts, as at Sea. . . .

For foure and twenty houres the storme in a restlesse tumult, had blowne so exceedingly, as we could not apprehend in our imaginations any possibility of greater violence, yet did wee still finde it, not onely more terrible, but more constant, fury added to fury, and one storme urging a second more outragious then the former; whether it so wrought upon our feares, or indeede met with new forces: Sometimes strikes in our Ship amongst women, and passengers, not used to such hurly and discomforts, made us looke one upon the other with troubled hearts, and panting bosomes: our clamours dround in the windes, and the windes in thunder. Prayers might well be in the heart and lips, but drowned in the outcries of the Officers: nothing heard that could give comfort, nothing seene that might incourage hope. It is impossible for me, had I the voyce of *Stentor*,[1] and expression of as many tongues, as his throate of voyces, to expresse the outcries and miseries, not languishing, but wasting his spirits, and art constant to his owne principles, but not prevailing. Our sailes wound up lay without their use, and if at any time wee bore but a Hollocke,[2] or halfe forecourse, to guide her

---

1 The *Iliad* described the Greek herald Stentor as having the voice of fifty men.

2 '[L]et us trie if she will endure the *Hullocke* of a Saile, which sometimes is a peece of the mizen saile or some other little saile part opened, to keepe her head to the sea' (J. Smith, *Sea Grammar*, 41).

before the Sea, six and sometimes eight men were not inough to hold the whipstaffe[1] in the steerage, and the tiller below in the Gunner roome, by which may be imagined the strength of the storme: In which, the Sea swelled above the Clouds, and gave battell unto Heaven. It could not be said to raine, the waters like whole Rivers did flood in the ayre. And this I did still observe, that whereas upon the Land, when a storme hath powred it selfe forth once in drifts of raine, the winde as beaten downe, and vanquished therewith, not long after indureth: here the glut of water (as if throatling the winde ere while) was no sooner a little emptied and qualified, but instantly the windes (as having gotten their mouthes now free, and at liberty) spake more loud, and grew more tumultuous, and malignant. What shall I say? Windes and Seas were as mad, as fury and rage could make them; for mine owne part, I had bin in some stormes before, as well upon the coast of *Barbary* and *Algeere*, in the *Levant*, and once more distresfull in the *Adriatique* gulfe....

It pleased God to bring a greater affliction yet upon us; for in the beginning of the storme we had received likewise a mighty leake. And the Ship in every joynt almost, having spued out her Okam, before we were aware (a casualty more desperate then any other that a Voyage by Sea draweth with it) was growne five foote suddenly deepe with water above her ballast, and we almost drowned within, whilest we sat looking when to perish from above. This imparting no lesse terrour then danger, ranne through the whole Ship with much fright and amazement, startled and turned the bloud, and tooke downe the braves of the most hardy Marriner of them all, insomuch as he that before happily felt not the sorrow of others, now began to sorrow for himselfe, when he saw such a pond of water so suddenly broken in, and which he knew could not (without present avoiding) but instantly sinke him. So as joyning (onely for his owne sake, not yet worth the saving) in the publique safety; there might be seene Master, Masters Mate, Boateswaine, Quarter Master, Coopers, Carpenters, and who not, with candels in their hands, creeping along the ribs viewing the sides, searching every corner, and listening in every place, if they could heare the water runne....

I am not able to give unto your Ladiship every mans thought in this perplexity, to which we were now brought; but to me, this Leakage appeared as a wound given to men that were before dead. The Lord

---

1 The whipstaff was attached to the tiller, which in turn controlled the rudder.

knoweth, I had as little hope, as desire of life in the storme, & in this, it went beyond my will; because beyond my reason, why we should labour to preserve life; yet we did, either because so deare are a few lingring houres of life in all mankinde, or that our *Christian* knowledges taught us, how much we owed to the rites of Nature, as bound, not to be false to our selves, or to neglect the meanes of our owne preservation; the most despairefull things amongst men, being matters of no wonder nor moment with him, who is the rich Fountaine and admirable Essence of all mercy.

Our Governour, upon the tuesday morning (at what time, by such who had bin below in the hold, the Leake was first discovered) had caused the whole Company, about one hundred and forty, besides women, to be equally divided into three parts, and opening the Ship in three places (under the forecastle, in the waste, and hard by the Bitacke[1]) appointed each man where to attend; and thereunto every man came duely upon his watch, tooke the Bucket, or Pumpe for one houre, and rested another. Then men might be seene to labour, I may well say, for life, and the better sort, even our Governour,[2] and Admirall[3] themselves, not refusing their turne, and to spell each the other, to give example to other. The common sort stripped naked, as men in Gallies, the easier both to hold out, and to shrinke from under the salt water, which continually leapt in among them, kept their eyes waking, and their thoughts and hands working, with tyred bodies, and wasted spirits, three dayes and foure nights destitute of outward comfort, and desperate of any deliverance, testifying how mutually willing they were, yet by labour to keepe each other from drowning, albeit each one drowned whilest he laboured....

During all this time, the heavens look'd so blacke upon us, that it was not possible the elevation of the Pole might be observed: nor a Starre by night, not Sunne beame by day was to be seene. Onely upon the thursday night Sir *George Summers* being upon the watch, had an

1 Bitacke: binnacle, the case that housed the compass
2 Thomas Gates (*c*.1560–1621), a founding member of the Virginia Company which in 1609 appointed him governor of its colony, where he served in 1610 and, after a return to England that year, resumed office in 1611–14
3 Sir George Somers (1554–1610), a founding member of the Virginia Company which in 1609 appointed him admiral of the expedition to Virginia. A month after his arrival at Jamestown in one of the vessels he helped to construct on Bermuda, he returned to the islands for food supplies and died there from – according to a contemporaneous report – excessive consumption of pig meat.

apparition of a little round light, like a faint Starre, trembling, and streaming along with a sparkeling blaze, halfe the height upon the Maine Mast, and shooting sometimes from Shroud to Shroud, tempting to settle as it were upon any of the foure Shrouds: and for three or foure houres together, or rather more, halfe the night it kept with us, running sometimes along the Maine-yard to the very end, and then returning. At which, Sir *George Summers* called divers about him, and shewed them the same, who observed it with much wonder, and carefulnesse: but upon a sodaine, towards the morning watch, they lost the sight of it, and knew not what way it made. The superstitious Sea-men make many constructions of this Sea-fire, which neverthelesse is usuall in stormes: the same (it may be) which the *Graecians* were wont in the *Mediterranean* to call *Castor* and *Pollux*, of which, if one onely appeared without the other, they tooke it for an evill signe of great tempest. The *Italians*, and such, who lye open to the *Adriatique* and *Tyrrene* Sea, call it (a *sacred Body*) *Corpo sancto*: the *Spaniards* call it Saint *Elmo*, and have an authentique and miraculous Legend for it. Be it what it will, we laid other foundations of safety or ruine, then in the rising or falling of it, could it have served us now miraculously to have taken our height by, it might have strucken amazement, and a reverence in our devotions, according to the due of a miracle. But it did not light us any whit the more to our knowne way, who ran now (as doe hoodwinked men) at all adventures, sometimes North, and North-east, then North and by West, and in an instant againe varying two or three points, and sometimes halfe the Compasse. East and by South we steered away as much as we could to beare upright, which was no small carefulnesse nor paine to doe, albeit we much unrigged our Ship, threw over-boord much luggage, many a Trunke and Chest (in which I suffered no meane losse) and staved many a Butt of Beere, Hogsheads of Oyle, Syder, Wine, and Vinegar, and heaved away all our Ordnance on the Starboord side, and had now purposed to have cut downe the Maine Mast, the more to lighten her, for we were much spent, and our men so weary, as their strengths together failed them, with their hearts, having travailed now from Tuesday till Friday morning, day and night, without either sleepe or foode; for the leakeage taking up all the hold, wee could neither come by Beere nor fresh water; fire we could keepe none in the Cookeroome to dresse any meate, and carefulnesse, griefe, and our turne at the Pumpe or Bucket, were sufficient to hold sleepe from our eyes....

[A]nd it being now Friday, the fourth morning, it wanted little, but that there had bin a generall determination, to have shut up hatches, and commending our sinfull soules to God, committed the Shippe to the mercy of the Sea: surely, that night we must have done it, and that night had we then perished: but see the goodnesse and sweet introduction of better hope, by our mercifull God given unto us. Sir *George Summers*, when no man dreamed of such happinesse, had discovered, and cried Land. Indeede the morning now three quarters spent, had wonne a little cleerenesse from the dayes before, and it being better surveyed, the very trees were seene to move with the winde upon the shoare side: whereupon our Governour commanded the Helme-man to beare up, the Boateswaine sounding at the first, found it thirteene fathome, & when we stood a little in seven fatham; and presently heaving his lead the third time, had ground at foure fathome, and by this, we had got her within a mile under the South-east point of the land, where we had somewhat smooth water. But having no hope to save her by comming to an anker in the same, we were inforced to runne her ashoare, as neere the land as we could, which brought us within three quarters of a mile of shoare, and by the mercy of God unto us, making out our Boates, we had ere night brought all our men, women, and children, about the number of one hundred and fifty, safe into the Iland.

We found it to be the dangerous and dreaded Iland, or rather Ilands of the *Bermuda*: whereof let mee give your Ladyship a briefe description, before I proceed to my narration. And that the rather, because they be so terrible to all that ever touched on them, and such tempests, thunders, and other fearefull objects are seene and heard about them, that they be called commonly, *The Devils Ilands*, and are feared and avoyded of all sea travellers alive, above any other place in the world. Yet it pleased our mercifull God, to make even this hideous and hated place, both the place of our safetie, and meanes of our deliverance.

And hereby also, I hope to deliver the world from a foule and generall errour: it being counted of most, that they can be no habitation for Men, but rather given over to Devils and wicked Spirits; whereas indeed wee find them now by experience, to bee as habitable and commodious as most Countries of the same climate and situation: insomuch as if the entrance into them were as easie as the place it selfe is contenting, it had long ere this beene inhabited, as well as other Ilands. . . .

It should seeme by the testimony of *Gonzalus Ferdinandus Oviedus*,

315

in his Booke intituled, *The Summary or Abridgement of his generall History of the West* Indies, written to the Emperor *Charles* the Fift, that they have beene indeed of greater compasse (and I easily beleeve it) then they are now. . . .

These Ilands are often afflicted and rent with tempests, great strokes of thunder, lightning and raine in the extreamity of violence: which (and it may well bee) hath so sundred and torne downe the Rockes, and whurried whole quarters of Ilands into the maine Sea (some sixe, some seven leagues, and is like in time to swallow them all) so as even in that distance from the shoare there is no small danger of them and with them, of the stormes continually raging from them, which once in the full and change commonly of every Moone (Winter or Summer) keepe their unchangeable round, and rather thunder then blow from every corner about them, sometimes fortie eight houres together. . . .

The soile of the whole Iland is one and the same, the mould, dark, red, sandie, dry, and uncapable I beleeve of any of our commodities or fruits. Sir *George Summers* in the beginning of August, squared out a Garden by the quarter, the quarter being set downe before a goodly Bay, upon which our Governour did first leape ashoare, and therefore called it (as aforesaid) *Gates his Bay*, which opened into the East, and into which the Sea did ebbe and flow, according to their tides, and sowed Muske Melons, Pease, Onyons, Raddish, Lettice, and many *English* seeds, and Kitchen Herbes. All which in some ten daies did appeare above ground, but whether by the small Birds, of which there be many kindes, or by Flies (Wormes I never saw any, nor any venomous thing, as Toade, or Snake, or any creeping beast hurtfull, onely some Spiders, which as many affirme are signes of great store of Gold: but they were long and slender legge Spiders, and whether venomous or no I know not; I beleeve not, since wee should still find them amongst our linnen in our Chests, and drinking Cans; but we never received any danger from them: A kind of *Melontha*, or blacke Beetell there was, which bruised, gave a savour like many sweet and strong gums punned together) whether, I say, hindred by these, or by the condition or vice of the soyle they came to no proofe, nor thrived. It is like enough that the commodities of the other Westerne Ilands would prosper there, as Vines, Lemmons, Oranges, and Sugar Canes: Our Governour made triall of the later, and buried some two or three in the Garden mould, which were reserved in the wracke amongst many which wee carried to

plant here in *Virginia*, and they beganne to grow, but the Hogs breaking in, both rooted them up and eate them: there is not through the
whole Ilands, either Champion ground, Valleys, or fresh Rivers. They
are full of Shawes of goodly Cedar, fairer then ours here of *Virginia*: the
Berries, whereof our men seething, straining, and letting stand some
three or foure daies, made a kind of pleasant drinke....

Likewise there grow great store of Palme Trees, not the right *Indian*
Palmes, such as in Saint *John Port-Rico* are called *Cocos*, and are there
full of small fruites like Almonds (of the bignesse of the graines in
Pomgranates) nor of those kind of Palmes which beares Dates, but a
kind of Simerons[1] or wild Palmes in growth, fashion, leaves, and
branches, resembling those true Palmes: for the Tree is high, and
straight, sappy and spongious, unfirme for any use, no branches but in
the uppermost part thereof, and in the top grow leaves about the head
of it (the most inmost part whereof they call *Palmeto*, and it is the heart
and pith of the same Trunke, so white and thin, as it will peele off into
pleates as smooth and delicate as white Sattin into twentie folds, in
which a man may write as in paper) where they spread and fall down-
ward about the Tree like an overblowne Rose, or Saffron flower not
early gathered; so broad are the leaves, as an *Italian Umbrello*, a man
may well defend his whole body under one of them, from the greatest
storme raine that falls. For they being stiffe and smooth, as if so many
flagges were knit together, the raine easily slideth off....

Other kindes of high and sweet smelling Woods there bee, and divers
colours, blacke, yellow, and red, and one which beares a round blew
Berry, much eaten by our owne people, of a stiptick qualitie and rough
taste on the tongue like a Slow to stay or binde the Fluxe, which the
often eating of the luscious Palme berry would bring them into, for the
nature of sweet things is to clense and dissolve. A kinde of Pease of the
bignesse and shape of a *Katherine* Peare, wee found growing upon the
Rockes full of many sharpe subtill prickes (as a Thistle) which wee
therefore called, *The Prickle Peare*, the outside greene, but being
opened, of a deepe murrie, full of juyce like a Mulberry, and just of the
same substance and taste, wee both eate them raw and baked.

Sure it is, that there are no Rivers nor running Springs of fresh water
to bee found upon any of them: when wee came first wee digged and

1 Simerons: cimarron, an American-Spanish word for wild, unruly

317

found certaine gushings and soft bublings, which being either in bottoms, or on the side of hanging ground, were onely fed with raine water, which neverthelesse soone sinketh into the earth and vanisheth away, or emptieth it selfe out of sight into the Sea, without any channell above or upon the superficies of the earth: for according as their raines fell, we had our Wels and Pits (which we digged) either halfe full, or absolute exhausted and dry, howbeit some low bottoms (which the continuall descent from the Hills filled full, and in those flats could have no passage away) we found to continue as fishing Ponds, or standing Pooles, continually Summer and Winter full of fresh water.

The shoare and Bayes round about, when wee landed first afforded great store of fish, and that of divers kindes, and good, but it should seeme that our fiers, which wee maintained on the shoares side drave them from us, so as wee were in some want, untill wee had made a flat bottome Gundall of Cedar with which wee put off farther into the Sea, and then daily hooked great store of many kindes, as excellent Angellfish, Salmon Peale, Bonetas, Stingray, Cabally, Scnappers, Hogge-fish, Sharkes, Dogge-fish, Pilcherds, Mullets, and Rock-fish, of which bee divers kindes: and of these our Governour dryed and salted....

Wee have taken also from under the broken Rockes, Crevises oftentimes greater then any of our best *English* Lobsters; and likewise abundance of Crabbes, Oysters, and Wilkes. True it is, for Fish in everie Cove and Creeke wee found Snaules, and Skulles in that abundance, as (I thinke) no Iland in the world may have greater store or better Fish. For they sucking of the very water, which descendeth from the high Hills mingled with juyce and verdor of the Palmes, Cedars, and other sweet Woods (which likewise make the Herbes, Roots, and Weeds sweet which grow about the Bankes) become thereby both fat and wholsome. As must those Fish needes bee grosse, slimy, and corrupt the bloud, which feed in Fennes, Marishes, Ditches, muddy Pooles, and neere unto places where much filth is daily cast forth....

Fowle there is great store, small Birds, Sparrowes fat and plumpe like a Bunting, bigger then ours, Robbins of divers colours greene and yellow, ordinary and familiar in our Cabbins, and other of lesse sort ... and Battes in great store. And upon New-yeeres day in the morning, our Governour being walked foorth with another Gentleman Master *James Swift*, each of them with their Peeces killed a wild Swanne, in a great Sea-water Bay or Pond in our Iland. A kinde of webbe-footed

Fowle there is, of the bignesse of an *English* greene Plover, or Sea-Meawe, which all the Summer wee saw not, and in the darkest nights of November and December (for in the night they onely feed) they would come forth, but not flye farre from home, and hovering in the ayre, and over the Sea, made a strange hollow and harsh howling... which Birds with a light bough in a darke night (as in our Lowbelling) wee caught. I have beene at the taking of three hundred in an houre, and wee might have laden our Boates. Our men found a prettie way to take them, which was by standing on the Rockes or Sands by the Sea side, and hollowing, laughing, and making the strangest out-cry that possibly they could: with the noyse whereof the Birds would come flocking to that place, and settle upon the very armes and head of him that so cryed, and still creepe neerer and neerer, answering the noyse themselves: by which our men would weigh them with their hand, and which weighed heaviest they tooke for the best and let the others alone, and so our men would take twentie dozen in two houres of the chiefest of them; and they were a good and well relished Fowle, fat and full as a Partridge....

[O]ur people would goe a hunting with our Ship Dogge, and sometimes bring home thirtie, sometimes fiftie Boares, Sowes, and Pigs in a weeke alive: for the Dog would fasten on them and hold, whilest the Hunts-men made in: and there bee thousands of them in the Ilands, and at that time of the yeere, in August, September, October, and November, they were well fed with Berries that dropped from the Cedars and the Palmes, and in our quarter wee made styes for them, and gathering of these Berries served them twice aday, by which meanes we kept them in good plight: and when there was any fret of weather (for upon every increase of wind the billow would be so great, as it was no putting out with our Gundall or Canow) that we could not fish nor take Tortoyses, then wee killed our Hogs. But in February when the Palme Berries began to be scant or dry, and the Cedar Berries failed two moneths sooner. True it is the Hogs grew poore, and being taken so, wee could not raise them to be better, for besides those Berries, we had nothing wherewith to franke them: but even then the Tortoyses came in againe, of which wee daily both turned up great store, finding them on Land, as also sculling after them in our Boate strooke them with an Iron goad, and sod, baked, and roasted them. The Tortoyse is reasonable toothsom (some say) wholsome meate. I am sure our Company liked the meate of them verie well, and one Tortoyse would goe further amongst them, then three Hogs. One Turtle (for so we called them) feasted well a dozen Messes, appointing sixe to every Messe. It is such a kind of meat, as a man can neither absolutely call Fish nor Flesh, keeping most what in the water, and feeding upon Sea-grasse like a Heifer, in the bottome of the Coves and Bayes, and laying their Egges (of which wee should finde five hundred at a time in the opening of a shee Turtle) in the Sand by the shoare side, and so covering them close leave them to the hatching of the Sunne. . . .

II

Actions and Occurrents whiles they continued in the Ilands: Ravens sent for Virginia; *Divers mutinies;* [HENRY] PAINE *executed: Two Pinnaces built.*

. . . And sure it was happy for us, who had now runne this fortune, and were fallen into the bottome of this misery, that we both had our Governour with us, and one so solicitous and carefull, whose both example (as I said) and authority, could lay shame, and command upon our people: else, I am perswaded, we had most of us finished our dayes there, so willing were the major part of the common sort (especially when they found such a plenty of victuals) to settle a foundation of ever inhabiting there; as well appeared by many practises of theirs (and perhaps of some of the better sort) Loe, what are our affections and passions, if not rightly squared? how irreligious, and irregular they expresse us? not perhaps so ill as we would be, but yet as wee are; some dangerous and secret discontents nourished amongst us, had like to have bin the parents of bloudy issues and mischiefes; they began first in the Sea-men, who in time had fastened unto them (by false baits) many of our land-men likewise, and some of whom (for opinion of their Religion) was carried an extraordinary and good respect. The Angles wherewith chiefly they thus hooked in these disquieted Pooles, were, how that *in Virginia, nothing but wretchednesse and labour must be expected, with many wants, and a churlish intreaty, there being neither that Fish, Flesh, nor Fowle, which here (without wasting on the one part, or watching on theirs, or any threatning, and are of authority) at ease, and pleasure might be injoyed: and since both in the one, and the other place, they were (for the time) to loose the fruition both of their friends and Countrey, as good, and better were it for them, to repose and seate them where they should have the least outward wants the while.* This, thus preached, and published each to other, though by such who never had bin more onward towards *Virginia*, then (before this Voyage) a Sculler could happily rowe him (and what hath a more adamantive power to draw unto it the consent and attraction of the idle, untoward, and wretched number of the many, then liberty, and fulnesse of sensuality?) begat such a murmur, and such a discontent, and disunion of hearts and hands from this labour, and forwarding the meanes of redeeming us from hence, as each one wrought with his Mate how to divorse him from the same.

And first (and it was the first of September) a conspiracy was discovered, of which six were found principals, who had promised each unto the other, not to set their hands to any travaile or endeavour which might expedite or forward this Pinnace: and each of these had severally (according to appointment) sought his opportunity to draw the Smith, and one of our Carpenters, *Nicholas Bennit*, who made much profession of Scripture, a mutinous and dissembling Imposter; the Captaine, and one of the chiefe perswaders of others, who afterwards brake from the society of the Colony, and like outlawes retired into the Woods, to make a settlement and habitation there, on their party, with whom they purposed to leave our Quarter, and possesse another Iland by themselves: but this happily found out, they were condemned to the same punishment which they would have chosen (but without Smith or Carpenter) and to an Iland farre by it selfe, they were carried, and there left.... [B]ut soone they missed comfort (who were farre removed from our store) besides, the society of their acquaintance had wrought in some of them, if not a loathsomenesse of their offence, yet a sorrow that their complement was not more full, and therefore a wearinesse of their being thus untimely prescribed; insomuch, as many humble petitions were sent unto our Governor, fraught full of their seeming sorrow and repentance, and earnest vowes to redeeme the former trespasse, with example of dueties in them all, to the common cause, and generall businesse; upon which our Governour (not easie to admit any accusation, and hard to remit an offence, but at all times sorry in the punishment of him, in whom may appeare either shame or contrition) was easily content to reacknowledge them againe....

In these dangers and divellish disquiets (whilest the almighty God wrought for us, and sent us miraculously delivered from the calamities of the Sea, all blessings upon the shoare, to content and binde us to gratefulnesse) thus inraged amongst our selves, to the destruction each of other, into what a mischiefe and misery had wee bin given up, had wee not had a Governour with his authority, to have suppressed the same? Yet was there a worse practise, faction, and conjuration a foote, deadly and bloudy, in which the life of our Governour, with many others were threatned, and could not but miscarry in his fall. But such is ever the will of God (who in the execution of his judgements, breaketh the firebrands upon the head of him, who first kindleth them) there were, who conceived that our Governour indeede neither durst, nor had authority to put in execution, or passe the act of Justice upon any one, how treacherous or impious so ever; their owne opinions so much deceiving them for the unlawfulnesse of any act, which they would execute: daring to justifie among themselves, that if they should be apprehended, before the performance, they should happily suffer as Martyrs. They persevered therefore not onely to draw unto them such a number, and associates as they could worke in, to the abandoning of our Governour, and to the inhabiting of this Iland. They had now purposed to have made a surprise of the Store-house, and to have forced from thence, what was therein either of Meale, Cloath, Cables, Armes, Sailes, Oares, or what else it pleased God that we had recovered from the wracke, and was to serve our generall necessity and use, either for the reliefe of us, while wee staied here, or for the carrying of us from this place againe, when our Pinnace should have bin furnished.

But as all giddy and lawlesse attempts, have alwayes something of imperfection, and that as well by the property of the action, which holdeth of disobedience and rebellion (both full of feare) as through the ignorance of the devisers themselves; so in this (besides those defects) there were some of the association, who not strong inough fortified in their owne conceits, brake from the plot it selfe, and (before the time was ripe for the execution thereof) discovered the whole order, and every Agent, and Actor thereof, who neverthelesse were not suddenly apprehended, by reason the confederates were divided and seperated in place, some with us, and the chiefe with Sir *George Summers* in his Iland (and indeede all his whole company) but good watch passed upon them, every man from thenceforth commanded to weare his weapon, without which before, we freely walked from quarter to quarter, and conversed among our selves, and every man advised to stand upon his guard, his owne life not being in safety, whilest his next neighbour was not to be trusted. The Centinels, and nightwarders doubled, the passages of both the quarters were carefully observed, by which meanes nothing was further attempted; untill a Gentleman amongst them, one *Henry Paine*, the thirteenth of March, full of mischiefe, and every houre preparing something or other, stealing Swords, Adises, Axes, Hatchets, Sawes, Augers, Planes, Mallets, &c. to make good his owne bad end, his watch night comming about, and being called by the Captaine of the same, to be upon the guard, did not onely give his said Commander evill language, but strucke at him, doubled his blowes, and when hee was not suffered to close with him, went off the Guard, scoffing at the double diligence and attendance of the Watch, appointed by the Governour for much purpose, as hee said: upon which, the Watch telling him, if the Governour should understand of this his insolency, it might turne him to much blame, and happily be as much as his life were worth. The said *Paine* replyed with a setled and bitter violence, and in such unreverent tearmes, as I should offend the modest eare too much to expresse it in his owne phrase; but the contents were, how *that the Governour had no authoritie of that qualitie, to justifie upon any one (how meane soever in the Colonie) an action of that nature, and therefore let the Governour* (said hee) *kisse*, &c. Which words, being with the omitted additions, brought the next day unto every common and publique discourse, at length they were delivered over to the Governour, who examining well the fact (the transgression so much the more exemplary and odious, as being in a dangerous time, in a Confederate, and the successe of the same wishtly listened after, with a doubtfull conceit, what might be the issue of so notorious a boldnesse and impudency) calling the said *Paine* before him, and the whole Company, where (being soone convinced both by the witnesse, of the Commander, and many which were upon the watch with him) our Governour, who had now the eyes of the whole Colony fixed upon him, condemned him to be instantly hanged; and the ladder being ready, after he had made many confessions, hee earnestly desired, being a Gentleman, that hee might be shot to death, and towards the evening he had his desire, the Sunne and his life setting together....

III

Their departure from Bermuda *and arrivall in* Virginia: *miseries there, departure and returne upon the Lord* LAWARRES *arriving.* JAMES *Towne described.*

...Unto such calamity can sloath, riot, and vanity, bring the most setled and plentifull estate. Indeede (right noble Lady) no story can remember unto us, more woes and anguishes, then these people, thus governed, have both suffered and puld upon their owne heads. And yet true it is, some of them, whose voyces and command might not be heard, may easily be absolved from the guilt hereof, as standing untouched, and upright in their innocencies; whilest the privie factionaries shall never find time nor darknesse, to wipe away or cover their ignoble and irreligious practises, who, it may be, lay all the discredits, and imputations the while upon the Countrie. But under pardon, let me speake freely to them: let them remember that if riot and sloth should both meet in any one of their best Families, in a Countrey most stored with abundance and plentie in *England*, continuall wasting, no Husbandry, the old store still spent on, no order for new provisions, what better could befall unto the Inhabitants, Land-lords, and Tenants of that corner, then necessarily following cleannesse of teeth, famine and death? Is it not the sentence and doome of the Wiseman? *Yet a little sleepe, a little slumber, and a little folding of the hands to sleepe: so thy poverty commeth, as one that travelleth by the way, and thy necessitie like an armed man.*[1] And with this Idlenesse, when some thing was in store, all wastfull courses exercised to the heigth, and the headlesse multitude, (some neither of qualitie nor Religion) not imployed to the end for which they were sent hither, no not compelled (since in themselves unwilling) to sowe Corne for their owne bellies, nor to put a Roote, Herbe, &c. for their owne particular good in their Gardens or elsewhere: I say in this neglect and sensuall Surfet, all things suffered to runne on, to lie sicke and languish; must it be expected, that health, plentie, and all the goodnesse of a well ordered State, of necessitie for all this to flow in this Countrey? You have a right and noble heart (worthy Lady) bee judge of the truth herein. Then suffer it not bee concluded unto you, nor beleeve, I beseech you, that the wants and wretchednesse which they have indured, ascend out of the povertie and vilenesse of the Countrey, whether bee respected the Land or Rivers: the one, and the other, having not only promised, but powred enough in their veines, to convince them in such calumnies, and to quit those common calamities, which (as the shadow accompanies the body) the precedent neglects touched at, if truely followed, and wrought upon....

1 marginal note: *Proverbs* 6

2 *Montaigne, 'Of the Caniballes'*

Michel Eyquem, seigneur de Montaigne[1] (1533–92), the renowned French essayist and sometime mayor of Bordeaux, published the first volume of his collected *Essais* in 1580; expanded editions followed in 1588 and 1595. The essay on cannibals was written in 1578–80 and is based in large part on information that Montaigne gleaned from one of his servants, who had spent several years among the Tupinambas, and to a much lesser extent on his own conversation, imperfectly translated, with a Brazilian Indian at Rouen in 1562. In 1603, *The Essayes* were published in London, 'done into English By... John Florio' (1545–1625), the Oxford-educated son of an Italian immigrant, and later tutor to Prince Henry. The following selection is taken from chapter 30 (31 in later editions) of Florio's translation, pp. 100–7.

Of the Caniballes

...I finde (as farre as I have beene informed) there is nothing in that nation [Brazil], that is either barbarous or savage, unlesse men call that barbarisme, which is not common to them. As indeede, we have no other ayme of truth and reason, then the example and *Idea* of the opinions and customes of the countrie we live in. Where is ever perfect religion, perfect policie, perfect and compleate use of all things. They are even savage, as we call those fruites wilde, which nature of hir selfe, and of hir ordinarie progresse hath produced: whereas indeede, they are those which our selves have altered by our artificiall devises, and diverted from their common order, we should rather terme savage. In those are the true and most profitable vertues, and naturall proprieties most livelie and vigorous, which in these we have bastardized, applying them to the pleasure of our corrupted taste. And if notwithstanding, in divers fruites of those countries that were never tilled, we shall finde, that in respect of ours they are most excellent, and as delicate unto our

---

1 For further information on the author, see Donald M. Frame, *Montaigne, A Biography* (New York, 1965); modern translations appear in *The Complete Essays of Montaigne*, trans. Donald M. Frame (Stanford, 1957).

taste; there is no reason, arte should gaine the point of honour of our great and puissant mother Nature. We have so much by our inventions, surcharged the beauties and riches of hir workes, that we have altogether over-choaked hir: yet where ever hir puritie shineth, she makes our vaine, and frivolus enterprises wonderfully ashamed.

> *Et veniunt hederae sponte sua melius,*
> *Surgit & in solis formosior arbutus antris,*
> *Et volucres nulla dulcius arte canunt.*[1]

> Ivies spring better of their owne accord,
> Un-hanted plots much fairer trees afford,
> Birdes by no arte much sweeter notes record.

Al our endevours or wit, cannot so much as reach to represent the neast of the least birdlet, it's contexture, beautie, profit and use, no nor the webbe of a seelie spider. *All things* (saith *Plato*) *are produced, either by nature, by fortune, or by arte. The greatest and fairest by one or other of the two first, the least and imperfect by the last.* Those nations seeme therefore so barbarous unto mee, because they have received very little fashion from humane wit, and are yet neere their originall naturalitie. The lawes of nature do yet commaund them, which are but little bastardized by ours. And that with such puritie, as I am sometimes grieved the knowlege of it came no sooner to light, at what time ther were men, that better than we could have judged of it. I am sorie, *Licurgus* and *Plato*[2] had it not: for meseemeth that what in those nations wee see by experience, doth not onelie exceede all the pictures wherewith licentious Poesie hath prowdly imbellished the golden age, & al hir quaint inventions to faine a happy condition of man, but also the conception & desire of Philosophie. They could not imagine a genuitie[3] so pure and simple, as we see it by experience; nor ever beleeve our societie might be maintained with so little arte and humane combination. It is a nation, would I answere *Plato*, that hath no kinde of traffike, no knowledge of Letters, no intelligence of numbers, no name of magistrate, nor of politike superioritie; no use of service, of riches, or of poverty; no contracts, no successions, no dividences,[4] no occupation but idle; no respect of kinred,

1 Elegies, 1.2 from Roman poet Sextus Propertius (*c.* 50 BC–*c.* 16 BC).
2 Plato, *Laws*, 2
3 genuity: simplicity
4 Subsequent editions read 'partitions'.

but common, no apparrell but naturall, no manuring of lands, no use of wine, corne, or mettle. The very words that import lying, falshood, treason, dissimulation, covetousnes, envie, detraction, and pardon, were never heard of amongst them. How dissonant would hee finde his imaginary common-wealth from this perfection?

Hos natura modos primùm dedit.[1]

Nature at first uprise,
These manners did devise.

Furthermore, they live in a country of so exceeding pleasant and temperate situation, that as my testimonies have tolde me, it is very rare to see a sicke body amongst them; and they have further assured me, they never saw any man there, either shaking with the palsie, toothlesse, with eyes dropping, or crooked and stooping through age. They are seated alongst the sea-coast, encompassed toward the land with huge and steepie mountaines, having betweene both, a hundred leagues or there abouts of open and champaine[2] ground. They have great abundance of fish and flesh, that have no resemblance at all with ours, and eate them without any sawces, or skill of Cookerie, but plaine boiled or broyled. The first man that brought a horse thither, although he had in many other voyages conversed with them, bred so great a horror in the land, that before they could take notice of him, they slew him with arrowes. Their buildings are very long, and able to containe two or three hundred soules, covered with barkes of great trees, fastned in the ground at one end, enterlaced and joyned close together by the toppes, after the manner of some of our Granges; the covering wherof hangs downe to the ground, and steadeth them as a flancke. They have a kinde of wood so hard, that ryving and cleaving the same, they make blades, swords, and grid-yrons to broile their meate with. Their beddes are of a kind of cotten cloth, fastened to the house-roofe, as our shippe-cabbanes: every one hath his severall cowch; for the women lie from their husbands. They rise with the Sunne, and feede for all day, as soone as they are up: and make no meales after that. They drinke not at meat, as *Suidas*[3] reporteth of some other people of the East, which dranke after

---

1 from Virgil, *Georgics*, 2
2 champaine (champaign): flat, broad countryside
3 Suidas, tenth-century AD Greek encyclopedist

meales, but drinke manie times a day, and are much given to pledge carowses.[1] Their drinke is made of a certaine roote, and of the colour of our Claret wines, which lasteth but two or three dayes; they drinke it warme: It hath somewhat a sharp taste, wholsome for the stomake, nothing headie, but laxative for such as are not used unto it, yet verie pleasing to such as are accustomed unto it. Instead of bread, they use a certain white composition, like unto Corianders confected. I have eaten some, the taste whereof is somwhat sweete and wallowish.[2] They spend the whole day in dancing. Their yong men goe a hunting after wilde beastes with bowes and arrowes. Their women busie themselves therewhil'st with warming of their drinke, which is their chiefest office. Some of their old men, in the morning before they goe to eating, preach in common to all the householde, walking from one end of the house to the other, repeating one selfe-same sentence many times, till he have ended his turne (for their buildings are a hundred paces in length) hee commends but two things unto his auditorie; *First, valour against their enemies, then lovingnesse unto their wives.* They never misse (for their restraint) to put men in minde of this duetie, that it is their wives which keepe their drincke luke-warme and well-seasoned. The forme of their beddes, cordes, swordes, blades, and woodden bracelets, wherewith they cover their hand-wrists when they fight, and great Canes open at one end, by the sound of which they keepe time and cadence in their da;uncing, are in many places to be seene, and namely in mine own house. They are shaven all-over, much more close and cleaner than wee are, with no other Razers than of wood or stone. They beleeve their soules to be eternall, and those that have deserved well of their Gods, to be placed in that part of heaven where the Sunne riseth; and the cursed toward the West in opposition. They have certaine Prophets and Priests, which commonly abide in the mountaines, & very seldome shew them-selves unto the people; but when they come downe, there is a great feast prepared, and a solemne assembly of manie towneships together (each Grange as I have described maketh a village, and they are about a French league one from an other.) The Prophet speakes to the people in publike, exhorting them to embrace vertue, and follow their duetie. All their morall discipline containeth but these two articles; first

1 pledge carowses (carouses): indulge in excessive toasts or drinking parties
2 wallowish: tasteless

an undismayed resolution to warre, then an inviolable affection to their wives. Hee dooth also prognosticate of things to come, and what successe they shall hope for in their enterprises: hee either perswadeth or disswadeth them from warre; but if hee chance to misse of his divination, and that it succeede other-wise than hee fore-tolde them, if hee be taken, hee is hewen in a thousand peeces, and condemned for a false prophet. And therefore he that hath once mis-reckoned him selfe is never seene againe. Divination is the gift of God; the abusing wherof should be a punishable imposture. When the Divines amongst the Scithians had foretolde an untruth, they were couched along upon hurdles full of heath or brush-wood, and so manicled hand and foote, burned to death. Those which manage matters subject to the conduct of mans sufficiencie, are excusable, although they shew the utmost of their skill. But those that gull and coni-catch[1] us with the assurance of an extraordinarie facultie, and which is beyond our knowledge, ought to be double punished; first because they performe not the effect of their promise, then for the rashnes of their imposture and unadvisednes of their fraude. They warre against the nations, that lye beyond their mountaines, to which they goe naked, having no other weapons, then bowes, or woodden swords, sharpe at one ende, as our broaches are. It is an admirable thing to see the constant resolution of their combates, which never ende but by effusion of bloud & murther: for they know not what feare or rowts are. Every Victor brings home the head of the enimie he hath slaine as a Trophey of his victorie, and fastneth the same at the entrance of his dwelling-place. After they have long time used and entreated their prisoners well, and with all commodities they can devise, hee that is the Maister of them, summoning a great assembly of his acquaintance; tieth a corde to one of the prisoners armes, by the end whereof hee holdes him fast, with some distance from him, for feare he might offend him, and giveth the other arme, bound in like maner, to the dearest friend he hath, and both in the presence of all the assemblie kill him with swordes: which doone, they roste, and then eate him in common, and send some slices of him to such of their friendes as are absent. It is not as some imagine, to nourish themselves with it, (as anciently the Scithians wont to do,) but to represent an extreame, and inexpiable revenge. Which we prove thus; some of them perceiving the

---

1 coni-catch (conycatch): to dupe or swindle

Portugales, who had confederated themselves with their adversaries, to use another kinde of death, when they tooke them prisoners; which was, to burie them up to the middle, and against the upper part of the body to shoote arrowes, and then being almost dead, to hang them up; they supposed, that these people of the other world (as they who had sowed the knowledge of many vices amongst their neighbours, and were much more cunning in all kindes of evilles and mischiefe then they) undertooke not this maner of revenge without cause, and that consequently it was more smartfull, and cruell then theirs, and thereupon began to leave their olde fashion to followe this. I am not sory we note the barbarous horror of such an action, but grieved, that prying so narrowly into their faults, we are so blinded in ours. I think there is more barbarisme in eating men alive, than to feede upon them being dead; to mangle by tortures and torments a body full of lively sense, to roast him in peeces, to make dogges and swine to gnawe and teare him in mammockes (as we have not onely read, but seene very lately, yea and in our owne memorie, not amongst ancient enemies, but our neighbours and fellow-citizens; and which is worse, under pretence of piety and religion) then to roast and teare him after he is dead. *Chrysippus* and *Zeno*, Arch-pillers of the Stoicke sect, have supposed that it was no hurt at all, in time of neede, and to what end soever, to make use of our carrion bodies, and to feede upon them, as did our forefathers, who being besieged by *Caesar* in the Cittie of *Alexia*, resolved to sustaine the famine of the siege, with the bodies of old men, women, and other persons unserviceable & unfit to fight.

> *Vascones (fama est) alimentis talibus usi*
> *Produxere animas.*[1]

> *Gascoynes* (as fame reportes)
> Liv'd with meates of such sortes.

And Phisitians feare not, in all kindes of compositions availefull to our health, to make use of it, be it for outward or inward applications: But there was never any opinion found so unnaturall and immodest, that would excuse treason, treachery, disloyalty, tyrannie, crueltie, and such like, which are our ordinary faults. We may then well call them barbarous, in regarde of reasons rules, but not in respect of us that

1 from Decimus Junius Juvenalis (Juvenal), first/second-century AD Roman poet, *Satires*, 15

exceede them in all kinde of barbarisme. Their warres are noble and generous, and have as much excuse and beautie, as this humane infirmitie may admit: they ayme at nought so much, and have no other foundation amongst them, but the meere jealosie of vertue. They contend not for the gaining of new landes; for to this day they yet enjoy that naturall ubertie[1] and fruitefulnesse, which without labouring-toyle, doth in such plenteous aboundance furnish them with all necessary things, that they neede not enlarge their limites. They are yet in that happy estate, as they desire no more, then what their naturall necessities direct them: whatsoever is beyond it, is to them superfluous. Those that are much about one age, doe generally enter-call one another brethren, and such as are yonger, they call children, and the aged are esteemed as fathers to all the rest. These leave this full possession of goods in common, and without individuitie[2] to their heires, without other claime or title, but that which nature doth plainely imparte unto all creatures, even as she brings them into the world. If their neighbours chance to come over the mountaines to assaile or invade them, and that they get the victory over them, the Victors conquest is glorie, and the advantage to be and remaine superiour in valour and vertue: else have they nothing to doe with the goods and spoyles of the vanquished, and so returne into their countrie, where they neither want any necessary thing, nor lacke this great portion, to know how to enjoy their condition happily, and are contented with what nature affordeth them. So doe these when their turne commeth. They require no other ransome of their prisoners, but an acknowledgement and confession that they are vanquished. And in a whole age, a man shall not finde one, that doth not rather embrace death, then either by word or countenance remissely to yeeld one jot of an invincible courage. There is none seene that would not rather be slaine and devoured, then sue for life, or shew any feare: They use their prisoners with all libertie, that they may so much the more holde their lives deare and precious, and commonly entertaine them with threates of future death, with the torments they shall endure, with the preparations intended for that purpose, with mangling and slicing of their members, and with the feast that shall be kept at their charge. All which is done, to wrest some remisse, and exact some faint-yeelding speech of submission from them, or to possesse them with a

1 ubertie (uberty): fertility, abundance
2 individuitie: subsequent editions read 'divisions'.

desire to escape or runne away; that so they may have the advantage to have danted and made them afraide, and to have forced their constancie. For certainely true victory consisteth in that onely point.

> *– Victoria nulla est*
> *Quàm quae confessos animo quoque subjugat hostes.*[1]

No conquest such, as to suppresse
Foes hearts, the conquest to confesse.

The Hungarians, a most warre-like nation, were whilome woont to pursue their pray no longer then they had forced their enemie to yeeld unto their mercie. For, having wrested this confession from him, they set him at libertie without offence or ransome, except it were to make him sweare, never after to beare armes against them. Wee get many advantages of our enemies, that are but borrowed and not ours: It is the qualitie of a porterly rascall, and not of vertue, to have stronger armes, and sturdier legs: Disposition is a dead and corporall qualitie. It is a tricke of fortune to make our enemie stoope, and to bleare his eyes with the Sunnes-light: It is a pranke of skill and knowledge to be cunning in the arte of fencing, and which may happen unto a base and worthlesse man. The reputation and worth of a man consisteth in his heart and will: therein consists true honour: Constancie is valour, not of armes and legs, but of minde and courage: it consisteth not in the spirit and courage of our horse, nor of our armes, but in ours. Hee that obstinately faileth in his courage, *Si succiderit, de genu pugnat, If he slip or fall, he fights upon his knee.*[2] He that in danger of iminent death, is no whit danted in his assurednesse; he that in yeelding up his ghost beholdeth his enemie with a scornefull and fierce looke, he is vanquished, not by us, but by fortune: he is slaine, but not conquered. The most valiant, are often the most unfortunate. So are there triumphant losses in envie of victories. Not those foure sister-victories, the fairest that ever the Sunne beheld with his all-seeing eye, of *Salamine*, of *Platea*, of *Mycale*, and of *Sicilia*,[3] durst ever dare to oppose all their glorie together, to the

---

1 from the Latin poet Claudius Claudianus (Claudian), *c.* 370–*c.* 404), quoted from Justus Lipsius, *Politics*, 5

2 from Seneca, *De Providentia*, 2

3 Salamis, Platea, Micale, and Sicilia, sites of Greek victories in the Persian wars of the fifth century BC. For these and other episodes referred to by Montaigne in the following lines, see Herodotus, *Histories*, 4.59

glory of the King *Leonidas* his discomfiture and of his men, at the passage of *Thermopyles*: what man did ever runne with so glorious an envie, or more ambitious desire to the goale of a combat, than Captaine *Ischolas* to an evident losse and overthrow? who so ingeniously or more politikely did ever assure him-selfe of his wel-fare, than he of his ruine? He was appointed to defend a certaine passage of *Peloponensus* against the *Arcadians*, which finding himselfe altogether unable to performe, seeing the nature of the place, and inequalitie of the forces, and resolving, that whatsoever should present it selfe unto his enemie, must necessarily be utterly defeated: On the other side, deeming it unworthy both his vertue and magnanimitie, and the Lacedemonian name, to faile or faint in his charge, betweene these two extremities he resolved upon a meane and indifferent course, which was this. The yongest and best disposed of his troupe, he reserved for the service and defence of their countrie, to which hee sent them backe; and with those whose losse was least, and who might best be spared, hee determined to maintaine that passage, and by their death to force the enemie, to purchase the entrance of it as deare as possibly he could; as indeede it followed. For being sodainely environed round by the Arcadians: After a great slaughter made of them, both himselfe and all his were put to the sword. Is any Trophey assigned for conquerours, that is not more duly due unto these conquered? A true conquest respecteth rather an undanted resolution, and honourable end, then a faire escape, and the honour of vertue doth more consist in combating then in beating. But to returne to our History, these prisoners, howsoever they are dealt withall, are so farre from yeelding, that contrariwise during two or three moneths that they are kept, they ever carry a cheerefull countenance, and urge their keepers to hasten their triall, they outragiously defie, and injure them. They upbray them with their cowardlinesse, and with the numbers of battels, they have lost against theirs. I have a song made by a prisoner, wherein is this clause, Let them boldly come altogether, and flocke in multitudes, to feede on him; for, with him they shall feede upon their fathers, and grandfathers, that heretofore have served his body for foode and nourishment: These muscles, (saith he) this flesh, and these veines, are your owne; fond men as you are, know you not that the substance of your forefathers limbes is yet tied unto ours? Taste them well, for in them shall you finde the rellish of your owne flesh: An invention, that hath no shew of barbarisme. Those that paint them dying, and that represent this action, when they are put to execution, delineate the prisoners spitting in their executioners faces, and making mowes at them. Verily, so long as breath is in their bodie, they never cease to brave and defie them, both in speech and countenance. Surely, in respect of us these are very savage men: for either they must be so in good sooth, or we must bee so indeede: There is a wondrous distance betweene their forme and ours. Their men have many wives, and by how much more they are reputed valiant, so much the greater is their number. The maner and beautie in their marriages is woondrous strange and remarkable: For, the same jealosie our wives have to keepe us from the love and affection of other women, the same have theirs to procure it. Being more carefull for their husbands honour and content, then of any thing else: They endevour and apply all their industry, to have as many rivalls as possibly, they can, forasmuch as it is a testimonie of their husbands vertue. Our women would count it a wonder, but it is not so: It is a vertue properly Matrimoniall; but of the highest kinde. And in the Bible, *Lea*, *Rachel*, *Sara*, and *Jacobs* wives, brought their fairest maiden-servants unto their husbands beds. And *Livia* seconded the lustfull appetites of *Augustus* to her great prejudice. And *Stratonica* the wife of King *Dejotarus* did not onely bring a most beauteous chambermaide, that served her to her husbands bed, but very carefully brought up the children he begot on her, and by all possible meanes ayded and furthered them to succeede in their fathers royaltie. And least a man should thinke, that all this is done by a simple, and servile, or awefull dutie unto their custome, and by the impression of their ancient customes authoritie, without discourse or judgement, and because they are so blockish, and dull-spirited, that they can take no other resolution, it is not amisse, wee alleadge some evidence of their sufficiencie. Besides what I have saide of one of their warlike songs, I have another amorous canzonet, which beginneth in this sence: *Adder stay, stay good adder, that my sister may by the patterne of thy partie-coloured coate drawe the fashion and worke of a rich lace, for me to give unto my love; so may thy beautie, thy nimblenesse or disposition be ever preferred before al other serpents.* This first couplet is the burthen of the song. I am so conversant with Poesie, that I may judge, this invention hath no barbarisme at all in it, but is altogether Anacreontike.[1] Their language is a kinde of pleasant speech,

---

1 Anacreontike (Anachreontic): like the lyric poetry of the sixth-century BC Greek, Anacreon

and hath a pleasing sound, and some affinitie with the Greeke terminations. Three of that nation, ignoring how deare the knowledge of our corruptions will one day cost their repose, securitie, and happinesse, and how their ruine shall proceede from this comerce, which I imagine is already well advanced, (miserable as they are to have suffered themselves to be so cosoned by a desire of new-fangled novelties, and to have quit the calmenesse of their climate, to come and see ours) were at *Roane* in the time of our late King *Charles* the ninth, who talked with them a great while. They were shewed our fashions, our pompe, and the forme of a faire Cittie; afterward some demanded their advise, and would needes knowe of them what things of note and admirable they had observed amongst us: they answered three things, the last of which I have forgotten, and am very sorie for it, the other two I yet remember. They saide, *First, they found it very strange, that so many tall men with long beardes, strong and well armed, as were about the Kings person (it is very likely they meant the Swizzers of his guarde) would submit themselves to obey a beardlesse childe, and that we did not rather chuse one amongst them to commaund the rest.* Secondly (they have a maner of phrase whereby they call men but a moytie of men from others.[1]) *They had perceived, there were men amongst us full gorged with all sortes of commodities, and others which hunger-starven, and bare with neede and povertie, begged at their gates: and found it strange, these moyties so needie could endure such an injustice, and that they tooke not the others by the throte, or set fire on their houses.* I talked a good while with one of them, but I had so bad an interpreter: and who did so ill apprehend my meaning, and who through his foolishnesse was so troubled to conceive my imaginations, that I could drawe no great matter from him. Touching that point, wherein I demaunded of him, what good he received by the superioritie hee had amongst his countriemen (for he was a Captaine and our Marriners called him King) he told me, it was to march formost in any charge of warre: further, I asked him, how many men did follow him; he shewed me a distance of place, to signifie they were as many as might be contained in so much ground, which I guessed to be about 4. or 5. thousand men: moreover I demanded, if when warres were ended, all his authoritie expired? he answered, that hee had onely this left him,

1 moiety: half; Montaigne seems to be saying that the Indians believe that men are half of each other, though he may refer to the widespread American native custom of dividing nations or tribes into halves for a variety of structural and social functions.

335

which was, that when he went on progresse, and visited the villages depending of him, the inhabitants prepared paths and high-wayes athwart the hedges of their woodes, for him to passe through at ease. All that is not very ill; but what of that? They weare no kinde of breeches or hosen.

APPENDIX 2
APPROPRIATIONS

Shakespeare's dramas, like those of any playwright, are frequently adapted – rewritten or performed in ways that veer, sometimes sharply, from the original text but are similar enough to retain a clear identification with it. *Appropriations*, by contrast, borrow characters (usually) or themes or specific language from a well-known play for philosophical, political or social purposes which may have no relation to the drama itself apart from the widespread recognition of the borrowed symbol – Hamlet as indecisive, for example, or Lady Macbeth as manipulative. *The Tempest*, as we argue in the Introduction, has been uncommonly susceptible to appropriation for well over a century.

The following examples are representative. In the first, the English philosophical poet Robert Browning makes Caliban his spokesman in a late nineteenth-century meditation on divinity; in the second, the Uruguayan ideological sociologist José Enrique Rodó invokes Ariel as his early twentieth-century symbol of spiritual perfection; in the third, the French psychoanalyst and civil servant Octave Mannoni uses Prospero and Caliban to exemplify mid-twentieth-century colonialism's human dynamics. The three works were widely influential in their times, and were often emulated in their application of *Tempest* tropes to a variety of literary forms – dramatic poetry, philosophical essays, political treatises – and to a wide variety of topics. We reprint this illustrative sample to exemplify *The Tempest*'s rich afterlife.

1 *Robert Browning, 'Caliban upon Setebos'*

Robert Browning (1812–89) began writing 'Caliban upon Setebos' as early as 1859, the same year that Charles Darwin published *On the Origin of Species by means of Natural Selection.* Browning's poem was not published, however, until 1864, when it was included in a collection of dramatic monologues, *Dramatis Personae.* Although many commentators have assumed Browning's Caliban is a Darwinian 'missing link', the poem is not about evolution. Browning's dramatic monologue reveals Caliban's secret thoughts about his god Setebos. Caliban's 'natural theology' is based on the ecological phenomena he observes around him, not upon any supernatural revelations. The poem's central organizing principle is analogy: Caliban reasons that his god Setebos is similar to himself. Whatever Caliban would think or do, so would He (see *Constellation*, 120–43). Caliban's speculations are carefully framed. The poem's first twenty-three lines set the scene (and are distinguished by the author's square brackets at either end of the passage); Prospero and Miranda are sleeping, and, for the moment, Caliban is free to gaze at the sea and ponder. Because he is so afraid that Setebos, a cruel deity at best, might hear him, Caliban speaks of himself in the third person. The capitalized 'He' is Setebos. In the final twelve lines (also bracketed in the original), Caliban fears that a raven flying overhead will report his remarks back to Setebos; in anticipation of Setebos' wrath, he fearfully falls flat.

'Caliban upon Setebos' is taken from volume 7 of *The Poetical Works of Robert Browning* of 1888; this is the last edition published in the poet's lifetime, and it includes his final revisions.

Caliban upon Setebos; or, Natural Theology in the Island

'Thou thoughtest that I was altogether such a one as thyself.'[1]

> ['WILL sprawl, now that the heat of day is best,
> Flat on his belly in the pit's much mire,
> With elbows wide, fists clenched to prop his chin.
> And, while he kicks both feet in the cool slush,

1 The epigraph is from Psalm 50:21 where God reproves the wicked for their errors.

And feels about his spine small eft-things[1] course,
Run in and out each arm, and make him laugh:
And while above his head a pompion-plant,[2]
Coating the cave-top as a brow its eye,
Creeps down to touch and tickle hair and beard,
And now a flower drops with a bee inside,
And now a fruit to snap at, catch and crunch, –
He looks out o'er yon sea which sunbeams cross
And recross till they weave a spider-web
(Meshes of fire, some great fish breaks at times)
And talks to his own self, howe'er he please,
Touching that other, whom his dam called God.[3]
Because to talk about Him, vexes – ha,
Could He but know! and time to vex is now,
When talk is safer than in winter-time.
Moreover Prosper and Miranda sleep
In confidence he drudges at their task,
And it is good to cheat the pair, and gibe,
Letting the rank tongue blossom into speech.]

Setebos, Setebos, and Setebos!
'Thinketh, He dwelleth i' the cold o' the moon.

'Thinketh He made it, with the sun to match,
But not the stars; the stars came otherwise;
Only made clouds, winds, meteors, such as that:
Also this isle, what lives and grows thereon,
And snaky sea which rounds and ends the same.

'Thinketh, it came of being ill at ease:
He hated that He can not change His cold,
Nor cure its ache. 'Hath spied an icy fish
That longed to 'scape the rock-stream where she lived,
And thaw herself within the lukewarm brine
O' the lazy sea her stream thrusts far amid,
A crystal spike 'twixt two warm walls of wave;

---

1 eft-things: an *eft* is a newt; Caliban refers to water lizards who swim about him.
2 pompion: pumpkin
3 Caliban refers to his mother's god Setebos in *Tem* 1.2.374.

Only, she ever sickened, found repulse
At the other kind of water, not her life,
(Green-dense and dim-delicious, bred o' the sun)
Flounced back from bliss she was not born to breathe,
And in her old bounds buried her despair,
Hating and loving warmth alike: so He.

'Thinketh, He made thereat the sun, this isle,
Trees and the fowls here, beast and creeping thing.
Yon otter, sleek-wet, black, lithe as a leech;
Yon auk,[1] one fire-eye in a ball of foam,
That floats and feeds; a certain badger brown
He hath watched hunt with that slant white-wedge eye
By moonlight; and the pie[2] with the long tongue
That pricks deep into oakwarts for a worm,
And says a plain word when she finds her prize,
But will not eat the ants; the ants themselves
That build a wall of seeds and settled stalks
About their hole – He made all these and more,
Made all we see, and us, in spite: how else?
He could not, Himself, make a second self
To be His mate; as well have made Himself:
He would not make what he mislikes or slights,
An eyesore to Him, or not worth His pains:
But did, in envy, listlessness or sport,
Make what Himself would fain, in a manner, be –
Weaker in most points, stronger in a few,
Worthy, and yet mere playthings all the while,
Things He admires and mocks too, – that is it!
Because, so brave, so better tho' they be,
It nothing skills if He begin to plague.
Look now, I melt a gourd-fruit into mash,
Add honeycomb and pods, I have perceived,
Which bite like finches when they bill and kiss, –
Then, when froth rises bladdery, drink up all,
Quick, quick, till maggots scamper thro' my brain;

1 auk: a seabird with small narrow wings
2 pie: magpie

Last, throw me on my back i' the seeded thyme,
And wanton, wishing I were born a bird.
Put case, unable to be what I wish,
I yet could make a live bird out of clay:
Would not I take clay, pinch my Caliban
Able to fly? – for, there, see, he hath wings,
And great comb like the hoopoe's[1] to admire,
And there, a sting to do his foes offence,
There, and I will that he begin to live,
Fly to yon rock-top, nip me off the horns
Of grigs[2] high up that make the merry din,
Saucy thro' their veined wings, and mind me not.
In which feat, if his leg snapped, brittle clay,
And he lay stupid-like, – why, I should laugh;
And if he, spying me, should fall to weep,
Beseech me to be good, repair his wrong,
Bid his poor leg smart less or grow again, –
Well, as the chance were, this might take or else
Not take my fancy: I might hear his cry,
And give the mankin[3] three sound legs for one,
Or pluck the other off, leave him like an egg,
And lessoned he was mine and merely clay.
Were this no pleasure, lying in the thyme,
Drinking the mash, with brain become alive,
Making and marring clay at will? So He.

'Thinketh, such shows nor right nor wrong in Him,
Nor kind, nor cruel: He is strong and Lord.
'Am strong myself compared to yonder crabs
That march now from the mountain to the sea,
'Let twenty pass, and stone the twenty-first,
Loving not, hating not, just choosing so.
'Say, the first straggler that boasts purple spots
Shall join the file, one pincer twisted off;
'Say, this bruised fellow shall receive a worm,

---

1 hoopoe: a bird with distinctively patterned plumage and a fanlike crest
2 grigs: crickets or grasshoppers
3 mankin: diminutive of 'man'; a puny man

And two worms he whose nippers end in red;
As it likes me each time, I do: so He.

Well then, 'supposeth He is good i' the main,
Placable if His mind and ways were guessed,
But rougher than His handiwork, be sure!
Oh, He hath made things worthier than Himself,
And envieth that, so helped, such things do more
Than He who made them! What consoles but this?
That they, unless thro' Him, do naught at all,
And must submit: what other use in things?
'Hath cut a pipe of pithless elder-joint
That, blown through, gives exact the scream o' the jay
When from her wing you twitch the feathers blue:
Sound this, and little birds that hate the jay
Flock within stone's throw, glad their foe is hurt:
Put case such pipe could prattle and boast forsooth
'I catch the birds, I am the crafty thing,
'I make the cry my maker can not make
'With his great round mouth; he must blow thro' mine!'
Would not I smash it with my foot? So He.

But wherefore rough, why cold and ill at ease?
Aha, that is a question! Ask, for that,
What knows, – the something over Setebos
That made Him, or He, may be, found and fought,
Worsted, drove off and did to nothing, perchance.
There may be something quiet o'er His head,
Out of His reach, that feels nor joy nor grief,
Since both derive from weakness in some way.
I joy because the quails come; would not joy
Could I bring quails here when I have a mind:
This Quiet, all it hath a mind to, doth.
'Esteemeth stars the outposts of its couch,
But never spends much thought nor care that way.
It may look up, work up, – the worse for those
It works on! 'Careth but for Setebos
The many-handed as a cuttle-fish,[1]

1 cuttle-fish: also called inkfish, the cuttle-fish has many tentacles

Who, making Himself feared thro' what He does,
Looks up, first, and perceives he cannot soar
To what is quiet and hath happy life;
Next looks down here, and out of very spite
Makes this a bauble-world to ape yon real,
These good things to match those as hips[1] do grapes.
'T is solace making baubles, ay, and sport.
Himself peeped late, eyed Prosper at his books
Careless and lofty, lord now of the isle:
Vexed, 'stitched a book of broad leaves, arrow-shaped,
Wrote thereon, he knows what, prodigious words;
Has peeled a wand and called it by a name;
Weareth at whiles for an enchanter's robe
The eyed skin of a supple oncelot;[2]
And hath an ounce sleeker than youngling mole,
A four-legged serpent he makes cower and couch,
Now snarl, now hold its breath and mind his eye,
And saith she is Miranda and my wife:
'Keeps for his Ariel a tall pouch-bill crane
He bids go wade for fish and straight disgorge;
Also a sea-beast, lumpish, which he snared,
Blinded the eyes of, and brought somewhat tame,
And split its toe-webs, and now pens the drudge
In a hole o' the rock and calls him Caliban;
A bitter heart that bides its time and bites.
'Plays thus at being Prosper in a way,
Taketh his mirth with make-believes: so He.

His dam held that the Quiet made all things
Which Setebos vexed only: 'holds not so.
Who made them weak, meant weakness He might vex.
Had He meant other, while His hand was in,
Why not make horny eyes no thorn could prick,
Or plate my scalp with bone against the snow,
Or overscale my flesh 'neath joint and joint,

---

1 hips: the hard fruits of the rose plant
2 oncelot: a spotted wildcat, like the French *ocelot* or the Spanish *oncela*

Like an orc's[1] armour? Ay, – so spoil His sport!
He is the One now: only He doth all.

'Saith, He may like, perchance, what profits Him.
Ay, himself loves what does him good; but why?
'Gets good no otherwise. This blinded beast
Loves whoso places flesh-meat on his nose,
But, had he eyes, would want no help, but hate
Or love, just as it liked him: He hath eyes.
Also it pleaseth Setebos to work,
Use all His hands, and exercise much craft,
By no means for the love of what is worked.
'Tasteth, himself, no finer good i' the world
When all goes right, in this safe summer-time,
And he wants little, hungers, aches not much,
Than trying what to do with wit and strength.
'Falls to make something: 'piled yon pile of turfs,
And squared and stuck there squares of soft white chalk,
And, with a fish-tooth, scratched a moon on each,
And set up endwise certain spikes of tree,
And crowned the whole with a sloth's skull a-top,
Found dead i' the woods, too hard for one to kill.
No use at all i' the work, for work's sole sake;
'Shall some day knock it down again: so He.

'Saith He is terrible: watch His feats in proof!
One hurricane will spoil six good months' hope.
He hath a spite against me, that I know,
Just as He favours Prosper, who knows why?
So it is, all the same, as well I find.
'Wove wattles half the winter, fenced them firm
With stone and stake to stop she-tortoises
Crawling to lay their eggs here: well, one wave,
Feeling the foot of Him upon its neck,
Gaped as a snake does, lolled out its large tongue,
And licked the whole labour flat: so much for spite!
'Saw a ball[2] flame down late (yonder it lies)

1 orc: killer whale
2 ball: asteroid or meteorite

Where, half an hour before, I slept i' the shade:
Often they scatter sparkles: there is force!
'Dug up a newt He may have envied once
And turned to stone, shut up inside a stone.
Please Him and hinder this? – What Prosper does?
Aha, if He would tell me how! Not He!
There is the sport: discover how or die!
All need not die, for of the things o' the isle
Some flee afar, some dive, some run up trees;
Those at His mercy, – why, they please Him most
When . . when . . well, never try the same way twice!
Repeat what act has pleased, He may grow wroth.
You must not know His ways, and play Him off,
Sure of the issue. 'Doth the like himself:
'Spareth a squirrel that it nothing fears
But steals the nut from underneath my thumb,
And when I threat, bites stoutly in defence:
'Spareth an urchin[1] that contrariwise,
Curls up into a ball, pretending death
For fright at my approach: the two ways please.
But what would move my choler more than this,
That either creature counted on its life
To-morrow, next day and all days to come,
Saying forsooth in the inmost of its heart,
'Because he did so yesterday with me,
'And otherwise with such another brute,
'So must he do henceforth and always.' – Ay?
'Would teach the reasoning couple what 'must' means!
'Doth as he likes, or wherefore Lord? So He.

'Conceiveth all things will continue thus,
And we shall have to live in fear of Him
So long as He lives, keeps His strength: no change,
If He have done His best, make no new world
To please Him more, so leave off watching this, –
If He surprise not even the Quiet's self

---

1 urchin: hedgehog; see *Tem* 2.2.5 and note.

Some strange day, – or, suppose, grow into it
As grubs grow butterflies: else here are we,
And there is He, and nowhere help at all.

'Believeth with the life, the pain shall stop.
His dam held different, that after death
He both plagued enemies and feasted friends:
Idly! He doth His worst in this our life,
Giving just respite lest we die thro' pain,
Saving last pain for worst, – with which, an end.
Meanwhile, the best way to escape His ire
Is, not to seem too happy. 'Sees, himself,
Yonder two flies, with purple films and pink,
Bask on the pompion-bell above: kills both.
'Sees two black painful beetles roll their ball
On head and tail as if to save their lives:
Moves them the stick away they strive to clear.

Even so, 'would have Him misconceive, suppose
This Caliban strives hard and ails no less,
And always, above all else, envies Him;
Wherefore he mainly dances on dark nights,
Moans in the sun, gets under holes to laugh,
And never speaks his mind save housed as now:
Outside, 'groans, curses. If He caught me here,
O'erheard this speech, and asked 'What chucklest at?'
'Would, to appease Him, cut a finger off,
Or of my three kid yearlings burn the best,
Or let the toothsome apples rot on tree,
Or push my tame beast for the orc to taste:
While myself lit a fire, and made a song
And sung it, '*What I hate, be consecrate*
'*To celebrate Thee and Thy state, no mate*
'*For Thee; what see for envy in poor me?*'
Hoping the while, since evils sometimes mend,
Warts rub away and sores are cured with slime,
That some strange day, will either the Quiet catch
And conquer Setebos, or likelier He
Decrepit may doze, doze, as good as die.

[What, what? A curtain o'er the world at once!
Crickets stop hissing; not a bird – or, yes,
There scuds His raven that has told Him all!
It was fool's play, this prattling! Ha! The wind
Shoulders the pillared dust, death's house o' the move,
And fast invading fires begin! White blaze –
A tree's head snaps – and there, there, there, there, there,
His thunder follows! Fool to gibe at Him!
Lo! 'Lieth flat and loveth Setebos!
'Maketh his teeth meet thro' his upper lip,
Will let those quails fly, will not eat this month
One little mess of whelks,[1] so he may 'scape!]

2 *José Enrique Rodó*, Ariel

José Enrique Rodó (1872–1917), prominent Uruguayan philosopher and writer, was a major figure in Latin America's *modernismo* movement of the early twentieth century and was the editor for many years of one of its leading journals, *La Revista Nacional de Literatura y Ciencias Sociales,* published in Montevideo. His *Ariel* (1900) expressed Latin American yearnings for spiritual and intellectual identity and for a cultural future that would not be dominated by the United States. Rodó's brief, idealistic book was an instant bestseller in Latin America and remained a pervasive cultural document throughout the twentieth century (an annotated list of its many editions appears on pp. 115–23 of the edition cited below). Among Rodó's collections of essays is *El mirador de Prospero* (Prospero's balcony), published in 1913.

The following selection from *Ariel* includes the opening and closing pages, with some omissions.

Reproduced from *Ariel* by José Enrique Rodó, translated by Margaret Sayers Peden, © 1988, pp. 31–33, 96–101; by permission of the University of Texas Press.

1 whelks: sea molluscs

That afternoon, at the end of a year of classes, the venerable old teacher, who by allusion to the wise magician of Shakespeare's *Tempest* was often called Prospero, was bidding his young disciples farewell, gathering them about him one last time.

The students were already present in the large classroom in which an exquisite yet austere decor honored in every fastidious detail the presence of Prospero's books, his faithful companions. An exquisite bronze of *The Tempest*'s Ariel, like the presiding spirit of that serene atmosphere, dominated the room. It was the teacher's custom to sit beside this statue, and this is why he had come to be called Prospero, the magician who in the play is attended and served by the fanciful figure depicted by the sculptor. Perhaps, however, an even deeper reason and meaning for the name lay in the master's teaching and character.

Shakespeare's ethereal Ariel symbolizes the noble, soaring aspect of the human spirit. He represents the superiority of reason and feeling over the base impulses of irrationality. He is generous enthusiasm, elevated and unselfish motivation in all actions, spirituality in culture, vivacity and grace in intelligence. Ariel is the ideal toward which human selection ascends, the force that wields life's eternal chisel, effacing from aspiring mankind the clinging vestiges of Caliban, the play's symbol of brutal sensuality.

The regal statue represented the 'airy spirit' at the very moment when Prospero's magic sets him free, the instant he is about to take wing and vanish in a flash of light. Wings unfolded; gossamer, floating robes damascened by the caress of sunlight on bronze; wide brow uplifted; lips half-parted in a serene smile – everything in Ariel's pose perfectly anticipated the graceful beginnings of flight. Happily, the inspired artist who formed his image in solid sculpture had also preserved his angelic appearance and ideal airiness.

Deep in thought, Prospero stroked the statue's brow. Then he seated the young men about him and in a firm voice – a *masterful* voice capable of seizing an idea and implanting it deep within the listener's mind with all the penetrating illumination of a beam of light, the incisive ring of chisel on marble, or the life-infusing touch of brush upon canvas or sculpting wave upon sand – he began to speak, surrounded by his affectionate and attentive students.

Here beside the statue that has daily witnessed our friendly gatherings – from which I have tried to remove any unwelcome austerity – I am going to speak with you one last time, so that our farewell may be the seal stamped on a covenant of emotions and ideas.

I call upon Ariel to be my numen,[1] so that my words will be the most subtle and most persuasive I have ever spoken. I believe that to address the young on any noble and elevated subject is a kind of sacred discourse. I also believe that a young mind is hospitable soil in which the seed of a single timely word will quickly yield immortal fruit.

It is my wish to collaborate on but one page of the agenda that you will draw up in your innermost being and shape with your personal moral character and strength while preparing to breathe the free air of action. This individual agenda – which sometimes may be formulated or written but sometimes is revealed only during the course of action itself – is always to be found in the spirit of those groups and peoples who rise above the multitudes. If, when referring to the philosophy of individual choice, Goethe[2] could say with such profundity that the only man worthy of liberty and life is the man capable of winning them for himself with each new day, can it not also be said – with even greater truth – that the honor of each generation requires it to win liberty and life through its increasing intellectual activity, its own particular efforts, its faith in resolutely expressing the ideal, and its place in the evolution of ideas? . . .

Perhaps it is a rash and ingenuous hope to believe that with a continuous and felicitous acceleration of evolution, with efficacious effort on your part, the period of one generation might suffice to transform the conditions of intellectual life in America[3] from the early stages at which we now find ourselves to a level that would truly benefit society, to a truly dominant peak of achievement. But even when a total transformation is not within the realm of possibility, there can be progress. Even if you know that the first fruits of the soil you so laboriously worked were never to be served on your table, the work itself, if you are generous and strong, would be its own satisfaction. The most invigorating work is that which is realized without anticipation of immediate

1 numen: guiding spirit
2 Johann Wolfgang von Goethe (1749–1832), prolific German poet, novelist and dramatist, best known for the dramatic poem *Faust*
3 Rodó here means primarily Latin America.

349

success. The most glorious effort is that which places hope just beyond the visible horizon. And the purest abnegation is that which denies in the present, not merely resounding applause and the reward of the laurel, but even the moral voluptuousness of satisfaction in a job well done.

There were in antiquity altars for the 'unknown gods.' I urge you to dedicate a part of your soul to the unknown future. As a society advances, concern about the future becomes a major factor in its evolution, an inspiration in its labors. From the confusion and lack of foresight of the savage, who can see into the future only as far as the hours remaining until sunset, and who has no concept that it is possible to have partial control over the days ahead, to our own thoughtful and prudent preoccupation with posterity, there is an enormous distance that some day may seem brief and insignificant. We are capable of progress only to the degree that we become capable of adapting our acts to conditions that are increasingly distant from us in space and time. The certainty that we are contributing to work that will survive us, work that will benefit the future, enhances our sense of human dignity, helping us to triumph over the limitations of our nature. If, through some calamity, humanity were to despair of the immortality of the individual consciousness, the most religious sentiment that could replace it would be the one born from the belief that even after the dissolution of the soul, the best of what it has felt and dreamed – its most personal, its purest, essence – will persist in the heritage transmitted by generations of human beings, in the same way that the shining ray of a dead star lives on in infinity to touch us with its tender and melancholy light.

In the life of human societies, the future is a perfect equivalence of visionary thought. From the pious veneration of the past and the cult of tradition, on the one hand, and, on the other, from bold movement toward what is to come, is composed the noble strength that in raising the collective spirit above the limitations of the present communicates the sentiments and agitations of a society. Men and nations, in the opinion of Fouillée,[1] work under the inspiration of ideas, while irrational beings react to the stimulus of the instincts. According to that same thinker, the society that struggles and labors, often unknowingly, to

1 Alfred Jules Emile Fouillée (1838–1912), a French sociologist and philosopher who argued that ideas were almost autonomous entities in the evolution of societies. His *L'idée moderne du droit en Allemagne, en Angleterre et en France* (1878) invoked symbols from *The Tempest*, especially Ariel.

make an idea reality is imitating the instinctive work of a bird that, as it constructs its nest, obsessed by an imperious internal image, is obeying both an unconscious memory of the past and a mysterious presentiment of the future.

...I have taken my inspiration from the gentle and serene image of my Ariel. The beneficent spirit that Shakespeare – perhaps with the divine unawareness frequent in inspired intuitions – imbued with such high symbolism is clearly represented in the statue, his ideals magnificently translated by art into line and contour. Ariel is reason and noble sentiment. Ariel is the sublime instinct for perfectibility, by virtue of which human clay – the *miserable clay* of which Arimanes' spirits spoke to Manfred[1] – is exalted and converted into a creature that lives in the glow of Ariel's light: the center of the universe. Ariel is for Nature the crowning achievement of her labors, the last figure in the ascending chain, the spiritual flame. A triumphant Ariel signifies idealism and order in life; noble inspiration in thought; selflessness in morality; good taste in art; heroism in action; delicacy in customs. He is the eponymous hero in the epic of the species. He is the immortal protagonist: his presence inspired the earliest feeble efforts of rationalism in the first prehistoric man when for the first time he bowed his dark brow to chip at rock or trace a crude image on the bones of the reindeer; his wings fanned the sacred bonfire that the primitive Aryan, progenitor of civilized peoples, friend of light, ignited in the mysterious jungles of the Ganges in order to forge with his divine fire the scepter of human majesty. In the later evolution of superior races, Ariel's dazzling light shines above souls that have surpassed the natural limits of humankind, above heroes of thought and fantasy, as well as those of action and sacrifice, above Plato on the promontory of Sunium, as well as above St. Francis of Assisi in the solitude of Monte della Verna. Ariel's irresistible strength is fueled by the ascendant movement of life. Conquered a thousand times over by the indomitable rebellion of Caliban, inhibited by victorious barbarism, asphyxiated in the smoke of battles, his transparent wings stained by contact with the 'eternal dunghill of Job,' Ariel rebounds, immortal; Ariel recovers his youth and beauty and responds with agility to Prospero's call, to the call of all those who love him and invoke him in reality. At times his beneficent empire reaches even those

1 in Lord Byron's *Manfred: A Dramatic Poem* (1816), which draws on themes from Goethe's *Faust*

who deny him and ignore him. He often directs the blind forces of evil and barbarism so that, like others, they will contribute to the work of good. Ariel will pass through human history, humming, as in Shakespeare's drama, his melodious song to animate those who labor and those who struggle, until the fulfillment of the unknown plan permits him – in the same way that in the drama he is liberated from Prospero's service – to break his material bonds and return forever to the center of his divine fire.

I want you to remember my words, but even more, I beseech you to cherish the indelible memory of my statue of Ariel. I want the airy and graceful image of this bronze to be imprinted forever in the innermost recesses of your mind. I remember that once while enjoying a coin collection in a museum my attention was captured by the legend on an ancient coin: the word *Hope*, nearly effaced from the faded gold. As I gazed at that worn inscription, I pondered what its influence might have been. Who knows what noble and active role in forming the character and affecting the lives of human generations we could attribute to that simple theme's working its insistent suggestion upon those who held it in their hands? Who knows, as it circulated from hand to hand, how much fading joy was renewed, how many generous plans brought to fruition, how many evil proposals thwarted, when men's gaze fell upon the inspiring word incised, like a graphic cry, on the metallic disc. May this image of Ariel – imprinted upon your hearts – play the same imperceptible but decisive role in your own lives. In darkest hours of discouragement, may it revive in your consciousness an enthusiasm for the wavering ideal and restore to your heart the ardor of lost hope. Once affirmed in the bastion of your inner being, Ariel will go forth in the conquest of souls. I see him, far in the future, smiling upon you with gratitude from above as your spirit fades into the shadows. I have faith in your will, in your strength, even as I have faith in the will and strength of those to whom you will give life, to whom you will transmit your work. Often I am transported by the dream that one day may be a reality: that the Andes, soaring high above our America, may be carved to form the pedestal for this statue, the immutable altar for its veneration.

These were the words of Prospero. After pressing the master's hand with filial affection, the youthful disciples drifted away. His gently spoken words, like the lament of ringing crystal, lingered in the air. It was the last hour of the day. A ray from the dying sun penetrated the room, pierced the shadows, and fell upon the bronze brow of the statue, seeming to strike a restless spark of life in Ariel's exalted eyes. Lingering in the gloom, the beam of light suggested the gaze the spirit, captive in the bronze, cast upon the departing youths. They left in silent unanimity, each absorbed in serious thought – the delicate distillation of meditation that a saint exquisitely compared to the slow and gentle fall of dewdrops upon the fleece of a lamb. When their harsh encounter with the throng brought them back to the surrounding reality, it was night. A warm, serene summer night. The grace and quietude the night spilled upon the earth from its ebony urn triumphed over the rudeness of man's accomplishments. Only the presence of the multitude forbade ecstasy.

A warm breeze rippled the evening air with languid and delicious abandon, like wine trembling in the goblet of a bacchant. The shadows cast no darkness on the pure night sky, but painted its blue with a shade that seemed to reflect a pensive serenity....

3 *Octave Mannoni,* Prospero and Caliban: The Psychology of Colonization

Octave Mannoni (1899–1989), a French official in Madagascar, wrote *Psychologie de la Colonisation* in 1948. By training and usually by vocation, Mannoni was a social scientist, especially a psychoanalyst, but in the widespread European tradition of intellectuals-as-public servants, he was for several years an administrator in France's largest colony. His book is partly a response to the island's anti-colonial uprising and its lethal suppression, and partly a theoretical analysis of 'colonial situations', to which Mannoni had already devoted articles in the French journal *Psyché* in 1947 and 1948. Mannoni's book was first published in Paris in 1950; it was translated into English in 1956 by Pamela Powesland as *Prospero and Caliban: The Psychology of Colonization,* with a brief Author's Note by Mannoni and a Foreword by Philip Mason; the same translation was reissued in 1964, supplemented by an Author's Note to the second edition; and reissued again in 1990, with all of the foregoing front matter plus a critical New Foreword by Maurice Bloch.

Part I of *Prospero and Caliban* describes what Mannoni perceives as 'the general characteristics most typical of the Malagasy personality in relation to the structure of the family and the cult of the ancestors'; Part II analyses 'the attitude of the European colonial to the image of the native'; and Part III is 'an examination of the different aspects of the interhuman relationship which arises in a colonial situation' (pp. 34–5). The following selection comprises most of the first chapter (pp. 97–102, 104–9), entitled 'Crusoe and Prospero', of Part II, from the edition of 1956.

The dependence relationship requires at least two members, and where a colonial situation exists, if one of them is the native of the colony, the other is likely to be the colonizer, or rather the colonial, for he it is who offers us the more interesting subject of study. The real colonizer is almost of necessity a man of strong character, a creator rather than an accepter of relationships, at least at the outset. It is only later that he becomes a colonial. The typical colonial, on the other hand, finds the relationship ready made; he takes it up, adapts himself to it, and very often exploits it. And in any case, whether he accepts it passively or seizes upon it greedily, the relationship changes him more than he it. It is precisely this transformation which sets a stamp on him, which makes him a colonial. And it is this which we must now study if we are to find out the exact psychological nature of the relations which form between the European colonial and the dependent native – if we are to understand how and why these relations change with time and what effect they have on the two members.

The reader will see that in trying to discover how it is that a European, to all appearances indistinguishable from other Europeans, can become, sometimes in a very short space of time, a typical colonial and very different from his former self, I have reached a conclusion which is at first sight paradoxical – namely, that the personality of the colonial is made up, not of characteristics acquired during and through experience of the colonies, but of traits, very often in the nature of a complex, already in existence in a latent and repressed form in the European's psyche, traits which the colonial experience has simply brought to the surface and made manifest. Social life in Europe exerts a certain pressure on the individual, and that pressure keeps the personality in a given shape; once it is removed, however, the outlines of the personality change and swell, thus revealing the existence of internal pressures which had up to then passed unnoticed.

Of course that is simply a metaphor; what I want to bring out is that what happens to a European when he becomes a colonial is the result of unconscious complexes, and these I propose to analyse. The shape assumed by a deep-sea fish when it is brought up to the surface is due to differences in pressure, certainly, but it is also due to its own internal anatomical structure. Logically, what my theory amounts to is this, that a person free from complexes – if such a person can be imagined – would not undergo change as a result of experience of the colonies. He would not in the first place feel the urge to go to the colonies, but even should he find himself there by chance, he would not taste those emotional satisfactions which, whether consciously or unconsciously, so powerfully attract the predestined colonial.

These complexes are formed, necessarily, in infancy; their later history varies according to whether they are resolved, repressed, or satisfied in the course of a closer and closer contact with reality as the age of adulthood is reached. The best description of them is to be found in the works of some of the great writers who projected them on to imaginary characters placed in situations which, though imaginary, are typically colonial. The material they drew directly from their own unconscious desires. This is proof enough that the complexes exist even before the colonial situation is experienced. . . . [Two omitted paragraphs discuss Daniel Defoe's *Robinson Crusoe.*]

Shakespeare's *The Tempest* – he, too [like Defoe], wrote it in his old age – presents a situation which is, psychoanalytically, almost identical with that of Crusoe. We can be sure that Shakespeare had no other model but himself for his creation of Prospero.

It is characteristic of this type of story – the remark applies equally, for instance, to the *Odyssey, Sinbad the Sailor* and *Gulliver's Travels* – that the hero has to face either the perils or the miseries of exile; they are either punishments or, as it were, scarecrows, the two ideas being easily linked in that of prohibition. The reason for them is usually a wrongdoing, deliberate or otherwise, and it constitutes disobedience of the gods, the customs, or more generally the father. Prospero had neglected the duties of his office and had been betrayed by his brother in complicity with a king – psychoanalytically a king is a father-image. Even the real travellers, Baudelaire,[1] Trelawny[2] and many others, obediently conform to the unconscious schema.[3] The story-book travellers encounter parental prohibitions in the form of monsters: Cyclops, the Roc bird, the cannibals. They are full of regrets – 'Ah, how much better it would have been...!' and so on. When they get back they have nothing but misfortunes to relate: 'So we worked at the oar' says Robinson, 'and the wind driving us towards the shore, we hastened our destruction with our own hands....' Nevertheless their adventures rouse envy in their stay-at-home readers, especially if they are young.

Prospero is the least evolved of all these literary figures, according to the criteria of psychoanalysis, for he is endowed with magical power, and so is not required to display those virile and adult qualities to which Ulysses and Crusoe owe their salvation. Crusoe is psychologically the least archaic, as is shown by his faith in technical skill – he is a veritable Jack-of-all-trades. He is in line with the current of ideas flowing from Locke to the Encyclopaedists; Prospero, on the other hand, is reminiscent rather of Bacon, who thought in terms of experiment but dreamed of magic; nor is he the only character in the play to repudiate technique, for there is Gonzalo, too, the Utopist. Between them, therefore, these characters appear to cover the whole of the subject we are studying. Chronology is of no importance, and so we shall begin with an analysis of Crusoe and see what we can learn from it.

First, it is very significant that he is much less unhappy when he is absolutely alone than when he is afraid he may not be. I must dwell on this paradox, for our familiarity with it dulls our surprise at it; man is afraid because he is alone and his fear is the fear of other men. Fear of solitude is fear of intrusion upon that solitude. (It is the same in *The Tempest*: Prospero's solitude is finally broken in upon.) Contemporary critics even pointed out this 'contradiction' in Robinson Crusoe. But perhaps it was not a contradiction, after all.

At all events, every sign of another living thing, a goat, a footprint, anything put fear into the heart of Crusoe – even his parrot, which was

---

1 Charles Baudelaire (1821–67), French poet and critic
2 Edward John Trelawny (1792–1881), English writer
3 [Mannoni:] A particularly interesting traveller to study is R.L. Stevenson. In his story Ariel and Caliban are called Jekyll and Hyde. In the remote Pacific he found courage to grapple with the image which had driven him that far, and began writing the *Weir of Hermiston*. He died before victory was won, leaving his *chef-d'oeuvre* incomplete.

nonetheless a first configuration of the companion he both dreaded and desired in an ambivalent complex of feelings. (It will be easier to understand the role of this parrot, which learns to talk, after reading the passage from the *Serious Reflections*, which I shall quote later on.) In fact, Daniel Defoe's story recounts *the long and difficult cure of a misanthropic neurosis.* His hero, who is at first at odds with his environment, gradually recovers psychological health in solitude. He comes to accept the presence of creatures upon whom he tries to project the image – at once terrifying and reassuring – of *another.* Then he has a friend, 'dumb' at first, like his parrot. Later he has the courage to fight against the 'others' in the form of hostile cannibals. Finally he has to deal with a terribly bad lot who are, however, more akin to himself, and he manages to subdue them by his authority. He even assumes the title of governor of the island. His cure is assured; he is even reconciled with the father-image, and, by the same token, with God (God is also mentioned in the *Serious Reflections*). So, then, Crusoe can return, like Ulysses, '*plein d'usage et raison*' – and money, too, gained chiefly through slave-trading.

Let us leave Defoe's case for a moment to consider that of his reader and discover why he finds Defoe's book so interesting. His interest itself is enough to show that there is in the child some trait which is partly misanthropic, or at any rate anti-social, a trait which, for lack of a better term, I would call 'the lure of a world without men'. It may be repressed to a greater or less extent, but it will remain, nonetheless, in the unconscious.

It is the existence of this trait which makes the idea of the desert island so attractive, whereas in reality there is little to be said for it, as the real Robinsons discovered. The desert islands of the imagination are, it is true, peopled with imaginary beings, but that is after all their *raison d'être.* Some of the semi-human creatures the unconscious creates, such as Caliban or the Lilliputians, reveal their creator's desire to denigrate the whole of mankind. Others are a compound of the bad creatures on whom the child projects his own desire to be naughty and the parents who forbid him to be naughty – for the father who tells his child that the wicked bogey-man will get him if he does not behave, himself becomes a bogey-man in the eyes of the child. And all external dangers, such as the wolf and the policeman, are felt to be his allies, especially as they are specifically referred to by the parents. We have already seen how often this fusion occurs in the dreams of Malagasy children where the 'naughty' (i.e. guilty) child is pursued by the wicked Senegalese soldier who is at the same time his father, both being represented by the bull.[1]

It is a fact, however, that in spite of prohibitions, or perhaps because of them, the child longs to escape. Some time after he is four years of age he makes surreptitious attempts to venture out alone. Sometimes he 'loses' himself or he makes a tour of a block of houses and returns to his starting-point, as if he wanted to verify some topographical intuition or prove that the world is round. Sometimes he longs to be invisible, and hides himself; when his mother calls him anxiously he does not reply. She calls these escapades silly, but perhaps they are something more than mere games. Or again the child may long to go and hide far away from everybody, and so he goes to the bottom of the garden to play at being Robinson; the fact that several children may take part in this game makes no difference – it is still a flight from mankind, and intrusion must be guarded against.

The real attraction of solitude, however, is that if the world is emptied of human beings as they really are, it can be filled with the creatures of our own imagination: Calypso, Ariel, Friday. But if we are to achieve a complete and adult personality it is essential that we should make the images of the unconscious tally, more or less, with real people; flight into solitude shows that we have failed to do so. In *The Tempest*, when Miranda cries:

> ... O brave new world,
> That has such people in't

we realize, with an emotion which reveals the importance of the fact, that she has accomplished in one step that adjustment of the archetypes to reality which her neurotic father had so surely missed. His scornful reply, ''Tis new to thee', proves that he is not yet cured. Where there is a preference for Ariel or Friday to real persons, it is clear that there has been a failure in adaptation, resulting usually from a grave lack of sociability combined with a pathological urge to dominate. These characteristics, which are traceable in the unconscious of Prospero–Shakespeare and Crusoe–Defoe, are very probably present in all

1 discussed by Mannoni on pp. 89–93 of *Prospero and Caliban*

children too, but they may develop in one of many ways.... [The omitted section pertains to *Robinson Crusoe.*]

[A] tendency towards misanthropy, which may first be expressed in a flight from other people, may, it is clear, later lead to a serious rupture of the image of these others or to a failure in the process of synthesis whereby that image is formed. The image falls into two parts which recede farther and farther from one another instead of coalescing; on the one hand there are pictures of monstrous and terrifying creatures, and on the other visions of gracious beings bereft of will and purpose – Caliban and the cannibals at one extreme (Caliban is surely a deliberate anagram); Ariel and Friday at the other. But man is both Ariel and Caliban; we must recognize this if we are to grow up. For a period during childhood we refuse to believe it, and it is the traces of this phase which remain in the unconscious that led Defoe and Shakespeare to write the works to which I have referred. The same unconscious tendency has impelled thousands of Europeans to seek out oceanic islands inhabited only by Fridays or, alternatively, to go and entrench themselves in isolated outposts in hostile countries where they could repulse by force of arms those same terrifying creatures whose image was formed in their own unconscious.

It would, of course, be possible to put forward all sorts of historical reasons to explain the success of colonization, and there is no denying the importance of the phenomena of economic expansion. But these causes were brought to bear on minds psychologically prepared, and if my analysis is correct no one becomes a real colonial who is not impelled by infantile complexes which were not properly resolved in adolescence. The gap between the dependent personality of the native and the independent personality of the European affords these complexes an opportunity of becoming manifest; it invites the projection of unconscious images and encourages behaviour which is not warranted by the objective situation, but is ultimately explainable in terms of the most infantile subjectivity. Colonial countries are still the nearest approach possible to the archetype of the desert island, and the native still best represents the archetype of the *socius* and the enemy, Friday and the cannibals. So, then, colonial life is simply a substitute to those who are still obscurely drawn to a world without men – to those, that is, who have failed to make the effort necessary to adapt infantile images to adult reality.

This is the conclusion to which my analysis of Robinson Crusoe has led me: I shall now consider the case of Prospero, and the reader will find my interpretation confirmed and given more precision.

The colonial situation is even more clearly portrayed in *The Tempest*[1] than in *Robinson Crusoe*, which is the more remarkable in that Shakespeare certainly thought less about it than did Defoe. Shakespeare's theme is the drama of the renunciation of power and domination, which are symbolized by magic, a borrowed power which must be rendered up. Man must learn to accept himself as he is and to accept others as they are, even if they happen to be called Caliban. This is the only wise course, but the path towards wisdom is long and infinitely painful for Prospero.

There is no doubting the nature of Prospero's magical power, for at his side we find his obedient daughter – and magic is the child's image of paternal omnipotence. Whenever his absolute authority is threatened, and however slight the threat, Prospero – our aspirant to wisdom – always becomes impatient and almost neurotically touchy. The essence of the problem is revealed at the outset; Prospero lays down his magic garment and prepares to tell Miranda the story of his life. In other words, he tries to treat Miranda as an equal; but he fails. He begins with 'Obey and be attentive,' and the recital is punctuated with other orders of the same kind, all absurd and quite unwarranted; later in the play he even goes so far as to threaten Miranda with his hatred. It is the same with Ariel; Prospero has promised him his liberty, but fails to give it to him. He constantly reminds Ariel that he freed him from the knotty entrails of a cloven pine in which the terrible mother, Sycorax, had confined him. This again means that Prospero has the absolute authority of the father. Caliban is the unruly and incorrigible son who is disowned. Prospero says he was 'got by the devil himself'. At the same time he is the useful slave who is ruthlessly exploited. But Caliban does not complain of being exploited; he complains rather of being betrayed, in Künkel's[2] sense of the word: he says, explicitly,

> ... When thou camest first,
> Thou strok'dst me, and mad'st much of me; wouldst give me

1 [Mannoni:] On the analytical interpretation of the text of Shakespeare's play, see Abenheimer: 'Shakespeare's Tempest', in the *Psychoanalytic Review* of October 1946.

2 Fritz Künkel, a German psychoanalyst on whose works Mannoni drew in Part I

Water with berries in't; and teach me how
To name the bigger light, and how the less,
That burn by day and night: and then I lov'd thee,

but now

        ... you sty me
In this hard rock, whiles you do keep from me
The rest o' the island.

Caliban has fallen prey to the resentment which succeeds the break-down of dependence. Prospero seeks to justify himself: did Caliban not attempt to violate the honour of his child? After such an offence, what hope is there? There is no logic in this argument. Prospero could have removed Caliban to a safe distance or he could have continued to civi-lize and correct him. But the argument: you tried to violate Miranda, *therefore* you shall chop wood, belongs to a non-rational mode of think-ing. In spite of the various forms this attitude may take (it includes, for instance, working for the father-in-law, a common practice in patriar-chal communities), it is primarily a justification of hatred on grounds of sexual guilt, and it is at the root of colonial racialism.

I was given a clue to the explanation of this racialism while ques-tioning a European colonial, who expressed the belief that the black race had become inferior to the white through excessive masturbation! The man himself was troubled by parental prohibitions in this respect. The 'inferior being' always serves as scapegoat; our own evil intentions can be projected on to him. This applies especially to incestuous intentions; Miranda is the only woman on the island, and Prospero and Caliban the only men. It is easy to see why it is always his daughter or his sister or his neighbour's wife (never his own) whom a man imagines to have been violated by a negro; he wants to rid himself of guilt by putting the blame for his bad thoughts on someone else. Caliban, in this hopeless situation, begins plotting against Prospero – not to win his freedom, for he could not support freedom, but to have a new master whose 'foot-licker' he can become. He is delighted at the prospect. It would be hard to find a better example of the dependence complex in its pure state. In the play the complex must be a projection, for where else could it have come from? The dependence of colonial natives is a matter of plain fact. The ensuing encounter between the European's unconscious and a reality only too well prepared to receive its projections is in practice full of dangers. Colonials live in a less real social world, and this diminished reality is less able to wake the dreamer....

Among the castaways in *The Tempest* there is one rather strangely-drawn character: Gonzalo. The list of *dramatis personae* describes him as an 'honest old counsellor'. He once rendered Prospero great service, and Prospero treats him with immense respect. He is, however, simply a variant of Polonius, a garrulous old dotard, but more of a caricature. *The Tempest* repeats, in order to resolve it, the Hamlet situation: brother ousted by brother, guilty father (here the King of Naples), hatred of the mother, brooding instead of action – the latter a regression due to loss of real power. And in both cases, alongside the father, there is the uncle or some other father-image: a doddering and impotent old man. Gonzalo, the Utopist, dreams of turning the island into a Land of Cockaigne:[1]

> All things in common nature should produce
> Without sweat or endeavour...

no toil, no government, no institutions. His attitude is in fact identical with Prospero's and shows the same infantile regression – but he lacks the omnipotence of the father, that is to say magic, the power which is the cause of all difficulties and must be rejected. How reluctantly Prospero gives up his daughter to Ferdinand! And he cannot restore Ariel to liberty without asking him to perform yet one more task. He forgives his enemies, but only after he has avenged himself on them and thoroughly humiliated them. In Milan, where he will be duke in name only, he says, 'Every third thought shall be my grave'. In the Epilogue Prospero declares

> Now my charms are all o'erthrown,
> And what strength I have's mine own;
> Which is most faint.

In this, his will, he gives back everything he acquired by magic – all, that is, that he lost by betrayal, including his birthright. Surely the man

1 Land of Cockaigne: an imaginary place of idyllic luxury. [Mannoni:] We shall see in a later chapter (Part III, Ch. V) with regard to the *Fokon'olona*, how the image of the Land of Cockaigne emerges after the suppression of paternalist power, like a more distant memory of childhood.

who wrote this play must have harboured in his unconscious a strange and potent desire to possess power over men, if only by prestige, and this desire must in its way have been as powerful and as difficult to overcome as that of Defoe.

In any case it was from the unconscious that the two islands of these tales emerged. The parallels between the two works assure us that we are in the presence of archetypes: Ariel, Friday, Caliban, the cannibals. And as in these works of art these archetypes governed the imagination, so in real life they govern behaviour. The typical colonial is compelled to live out Prospero's drama, for Prospero is in his unconscious as he was in Shakespeare's; only the former lacks the writer's capacity for sublimation. The colonial's personality is wholly unaffected by that of the native of the colony to which he goes; it does not adapt itself, but develops solely in accordance with its own inner structure. It is inevitable, therefore, that misunderstandings should arise, for there can be no harmony between monads.

It is always worth while considering the opinions of the colonialists, for they are necessarily very revealing, and in this case they confirm my views. What they say in effect is: there is no misunderstanding to clear up; it would not be worth the trouble, anyway; the Malagasy personality is whatever you like to make of it – for in fact it does not exist; ours alone counts. In other words, they do not acknowledge the Malagasy personality. Nothing outside themselves affects them. After all, what sorts of personalities have Miranda, Ariel, and Friday? None at all, so long as they remain submissive. Caliban, it is true, asserts himself by opposing, but he is mere bestiality.

What the colonial in common with Prospero lacks, is awareness of the world of Others, a world in which Others have to be respected. This is the world from which the colonial has fled because he cannot accept men as they are. Rejection of that world is combined with an urge to dominate, an urge which is infantile in origin and which social adaptation has failed to discipline. The reason the colonial himself gives for his flight – whether he says it was the desire to travel, or the desire to escape from the cradle or from the 'ancient parapets', or whether he says that he simply wanted a freer life – is of no consequence, for whatever the variant offered, the real reason is still what I have called very loosely the colonial vocation. It is always a question of compromising with the desire for a world without men. As for the man who chooses a colonial career by chance and without specific vocation, there is nevertheless every possibility that he too has a 'Prospero complex', more fully repressed, but still ready to emerge to view in favourable conditions. . . .

ABBREVIATIONS
AND REFERENCES

The majority of biblical citations are taken from the Geneva Bible, which Shakespeare used more frequently in his later years (see Richmond Noble, *Shakespeare's Biblical Knowledge* (London, 1935), 75–6), and are so noted in the text. In other cases, citations are from the Bishops' Bible (London, 1568), which was readily available in parish churches during Shakespeare's lifetime. Line references for Shakespearean works other than *The Tempest* are to *The Riverside Shakespeare*, to which the *Harvard Concordance to Shakespeare* is keyed. For the reader's convenience, we have modernized the usage of *i, j, u* and *v* and substituted *th* for the thorn in our quotations from pre-modern texts. Quotations from the Folio retain their original orthography.

ABBREVIATIONS
ABBREVIATIONS USED IN NOTES

edn	edition
Fc	corrected state of F
Fu	uncorrected state of F
n.s.	new series
om.	omitted
opp.	opposite
SD	stage direction
sig., sigs	signature, signatures
SP	speech prefix
this edn	a reading adopted for the first time in this edition
t.n.	textual note

SHAKESPEARE'S WORKS AND WORKS PARTLY
BY SHAKESPEARE

AC	*Antony and Cleopatra*
AW	*All's Well that Ends Well*
AYL	*As You Like It*
CE	*The Comedy of Errors*
Cor	*Coriolanus*
Cym	*Cymbeline*
Ham	*Hamlet*

1H4	*King Henry IV Part 1*
2H4	*King Henry IV Part 2*
H5	*King Henry V*
1H6	*King Henry VI Part 1*
2H6	*King Henry VI Part 2*
3H6	*King Henry VI Part 3*
H8	*King Henry VIII*
JC	*Julius Caesar*
KJ	*King John*
KL	*King Lear*
LC	*A Lover's Complaint*
LLL	*Love's Labour's Lost*
Luc	*The Rape of Lucrece*
MA	*Much Ado about Nothing*
Mac	*Macbeth*
MM	*Measure for Measure*
MND	*A Midsummer Night's Dream*
MV	*The Merchant of Venice*
MW	*The Merry Wives of Windsor*
Oth	*Othello*
Per	*Pericles*
PP	*The Passionate Pilgrim*
R2	*King Richard II*
R3	*King Richard III*
RJ	*Romeo and Juliet*
Son	*Shakespeare's Sonnets*
STM	*Sir Thomas More*
TC	*Troilus and Cressida*
Tem	*The Tempest*
TGV	*The Two Gentlemen of Verona*
Tim	*Timon of Athens*
Tit	*Titus Andronicus*
TN	*Twelfth Night*
TNK	*The Two Noble Kinsmen*
TS	*The Taming of the Shrew*
VA	*Venus and Adonis*
WT	*The Winter's Tale*

REFERENCES

EDITIONS AND ADAPTATIONS OF
SHAKESPEARE COLLATED

Ard[1]	*The Tempest*, ed. Morton Luce, The Arden Shakespeare (London, 1901)
Ard[2]	*The Tempest*, ed. Frank Kermode, The Arden Shakespeare (London, 1954; rev. edn, 1961)
Bantam	*The Tempest*, ed. David Bevington (London, 1988)
Bell	*The Tempest*, ed. John Bell (London, 1773)
Cam[1]	*The Tempest*, ed. John Dover Wilson, The New Shakespeare (Cambridge, 1921)
Capell	*Comedies, Histories, and Tragedies*, ed. Edward Capell, 10 vols (London, 1767–8)
Dryden & Davenant	*The Tempest, or, The Enchanted Island*, by John Dryden and William Davenant (London, 1670)
Dyce	*Works*, ed. Alexander Dyce, 6 vols (London, 1857)
Everyman	*The Tempest*, ed. John F. Andrews, The Everyman Shakespeare (London, 1991)
F	*Comedies, Histories, and Tragedies*, First Folio (London, 1623)
F2	*Comedies, Histories, and Tragedies*, Second Folio (London, 1632)
F3	*Comedies, Histories, and Tragedies*, Third Folio (London, 1663)
F4	*Comedies, Histories, and Tragedies*, Fourth Folio (London, 1685)
Folg[2]	*The Tempest*, ed. Barbara A. Mowat and Paul Werstine, The New Folger Library Shakespeare (New York, 1994)
Hanmer	*Works*, ed. Thomas Hanmer, 6 vols (London, 1744)
Johnson	*Plays*, ed. Samuel Johnson, 10 vols (London, 1766)
Johnson & Steevens	*Plays*, ed. Samuel Johnson and George Steevens, 10 vols (London, 1773)
Johnson & Steevens[1]	*Plays*, ed. Samuel Johnson and George Steevens, 15 vols (London, 1793)
Malone	*Plays and Poems*, ed. Edmond Malone, 10 vols (London, 1790)
Oxf	*Complete Works*, ed. Stanley Wells *et al.* (Oxford, 1986)
Oxf[1]	*The Tempest*, ed. Stephen Orgel, The Oxford Shakespeare (Oxford, 1987)
Penguin	*The Tempest*, ed. Anne Barton, The New Penguin Shakespeare (Harmondsworth, 1968)
Pope	*Works*, ed. Alexander Pope, 6 vols (London, 1723–5)

Rann	*Works*, ed. Joseph Rann, 6 vols (Oxford, 1786)
Riv	*The Riverside Shakespeare*, ed. G. Blakemore Evans (Boston, 1974; rev. edn 1997)
Rowe*	*The Tempest: A Comedy* (a proof-sheet), ed. Nicholas Rowe(?) (London, 1708)
Rowe[1]	*Works*, ed. Nicholas Rowe, 6 vols (London, 1709)
Rowe[2]	*Works*, ed. Nicholas Rowe, 2nd edn, 6 vols (1709)
Rowe[3]	*Works*, ed. Nicholas Rowe, 8 vols (London, 1714)
Signet	*The Tempest*, ed. Robert Langbaum, The Signet Shakespeare (New York, 1964)
Theobald[1]	*Works*, ed. Lewis Theobald, 7 vols (London, 1733)
Theobald[2]	*Works*, ed. Lewis Theobald, 8 vols (London, 1740)
Var	*The Tempest*, ed. H.H. Furness, New Variorum Edition (Philadelphia, 1892)
Warburton	*Works*, ed. William Warburton, 8 vols (London, 1747)
White, R.G.	*Works*, ed. Richard Grant White, 12 vols (Boston, 1857)

OTHER WORKS

Abbott	E.A. Abbott, *A Shakespearian Grammar* (London, 1869)
Aeneid	Virgil, *The Aeneid*, trans. H. Rushton Fairclough, 2 vols (Cambridge, Mass., 1916)
Aercke	Kristiaan P. Aercke, ' "An odd angle of the isle": the courtly art of *The Tempest*', in *Approaches to Teaching Shakespeare's 'The Tempest' and Other Late Romances*, ed. Maurice Hunt (New York, 1992), 146–52
Allen	Harold B. Allen, 'Shakespeare's "Lay her a-hold"', *MLN*, 52 (1937), 96–100
Auberlen	Eckhard Auberlen, '*The Tempest* and the concerns of the Restoration court: a study of *The Enchanted Island* and the operatic *Tempest*', *Restoration*, 15 (1991), 71–88
Auden	W.H. Auden, *The Sea and the Mirror*, in *Collected Poems* (New York, 1976), 309–41
Bacon	Wallace A. Bacon, 'A note on "The Tempest", IV.i', *N&Q*, 192 (1947), 343–4
Baker	David J. Baker, 'Where is Ireland in *The Tempest*?', in *Shakespeare and Ireland: History, Politics, Culture*, ed. Mark Thornton Burnett and Ramona Wray (Houndmills, Hants., 1997), 68–88
Ball	Robert Hamilton Ball, *Shakespeare on Silent Film* (London, 1968)
Bate, 'Caliban'	Jonathan Bate, 'Caliban and Ariel write back', *SS 48* (1995), 155–62
Bate, *Genius*	Jonathan Bate, *The Genius of Shakespeare* (London, 1997)

Bate, *Ovid*	Jonathan Bate, *Shakespeare and Ovid* (Oxford, 1993)
Beaumont & Fletcher	*The Dramatic Works in the Beaumont and Fletcher Canon*, ed. Fredson Bowers, 10 vols (Cambridge, 1966–96)
Beresford-Howe	Constance Beresford-Howe, *Prospero's Daughter* (Toronto, 1988)
Berger	Karol Berger, 'Prospero's art', *SSt*, 10 (1977), 211–39
Bergeron	David M. Bergeron, *Royal Family, Royal Lovers: King James of England and Scotland* (Columbia, Mo., 1991)
Bible	*The Geneva Bible; A Facsimile of the 1560 Edition* (Madison, Wis., 1969)
Blayney, *Folio*	Peter W.M. Blayney, *The First Folio of Shakespeare* (Washington, D.C., 1991)
Blayney, *Norton*	Peter W.M. Blayney, 'Introduction to the Second Edition', *The Norton Facsimile [of] The First Folio of Shakespeare*, prepared by Charlton Hinman, 2nd edn (New York, 1996), xxvii–xxxv
Brathwaite, 'Caliban'	Edward Kamau Brathwaite, 'Caliban, Ariel, and Unprospero in the conflict of Creolization: a study of the slave revolt in Jamaica 1831–32', in *Comparative Perspectives on Slavery in New World Plantation Society*, ed. Vera Rubin and Arthur Tuden (New York, 1977), 41–62
Brathwaite, *Islands*	Edward Kamau Brathwaite, *Islands* (London, 1969)
Bristol	Frank M. Bristol, *Shakespeare and America* (Chicago, 1898)
Brockbank	Philip Brockbank, '*The Tempest*: conventions in art and empire', in *Later Shakespeare*, ed. John Russell Brown and Bernard Harris (London, 1966), 183–201
Brooks	Harold F. Brooks, '*The Tempest*: what sort of play?', *Proceedings of the British Academy* (London, 1980), 27–54
Brotton	Jerry Brotton, '"This Tunis, Sir, was Carthage": contesting colonialism in *The Tempest*', in *Post-Colonial Shakespeares*, ed. Ania Loomba and Martin Orkin (London, 1998), 23–42
Brown	Paul Brown, '"This thing of darkness I acknowledge mine": *The Tempest* and the discourse of colonialism', in *Political Shakespeare*, ed. Jonathan Dollimore and Alan Sinfield (Ithaca, N.Y., 1985), 48–71
Browning	Robert Browning, 'Caliban upon Setebos', in *The Poetical Works*, vol. 7 (London, 1888), 149–61
Brydon, 'Re-writing'	Diana Brydon, 'Re-writing *The Tempest*', *World Literature Written in English*, 23 (1984), 75–88
Brydon, 'Sister'	Diana Brydon, 'Sister letters: Miranda's *Tempest* in Canada', in *Cross-Cultural Performances: Differences in Women's Re-Visions of Shakespeare*, ed. Marianne Novy (Urbana, Ill., 1993), 165–84

Bullough	Geoffrey Bullough, *Narrative and Dramatic Sources of Shakespeare*, 8 vols (London, 1975)
Byrne	St Geraldine Byrne, *Shakespeare's Use of the Pronoun of Address: Its Significance in Characterization and Motivation* (Washington, D.C., 1936)
Callaghan	Dympna Callaghan, 'Irish memories in *The Tempest*', in *Shakespeare Without Women* (London, 2000), 97–138
Canny	Nicholas Canny, ed., *The Origins of Empire*, The Oxford History of the British Empire, 1 (Oxford, 1998)
Carlton	Bob Carlton, *Return to the Forbidden Planet* (London, 1985)
Cartari	Vincenzo Cartari, *The Fountaine of Ancient Fiction*, trans. Richard Linch (London, 1599)
Cartelli	Thomas Cartelli, 'Prospero in Africa: *The Tempest* as colonialist text and pretext', in *Shakespeare Reproduced*, ed. Jean E. Howard and Marion F. O'Connor (London, 1987), 99–115
Cawley	Robert Ralston Cawley, 'Shakespeare's use of the voyagers in *The Tempest*', *PMLA*, 41 (1926), 688–726
Césaire	Aimé Césaire, *Une Tempête: d'Après 'La Tempête' de Shakespeare* (Paris, 1969)
Chambers	E.K. Chambers, *William Shakespeare: A Study of Facts and Problems*, 2 vols (Oxford, 1930)
Chedgzoy	Kate Chedgzoy, *Shakespeare's Queer Children: Sexual Politics and Contemporary Culture* (Manchester, 1995)
Cheyfitz	Eric Cheyfitz, *The Poetics of Imperialism: Translation and Colonization from 'The Tempest' to 'Tarzan'* (Philadelphia, Pa., 1991)
Coleridge	Samuel Taylor Coleridge, *Shakespearean Criticism*, ed. Thomas Middleton Raysor, 2 vols (London, 1960)
Constellation	Nadia Lie and Theo D'haen, eds, *Constellation Caliban; Figurations of a Character* (Amsterdam, 1997)
Coursen	H.R. Coursen, '*The Tempest* on television', in *Shakespearean Performance as Interpretation* (Newark, Del., 1992), 227–52
Crosse	Gordon Crosse, *Shakespearean Playgoing, 1890–1952* (London, 1953)
Croyden	Margaret Croyden, 'Peter Brook's *Tempest*', *Drama Review*, 13 (1968–9), 125–8
Cuningham	William Cuningham, *The Cosmographical Glasse* (London, 1559)
Curry	Walter Clyde Curry, *Shakespeare's Philosophical Patterns* (Baton Rouge, La., 1937)
Dante	Dante Alighieri, *Inferno*, trans. Charles Singleton, 2 vols (Princeton, N.J., 1970)

Darío	Rubén Darío, 'El triunfo de Caliban', in *Escritos ineditos de Rubén Darío*, ed. E.K. Mapes (New York, 1938)
Demaray	John G. Demaray, *Shakespeare and the Spectacles of Strangeness: 'The Tempest' and the Transformation of Renaissance Theatrical Forms* (Pittsburgh, Pa., 1998)
Dent	R.W. Dent, *Shakespeare's Proverbial Language* (Berkeley, 1981)
Dessen	Alan C. Dessen, *Recovering Shakespeare's Theatrical Vocabulary* (Cambridge, 1995)
Dessen & Thomson	Alan C. Dessen and Leslie Thomson, *A Dictionary of Stage Directions in English Drama, 1580–1642* (Cambridge, 1999)
Dobson	Michael Dobson, '"Remember / First to possess his books": the appropriation of *The Tempest*, 1700–1800', *SS43* (1990), 99–107
Dorsinville	Max Dorsinville, *Caliban Without Prospero: Essays in Quebec and Black Literature* (Erin, Ont., 1974)
Dowden	Edward Dowden, *Shakespere: His Mind and Art* (New York, 1899)
Downes	John Downes, *Roscius Anglicanus; Or an Historical Review of the Stage* (London, 1708)
Dryden	John Dryden, *Of Dramatic Poesy and Other Critical Essays*, ed. George Watson, 2 vols (London, 1962)
Dymkowski	Christine Dymkowski, ed., *'The Tempest': Shakespeare in Production* (Cambridge, 2000)
Eden	Richard Eden, ed. and trans., *The Decades of the Newe Worlde or West India* (London, 1555); *The History of Travayle in the West and East Indies*, ed. Richard Eden and Richard Willies (London, 1577)
Edwards	Philip Edwards, 'Shakespeare's romances: 1900–1957', *SS 11* (1958), 1–18
Elze	Theodor Elze, 'Die Insel der Sycorax', *SJ*, 15 (1880), 251–3
Falconer	Alexander Frederick Falconer, *Shakespeare and the Sea* (London, 1964)
Felperin	Howard Felperin, *Shakespearean Romance* (Princeton, N.J., 1972)
Fernández Retamar	Roberto Fernández Retamar, 'Caliban: notes towards a discussion of culture in America', *Massachusetts Review*, 15 (1973–4), 11–16
Fiedler	Leslie A. Fiedler, *The Stranger in Shakespeare* (New York, 1972)
Fletcher	Francis Fletcher, *The World Encompassed by Sir Francis Drake*, ed. W.S.W. Vaux (London, 1854)

Forster	John Forster and George Henry Lewes, *Dramatic Essays* (London, 1896)
Fox	Charles O. Fox, 'A crux in "The Tempest"', *N&Q*, 202, n.s. 4 (1957), 515–16
FQ	Edmund Spenser, *The Faerie Queene*, ed. A.C. Hamilton (London, 1977)
Franck	Jane P. Franck, 'Caliban at Lewisohn Stadium, 1916', in *Shakespeare Encomium*, ed. Anne Paolucci (New York, 1964), 154–68
French	Peter J. French, *John Dee: The World of the Elizabethan Magus* (London, 1972)
Frey, 'New World'	Charles H. Frey, '*The Tempest* and the New World', *SQ* 30 (1979), 29–41
Frey, 'Play'	Charles H. Frey, 'Embodying the play', in Wood, 67–96
Fuller	Mary C. Fuller, *Voyages in Print: English Travel to America, 1576–1624* (Cambridge, 1995)
Gerard	John Gerard, *The Herball or Generall Historie of Plantes* (London, 1597)
Gillies	John Gillies, 'Shakespeare's Virginian masque', *English Literary History*, 53 (1986), 673–707
Goldberg	Jonathan Goldberg, 'Under the covers with Caliban', in *The Margins of the Text*, ed. D.C. Greetham (Ann Arbor, Mich., 1997), 105–28
Greenaway	Peter Greenaway, *Prospero's Books* (filmscript) (New York, 1991)
Greenblatt	Stephen Greenblatt, 'Learning to curse: aspects of linguistic colonialism in the sixteenth century', in *Learning to Curse: Essays in Early Modern Culture* (New York, 1990), 16–39
Greene	Gayle Greene, 'Margaret Laurence's *Diviners* and Shakespeare's *Tempest*', in *Women's Re-visions of Shakespeare*, ed. Marianne Novy (Urbana, Ill., 1990), 164–82
Griffiths	Trevor R. Griffiths, '"This island's mine": Caliban and colonialism', *Yearbook of English Studies*, 13 (1983), 159–80
Guffey	George Robert Guffey, ed., *After the Tempest*, Augustan Reprint Society, Special Series No. 4 (Los Angeles, 1969)
Hakluyt, 1589	Richard Hakluyt, *The Principall Navigations, Voyages and Discoveries of the English Nation* (London, 1589)
Hakluyt, 1598–1600	Richard Hakluyt, *The Principal Navigations, Voyages Traffiques & Discoveries of the English Nation*, 3 vols (London, 1598–1600; repr. in 12 vols, Glasgow, 1903–5)
Hall	Kim F. Hall, *Things of Darkness: Economies of Race and Gender in Early Modern England* (Ithaca, N.Y., 1995)

Halliwell, *Memoranda*	J.O. Halliwell-Phillips, *Memoranda on Shakespeare's Tempest* (Brighton, Sussex, 1880)
Halliwell, *Notes*	J.O. Halliwell-Phillips, *Selected Notes upon Shakespeare's The Tempest* (London, 1868)
Halpern	Richard Halpern, '"The picture of Nobody": white cannibalism in *The Tempest*', in *The Production of English Renaissance Culture*, ed. David Lee Miller, Sharon O'Dair and Harold Weber (Ithaca, N.Y., 1994), 262–92
Hamilton	Donna B. Hamilton, *Virgil and 'The Tempest': The Politics of Imitation* (Columbus, Oh., 1990)
Harrison	Thomas P. Harrison, 'A note on *The Tempest*: a sequel', *MLN*, 58 (1943), 422–6
Hartwig	Joan Hartwig, *Shakespeare's Tragicomic Vision* (Baton Rouge, La., 1972)
Hazlitt	William Hazlitt, *Lectures on the Literature of the Age of Elizabeth and Characters of Shakespear's Plays* (London, 1901)
H.D.	H.D. [Hilda Doolittle], *By Avon River* (New York, 1949)
Heywood	Thomas Heywood, *The Brazen Age* (London, 1613)
Highfill	Philip H. Highfill, Kalman Burnim and Edward A. Langhans, *A Biographical Dictionary of Actors . . . 1660–1800*, 16 vols (Carbondale, Ill., 1973–93)
Hinman	Charlton Hinman, *The Printing and Proof-reading of the First Folio of Shakespeare*, 2 vols (Oxford, 1963)
Hirst	David L. Hirst, *The Tempest: Text and Performance* (Houndmills, Hants., 1984)
Honigmann	E.A.J. Honigmann, *The Texts of 'Othello' and Shakespearian Revision* (London, 1996)
Horowitz	Arthur Horowitz, *Prospero's 'True Preservers': Peter Brook, Yukio Ninagawa, and Giorgio Strehler* (Newark, Del., 2004)
Howard-Hill, *Crane*	Trevor Howard-Hill, *Ralph Crane and Some Shakespeare First Folio Comedies* (Charlottesville, Va., 1972)
Howard-Hill, 'Editor'	Trevor Howard-Hill, 'Shakespeare's earliest editor, Ralph Crane', *SS 44* (1992), 113–29
Howard-Hill, 'Parentheses'	Trevor Howard-Hill, 'Ralph Crane's parentheses', *N&Q*, 210 n.s. 12 (1965), 334–40
Hulme, H.	Hilda M. Hulme, *Explorations in Shakespeare's Language* (London, 1962)
Hulme, P.	Peter Hulme, *Colonial Encounters: Europe and the Native Caribbean, 1492–1797* (London, 1986)
Hulme, P. & Sherman	Peter Hulme and William H. Sherman, eds., *'The Tempest' and its Travels* (London, 2000)

Hunter	Joseph Hunter, *A Disquisition on the Scene, Origin, Date, etc., of Shakespeare's Tempest* (London, 1839)
Hunter, G.K.	G.K. Hunter, 'English folly and Italian vice', in *Dramatic Identities and Cultural Tradition* (Liverpool, 1978), 103–32.
James I, *Daemonologie*	James I, *Daemonologie, in Forme of a Dialoge* (Edinburgh, 1597)
James I, *Political*	James I, *Political Works*, ed. Charles Howard Mclwain (Cambridge, Mass., 1918)
Jameson	Anna Jameson, *Shakespeare's Heroines: Characteristics of Women, Moral, Poetical, and Historical* (London, 1913)
Johnson, L., *Africa*	Lemuel A. Johnson, *Shakespeare in Africa* (Trenton, N.J., 1998)
Johnson, L., *Caliban*	Lemuel A. Johnson, *Highlife for Caliban* (Ann Arbor, Mich., 1973)
Johnson, S.	Samuel Johnson, *Poetry and Prose*, ed. Mona Wilson (Cambridge, 1967)
Jonson, *Masques*	Ben Jonson, *Selected Masques*, ed. Stephen Orgel (New Haven, 1970)
Jonson, *Works*	Ben Jonson, *Works of Ben Jonson*, ed. C.H. Herford and Percy and Evelyn Simpson, 11 vols (Oxford, 1925–52)
Jourda[i]n	Silvester Jourda[i]n, *A Discovery of the Burmudas, otherwise called the Ile of Divels* (London, 1610)
Jowett	John Jowett, 'New created creatures: Ralph Crane and the stage directions in "The Tempest"', *SS 36* (1983), 107–20
Kahn	Coppélia Kahn, 'The providential Tempest and the Shakespearean family', in *Representing Shakespeare: New Psychoanalytic Essays*, ed. Murry M. Schwartz and Coppélia Kahn (Baltimore, Md., 1980), 217–43
Kastan	David Scott Kastan, '"The Duke of Milan and his brave son": dynastic politics in *The Tempest*', in *Critical Essays on Shakespeare's 'The Tempest'*, ed. Virginia Mason Vaughan and Alden T. Vaughan (New York, 1998), 91–103
Kay	Dennis C. Kay, 'Gonzalo's "lasting pillars": The Tempest, V.i.208', *SQ*, 35 (1984), 322–4
Kipling	Rudyard Kipling, *How Shakspere Came to Write the 'Tempest'* (New York, 1916; first published 1898)
Knapp	Jeffrey Knapp, *An Empire Nowhere: England, America, and Literature from 'Utopia' to 'The Tempest'* (Berkeley, 1992)
Lamb	Charles Lamb, *The Dramatic Essays*, ed. Brander Matthews (New York, 1891)

Lamming	George Lamming, *The Pleasures of Exile* (London, 1960)
Latham	Jacqueline E.M. Latham, '"Standing water" in "The Tempest" and Joseph Hall's "Characters"', *N&Q*, 219 n.s. 21 (1974), 136
Laurence	Margaret Laurence, *The Diviners* (Toronto, 1974)
Law	Ernest Law, *Shakespeare's Tempest as Originally Produced at Court* (London, 1920)
Lea	Kathleen M. Lea, *Italian Popular Comedy*, 2 vols (Oxford, 1934)
Lee, 'Caliban'	Sidney Lee, 'Caliban's visits to England', *Cornhill Magazine*, n.s. 34 (1913), 333–45
Lee, 'Indian'	Sidney Lee, 'The Call of the West: America and Elizabethan England', Pt 3: 'The American Indian in Elizabethan England', *Scribner's Magazine* (Sept. 1907), 313–30; reprinted in *Elizabethan and Other Essays*, ed. Frederick S. Boas (Oxford, 1929)
Lee, *Life*	Sidney Lee, *Life of William Shakespeare* (London, 1898)
Levin, H.	Harry Levin, ' "The Tempest" and "The Alchemist" ', *SS 22* (1969), 47–58
Levin, R.	Richard Levin, 'Anatomical geography in "The Tempest", IV.i.235–38', *N&Q*, 209, n.s. 11 (1964), 142–6
Lewis	C.S. Lewis, *The Allegory of Love* (Oxford, 1936)
Lindley	David Lindley, *The Tempest: Shakespeare at Stratford* (London, 2003)
Liyong	Taban lo Liyong, *Frantz Fanon's Uneven Ribs* (London, 1971)
Long	John H. Long, *Shakespeare's Use of Music: The Final Comedies* (Gainesville, Fla., 1961)
Loughrey & Taylor	Bryan Loughrey and Neil Taylor, 'Ferdinand and Miranda at chess', *SS 35* (1982), 113–18
MacDonnell	Patrick MacDonnell, *An Essay on the Play of The Tempest* (London, 1840)
MacKaye	Percy MacKaye, *Caliban by the Yellow Sands* (New York, 1916)
Maguire	Nancy Klein Maguire, ed., *Renaissance Tragicomedy: Explorations in Genre and Politics* (New York, 1987)
Mahood	M. M. Mahood, *Bit Parts in Shakespeare's Plays* (Cambridge, 1992)
Malone, *Account*	Edmond Malone, *An Account of the Incidents, from which the Title and Part of the Story of Shakspeare's Tempest Were Derived* (London, 1808)
Mannoni	Octave Mannoni, *Prospero and Caliban*, trans. Pamela Powesland (New York, 1956)

Maquerlot & Willems	Jean-Pierre Maquerlot and Michèle Willems, eds, *Travel and Drama in Shakespeare's Time* (Cambridge, 1996)
Marcus	Leah Marcus, *Unediting the Renaissance: Shakespeare, Marlowe, Milton* (London, 1996)
Marlowe	Christopher Marlowe, *Dr Faustus*, ed. David Bevington and Eric Rasmussen (Manchester, 1993)
Márquez	Robert Márquez, 'Foreword', *Massachusetts Review*, 15 (1973–4), 6
Marston	John Marston, *The Malcontent*, ed. George K. Hunter (Manchester, 1975, repr. 1999)
Marx	Leo Marx, 'Shakespeare's American fable', *Massachusetts Review*, 2 (1960), 40–71
Maus	Katharine Eisaman Maus, '"Arcadia lost": politics and revision in the Restoration *Tempest*', *Renaissance Drama*, 13 (1982), 189–209
McDonald	Russ McDonald, 'Reading *The Tempest*', *SS 43* (1990), 15–28
McMullan & Hope	Gordon McMullan and Jonathan Hope, eds, *The Politics of Tragicomedy: Shakespeare and After* (London, 1992)
Mebane	John S. Mebane, *Renaissance Magic and the Return of the Golden Age* (Lincoln, Nebr., 1989)
Melchiori	Barbara Melchiori, 'Still harping on my daughter', *English Miscellany* (Rome), 11 (1960), 59–74
Middleton	Thomas Middleton, *The Complete Works*, ed. Gary Taylor, *et al.* (Oxford, 2007)
Mirror[1]	*The First Part of the Mirrour of Princely Deedes and Knighthood*, trans. Margaret Tyler (London, 1580)
Mirror[2]	*The Third Part of the First Booke of the Mirrour of Knighthood*, trans. R. Parry (London, 1586)
MLN	*Modern Language Notes*
Montaigne	Michel de Montaigne, *The Essayes, or Morall, Politicke and Militarie Discourses*, trans. John Florio (London, 1603)
Mowat, *Dramaturgy*	Barbara A. Mowat, *The Dramaturgy of Shakespeare's Romances* (Athens, Ga., 1976)
Mowat, 'Hocus'	Barbara A. Mowat, 'Prospero, Agrippa, and hocus pocus', *English Literary Renaissance*, 11 (1981), 281–303
Mowat, 'Tragicomedy'	Barbara A. Mowat, 'Shakespearean tragicomedy', in Maguire, 80–96
Murphy	Sarah Murphy, *The Measure of Miranda* (Edmonton, 1987)
Myers	James F. Myers, Jr, ed., *Elizabethan Ireland: A Selection of Writings by Elizabethan Writers on Ireland* (Hamden, Conn., 1983)

Namjoshi	Suniti Namjoshi, 'Snapshots of Caliban', in *Because of India* (London, 1989), 85–102
N&Q	*Notes and Queries*
Ngugi	Ngugi Wa Thiong'o, *Homecoming: Essays on African and Caribbean Literature, Culture, and Politics* (New York, 1973)
Nixon	Rob Nixon, 'Caribbean and African appropriations of *The Tempest*', *Critical Inquiry*, 13 (1987), 557–78
Noble	Richmond Noble, *Shakespeare's Use of Song* (Oxford, 1923)
Norbrook	David Norbrook, ' "What cares these roarers for the name of King?": language and Utopia in *The Tempest*', in McMullan & Hope, 21–54
Nosworthy	J.M. Nosworthy, 'The narrative sources of *The Tempest*', *Review of English Studies*, 24 (1948), 281–94
OED	*Oxford English Dictionary*, 2nd edn, prepared by J.A. Simpson and E.S.C. Weiner (Oxford, 1989)
Orgell, 'Poetics'	Stephen Orgel, 'Poetics of spectacle', *New Literary History*, 2 (1971), 367–89
Orgel, 'Wife'	Stephen Orgel, 'Prospero's wife', in *Rewriting the Renaissance*, ed. Margaret W. Ferguson, Maureen Quilligan and Nancy J. Vickers (Chicago, 1986), 50–64
Orgel & Strong	Stephen Orgel and Roy Strong, *Inigo Jones: The Theatre of the Stuart Court*, 2 vols (Berkeley, 1973)
Ovid	Publius Ovidius Naso, *The XV Books of Ovidius Naso Entytuled Metamorphosis*, trans. Arthur Golding (London, 1567)
Parker	John Parker, *Van Meteren's Virginia, 1607–1612* (Minneapolis, Minn., 1961)
Partridge, A.C.	A.C. Partridge, *Orthography in Shakespeare and Elizabethan Drama* (London, 1964)
Partridge, Eric	Eric Partridge, *A Dictionary of Slang and Unconventional English*, 5th edn, 2 vols (London, 1961)
Paster	Gail Paster, 'Montaigne, Dido, and *The Tempest*: "How came that widow in?" ', *SQ*, 35 (1984), 91–4
Pearson	D'Orsay Pearson, ' "Unless I be reliev'd by prayer": *The Tempest* in perspective', *SSt*, 7 (1974), 253–82
Pepys	*The Diary of Samuel Pepys*, ed. Robert Latham and William Matthews, 11 vols (Berkeley and Los Angeles, 1970–85)
Peterson	Douglas L. Peterson, *Time, Tide, and Tempest: A Study of Shakespeare's Romances* (San Marino, 1973)
Peyre	Yves Peyre, 'Les masques d'Ariel', *Cahiers Elisabethains*, 19 (1981), 53–71

Philaster	Francis Beaumont and John Fletcher, *Philaster*, ed. Andrew Gurr (London, 1969)
Philaster[1]	Francis Beaumont and John Fletcher, *Philaster*, ed. Suzanne Gossett (London, 2009)
Pitcher	John Pitcher, 'A theatre of the future: *The Aeneid* and *The Tempest*', *Essays in Criticism*, 34 (1984), 193–215
Pliny	Pliny (C. Plinius Secundus), *The Historie of the World*, trans. Philemon Holland (London, 1601)
PMLA	*Publications of the Modern Language Association of America*
Prosser	Eleanor Prosser, 'Shakespeare, Montaigne, and the rarer action', *SSt*, 1 (1965), 261–4
Purchas	Samuel Purchas, *Hakluytus Posthumus or Purchas his Pilgrimes. Contayning a History of the World in Sea Voyages & Lande-Travells by Englishmen & Others*, 4 vols (London, 1625)
Raleigh	Walter Alexander Raleigh, 'The English voyages of the sixteenth century', in Hakluyt, 1598–1600 (Glasgow, 1903–5), vol. 12, 1–120
Ranald	Margaret Loftus Ranald, review of the New York Shakespeare Festival's 1995 *Tempest*, *SBn* (Fall 1995), 10–11
Renan	Ernest Renan, *Caliban: A Philosophical Drama Continuing 'The Tempest' of William Shakespeare*, trans. Eleanor Vickery (New York, 1896)
Rich, B.	Barnabe Rich, *A New Description of Ireland* (London, 1610)
Rich, R.	Richard Rich, *Newes from Virginia: The Lost Flock Triumphant* (London, 1610)
Roberts, 'Crane'	Jeanne Addison Roberts, 'Ralph Crane and the text of *The Tempest*', *SSt*, 13 (1980), 213–33
Roberts, 'Wife'	Jeanne Addison Roberts, '"Wife" or "Wise" – *The Tempest*, 1.1786', *Studies in Bibliography*, 31 (1978), 203–8
RP	Richard Proudfoot, private communications
Saldívar	José David Saldívar, *The Dialectics of Our America: Genealogy, Cultural Critique and Literary History* (Durham, N.C., 1991)
SBn	*Shakespeare Bulletin*
Schmidgall	Gary Schmidgall, *Shakespeare and the Courtly Aesthetic* (Berkeley, 1981)
Schmidgall, *Primaleon*	Gary Schmidgall, '*The Tempest* and *Primaleon*: a new source', *SQ*, 39 (1986), 423–39
Semprúm	Jésus Semprúm, 'El Norte ye el Sur', *Cultura Venezolana*, 1 (1918), 132, quoted in Donald Marquand

	Dozer, *Are We Good Neighbors? Three Centuries of Inter-American Relations, 1930–1960* (Gainesville, Fla., 1959)
Seng	Peter J. Seng, *The Vocal Songs in the Plays of Shakespeare: A Critical History* (Cambridge, Mass., 1967)
Shawcross	John T. Shawcross, 'Tragicomedy as genre, past and present', in Maguire, 13–32
Shelley	Percy Bysshe Shelley, *Selected Prose and Poetry*, ed. Carlos Baker (New York, 1951)
Simonds, 'Charms'	Peggy Muñoz Simonds, '"My charms crack not": the alchemical structure of *The Tempest*', *Comparative Drama*, 32 (1998), 538–70
Simonds, 'Music'	Peggy Muñoz Simonds, '"Sweet power of music": the political magic of "The Miraculous Harp" in Shakespeare's *The Tempest*', *Comparative Drama*, 29 (1995), 61–90
Singh	Jyotsna G. Singh, 'Caliban versus Miranda: race and gender conflicts in postcolonial rewritings of *The Tempest*', *Feminist Readings of Early Modern Culture*, ed. Valerie Traub, Lindsay Kaplan and Dympna Callaghan (Cambridge, 1996), 191–209
SJ	*Shakespeare Jahrbuch*
Skura	Meredith Anne Skura, 'Discourse and the individual: the case of colonialism in *The Tempest*', *SQ*, 40 (1989), 42–69
Smith, H.	Hallett Smith, *Shakespeare's Romances* (San Marino, 1972)
Smith, J., *Gen. Hist.*	John Smith, *The Generall Historie of Virginia, New-England, and the Summer Isles* (London, 1624)
Smith, J., *Relation*	John Smith, *A True Relation of Such Occurrences and Accidents of Noate as Hath Hapned in Virginia* (London, 1608)
Smith, J., *Sea Grammar*	John Smith, *A Sea Grammar* (London, 1627)
Sokol	B. J. Sokol, *A Brave New World of Knowledge: Shakespeare's 'The Tempest' and Early Modern Epistemology* (Cranbury, N.J., 2003)
Speed	John Speed, *The Theatre of the Empire of Great Britaine*, 2 vols (London, 1611)
Spevack	Marvin Spevack, *The Harvard Concordance to Shakespeare* (Cambridge, Mass., 1973)
SQ	*Shakespeare Quarterly*
SS	*Shakespeare Survey*
SSt	*Shakespeare Studies*
Stoll	Elmer Edgar Stoll, *Poets and Playwrights: Shakespeare, Jonson, Spenser, Milton* (Minneapolis, 1930)

Stone	George Winchester Stone, Jr, 'Shakespeare's *Tempest* at Drury Lane during Garrick's management', *SQ*, 7 (1956), 1–7
Strachey	William Strachey, 'A True Reportory of the Wracke and Redemption of Sir Thomas Gates', Samuel Purchas, *Purchas his Pilgrimes* (London, 1625), vol. 4, 1734–58
Sturgess	Keith Sturgess, '"A quaint device": *The Tempest* at the Blackfriars', in Sturgess, *Jacobean Private Theatre* (London, 1987), 73–96
Takaki	Ronald T. Takaki, *Iron Cages: Race and Culture in Nineteenth-Century America* (New York, 1979)
Taylor	Gary Taylor, 'The structure of performance: act intervals in the London theatres, 1576–1642', in *Shakespeare Reshaped, 1606–1623*, ed. Gary Taylor and John Jowett (Oxford, 1993), 1–50
Thevet	André Thevet, *The New Found Worlde, or Antartike*, trans. T. Hacket (London, 1568)
Thomas	William Thomas, *Historie of Italie* (London, 1549)
Thompson	Ann Thompson, '"Miranda, where's your sister?": reading Shakespeare's *The Tempest*', in *Feminist Criticism: Theory and Practice*, ed. Susan Sellers (Hemel Hempstead, Herts., 1991), 45–55
Tippett	Michael Tippett, *The Knot Garden* (libretto) (London, n.d.)
Traister	Barbara Howard Traister, *Heavenly Necromancers: The Magician in English Renaissance Drama* (Columbia, Mo., 1984)
Tree	Herbert Beerbohm Tree, *Shakespeare's 'The Tempest' as Arranged for the Stage by Herbert Beerbohm Tree* (London, 1904)
True Declaration	*A True Declaration of the Estate of the Colonie in Virginia* (London, 1610)
TxC	Stanley Wells, Gary Taylor *et al.*, *William Shakespeare: A Textual Companion* (Oxford, 1987)
Udall	Joanna Udall, *A Critical, Old-Spelling Edition of 'The Birth of Merlin'* (London, 1991)
Van Lennep	William Van Lennep *et al.*, *The London Stage, 1660–1800*, 11 vols (Carbondale, Ill., 1960–8)
Vaughan, A.	Alden T. Vaughan, 'William Strachey's "True Reportory" and Shakespeare: a closer look at the evidence', *SQ*, 59 (2008), 245–73
Vaughan, 'Africans'	Alden T. Vaughan and Virginia Mason Vaughan, 'Before *Othello*: Elizabethan representations of sub-Saharan

	Africans', *William and Mary Quarterly*, 3rd series, 54 (1997), 19–14
Vaughan, *Caliban*	Alden T. Vaughan and Virginia Mason Vaughan, *Shakespeare's Caliban: A Cultural History* (Cambridge, 1991)
Vaughan, V.	Virginia Mason Vaughan, 'Literary invocations of *The Tempest*', in *The Cambridge Companion to Shakespeare's Last Plays*, ed. Catherine M.S. Alexander (Cambridge, 2009), 155–72
Wallace	David Wallace, *Do You Love Me, Master?* (Lusaka, Zambia, 1977)
Warner	Marina Warner, *Indigo, or, Mapping the Waters* (London, 1992)
Warren	Michael J. Warren, 'Textual problems, editorial assertions in editions of Shakespeare', in *Textual Criticism and Literary Interpretation*, ed. Jerome J. McGann (Chicago, 1985), 23–37
Wayne	Valerie Wayne, 'The sexual politics of textual transmission', in *Textual Formations and Reformations*, ed. Laurie Maguire and Thomas L. Berger (Newark, Del., 1998), 179–210
Wells	Stanley Wells, *Shakespeare and Co.* (New York, 2006)
Wells[1]	Stanley Wells, 'Shakespeare and romance', in *Later Shakespeare*, ed. John Russell Brown and Bernard Harris (London, 1966), 49–79
Whall	W.B. Whall, *Shakespeare's Sea Terms Explained* (Bristol, 1910)
White	Hayden White, 'The forms of wildness: archaeology of an idea', in *The Wild Man Within: An Image in Western Thought from the Renaissance to Romanticism*, ed. Edward Dudley and Maximillian E. Novak (Pittsburgh, Pa., 1973)
Wickham	Glynne Wickham, 'Masque and anti-masque in "The Tempest"', *Essays and Studies* (1975), 1–14
Wikander	Matthew H. Wikander, '"The Duke My Father's wrack": the innocence of the Restoration *Tempest*', *SS 43* (1990), 91–8
Wilson, D.	Daniel Wilson, *Caliban: The Missing Link* (London, 1873)
Wilson, J.D., *Hamlet*	John Dover Wilson, *What Happens in Hamlet* (New York, 1935)
Wilson, J.D., *Meaning*	John Dover Wilson, *The Meaning of The Tempest* (Newcastle-upon-Tyne, 1936)
Wiltenburg	Robert Wiltenburg, '"The Aeneid" in "The Tempest"', *SS 39* (1986), 159–68
Wood	Nigel Wood, ed., *The Tempest: Theory and Practice* (Buckingham, 1995)

Wordsworth	William Wordsworth, *Selected Poems and Prefaces*, ed. Jack Stillinger (Boston, 1965)
Wright, G.	George T. Wright, *Shakespeare's Metrical Art* (Berkeley, 1988)
Wright, L.	Louis B. Wright, ed., *A Voyage to Virginia in 1609* (Charlottesville, Va., 1965)
Yates	Frances A. Yates, *Shakespeare's Last Plays: A New Approach* (London, 1975)
Zabus	Chantal Zabus, 'A Calibanic *Tempest* in Anglophone and Francophone New World writings', *Canadian Literature*, 104 (1985), 35–50
Zabus, *Tempests*	Chantal Zabus, *Tempests after Shakespeare* (New York, 2002)
Zeeveld	W. Gordon Zeeveld, *The Temper of Shakespeare's Thought* (New Haven, 1974)

INDEX